Astronomy

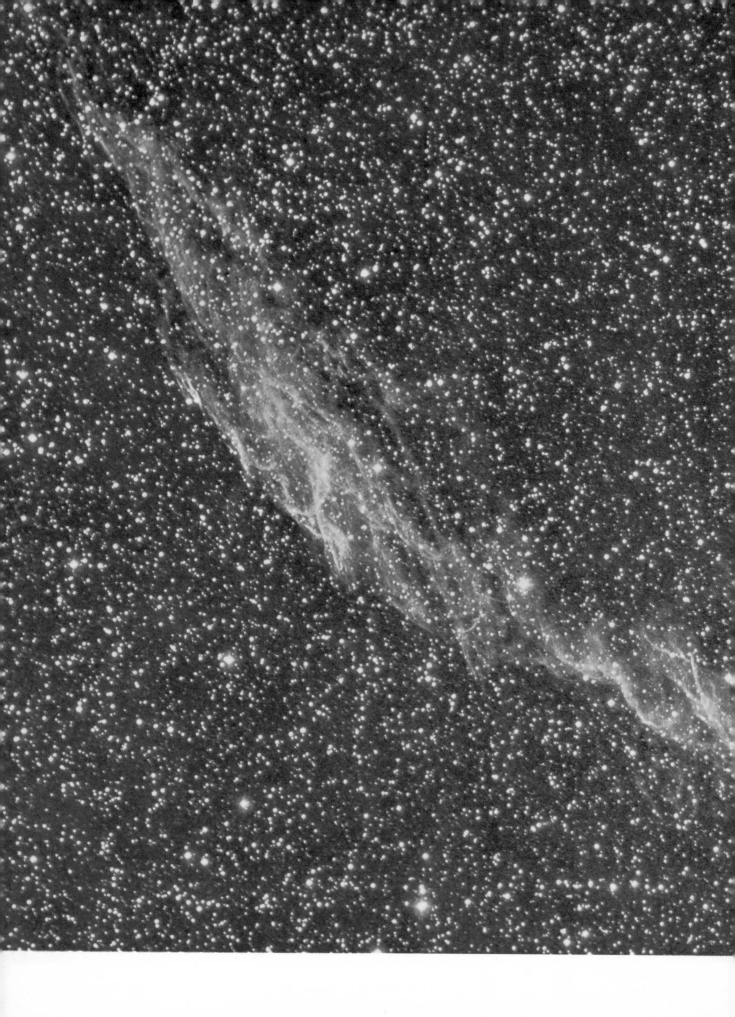

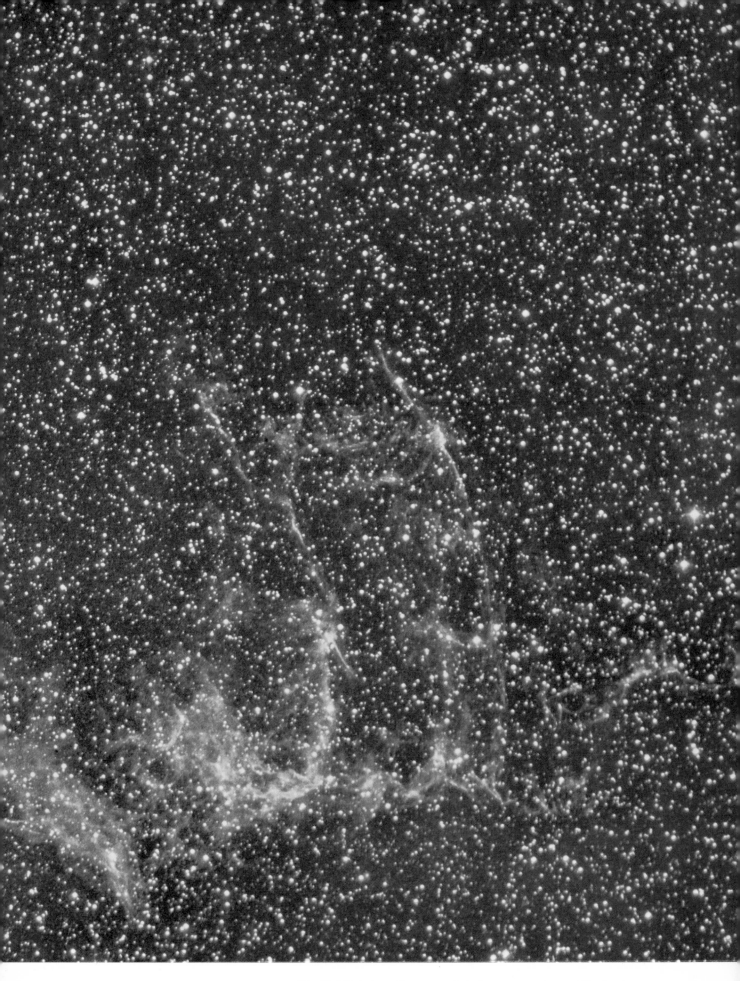

The Veil Nebula in Cygnus   © California Institute of Technology

Editor: M. H. Chandler
Art Editor: M. Kitson
Assistant: V. Zweig
Research: A. F. Walker
Research Consultants: Francis Maddison, Colin Ronan

ISBN 0-517-064197

Library of Congress Catalog Card No. 62-14108
© MCMLXII Rathbone Books Limited, London

Printed and bound in Yugoslavia by
Mladinska Knjiga, Ljubljana

Astronomy

Fred Hoyle

Crescent Books, Inc.

Foreword

In this book I have attempted to take the reader from the earliest-known astronomical discoveries up to the latest modern developments. The illustrations, so amply and effectively provided by my colleagues in this enterprise, are intended as a real aid to following the text, not just as a means of making the book look well.

Astronomy is the oldest of the sciences, as has often been said. What has not been so often realized is that, in a certain sense, astronomy is also the newest of the sciences. The great advances in physics during the first third of this century are bearing fruit in astronomy at the present day. Scientists are coming more and more to realize that only a very limited range of experiments can be performed in the terrestrial laboratory. The universe itself supplies a far subtler laboratory, and a far wider ranging one, with possibilities that can never be realized here on the Earth. A supernova will never be produced in a terrestrial laboratory, although many of the processes governing the explosion of these stars have indeed been studied in local experiments. It is just here that the point lies; for local experiments have fortunately been sufficient to discover physical laws which then turn out to have a wider range of application on the stage of the whole universe.

This situation is not wholly new, however. Already in the nineteenth century, discoveries concerning the nature and properties of light had effects on astronomy, not only in extending the scope of already-existing lines of research, but in starting new lines and in shifting the balance of "importance" within astronomy in general.

With these thoughts in mind, I felt it would be wrong to write purely from an astronomical point of view. In eight of the chapters I have been concerned with a history of the development of astronomy. Since this development has been so intimately affected by discoveries in physics, I have felt it essential to say something about the meaning of those discoveries.

The reader will find quite extensive discussions on light, and on electricity and magnetism. Nuclear physics appears in later chapters, where its important applications to modern astrophysics are described at some length. Quantum theory and relativity are briefly touched on.

I feel some personal comment on the historical chapters to be necessary. In a survey of astronomical discovery, Greek astronomy must be accorded a prominent place, since many major advances were quite certainly made by the Greeks. Yet an accurate description of exactly what occurred between, say, 500 B.C. and 200 B.C., is, I would think, irrecoverable by the modern world. Original manuscripts are few. Most of our knowledge of this period comes from corrupt Latin texts, which must be interpreted in the light of modern knowledge—and this may not always lead to a correct understanding of what really occurred! Eratosthenes' determination of the diameter of the Earth is a case in point. Was Eratosthenes 17 per cent wrong or was he only $\frac{1}{2}$ per cent wrong? A generation ago, scientific historians favored the worse result. On reading the evidence, I felt convinced of the opposite, however. The difference lies not in any change of documentary evidence but in a change of outlook. Nowadays, scientists are entirely willing to concede that men of the past, of the remote past too, were every bit as competent as we are. But to our grandfathers it seemed almost indecent that Eratosthenes, with only primitive instruments at his disposal, could have achieved a wonderfully accurate result. He had no business to be so good!

I have also found that hindsight has influenced many scientific histories, particularly the more popular expositions. Very great work has been slightingly condemned, whenever later developments turned research in new directions. Probably no great man has been so contemptuously dismissed by posterity as Ptolemy, the perfector of the epicyclic theory of planetary motions. His theory fitted closely to the known facts in his own day. It survived for over a thousand years as the best description of the observed motions; and even after its overthrow, Ptolemy's geometrical methods still played an important role at a decisive stage in the work of Kepler. Yet Ptolemy has been devalued, at any rate in the popular eye, to negligible stature. Such attitudes arise, I am convinced, from ignorance. A few scholarly presentations apart, it is not generally understood that Ptolemy was really grappling with the complexities of elliptic motion. Already in Greek times, the effects of the eccentricities of the planetary orbits had been observationally detected. A satisfactory theory could not treat the orbits as circles, even circles with the Sun as center. My suspicion is that even the most detailed descriptions of Ptolemy's work still fail to appreciate the mathematical basis of certain of his geometrical constructions. For this reason I have added a mathematical appendix at the end of the book in which I have attempted to explain why Ptolemy was led to these constructions.

Lastly, a few words about new techniques. There is a fairly widespread present belief that the traditional observational methods of astronomy will soon be replaced by space research. It may prove to be so, but for my own part, I doubt it. All important new techniques appear at first sight to have unlimited possibilities. But after a decade or two experience shows that a process of diminishing returns sets in. Each significant new result then costs more in time, effort and money than was the case in the beginning. This process is already operating in radio astronomy. A few years ago, discoveries could be made in radio astronomy with the aid of only rather primitive equipment. Today, this is no longer true. New radio telescopes, if they are to be effective, must now be financed and planned on a big scale. A similar situation must inevitably arise in space research. Moreover, we can hardly expect that the wealthiest nations will continue indefinitely to spend appreciable fractions of their incomes on the firing of instruments into space. For both these reasons I think space research, along with radio astronomy, will eventually reach an equilibrium in relation to more traditional methods, and I think that in this equilibrium the major part of astronomy will continue to advance in much the way it has done in the past.

This will explain why I have not written this book from the enthusiastic point of view that astronomy is due to be revolutionized tomorrow. I see astronomy as a continuing process, in which each new technique has a place in relation to the whole, but in which no particular technique overwhelms the rest.

Fred Hoyle

Contents

Chapter 1   Earth and Sky

In our modern world scientific discovery is in full spate. So strong is the current now running that nothing, it seems, short of the utter annihilation of man himself can hold back the flood. But this was not always so. The first steps in science were taken slowly and tentatively, thousands of years ago. And but for astronomy it is well-nigh certain that these early, hesitant steps would never have been taken at all. For astronomy is the progenitor of science.

So much is commonplace. What is not usually realized is that luck, in the sense of help from the heavens, has also been exceedingly important. At least four lucky circumstances made astronomy the ideal starting point for man's first major advance into an era in which natural phenomena can be explained and predicted, in which the world no longer presents itself as a stage for the playing out of a sequence of mysterious and uncorrelated events.

The Earth is not a cloud-bound planet. This is the first piece of luck, for if the Earth had been wholly cloud-bound, as the planet Venus is, man's intellectual emergence would scarcely have been possible. At any moment roughly half of the Earth's surface is cloud-covered and half is clear. The cloud cover shifts about, however, so that although cloud is much more frequent in some areas than in others there are times everywhere when an observer can look out into space. If man had not been able to do so, it is doubtful whether he would ever have established the directions north, south, east and west; and without that knowledge he would never have learned to find his way to and fro over any considerable part of the Earth's surface. Without sight of the regular rhythmical movements of Sun and stars across the sky, he would have found it next to impossible to grasp the very concept of time; and without attempting to measure time and direction it is highly improbable that he would have grappled with problems of simple geometry.

Simple geometry, often called Euclidean geometry, may be understood as geometry in which Pythagoras's Theorem is true. If ABC is a triangle with a right angle at B, Pythagoras's Theorem establishes that a square drawn on the line AC is equal in area to the sum of the squares drawn on lines AB and BC. (By *right angle* we mean simply the angle which results when we bisect a straight line by orthodox rule-and-compass procedure.)

However, systems of geometry exist in which Pythagoras's Theorem is not true. Such geometries

Top: Moving clouds over the south of Greece. Bottom: Rocket-camera view of Earth's cloud-cover at a single moment. Because this cover is partial and shifting, early man everywhere could look out into space and gain from the heavens a sense of time and direction. Had the Earth been wholly cloud-bound like Venus he could never have done so.

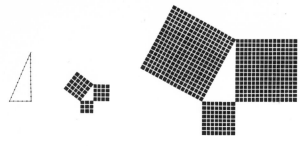 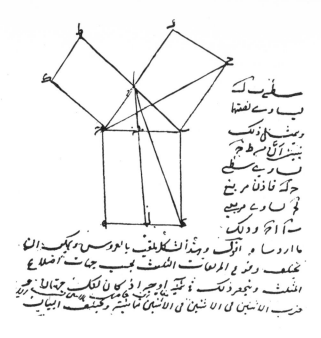

Mesopotamian mathematicians knew of many cases in which the square on the longest side of a right-angled triangle is equal in area to the sum of squares on the two shorter sides. This early Arabic edition of Euclid shows Pythagoras's proof that the same is true of *all* such triangles.

were first invented by Lobachevsky and by Riemann, in the middle of the nineteenth century. They are every bit as self-consistent as simple geometry, but they are much more difficult and complicated to work with.

The question arises as to which geometry must be used in the solution of problems of measurement in the everyday world. The answer is Euclidean geometry, not the more complicated geometries of Lobachevsky and Riemann. Many people interpret this welcome simplification as an indication that of all possible systems, Euclidean geometry is the only "true" one—that the others are mere intellectual exercises or figments of the imagination. But this view is entirely wrong. Euclidean geometry *cannot* be applied to the physical world *if the triangle ABC is very large*. In such cases the geometry of Riemann must be used. In fact, the "true" geometry of the universe is the complex geometry of Riemann!

This brings us to the second slice of luck. It is possible to prove mathematically that Riemannian geometry becomes indistinguishable from Euclidean geometry *whenever distances are small*, so that the more complicated geometry can then be replaced by simple geometry. Fortunately all distances involved in everyday problems of measurement are small enough to allow us to rely on simple geometry. If this had not been so, the problem of formulating Riemannian geometry would have provided a severe, and probably insuperable, obstacle to the development of mathematics in general. And

without mathematical tools, man would have attained little understanding of the world around him.

As an aside, we may ask: how big does a physical triangle have to become before Pythagoras's Theorem ceases to be approximately true? Bigger than the Earth, than the Solar System, and even than the Milky Way. Only when we come to problems concerning much vaster regions of the universe do geometrical complexities become severe. We shall encounter such problems in the last chapter.

The third lucky circumstance which contributed to man's intellectual emergence is more difficult to explain. Perhaps we can best begin by asking how, in a physical sense, we can delineate a triangle. (The existence of a triangle was *assumed implicitly* in the above argument.) One method might be with rulers; but obviously only very small triangles can be laid out with rulers. The method of delineating far larger triangles used in practice is by *light rays*. We make the initial assumption that light travels in straight lines, so that the sides of a triangle can then be determined by light rays emitted at the vertices. For example, a light ray emitted from a point A and received at a point B delineates the side AB of the triangle ABC.

But is our assumption correct? Does light really travel in straight lines? The strict answer is no. This can be demonstrated by the experiment shown in Figure 1.1. Let S be a small source of light, a so-called point source. Light from it falls on an observing screen at B after passing through a hole in an opaque screen at *A*. If the light really traveled consistently in straight lines the size of the patch of light on the observing screen would decrease steadily as the size of the hole at *A* decreased. Experiment shows that it actually does so, *provided that the hole remains greater than about 0.01 millimeters in diameter*. But when the hole becomes smaller than this, the patch of light on the observing screen, so far from diminishing, actually begins to increase again. Hence, when we are concerned with the behavior of light over distances of 0.01 mm. or less, the assumption that light travels in straight lines becomes altogether too crude. But provided we are not concerned with the passage of light through very small apertures, the assumption leads us into no appreciable errors.

The upshot is this. The delineation of a triangle by light rays is necessarily incomplete, since the positions of the vertices *A*, *B* and *C* cannot be determined within distances of about 0.01 mm. But for most practical purposes this indeterminacy of the vertices is unimportant, since the lengths of the sides of the triangle are so enormously greater. Indeed, in astronomy the sides of the triangle are often greater than a million million miles, in which case errors of a fraction of a millimeter are obviously entirely negligible. This, then, is man's third slice of luck. He can, for most practical purposes, reduce the highly complex way in which light actually travels to a very simple picture. And this simple picture is not only adequate for determining the positions and distances of the Moon, Sun, planets and stars, but is also sufficiently accurate for use in the design of many optical instruments, including the telescope, the microscope and the camera. Nevertheless, the fact remains that a physical triangle can never be determined with absolute precision. We cannot delineate a triangle in which the vertices are idealized points—Euclidean abstractions having position but no dimension.

A fourth circumstance which helped to develop man's intellect, by setting him a problem difficult enough to exercise his mental powers to the full but not so difficult as to discourage him altogether, arises from the tremendous distances of the stars and galaxies. The angle at which an observer views a very distant body hardly seems to change, even though both the distant body and the observer may be moving in different directions.

In Figure 1.2, *A* and *B* are two objects which move with the same speed along parallel tracks. *O* is the observer, moving at the same speed as *A* and *B* but along a track not parallel with theirs. Initially *O* is at O_1, *A* is at A_1, *B* is at B_1, so that *A* and *B* lie in the same direction from the observer. At some later time *O* is at O_2, *A* is at A_2, *B* is at B_2. (The distances A_1 to A_2, B_1 to B_2 and O_1 to O_2 are the same, since *A*, *B* and *O* move at the same speed.) Obviously the direction from *O* to the distant *B* has changed much less than the direction from *O* to the much nearer *A*.

To the ancients, the stars, because of their great distances, formed an apparently constant background—the background of the so-called fixed stars. Without that constant background they would never have found it possible to determine the motion of the Earth. Without that seemingly unchanging background, no direction whatever would have seemed fixed, and man would never have been able to orientate himself. Further, instead of aiming to

Figure 1.1
Here light from a point source passes through a hole in an opaque screen on to a viewing screen. If light travels in straight lines, the illuminated area should decrease as the size of the hole decreases. In fact it does so until the diameter of the hole is reduced to about 0.01 mm. Then it begins to *increase*.

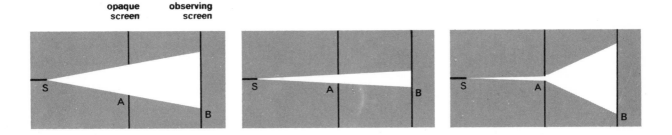

determine the motions of all the bodies of the universe—as the modern astronomer aims to do—the ancients could simplify the whole problem of astronomy to a discussion of the motions of only the Earth, Moon, Sun and planets. Even the solution of this restricted problem demanded the concentrated efforts of the finest intellects over a period covering several thousand years.

In fact the problem proved to be of just the right level of complexity. It is true that if it had been easier it would have been solved sooner. But then mathematics would not have developed to the stage where it served as a springboard for the advance of modern science. The great thing is that the problem was not so tough as to be insoluble but was yet tough enough to exercise the mind of man to the utmost. It was ideal as a stimulant to the achievement of maximum progress.

The Celestial Sphere

When we look at the stars with eyes and mind unprejudiced by preconceived notions about their relative distances from one another, they all appear to fall on a spherical surface, an upturned bowl. So striking is the illusion that the ancients believed the heavens were indeed a real sphere. One early Greek view was that a great spherical shield protected the Earth from a distant fire. Through holes in the shield—the holes being the stars—flames from the fire could be seen.

The somewhat naïve concept of a *celestial sphere* on which lie all the stars has always been, and still is, of vital importance to the astronomer. In Figure 1.3, an observer O is on the Earth, and A, B, C, and D are distant astronomical objects—stars, galaxies, and so on. The points where light from A to O, B to O, C to O and D to O cut a large sphere having its center at O are marked as a, b, c, and d. The observer's eye is quite incapable of informing him whether the light which reaches it really comes from A, B, C and D or whether it comes from a, b,

c and d. Indeed, if the observer is concerned only with describing the *directions* of astronomical objects, it is better for him to think of them all as lying on the sphere. We may say that a, b, c, etc., represent the *projections* on the sphere of the astronomical objects A, B, C, etc.

We should think of the sphere of Figure 1.3 as being very large compared with the Earth. This gives the advantage that when the observer O changes his position on the Earth the points a, b, c, etc., are not appreciably changed. Thus all observers everywhere on Earth can then agree (within practical limits) about the positions of a, b, c, etc., on the sphere.

Elementary textbooks sometimes state that we should think of the celestial sphere as being infinitely large. This is quite wrong. We must not think of it as being so large that simple Euclidean geometry ceases to be valid on its surface. In fact it can be as large as the Milky Way, but it must not be much larger. Galaxies very distant from the Milky Way must evidently then be taken to lie *outside* the celestial sphere, as, indeed, B and D are shown to do in the diagram. It is therefore wrong to imagine that all astronomical objects lie within the celestial sphere, as is often stated.

The Turning Earth

At any given moment the stars form a definite pattern on the celestial sphere. Observation, even with the naked eye and even extended over only an hour or two, shows clearly that this whole pattern moves with respect to our local surroundings on the Earth. It is as though the whole celestial sphere were spinning round. This, again, is an illusion. The apparent motion of the celestial sphere arises from the actual rotation of the Earth.

Strictly, this statement is subject to the proviso that we adhere to local Euclidean geometry. If we are prepared to depart from Euclidean geometry, not only over great distances but even locally, the

Figure 1.2
How, at two different moments, an observer (O) on our moving Earth sights (A) near and (B) more distant objects which are moving at equal speeds along parallel paths.

Figure 1.3
In describing apparent positions of objects A, B, C and D, a terrestrial observer (O) is not concerned with their distances. He need only define their projections—a, b, c and d—on the celestial sphere.

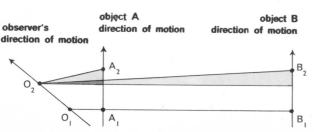

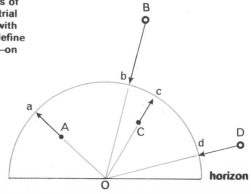

assertion cannot be made. At the expense of great geometrical complexity it is possible to regard the Earth as fixed and the heavens as spinning round it. When, in a later chapter, we come to discuss the problem of the Earth's motion round the Sun a similar situation will arise. We can then only assert the Copernican doctrine that the Earth moves round the Sun provided we specify that our geometry has the simple Euclidean form, based on Pythagoras's Theorem; the admission of a complex geometry into the context would allow us to say that the Sun moves around the Earth.

In fact, at the expense of appalling geometrical complexity, we can legitimately assert that the Earth is flat! The error of the flat-Earth faddist lies in the fact that he imagines he can combine the notion of a flat Earth with simple geometry. The latter positively demands that we regard the Earth as round, just as it demands that we regard the Earth as moving round the Sun and not *vice versa*. Similarly, simple Euclidean geometry demands that we explain our observations of the celestial sphere in terms of a rotating Earth.

When we take a long-exposure photograph of an area of the night sky, the rotation of the Earth causes light from the stars to leave a trailing arc on the plate. If we point the camera toward the north, at the correct elevation, these arcs become portions of circles, as shown on the following page. Moreover, all the arcs are portions of circles having the same center. The reason is easily seen. In Figure 1.4, P and Q are the geographical poles of the Earth and O is the observer. The rotation of the Earth about its geographical axis produces exactly the same apparent effect as would a rotation of the celestial sphere in the opposite direction about the axis from p to q. These are simply points lying along a straight line representing an extension of the Earth's axis, and are the two possible points toward which a camera must be pointed in order to produce a photograph of the kind we show. (In fact, of course, a camera pointed from O toward q, would be obstructed by the body of the Earth. We can point it toward q only from the southern hemisphere.)

The rotation of the Earth has no effect on the points p and q. They remain fixed. A star at a, however, will appear to move. It will appear to trail out a circular path on the celestial sphere, the center of the circle being on the line Pp. After a half-rotation the star will appear to have shifted to a_1, the angles a_1Op and pOa being essentially equal, because

the celestial sphere is very large compared with the Earth. After a full rotation the apparent position of the star returns to a.

A most important point emerges out of these simple considerations. If the observer O in Figure 1.5 takes the *projection* of the direction of p on to the horizontal plane, he obtains the direction ON. This gives him the direction along which he must travel in order to reach P, the Earth's north geographical pole, in the shortest possible distance. In other words, the direction of the pole p of the celestial sphere determines the points of the compass.

Evidently it would be highly convenient if a bright star were to lie exactly at p. Actually none does. But the star Polaris lies only a single degree away. The effect of the Earth's rotation is therefore to make Polaris appear to move in a very small circle, so small as not to be noticed by the casual eye. For all practical purposes in which accuracy to within one degree is unimportant, this star can therefore be used for determining the observer's northerly direction. Probably many people at one time or another, when lost in some trackless place, have cause to be thankful for the information supplied by this most useful star.

Measuring Positions on the Celestial Sphere

It is important, when referring to individual stars, to have some means of describing accurately their apparent positions on the celestial sphere. The few brightest stars can be referred to by name, as we have just referred to Polaris, and every astronomer knows exactly where to look for Polaris, Arcturus, Capella, Canopus, and so on. He identifies them from his *memory* of the pattern of the sky. But obviously he cannot depend on his memory when he is faced with the problem of identifying any one of the millions of faint stars which a powerful modern telescope may reveal.

Many of the most interesting stars are faint not because they are feeble specimens but because they are far distant. When an astronomer discovers an unusual case and wishes to talk about it to his colleagues, he must have some means of specifying precisely which among the multitude of stars is the one he has in mind. The only way to do this is by stating a precise position, so precise that there can be no possibility of confusion with nearby stars. In short, the accurate determination of the positions of stars is essential to the interchange of information among astronomers.

A long-exposure photograph of the
night sky taken with camera pointed
to the north shows that stars seem
to trail out circular arcs, all
having a common center.

$ap = pa_1$

Figure 1.4
The rotation of the Earth about PQ
explains the apparent rotation of
stars (in opposite sense) about pq.

Figure 1.5
By taking the projection of the
direction of p on to the horizontal
plane, the observer O obtains the
northerly direction ON.

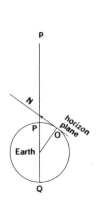

The problem is greatly simplified by the lucky
circumstance, already mentioned, that the star-
pattern is essentially unchanging. It is true that all
the stars are moving, and that their apparent positions relative to each other are therefore slowly
changing; but over short periods of time, up to four
or five years, these changes can be neglected. Hence
our problem is to determine the positions of fixed
points on the surface of the sphere. This is the kind
of problem with which mankind has long been
familiar, since the determining of positions on the
surface of the Earth is precisely similar.

Positions on the Earth's surface are normally
stated in latitudes and longitudes. Three quantities
play a crucial role in determining latitude and
longitude: the geographical equator, the polar axis,
and an arbitrary point on the equator. In Figure 1.6,
the polar axis cuts the surface of the Earth at the
two poles, marked P and Q; C is the Earth's center;
X is the arbitrary point. To determine the latitude
and longitude of any given point (here the point
marked A), we take a plane which passes through A
and through the polar axis. This plane cuts the
equator at B. We next join A, B, and the arbitrary
point X, all to the center, C. The angle ACB now
gives us the latitude of the point A, while the angle
BCX gives us its longitude.

This is not quite the end. Two further conventions are needed. If A, the point we wish to define,
is in the northern hemisphere we designate its latitude N, for example 50°N; if it is in the southern
hemisphere we designate its latitude S—50°S. The
second convention concerns the angle BCX. As
drawn in the figure, B lies to the west of X, and the
longitude is therefore designated W—say 110°W. If
B were to lie to the east of X then the longitude would
be designated E—say 110°E. What if the point B
should fall diametrically opposite to X? Should the
longitude be written 180°W or 180°E? The answer
is that either can be used. No longitude is ever
greater than 180°, while no latitude is ever greater
than 90°.

The last geographic question concerns the arbitrary point X. How is it chosen? For many years
different sovereign states chose the point at which
the plane through their administrative capitals and
the polar axis cuts the equator. This led to considerable confusion. For close on a century X has been
accepted, by international agreement, as the point
at which the plane through the polar axis and the
old Greenwich Observatory cuts the equator.

Before we go on to consider the determination of astronomical positions, a word about the measurement of angles may be useful. A movable straight arm OB is pivoted at O. Initially at OA, it is moved around until ultimately it comes back to OA. The arm thus sweeps out one complete rotation. In practice angles are commonly measured according to a scale in which a whole turn—one sweep through a complete rotation—is divided into 360 equal parts of a *degree* each. (There is another widely-used system of angular measurement, in which the unit is the radian, which does not here concern us.) In turn the degree is divided into 60 equal parts called *minutes*, and each minute is divided into 60 equal parts called *seconds*; and we can achieve still greater precision by using decimal fractions of a second.

The decision to divide angles in this way is very inconvenient. It would be far better to divide a complete turn into 1000 equal parts, and then to subdivide each such part into 1000. We should then have milliturns and microturns, and elementary calculations involving angles would consequently be much easier to perform.

The division of the circle into 360 equal parts was first made, perhaps 5000 years ago, in the river-valley civilization of Mesopotamia, though the circle was similarly divided elsewhere at different times—wherever and whenever men had succeeded in defining the length of the year as approximately 360 days. The division into 360 parts was far more convenient for the people of ancient Mesopotamia than it is for us today, since they used 60 as a fixed base in calculation, whereas we use 10; and as a general rule the units in which quantities are measured should always bear a simple and convenient relationship to the number currently used as a fixed base in calculation.

It seems that it is easier to achieve space flight than to change our archaic system of angular measure. The Mesopotamians imposed the number 60 on us, and we seem powerless to escape from it. The same kind of absurdity shows itself in the divisions of the clock into 24 hours, 60 minutes, and 60 seconds. It also shows itself in the British monetary system, and in British and American units of linear measurement. Man's inability to rid himself of inconvenient conventions is a trait that could lead to his undoing.

But to return to our theme of defining positions on the celestial sphere: one might expect this to be an extremely complicated business, but in fact the data can be even more limited than when we are defining terrestrial latitudes and longitudes. Provided we can specify the equator, it is not necessary initially to specify the polar axis. All we have to do is to take the plane of the equator, which passes through the center C, and draw a straight line through C perpendicular to this plane, as shown in Figure 1.7. This line *is* the required polar axis. Evidently, then, all we need in order to determine positions on the sphere is to specify an equator together with an arbitrary point on it.

Better still, we can simply specify any plane through C. This will cut the sphere in a great circle which we can regard as the equator. (A *great circle* is simply any circle of maximum diameter that can be drawn on the surface of a sphere, and the plane on which such a circle lies necessarily intersects the center of the sphere.) An arbitrary point on the equator must still be specified. So our recipe for determining positions on the celestial sphere is as follows: specify a plane through the center, that is, through the observer. Take the great circle in which this plane cuts the celestial sphere and specify a point on that circle. Then use a system of latitude and longitude.

In principle it is possible to choose the plane through the observer in an infinity of ways. In actual practice, however, there are four convenient

Figure 1.6
Principle of defining terrestrial latitude and longitude.

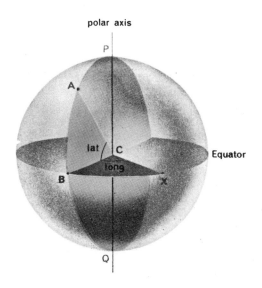

For centuries different map-makers
chose different meridians from
which to measure longitude. The top
map (*c.* 1650) measures from the
meridian of Cape Verde. That on
page 19 (1708) uses two zero meridians,
those of Paris and Ferro Island.

By international agreement longitude
everywhere is now reckoned from the
meridian of Greenwich Observatory.
A brass strip adjoining the building
marks a small segment of the line.

and feasible ways of doing so. The four feasible planes are:

(1) the horizontal plane, determined simply by using a spirit level;
(2) a plane parallel to the plane of the Earth's geographical equator;
(3) the plane of the Earth's motion round the Sun;
(4) the plane of the Milky Way.

Case (1), known as the altazimuth system, has the advantage that it is very easy to set up the horizontal plane. It has, however, two very serious disadvantages. In the first place, the horizontal planes will not, in general, be parallel for different observers, and the great circles in which the planes cut the celestial sphere will therefore be different for different observers. Hence there can be no common agreement about the way in which points on the celestial sphere are located. Each observer has his own private system.

To understand the second disadvantage we must notice that for each given observer the horizontal plane cuts the celestial sphere in the *horizon*. Now stars rise above the horizon and set below it. No star stays permanently *on* the horizon (unless the observer happens to be at one or other of the geographical poles). This means that no star can be used to determine the arbitrary point without which positions cannot be specified. The arbitrary point must therefore be chosen by a geographical criterion rather than by an astronomical one; for example, we may elect to choose that point on the horizon which

lies directly to the south. This procedure has the profound drawback that the rotation of the Earth causes the measured positions of astronomical objects to change from one moment to another. Hence the positions that each observer measures with his own private system are different at every moment of the day! As a basic method of cataloguing the positions of the stars the altazimuth system is therefore obviously useless.

Let us look next at Case (2), using a plane parallel to the plane of the Earth's equator. This is free from the disadvantages inherent in the altazimuth system and the basic circle is, moreover, readily determined. All that need be done is to find the direction of one of the poles and draw a plane perpendicular to this direction, as in Figure 1.8. The circle in which this plane cuts the celestial sphere is the required equatorial circle. The situation now is that any star lying on the equator at one moment of the day also lies on it at any other moment of the day. In other words, the rotation of the Earth about the polar direction does not alter the latitude of a star as measured in this system. Hence any star lying on the equator can conveniently be chosen as the arbitrary point. A description of how this choice is made in practice will be deferred for the moment, until we have examined Case (3).

So far we have been concerned only with how to measure the positions of the stars. Here the problem is simplified by the fact that, taken over any reasonably short period of time, such as a few years, the

stars maintain an unchanging pattern. Measuring the positions of the Moon, Sun and planets is made more difficult by the fact that these bodies do not form a part of that unchanging pattern. Their positions change from day to day. If we use Case (2) as a system of measuring their positions, both their latitude and their longitude will change with time. If we use Case (3), however, only the longitude changes in a first approximation. Hence Case (3) is more convenient than Case (2) for the purpose of describing positions within the Solar System.

To understand how this comes about, we must first notice that the Earth moves in an orbit round the Sun which, over not too long a period of time, can be taken as lying in a plane. This plane cuts the celestial sphere in a circle known as the *ecliptic*. A simplification now arises because it so happens that the planets and the Moon lie very nearly in the same plane. Hence their positions on the celestial sphere fall nearly on the ecliptic. This means that if the ecliptic circle is used to determine position, the planets will all have latitudes close to zero. Only their longitudes will change in any marked manner.

The ecliptic is readily determined by observation. The Sun lies always on the ecliptic, by the very definition of the word. As the Earth moves in its orbit, a line drawn from the Earth to the Sun changes in direction. This means that the Sun appears—as seen from the Earth—to move relative to the stars. In fact, the Sun simply moves along the ecliptic. So by tracing the path of the Sun among the stars we obtain the ecliptic itself.

The circle of Case (2) and the circle of Case (3) cut each other at two points. One of these two points, called the First Point of Aries, is marked by its traditional sign ♈ in Figure 1.9. When the Sun is at ♈, its direction is perpendicular to the polar direction. We then have the situation as shown in the small diagram, when every place on the Earth has the same length of day. That is to say ♈ indicates the position of the Sun at one or other of the equinoxes. If the polar direction is taken to point *north*, then ♈ denotes the *vernal*, or spring, *equinox*. The opposite point to ♈, where the two circles again intersect, denotes the *autumnal equinox*. In other words, the Sun reaches ♈ at about March 21. It reaches the point diametrically opposite to ♈ at about September 22.

The daily rotation of the Earth is equivalent to a rotation of the celestial sphere so far as the apparent motions of the heavenly bodies are concerned. Hence in relation to the observer's own horizon the Sun will appear to trace a diurnal path which is very nearly a small circle on the celestial sphere.

What this means to an observer living in the northern terrestrial hemisphere is shown in Figure 1.10.

Figure 1.7
As a step to defining positions on the celestial sphere we can specify the equator, then draw through its center (C) a line perpendicular to it. This line is the polar axis.

Figure 1.8
Alternatively, we can find the polar direction and draw a plane at right angles to it. The circle in which this plane cuts the celestial sphere is the equatorial circle.

Figure 1.9
Celestial longitudes are measured from the First Point of Aries(♈), one of the two points at which the circle of the equator cuts the plane of the ecliptic.

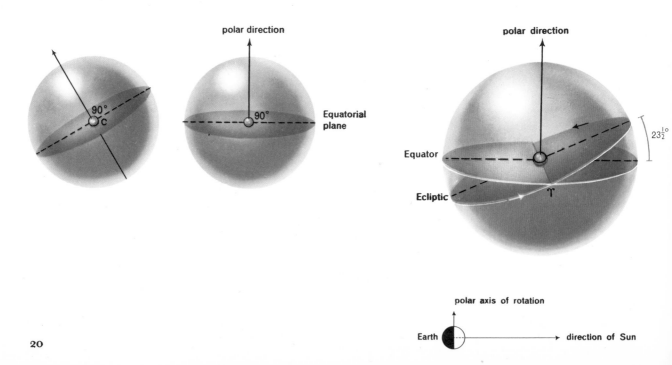

The observer's position (at the point O), the polar direction, the observer's zenith and his horizon are all to be regarded as fixed—the altazimuth system again. Suppose the Sun lies on the ecliptic at A. Then the Earth's diurnal rotation causes the Sun (and indeed the whole ecliptic) to appear to rotate about the polar direction. The Sun itself will appear to move nearly round the small circle $AXYZ$. (Actually the Sun does not *quite* come back to its starting point at the end of a day, because of the apparent solar motion along the ecliptic.) The points X and Y correspond to *sunset* and *dawn* respectively, while Z corresponds to midday. From Y to Z to X the Sun lies above the observer's horizon, so that the time taken for this part of the Sun's apparent motion corresponds to the observer's daytime. From X to Y the Sun lies below the observer's horizon, and this part of its apparent motion corresponds to his night-time.

The lengths of day and night are in general unequal. When the Sun lies on the ecliptic between C and D, the night is longer than the day, whereas the section between D and B gives a day longer than the night. Thus the Sun is at B in midsummer and at C in midwinter. The point D again shows the vernal equinox, one of the two occasions in the year when day and night are equal. The point diametrically opposite to D indicates the autumnal equinox.

The direction from the observer to D is the observer's west, which means that the Sun sets in the west (and rises in the east) at the equinoxes.

One point may seem puzzling. In the system in which the observer regards his own horizon as fixed —Case (1), the altazimuth system—the ecliptic has an apparent diurnal motion. This is also the case for our diagram (Figure 1.10). The ecliptic can lie in the position there shown only at one single moment of the day. But at what moment? Our diagram is drawn with the ecliptic in the position for midday at midsummer. The position would be the same at dawn at the autumnal equinox, at midnight at the winter solstice, or at sunset at the vernal equinox. Indeed, on any day there is always some moment when the ecliptic lies in the position depicted.

Returning once more to position measurement, we have still to see how the arbitrary point is chosen for Case (2) as well as for Case (3). If we choose the point ♈ (as shown in Figure 1.9 on page 20), it will serve equally well for *both* cases, since this point lies on both the fundamental circles concerned. Hence the position of the Sun among the stars at the vernal equinox defines the required arbitrary point for Case (2) as well as for Case (3).

We have examined the first three systems of position-measurement in ascending order of astronomical significance. Case (1) is entirely particular to the

Figure 1.10
Position of ecliptic at noon on midsummer day (northern hemisphere). The Earth's rotation makes the Sun and the ecliptic appear to move in the day round the circle AXYZ.

Figure 1.11
One system of celestial co-ordinates makes use of the galactic circle, the central line of the Milky Way. Here we see the angle at which it cuts the celestial equator.

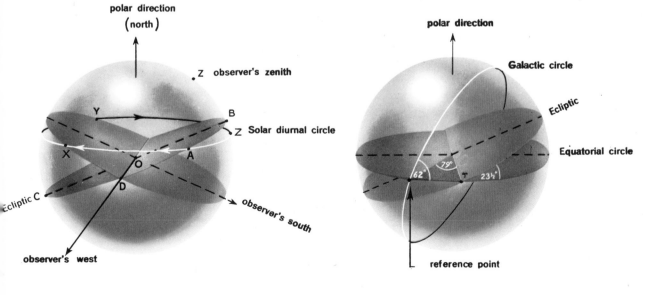

observer's location on the Earth. In contrast, Case (2) yields the same results for every location on the Earth. Even so, positions measured by this system have a special relation *only* to the Earth; they would have no significance for an observer not situated on the Earth. Positions measured according to Case (3) would have significance for observers on any planet within the Solar System, but they would not be significant for an observer living on a planet moving round any star other than the Sun. To obtain a system which would be equally meaningful for all observers within the Milky Way we must move on to Case (4), explained in Figure 1.11.

The central line of the Milky Way forms the basic circle of Case (4). Thus positions are referred in this case to the structure of the galaxy of stars in which we live. The circle of Case (2) cuts the circle of Case (4) at two points. One of these is chosen as the arbitrary point for Case (4). The angle at which the two circles cut is about 62°, as compared with the angle of about 23.5° which the plane of the ecliptic makes with the circle of Case (2).

In practice, the positions of astronomical objects are catalogued in accordance with Case (2). Although this system is related to the Earth's polar axis, and therefore has no general astronomical significance, the basic circle it employs is readily determined and is common to all observatories on the Earth. It is, moreover, a system that is convenient for use in relation to the setting and orientation of astronomical instruments.

A final point about Case (2). Although this is a system of latitude and longitude essentially similar to that used for determining geographical positions here on the Earth, two small differences have been introduced in the astronomical measures. Instead of latitudes being designated N or S, for example 30°N or 30°S, the corresponding astronomical latitudes are written + or −, *e.g.*, +30° or −30°. Written in this way, the latitudes are called *declinations*, for example a declination +30° or −30°. Longitudes are likewise written somewhat differently. Instead of being measured both east and west, they are measured only eastward, and thus run from 0° to 360°. Divided into 24 intervals of 15° each, longitudes may be expressed in hours. Thus 15° = 1 hour, 30° = 2 hours, 45° = 3 hours, and so on. Finer divisions into minutes and seconds are also used. Expressed in this way, a longitude is referred to as a *right ascension*.

An important feature of position-measurement is that references given in terms of one system can readily be converted into those of another by calculation. To convert measurements given in terms of Case (2) to measurements in terms of the other cases, the following data are used.

To obtain the altazimuth system, Case (1). Here we must know the location of the observer on the Earth, and also the time. (The latter is necessary since the position of an astronomical object changes with time in the altazimuth system.)

To obtain the ecliptic system, Case (3). The angle at which the ecliptic cuts the basic circle of Case (2) must be known. This is sufficient to enable the position in the ecliptic system to be calculated. The angle is about 23.5°.

To obtain the galactic system, Case (4). Here we must know the right ascension of the point at which the galactic circle cuts the basic circle of Case (2). (The declination of this point is of course 0°, as is the declination of ♈.) Together with the angle of 62° at which the two circles cut each other, this is sufficient to determine the galactic co-ordinates of an object whenever its right ascension and declination are specified.

Nowadays conversions from Case (2) to the other systems can be performed almost instantaneously with the aid of a high-speed computer. The extreme rapidity of modern methods of calculation permits the design of instruments which make special use of an altazimuth system of reference, as we shall see in the following chapter.

Sketch-Maps of the Heavens

In ancient times men divided the stars visible in adjacent portions of the sky into groups and gave each group a name—often the name of an animal, a deity or a hero. These *constellations* are still used in modern astronomy as a rough and ready means of referring to objects on the sky, though it should always be remembered that this grouping of stars in adjacent parts of the sky into constellations has no physical significance.

The constellations to which the modern astronomer refers are listed on the opposite page, and the positions of most of the main ones are plotted on pages 26 to 28. The decorative star maps on pages 24, 25 and 29 are fairly typical of the fanciful kind of way in which men have plotted the heavens over a period of several thousand years.

Constellation List

Name	Abbreviation	Name	Abbreviation
Andromeda	And	Lupus	Lup
*Antlia	Ant	*Lynx	Lyn
*Apus	Aps	Lyra	Lyr
Aquarius	Aqr	*Mensa	Men
Aquila	Aql	*Microscopium	Mic
Ara	Ara	*Monoceros	Mon
Aries	Ari	*Musca	Mus
Auriga	Aur	*Norma	Nor
Bootes	Boo	*Octans	Oct
*Caelum	Cae	Ophiuchus	Oph
*Camelopardalis	Cam	Orion	Ori
Cancer	Cnc	*Pavo	Pav
*Canes Venatici	CVn	Pegasus	Peg
Canis Major	CMa	Perseus	Per
Canis Minor	CMi	*Phoenix	Phe
Capricornus	Cap	*Pictor	Pic
*Carina	Car	Pisces	Psc
Cassiopeia	Cas	Piscis Australis	PsA
Centaurus	Cen	*Puppis	Pup
Cepheus	Cep	*Pyxis	Pyx
Cetus	Cet	*Reticulum	Ret
*Chamaeleon	Cha	Sagitta	Sge
*Circinus	Cir	Sagittarius	Sgr
*Columba	Col	Scorpius	Sco
*Coma Berenices	Com	*Sculptor	Scl
Corona Australis	CrA	*Scutum	Sct
Corona Borealis	CrB	Serpens	Ser
Corvus	Crv	*Sextans	Sex
Crater	Crt	Taurus	Tau
*Crux	Cru	*Telescopium	Tel
Cygnus	Cyg	Triangulum	Tri
Delphinus	Del	*Triangulum Australe	TrA
*Dorado	Dor	*Tucana	Tuc
Draco	Dra	Ursa Major	UMa
Equuleus	Equ	Ursa Minor	UMi
Eridanus	Eri	*Vela	Vel
*Fornax	For	Virgo	Vir
Gemini	Gem	*(Piscis) Volans	Vol
*Grus	Gru	*Vulpecula	Vul
Hercules	Her		
*Horologium	Hor		
Hydra	Hya		
*Hydrus	Hyi		
*Indus	Ind		
*Lacerta	Lac		
Leo	Leo		
*Leo Minor	LMi		
Lepus	Lep		
Libra	Lib		

*Of modern origin.

On the following two pages is a decorative map of the heavens made in 1660 by Andreas Cellerius.

Urfa Major

Auriga

Cancer
Afellus

Canis
minor
Procyon

Circulus

Cor Leonis

LEO

M A R

Iordani Flu.

Mogul

Capud
Leonis

Cor Leonis

I N D I A

Cor Hydra
Alphard

Crater Vas.
Torculum Apollinis

Nova Holland

Hydra
Aquaticus Alfugabh

Argo

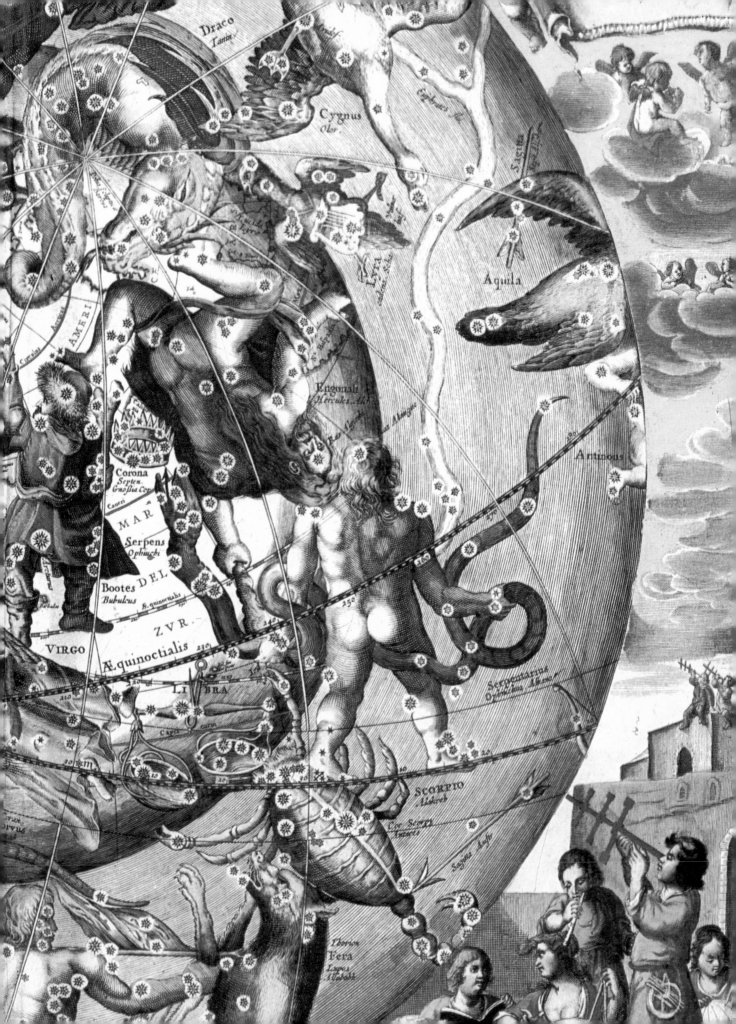

Star maps

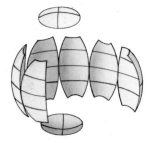

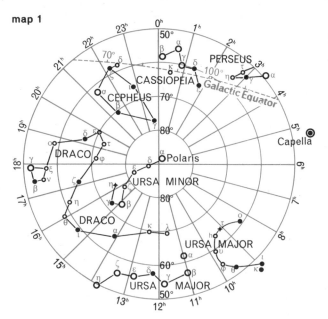

map 1

The maps here and on the next two pages show the main constellations in eight regions of the heavens. The diagram at the top shows the breakdown of the celestial sphere into the eight regions.

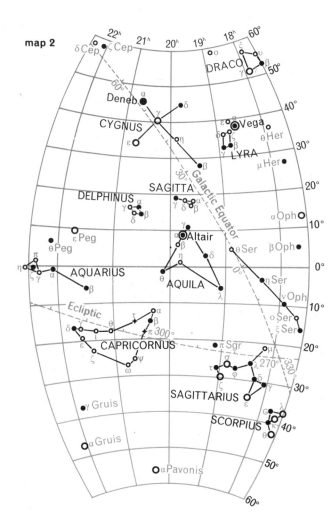

map 2

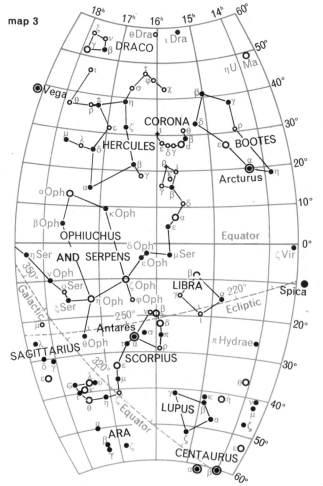

map 3

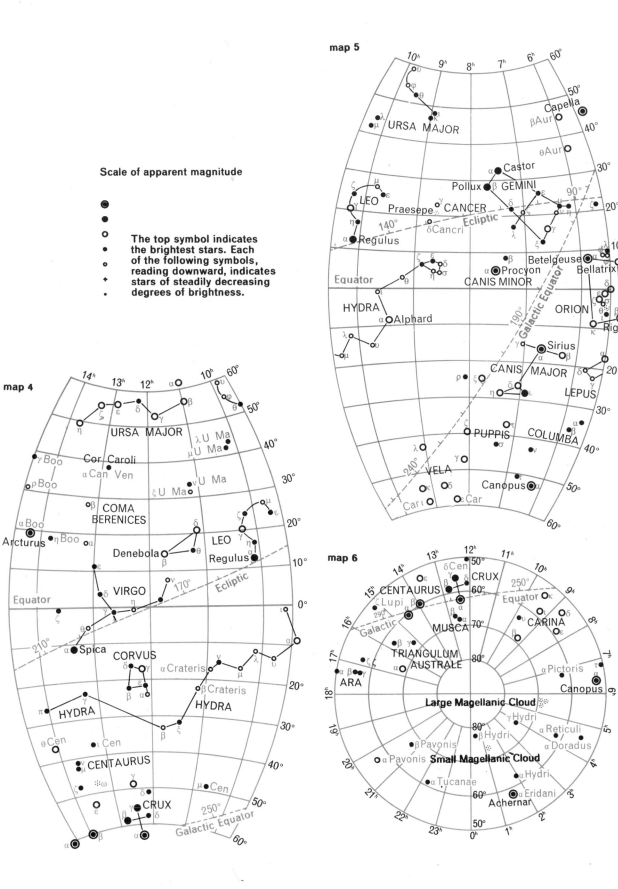

map 5

10ʰ 9ʰ 8ʰ 7ʰ 6ʰ 60°

Capella
βAur 50°
40°

θAur 30°

υ
φ
θ
κ
λ
μ URSA MAJOR

α Castor
Pollux β GEMINI 30°

ζ μ
LEO
η
α Regulus

Praesepe CANCER
δCancri
Ecliptic 140°
δ
90° ζ 20°

μ
λ
ξ
10°

Equator
HYDRA
θ

ζ δ
σ
α Procyon
CANIS MINOR

β Betelgeuse
Bellatrix γ
ε
Galactic Equator 190°
ORION
θ ι
κ
Rigel

Alphard

υ
μ

α Sirius
β

CANIS MAJOR
δ
20°
ρ ξ
η δ
LEPUS

ζ τ
PUPPIS
COLUMBA
α
β
240° λ γ σ
VELA
Canopus 40°

Car ι Car 50°
60°

---

map 4

14ʰ 13ʰ 12ʰ 10ʰ 60°
α υ
φ
δ γ β θ
ζ ε
η URSA MAJOR
λ U Ma
μ U Ma 40°
γ Boo
Cor Caroli
αCan Ven ν U Ma 30°
ρ Boo ξ U Ma
β COMA
BERENICES 20°
μ
ε
δ ζ
LEO γ θ
αBoo η Boo α Denebola β Regulus 10°
Arcturus
ε
VIRGO 170°
Equator γ η Ecliptic 0°
ζ θ
210° ι
α Spica
CORVUS 10°
δ γ αCrateris α
ε λ υ μ
β α γ βCrateris 20°
HYDRA
π γ HYDRA 30°
β ξ
θCen ι Cen 40°
ν CENTAURUS
μ ω γ μ Cen 50°
δ
γ CRUX
ε α 60°
β α

---

map 6

12ʰ
13ʰ 11ʰ
δCen 50°
14ʰ γ β CRUX 250° 10ʰ
15ʰ CENTAURUS β 60° Equator κ 9ʰ
ζLupi α γ δ
16ʰ ζ α MUSCA 70° ε CARINA 8ʰ
290° Galactic
β γ β
17ʰ α TRIANGULUM 80° α 7ʰ
ARA ζ AUSTRALE αPictoris
18ʰ α β τ
Large Magellanic Cloud Canopus 6ʰ
γHydri
19ʰ 80° βHydri αReticuli 5ʰ
βPavonis αDoradus
20ʰ αPavonis Small Magellanic Cloud αHydri 4ʰ
αTucanae 60° βEridani 3ʰ
21ʰ Achernar 2ʰ
22ʰ 50°
23ʰ 0ʰ 1ʰ

Scale of apparent magnitude

The top symbol indicates
the brightest stars. Each
of the following symbols,
reading downward, indicates
stars of steadily decreasing
degrees of brightness.

Star maps

map 7

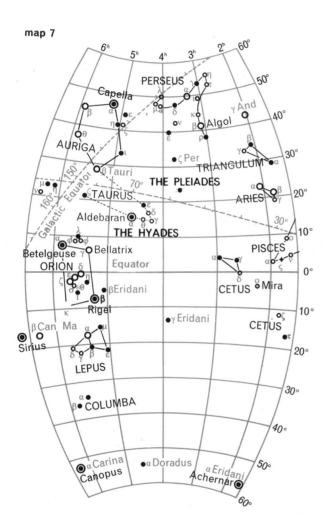

map 8

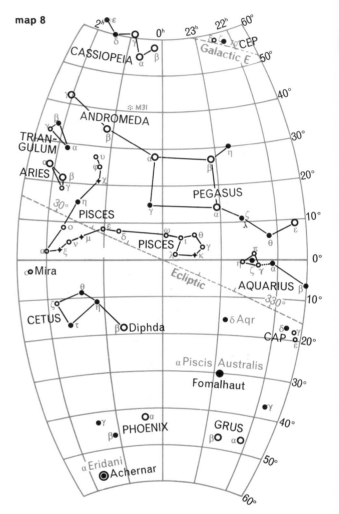

Scale of apparent magnitude

The top symbol indicates
the brightest stars. Each
of the following symbols,
reading downward, indicates
stars of steadily decreasing
degrees of brightness.

Part of the constellation Aquarius,
as depicted in a Persian manuscript
of about A.D. 1650.

Chapter 2 Some Tools of Astronomy

We have seen that it was only by observing the heavens that early man was able to develop a sense of time and to find direction. When we consider the complexity of the apparent motions of the Sun, Moon, stars and planets we may well wonder how he learned as much from them as he did. But it is astonishing just how much can be achieved with the simplest possible equipment. We can see how true this is if we imagine ourselves faced with the same problems and possessed of only the same tools as our early forebears.

Suppose you were stranded on a desert island with only one companion. How would you go about determining the time of day, the length of the year, the dates of midwinter, of midsummer, and of the equinoxes? How would you determine the points of the compass, measure the angle between the ecliptic and the equator, and fix your own geographical latitude? Could you possibly fix ♈, the point of intersection of the ecliptic and the equator? And could you state the positions of the Sun, Moon, stars and planets, using the system of declination and right ascension outlined in Chapter 1? The answer is that you could do all these things with very little apparatus. Provided you do not demand too high a standard of accuracy, most of them require only a plumb-line, a stick, two cans, a supply of water and a little help from your companion.

First fix the stick in an upright position, using the plumb-line to make sure that it is placed as nearly vertical as possible. Then, on a really bright day, keep a close watch on the length of the shadow cast by the stick, noticing the moment when it is shortest. At that moment the Sun is at its zenith—in other words it is just crossing your meridian. Assuming your island to lie in the northern hemisphere the Sun then lies to the south. (If your island were in the southern hemisphere the Sun would then be to the north.) Now take a bearing toward the Sun, using some fixed object in the distant landscape to give a permanent indication of the direction. That fixed object will always lie to the south of your primitive observatory, irrespective of the time of day, and irrespective of whether the Sun happens to be hidden by cloud or not.

But because the Sun is bright, and therefore blinding to the eye, your southerly direction would probably not yet be fixed very accurately. You could improve the result by observing some bright star, in the manner shown in Figure 2.1. Sit as nearly to the

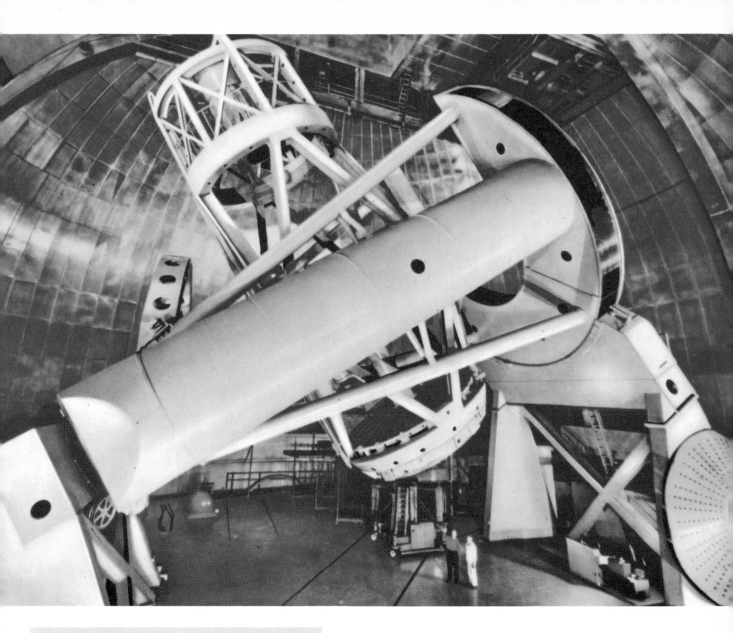

Accuracy of astronomical observation
depends largely on the degree of
refinement of the tools employed.
That, in turn, depends on technology.
Left: Borneo tribesmen using upright
gnomon to measure length of shadow
cast by sun near summer solstice.
Above: Interior photograph of the
200-inch Hale telescope on Palomar
Mountain, the most refined tool of
visual observation at the disposal
of the modern astronomer.

north of the plumb-line as you can, using your stick as a ruler to measure your distance from it. Next keep watch on one particular bright star in the southern sky until the rotation of the Earth causes it to cross behind the plumb-line. Get your assistant to mark the point A on the plumb-line where the star crosses, and also the point B where the line from your eye to the distant horizon intersects the plumb-line. Now measure the distance AB, and take the ratio of AB to BO (your measured distance from the plumb-line).

For any star this ratio will be greatest when you lie dead north of the plumb-line. So carry out the same observation on the same star for a number of nights, moving your position a little to right or left of the original position each time. When the ratio of AB to BO is greatest, take a bearing through the plumb-line to a distant fixed object. Your north-south direction will then be determined with tolerable accuracy.

Alternatively, with the plumb-line now to your north, you could make a similar series of observations of some bright star in the northern sky, but this time seeking the direction in which the ratio of AB to BO is *least*. The plumb-line then gives a reasonably accurate determination of the north. Once you have determined south and north, you can bisect the line joining them to obtain the approximate directions of west and east. This you could do either by eye or, if you wanted greater accuracy, by means of pegs and string used as a compass.

Next, using your stick placed vertically in the ground, measure the length of the shadow it casts at noon each day. (Still assuming that your island is north of the tropics, noon is, of course, the moment when the Sun is due south of you, and the stick is casting a shadow due north.) The length of the stick's noon shadow will vary a little from day to day. It will reach its longest at midwinter and its shortest at midsummer.

If you are sufficiently energetic you can also observe the position of the Sun at dawn each day. On two occasions only during the whole year it will lie due east. These are the times of the equinoxes, the vernal equinox occurring about halfway between midwinter and midsummer, and the autumnal equinox occurring about halfway between midsummer and midwinter. When you know the point at which the Sun lies at the vernal equinox you know ♈, for ♈ simply means that point. The Sun does not stay at ♈, of course, because of its apparent motion along

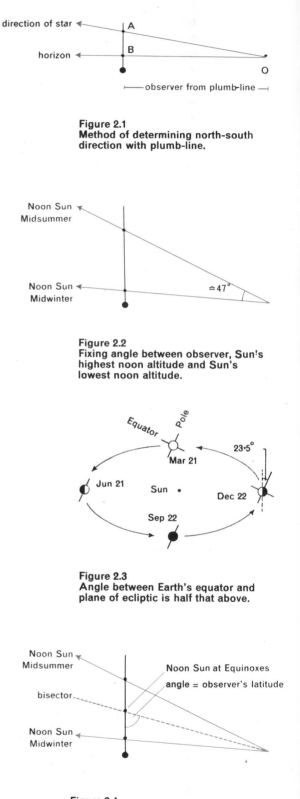

Figure 2.1
Method of determining north-south direction with plumb-line.

Figure 2.2
Fixing angle between observer, Sun's highest noon altitude and Sun's lowest noon altitude.

Figure 2.3
Angle between Earth's equator and plane of ecliptic is half that above.

Figure 2.4
Using observation of Figure 2.2 to determine terrestrial latitude.

the ecliptic; but any star that rises in the east at the moment of sundown at the autumnal equinox, *does* lie almost permanently close to ♈. When you have located such a star you can use it as a reference point for determining right ascensions. We shall see how later.

The length of the year can also be worked out from these observations. For example, the number of days that elapse between successive annual passages of the Sun through the vernal equinox, or the number of days that elapse between one midwinter-day and the next, gives the length of the year.

The length of the year, and the dates of midsummer and midwinter, could also be determined with the aid of your plumb-line, provided you could construct some simple device for cutting down the glare of the Sun. A hollow tube with a thin, semitransparent slice of some vegetable substance fitted across one end would suffice as a simple sighting tube. Sitting at a fixed point due north of the plumb-line, you would merely have to instruct your assistant to mark the point when the center of the Sun lies athwart the line at noon on each day. From midwinter to midsummer the point so determined moves up the plumb-line. From midsummer to midwinter it moves down again. The point is highest at midsummer, lowest at midwinter. The number of days required for one complete oscillation of the point determines the length of the year.

So far we have used only the most primitive equipment imaginable. To glean much further information from our observations we now need something more sophisticated—a large protractor for measuring angles. The highest and the lowest marks which our assistant made on the plumb-line during the last series of observations indicate the maximum change in the angle of elevation of the noon Sun during the course of the year. This change is equal to twice the angle between the plane of the Earth's equator and the plane of the ecliptic. Figure 2.2 shows that if you measure it you will find it to be about 47°, indicating that the Earth's equator makes an angle of about 23.5° with the ecliptic, as in Figure 2.3.

Furthermore, you can use these two extreme positions of the noon Sun to determine your latitude; for the line which bisects the angle between these positions—the line which marks the position of the noon Sun at the equinoxes, when it is directly overhead at the equator—itself makes an angle with the plumb-line. This latter angle, marked in Figure 2.4, *is* your geographical latitude.

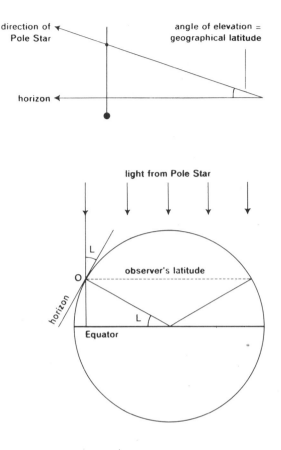

Figure 2.5
Measuring angle of elevation of Polaris gives observer's latitude.

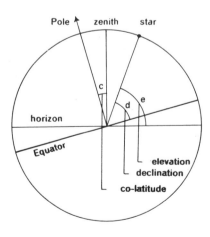

Figure 2.6
Principle of measuring declination.

Even more simply, you could place yourself in a position where the plumb-line lies due north of you, and pick out the star Polaris. Then with the plumb-line, and using the methods described above, you could measure the angle of elevation of that star. This angle, as Figure 2.5 shows, is again your geographical latitude.

By the time you had been stranded long enough to profit from all this do-it-yourself astronomy, you might well be fired with the ambition to compile a simple star catalog—one which would give the declination and right ascension of each of the brightest and most easily recognized stars. Declinations are easy, as we can see from Figure 2.6. You would only need to measure the angle of elevation of each star at the moment it lay due south of your position and this you would do by the now-familiar plumb-line method. You then obtain the declination of the star by the simple process of subtracting your *co-latitude* from the angle of elevation. (Your co-latitude is simply 90° minus your geographical latitude.)

The measurement of right ascensions would be equally easy *provided you had a reliable watch or clock.* If you have made your previous desert-island observations conscientiously, you will already have located some standard star near ♈, some star that rises in the east at sundown at the time of the autumnal equinox. All you need do now is to note the time when that standard star crosses your plumb-line and the time when the star to be catalogued crosses it. The time difference, expressed in hours and minutes, is the right ascension of the star you wish to catalog.

The snag, of course, is that you *don't* have a watch or clock. But it is here that your two cans and a supply of water come in handy. Fill one can with water and pierce a very small hole in the bottom of

Not until the fifteenth century A.D. were mechanical clocks at all common. This clock-dial of about 1500 was calibrated to show day-hours and night-hours at Nuremburg. In late November there were 16 night-hours and 8 day-hours, in late May 16 day-hours and 8 night-hours.

Two instruments used for measuring time in ancient Egypt, a shadow-clock and a water-clock. Both measured hours of unequal length.

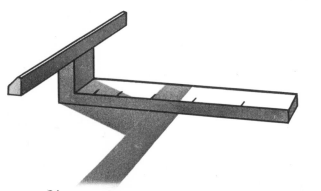

34

it, so that the water trickles slowly into the second can, placed just beneath. Mark the level to which the water rises in this second can during one complete day, measured from one noon to the next. Then, judging carefully by eye, divide the distance between the bottom of the can and the water-level into twenty-four equal divisions. Each division, marked on the side of the can, represents one hour. You now have a water-clock—a very crude one, no doubt, but better than no clock at all. If you use only clear water and take care that the hole in your top can does not become clogged, you should be able, over not too long a period, to measure time to within a quarter of an hour. An error of that amount corresponds to an error of about 4° of celestial longitude. By repeating the observations of a star many times, however, and by taking a final average of all the determinations, it might be possible to reduce the error to about 1°. In a primitive survey of the sky, this would be an entirely acceptable measure of accuracy.

Simple Instruments of Antiquity

We are now in a position to understand the enormous importance of very crude, simple instruments in the early history of astronomy. Indeed, throughout the second millennium B.C., the astronomer-priests of Egypt and Mesopotamia were concerned essentially with problems of the kind we set ourselves on our desert island, and the instruments at their command were seldom much more complicated than those we used there.

By night, and possibly by day as well, they measured time by means of simple water-clocks. The astronomers of Mesopotamia seem to have favored outflow models—vessels from which water escaped through a hole at a steady pace and in which the fall in water-level marked the passage of time. The Egyptians used both outflow and inflow models, the latter being vessels into which water dripped at a steady pace, the *rise* in water-level marking the passing of the hours.

The ambition to achieve ever-increasing standards of accuracy must have been as strong in ancient Mesopotamia as it is in the modern world, for the astronomers of 3000 years ago had already discovered one important way of improving on our desert-island water-clock. If we use a cylindrical can as a crude clepsydra, one drawback is that the water runs out of the hole faster when the can is nearly full than when it is nearly empty, for as the water-level falls the pressure of water falls with it. Astronomers of the ancient world overcame this difficulty by using vessels made in the shape of a truncated cone. The water still runs out of such a vessel faster when it is nearly full than when it is nearly empty, but for each inch of vertical height near the top of the vessel there is a greater volume to run out than for each inch of vertical height near the bottom of the vessel. Thus ten pints per hour may escape when the vessel is nearly full and only six pints per hour when it is nearly empty, but the fall in vertically-measured water-level is approximately the same in both cases. (On our desert island we could have come quite near this degree of accuracy simply by using a very large can with a very small outlet for the water, and by topping up frequently, so as to keep the head of water almost constant.) At a somewhat late stage in their development, water-clocks were frequently fitted with a floating pointer which rose or fell with the water-level, pointing toward a rod calibrated in hours.

Sundials with gnomons set at an angle equal to the latitude of their site measure hours of uniform length. When this one was drawn (about 1550), they were often used to check the accuracy of mechanical clocks.

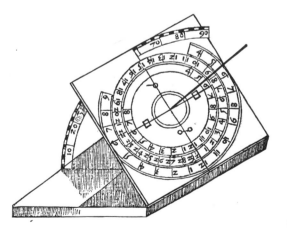

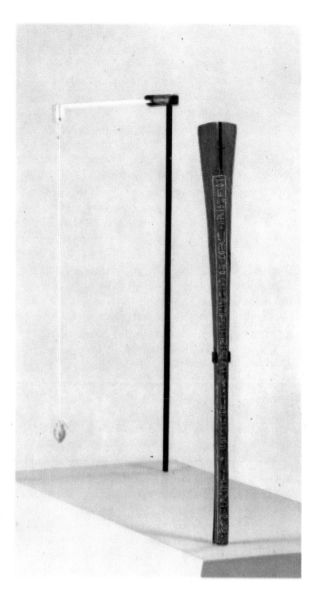

The merkhet, a device consisting of sighting rod and two plumb-lines, used in ancient Egypt for observing the transit of stars.

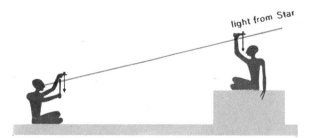

light from Star

To the priests of Egypt and Mesopotamia (as, indeed, to the citizens of ancient Greece and Rome or to the burgesses of medieval Europe) an hour did not commonly mean one twenty-fourth part of a whole day. Rather it meant one twelfth of the period between sunrise and sunset, or one twelfth of the period between sunset and sunrise. In the latitude of northern Egypt a daylight hour of midsummer was about 40 per cent longer than a daylight hour of midwinter. (In the latitude of the medieval Hanseatic ports the difference was about 110 per cent.) The business of calibrating a rod to measure hours at all seasons of the year was therefore a complicated one. Cuneiform tablets unearthed in Mesopotamia show that mathematicians sometimes tackled the problem another way. They worked out elaborate tables stating the amount of water that should be placed in water-clocks at each season of the year in order that they should empty between sunset and sunrise. One twelfth of the total fall in water-level during any night would then correspond to one twelfth of the period between sunset and sunrise at that particular season.

In both the great river-valley civilizations tall, slender columns of stone were commonly placed in the temple precincts. These, built more accurately vertical than any desert island dweller could place a stick in the ground, and throwing shadows of far greater length, provided an excellent means of fixing the time of noon with considerable precision, by noting the moment of the day when the shadow was shortest. The direction in which the shadow pointed at that precise moment also gave a very close approximation to the due northerly direction. The length, and to some extent the direction, of the shadow cast by such a tall column could also be used to measure the hour of day.

At some time between the tenth and eighth centuries B.C. the Egyptians developed a rather more advanced type of shadow-clock. It consisted of a long, horizontal bar fitted at one end with a shorter horizontal bar placed at right angles to it and raised a few inches above it. At dawn the instrument was placed so that the end fitted with the short bar faced due east. Now although the Sun rises in the east at the equinoxes, north of east in midsummer and south of east in midwinter, this short bar was of sufficient length to ensure that at any season at least part of the dawn shadow should fall on the longer horizontal bar. Throughout the morning, as the Sun climbed the heavens and moved steadily through south-east to due south at noon, the short bar would throw an ever-shortening shadow on the long one, and the long bar was calibrated so that the length of the shadow could be read off as the hour of the day. At noon the whole instrument was turned round so that the short bar now faced due west. Then, as the Sun declined in the sky, moving steadily through south-west toward west, the short bar cast an ever-lengthening shadow on the long one. Again the length of the shadow could be read off as the hour of day.

Incidentally, it was not until about the time of the Crusades that astronomers of the Islamic Empire devised sundials which, at any fixed latitude, could be calibrated to show hours of uniform length at every season of the year. Instead of placing the gnomon, or shadow-casting rod, vertically, as in earlier sundials, they now set it parallel to the Earth's axis—that is, at an angle equal to the latitude of the place where the instrument was to be used. Sundials of this kind were not common in Europe until the close of the fifteenth century A.D., by which time crude mechanical clocks were already coming into use.

For observing the transit of stars, the astronomers of ancient Egypt used a device known as the merkhet, which consisted of a simple sighting rod with a slit sight; and two plumb-lines suspended in the plane of the observer's meridian. The observations were made in essentially the same way as that used on our desert island.

The common feature of all these primitive instruments is that they contain no moving parts, in the engineer's sense of the term. To be sure movement does occur—the rise of the float in certain water clocks, for instance—but this demands no specially difficult process of manufacture. And in observing the transit of a star with a plumb-line there is certainly one very important movement—that of the assistant who marks the points of transit across the line! By using an assistant we can obviate the need for an instrument with moving mechanical parts. Equally, by using an instrument with moving mechanical parts, we can obviate the need for an assistant. Indeed, if we wanted to improve on our desert-island observations the next step in sophistication and convenience would be to dispense with the almost endless string of verbal instructions needed for the points of transit to be marked at all accurately by an assistant. We should seek to construct instruments that could be operated by a single observer.

Assuming we were still without workshop facilities, we should be obliged to confine ourselves to simple constructions in wood, perhaps with metal strips on which scales could be marked. In fact we should turn naturally to the sort of instrument used by the astronomers of the classical world, by men such as Hipparchus and Ptolemy. In particular we should want to construct instruments for measuring the angles of elevation of the Sun and the stars. Ptolemy describes an instrument used in his time—about A.D. 150—for measuring the angle of elevation of the Sun. A castaway on a desert island, equipped with only a few simple tools, could probably make a replica of it, though he would doubtless have to work in wood instead of in stone.

The plinth that Ptolemy describes (Figure 2.7) was simply a block of stone with one face cut as smooth and as square as possible. The block was set level on the ground with the help of wedges, and so placed that the smooth face looked due east. At the

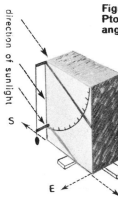

Figure 2.7
Ptolemy's plinth, for measuring the angle of elevation of the noon sun.

Figure 2.8
The triquetrum. This specimen, used by Copernicus, eventually passed into Tycho Brahe's possession.

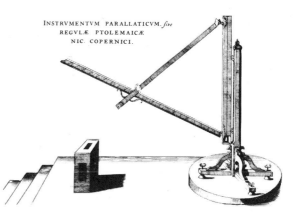

INSTRVMENTVM PARALLATICVM, _sive_
REGVLÆ PTOLEMAICÆ
NIC. COPERNICI.

top southern corner of this face was a horizontal peg, which served as a gnomon to cast a shadow on to a graduated quadrant of arc engraved on the face. About halfway down the southern edge of the face was a second peg. When a plumb-line suspended from the top peg just grazed the lower one, the observer could be sure that the plinth was set dead level. Since the smooth face looked due east, the top peg cast a shadow on it only until noon, when the Sun lay due south. At the moment immediately before the shadow disappeared, its angle, and therefore the angle of elevation of the noon Sun, could be read off from the quadrant. By using the Sun's shadow the problem of glare was solved.

Ptolemy also mentions another instrument, the triquetrum, or Ptolemy's rules (Figure 2.8), whose purpose was to enable the astronomer to measure the angle of elevation of a star as it made its transit across his meridian. One of the problems of making such an instrument was to provide it with a reliably calibrated scale of angular measurement; for at the stage of technological development reached in Ptolemy's time it was no easy matter to make a large arc of metal and to mark it off into small and equal angular divisions. The triquetrum by-passed the problem. It consisted of a vertical post with two arms hinged to it, an upper arm and a lower one. The upper arm was provided with a ring or slot through which the lower arm was fitted. The essential condition was that the distance between the upper and lower hinges on the vertical post had to be equal to the distance on the upper arm between the slot and the upper hinge, so that the two arms and the post formed an isosceles triangle. The upper arm was provided with sights at either end, through which a star or a planet could be viewed. Now if we know the lengths of all three sides of a triangle, it is easy, with the help of simple Euclidean geometry, to work out the angles of that triangle. In the case of the triquetrum, the lengths of two sides (the upper arm and the distance between the two hinges on the post) were known in advance. It only remained to measure the distance between the lower hinge and the point where the upper arm crossed the lower one; and the lower arm was calibrated in linear units to do just that job. So once the observer had taken a reading from the lower arm he had only to consult his table of chords (a simple trigonometrical table) to find out the angle at the apex of the triangle. He could thus find the angle of elevation of the star sighted.

It is true that the use of the triquetrum demands access to a table of chords, but the instrument itself is still of a kind that we could construct for ourselves on a desert island, using only bits of wood, scraps of metal and a few simple tools. Without far better facilities, however, that is probably as far as we should get. For the next step we should need some Swiss-Family-Robinson stroke of luck that would enable us to set up a well-equipped workshop with a plentiful supply of metal. Instead of confining our scale engraving to a line, as in Ptolemy's rules, we could then tackle the more difficult task of engraving a metal arc. This would allow the construction of an engraved quadrant ring with motion about a vertical axis, as shown in Figure 2.9. At the center, O, of the quadrant we could mount a movable arm in such a way that it could swing freely in the vertical plane of the quadrant. The free end of the arm would carry a pointer to facilitate the reading of the engraved scale. The arm would also carry two holes through which a star could be sighted.

Such an instrument would have the obvious advantage of rigidity, and of consequent greater accuracy, over Ptolemy's rules. And because of the possible motion of the quadrant about the vertical axis the observation of a star would not need to be confined to its transit of the southern meridian. We could follow a star continuously; and by noting the moment of maximum elevation we could, in fact, determine the southern meridian with far greater precision than was possible either with primitive immovable instruments or with wooden moving instruments.

Our instrument would have essentially the features of Tycho Brahe's movable quadrant. Ptolemy's rules belong to classical antiquity. Tycho Brahe's quadrant belongs to the sixteenth century. About fifteen hundred years were required to bridge the gap between them. The difficulty lay not at all in the intellectual concepts, but in the development of the necessary techniques of metalwork.

Early Analogue Computers

Analogue computer is the modern name for a model designed to simulate some feature of the natural world. We have already encountered one such analogue computer in the water-clock. The water-clock allows us to simulate the rotation of the Earth. We are able to estimate how much the Earth rotates between the transit of a star near ♈ and the transit of some other star by the simple process of measuring the amount of water that escapes from a vessel between the two transits.

Before the invention of the telescope many of the astronomical instruments in widespread use were skilfully-designed analogue computers. For the most part they depended on the simple fact that if we erect a plane disk, or a plane ring, parallel to the Earth's equator, the parallelism is not destroyed by the Earth's rotation. Nor is it destroyed by the motion of the Earth around the Sun.

The simplest instrument to make use of this property is a single rigidly-fastened thin metal ring. Such an instrument was probably used in the second century B.C. by Hipparchus, the great Alexandrian mathematician and astronomer, to determine the precise dates of the equinoxes. At the equinoxes the Sun lies in the plane of the Earth's equator, and at that time the shadow cast by the front of an Hipparchus ring therefore falls exactly on the back of the ring. At other times the shadow falls either above or below the back of the ring. It was probably in this simple way that Hipparchus was able to arrive at his great discovery of the precession of the equinoxes, a discovery that will be mentioned again in later chapters.

A far cry from the simple fixed circle of Hipparchus was Tycho Brahe's great equatorial armillary, another analogue computer type of instrument. Its construction can be understood from Figure 2.10. The rod PQ can rotate in bearings at P and Q, the direction of PQ being arranged parallel to the axis of rotation of the Earth. A metal circle is rigidly fastened to the rod PQ. The function of this circle is to carry the sight S, which can slide along the circumference of the circle. The sight is also fastened to an arm SC which turns about the center C as S slides along the circle. A cylindrical peg is mounted at C perpendicular to the plane of the circle, the peg being used for sighting in the manner shown in Figure 2.10A.

A star, or planet, was sighted in turn through each of two slits, the arm SC of Figure 2.10 being so turned that the star appeared equally bright through both slits, and so that it appeared on opposite sides of the cylinder in the two cases.

The position of the slide S on the circumference of the circle gave the declination of the star or planet, while the rotation of PQ gave the longitude. In order to read off the longitude a further reading scale had to be added to Figure 2.10. This is shown in Figure 2.11. The circle was simply read against this further scale. One single reading did not, of course, give the longitude. Since the reading changed continuously as the Earth rotated, a single reading evidently had no special significance. But if, in a short time interval, we make readings of two different stars, the difference between the readings is equal to the difference of longitude of the two stars. For a star at ♈ the longitude is 0°, since ♈ is the arbitrary point on the equator from which longitudes are measured. Hence, if we choose a star very near to ♈ as one of our two stars, our two readings give us the longitude of the other star.

Since longitude is simply the equivalent of right ascension—one hour of right ascension equals 15° of longitude—both the declinations and the right ascensions of the stars and planets are easily obtained with this important instrument. Indeed, it was through observations of the planets which Tycho Brahe made with the equatorial armillary and other instruments that Kepler was able to formulate his laws of planetary motions. And it was through these laws that Newton was able to arrive at his great system of universal dynamics.

The turning motion about PQ, necessary to follow any one particular star with the equatorial armillary, measures the passage of time, 15° to the hour. Hence the equatorial armillary could serve as a clock, a clock vastly more accurate than any mechanical timepiece available in the age of Tycho Brahe. It could therefore perform the important function of checking the accuracy of mechanical clocks, and Tycho Brahe did, in fact, so use it.

The equatorial armillary was a highly refined specialist instrument, however, as inaccessible to the average man as are the great modern telescopes. It therefore had no utility as an everyday method of time-measurement. This was the function of the sundial. But there was one other instrument which served the same purpose, and served it better, for a fairly wide range of professional men to whom time-measurement was important—the *astrolabe*. Although far less accurate in operation than the equatorial armillary, the astrolabe was of a convenient size to carry about, and it was not unduly expensive to manufacture. But the idea underlying its construction was of a level of subtlety hardly equalled in any other instrument of the period.

Some form of the astrolabe was probably known in antiquity, for Ptolemy seems to have referred to some such device. But no such instrument has survived from that period and we can speak of

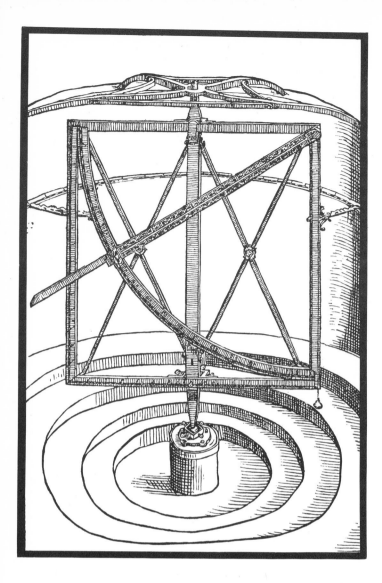

The Quadrant

star

O

rotation axis

Figure 2.9
Metal quadrant, marked with angular scale and fitted with movable sighting arm, capable of rotation about a vertical axis. With such an instrument the observer can follow a star continuously, reading off its elevation at any given moment.

Tycho Brahe's great steel quadrant with a radius of over six feet was readably calibrated in small fractions of a degree, thus enabling him to measure star positions with un-precedented accuracy.

Using quadrants in modern and in medieval times.

The Equatorial Armillary

The Hipparchus ring, a very simple analogue computer, relies on the fact that if a plane ring is set parallel to the Earth's equator the parallelism is not destroyed by the Earth's rotation. Only at the equinoxes does the shadow cast by the front of the ring fall on the back.

Engraving of Tycho Brahe's great equatorial armillary, from his book *Astronomiae Instruratae Mechanica*.

Figure 2.10
The key to the construction of the armillary is the rotating rod, PQ, aligned parallel to the Earth's axis of rotation. The graduated circle fastened to the rod carries a sliding sight. Position of sight on circle at moment of observation gives declination of star or planet.

Figure 2.10A
Star or planet was sighted in turn through two slits in the sight S. The arm SC of Figure 2.10 was so turned that the object appeared equally bright through both.

Figure 2.11
Here a second graduated circle is added. This measures the rotation of the rod PQ of Figure 2.10. From two readings of this scale it was possible to determine the longitude of the star or planet.

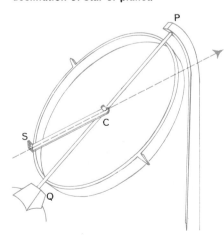

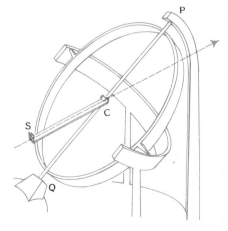

Tropic of Capricorn. Surrounding this projection is a scale for measuring the time in hours. Mounted above the main circular plate is a second plate, called the *rete*, cut away to form a kind of planisphere, or map of the brightest stars. On this star map (also bounded by the Tropic of Capricorn) the ecliptic is marked as an eccentric circle, divided according to the signs of the Zodiac. Worked into the tracery of the rete are several pointers, the tip of each marking the position of a bright star and each bearing the name of the star to which it points. The rete and a rule are pivoted to the center of the main plate. On the back of the astrolabe is a scale for measuring angles in degrees, together with a sighting arm.

The observer suspends the astrolabe vertically from its ring and measures the altitude of a star with the help of the sighting arm and the angular scale. He then turns the rete on its pivot until the position of that star, as marked on the rete, lies on the almucantar that corresponds with the altitude of the star. Next he rotates the rule until it lies over the point in the ecliptic that corresponds to the Sun's position in the ecliptic. (This has to be known for the day in question, since the Sun's position varies day by day throughout the year.) The pointer of the rule then gives the correct time, on the engraved scale of hours.

One particularly ingenious analogue computer, the *torquetum*, was developed in Islamic countries to meet a difficulty which now no longer exists. We saw in Chapter I that once the position of a star is known in the system of right ascension and declination, it is only a matter of calculation to determine its position in ecliptic co-ordinates (Case 3 of Chapter 1). Nowadays such calculations can be performed almost instantaneously with the aid of an automatic computer, but until long after the close of the Middle Ages these calculations were long and laborious. For this reason it was desirable to construct an instrument that enabled the observer to read off the ecliptic co-ordinates of a star (or more usually of a planet) directly. Perhaps the most highly-developed torquetum was that used by Regiomontanus.

To understand the curious construction of the torquetum we start with a plane fixed table, parallel to the Earth's equator. (This fixed plane is inclined to the horizontal by an angle equal to the observer's co-latitude.) On the table is mounted a cylindrical column capable of turning about its

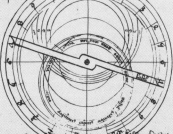

Part of a manuscript of Chaucer's *Treatise on the Astrolabe* compiled, probably in 1391, from Latin and English translations of far older Arabic works on astronomy.

the astrolabe only as we know it—a device owing much of its ingenuity, if not its original conception, to Arab and Persian astronomers and craftsmen of the ninth to eleventh centuries, and remaining virtually unchanged after its introduction into north-west Europe a century or two later.

It consists essentially of a circular metal plate engraved with a projection of the celestial sphere on a plane parallel with the equator. This projection shows azimuths (great-circle arcs from the zenith to the horizon), and almucantars (circles of altitude parallel to the horizon), and is bounded by the

Plate, carrying a projection of the celestial sphere, within a scale of hours numbered 1 to 12 twice.

The rete, which rotated within an engraved scale of hours.

The astrolabe, like the equatorial armillary, was used not only for observing but also for time-keeping. Unlike the armillary, it was portable and not prohibitively expensive. The two pictures above show first the front then the back of an astrolabe of about 1430.

Rule (on front of instrument, over the rete), sighting arm (on the back), and pivot pin.

central axis. The movable cylinder ends in a plane face inclined to the fixed table at an angle of 23.5°, the purpose being to orientate this end face parallel to the plane of the ecliptic. Mounted on the end face is a sighting arm, pivoted so that it can rotate about an axis perpendicular to the face. All this is shown in Figure 2.12. The plane end also carries a circular scale graduated from 0° to 360°, the scale being oriented in such a way that the sighting arm points to 0° when a star near ♈ is being sighted.

Because the fixed table is parallel to the Earth's equator, a star near ♈ lies essentially in the plane of the table. The observer's aim is to line up the movable cylinder so that such a star lies also in the plane of the inclined end of the cylinder. For this purpose the cylinder must be turned and the arm moved until the star at ♈ lies in the sights on the arm. The cylinder is then correctly orientated, and provided the pointer on the arm reads 0° the scale on the cylinder end is correctly positioned.

In Figure 2.13 we see the complete torquetum. The sighting arm is now attached to a plate that projects from the inclined end of the cylinder, and this plate carries a circular graduated scale at its upper end. A second movable sighting arm is attached to the center of this circular scale. With the cylinder correctly orientated, as just described, the ecliptic co-ordinates of any star or planet can immediately be read off by sighting the object in the second arm. To make such a sighting it will in general be necessary to make two motions. First there will be a turning of the whole plate structure, which will move the lower arm over the scale on the cylinder end. By reading the position of the lower arm on the scale on the cylinder end, the observer then obtains the ecliptic longitude of the star or planet. Next there will be a rotation of the upper sighting arm. The observer then reads off the position of the star or planet on the upper circular plate, and this reading gives him its ecliptic latitude.

It is abundantly clear that there has never been any lack of ingenuity in the design of astronomical instruments, nor in their use. Modern instruments are vastly superior to primitive devices for two reasons, neither being the product of superior intellect. Today we can handle much larger structures, we can divide far finer scales, and we can make reliable mechanical and electrical clocks. We also understand, as a consequence of the general advance of science, much more about the nature and behavior of light, and of the optical properties

of matter in general. It is because of this superior technology and superior knowledge that our modern instruments belong to a wholly different order of refinement from Tycho Brahe's moving quadrants and armillary spheres. The accuracy we can achieve nowadays is about a thousand times greater than that of Tycho Brahe's age. Instead of angular errors of about 1' of arc, we can now manage rather better than 0.1". Yet the problem of accuracy is as much with us today as it was with Tycho Brahe, for the modern astronomer would dearly like to push his margin of error down to 0.001". The instruments change, but the intellectual problems remain.

Refraction and Reflection

As we have seen, the development of the tools of astronomy since Tycho Brahe's time has been very largely conditioned by an increasing understanding of the properties of light itself. To begin with, it was sufficient to think of light as being a collection of bullets that travel in straight lines, except where they reach an interface between one medium and another—for example, an interface between air and glass. Here it was necessary to understand the laws of reflection and refraction.

Figure 2.14 shows light along *AB* incident on a glass block. There is a reflected ray *BC* that comes off the glass at an angle exactly equal to that made by the incident ray. There is also a refracted ray *BD* continuing on into the glass. This ray is bent toward the normal *XY*, the normal being an imaginary line which passes through *B* at right angles to the surface of the block. The three rays *AB*, *BC*, *BD*, and also the normal *XY*, all lie in the same plane.

The fact that a ray of light behaves in this way when it impinges on glass was doubtless known in ancient times. But the precise specification of the direction of the refracted ray was not discovered until 1621, more than a decade after the first telescopes were constructed. The man who made the discovery was Willebrord Snell, a Dutch astronomer and mathematician.

What Snell's discovery implies is shown in Figure 2.15. We see the incident ray, the normal and the refracted ray. The two points *A* and *D* are chosen so that the distances *AB* and *BD* are equal. Snell discovered that where this is so the ratio of *DY* to *AX* is always the same *for a given change of medium*. That is to say, if we change the angle which the incident ray makes with the normal, the ratio of

Figure 2.12
In the torquetum a fixed table is arranged parallel to the plane of the Earth's equator. The top face of the rotating cylinder mounted on the table is inclined to the table at an angle of 23.5°, thus lying in the plane of the ecliptic.

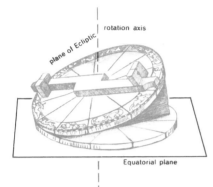

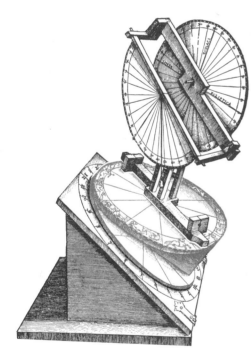

Figure 2.13
Here is the complete torquetum with the above portion picked out in blue. The instrument enabled the observer to read off not only declination and right ascension of stars but also ecliptic co-ordinates.

The oldest existing European torquetum, bought by Nicholas of Cusa in 1444.

DY to AX will remain unchanged. Once we know the value of that ratio for any specified change of medium it is therefore easy to determine the direction of the refracted ray for any one particular incident ray.

When we make use of any translucent material, such as glass, in optical instruments, we are far more concerned with the refracted ray than with the reflected ray, for the reasons shown in Figure 2.16. Light always undergoes some measure of absorption when it passes through matter, becoming progressively weaker the farther it penetrates. But in translucent materials the rate of loss is comparatively small, so that the refracted ray is a strong one. On the other hand, translucent materials also have the property of giving only a weak reflected ray whenever the angle of incidence is small; and in astronomical instruments we are almost always concerned with small angles of incidence. Thus, if we want to construct a refracting telescope, in which refracted rays are all-important and reflected rays of little or no importance, we shall obviously use lenses made of glass.

If we want to make a reflecting telescope, however, the choice of material for the mirror is not so obvious. Glass, as we have seen, gives only a weak reflected ray at small angles of incidence, and is therefore not suitable. Metals, on the other hand, give a very strong reflected ray and, because they are powerful absorbers of light, virtually no refracted ray. At first sight it might seem that the choice lies clearly on the side of metals. But unfortunately metals expand and contract very considerably with changes of temperature, and a mirror composed entirely of metal would have the grave disadvantage that it would be subject to large changes of size and shape, both of which would affect the direction of the reflected rays. Glass, on the other hand, is comparatively free from such thermal changes but is only a very poor reflector. The problem is to discover how the freedom from thermal variations of glass can be combined with the high reflectivity of metal. And this problem was not solved satisfactorily until the threshold of the present century. It was indeed the solution of this technological problem that opened the way to the construction of really large modern telescopes, the 60-inch Mount Wilson reflector, built in 1908, being the first of the new era.

The basis of a modern telescope mirror is a block or disk of glass shaped accurately to within about a millionth of an inch. Then on the surface of the glass a thin uniform layer of metal is deposited. Such a combination gives the best of both worlds. The shape of the surface is controlled by the glass and is hence not subject to much change with temperature, particularly if a special low-expansion form of glass is used. The metal coating, even though very thin, is sufficient to give high reflectivity at small angles of incidence.

The first metal surfaces were of silver. These gave a high reflectivity for red and green light, but the reflectivity was less good for blue light. It was soon found, however, that a layer of aluminum gave a uniform reflectivity over the whole normal color range of light, and for this reason aluminized mirrors are now used in all major observatories.

An aluminum coating does not, however, give good reflectivity for ultraviolet light. This is no embarrassment to the ground-based astronomer, for he is not concerned with ultraviolet light, since none penetrates the atmosphere. But the designer of equipment for satellites and space rockets may,

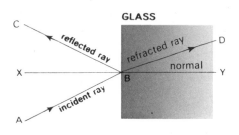

Figure 2.14
At interface between air and glass refracted ray is bent toward normal. Reflected ray comes off at an angle equal to that made by incident ray.

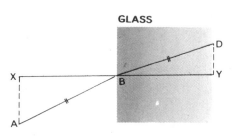

Figure 2.15
If segments of incident ray AB and refracted ray BD are equally long, the ratio of DY to AX is always the same for a given change of medium.

indeed, wish to work with ultraviolet light. He must, therefore, solve the problem of finding suitable new materials for coating his mirrors. Magnesium fluoride layers have already been used with considerable success for this purpose, but much research on this problem is still in progress.

Lenses and Refracting Telescopes

At the beginning of the seventeenth century, when the telescope first became a tool of astronomy, there was already an old-established industry of lens-making in Europe, but the time had not yet come when mirrors of high optical quality could be made. It is no wonder, therefore, that the first telescopes were all refractors. Before we can understand the principle of the refracting telescope we shall need to examine the behavior of light passing through glass lenses.

Figure 2.17 shows a cross section through a convex lens with central axis *OC*. (We assume that the lens is made so that the section would be the same for any plane containing the line *OCO'*.) *O* is an object emitting rays of light in all directions. We see that the ray along *OC* travels through the lens without deviation, but all other rays refracted by the lens are deviated. The measure of deviation of any particular refracted ray can readily be worked out from the rule of refraction which Snell discovered, for if the surfaces of the lens are quite smooth the curvature of the glass at the points *A* and *B* can be neglected. The ray is therefore turned toward the normal at *A*, and away from the normal at *B* in exactly the way we have discussed. Because of the symmetry of the lens, the ray emerging from *B* must continue to lie in the plane of *OC* and *OA*. It can thus intersect the axis at *O'*, say. The nearer

A is to the edge of the lens, the greater is the measure of deviation of *BO'* from *OA*.

An important question now arises. Can *all* the rays from *O* which pass through the lens be made to pass through the same point *O'*? The answer is that if the two surfaces of the lens are figured correctly the rays can indeed be made to pass through *O'* to an extremely high degree of accuracy. The accuracy is lost, however, if the distance of the object point *O* from the lens is changed at all markedly. For this reason, lenses are not usually given the complicated shapes that would be required to produce a well-nigh perfect focus for one particular and precise position of *O*. Instead, the lens surfaces are made spherical. This leads always to imperfect focusing, the defect known as *spherical aberration*. To minimize the spherical aberration, the two surfaces are ground to spherical shapes of different radii, as in Figure 2.17. This gives a much better result than a symmetrical lens would do. For the moment we shall ignore this question of spherical aberration. That is to say, we shall assume a perfect focus at *O'*. We shall also assume a perfect focus when the object is off-axis, as in Figure 2.18, although in actual fact further imperfections of focus are thereby introduced. These are known as *coma* for objects that are slightly off-axis, and as *astigmatism* for objects that are far off-axis.

In a first attempt to understand the broad principle of the refracting telescope we may indulge in the luxury of ignoring the practical imperfections of lenses, but it is important to recognize that such imperfections do exist and that spherical aberration, coma and astigmatism are not the only ones. Before we proceed it will be as well to look at the others. In Figure 2.19 the plane *p* is perpendicular to the

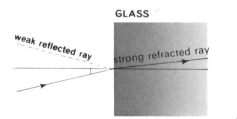

Figure 2.16
At small angles of incidence glass gives a strong refracted ray but a weak reflected ray. It is thus unsuitable for reflecting telescopes.

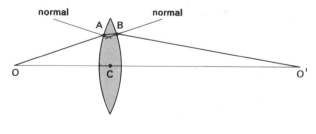

Figure 2.17
Top: Focusing with a convex lens.
Right: Surfaces of lens are given curved shapes of different radii to minimize *spherical aberration*.

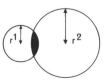

axis of the lens. Suppose that a number of points of p are emitting light, perhaps in the form of some picture. In accordance with what we have already assumed, each point of emission will be brought to a sharp focus to the right of the lens. Will all the focal points lie in the same plane, p', say? In fact, they will not lie in exactly the same plane but in a *curved field*. Will the picture formed on p' be a true representation of the picture on p, or will there be distortion? There will, in fact, be distortion. Lastly, does a lens behave the same way for light of different colors? It does not. Going back to the law of refraction illustrated in Figure 2.15, it is true that the ratio of AX to DY is independent of the angle of incidence, but the value of this ratio changes with the color of the light, because the glass changes its behavior with the color. This means that a given object point, such as O of Figure 2.17, will be brought to a different focal point O' according to the color of the light. This effect is known as *chromatic aberration*.

No practical optical system is entirely free from spherical aberration, coma, astigmatism, curvature of field, distortion, and chromatic aberration. These imperfections can, however, be minimized by a careful attention to the layout of the system and to the conditions under which it is to be operated. The history of the telescope is in large measure the history of attempts to free it as far as possible from these imperfections. For the moment, however, we may ignore all these difficulties, since our immediate aim is to understand the principle of the telescope, rather than the refinements of its design.

With that aim in mind we might look again at Figure 2.19 and ask how the size of the picture on p' compares with its size on p. Is the picture magnified or is it reduced? The answer depends on the distance of the lens from p. If the lens is far enough away from p the picture on p' is smaller than the original. But as the lens is moved toward p the size on p' increases, until eventually it is larger than the original. And the size on p' goes on increasing without limit as the lens is brought to a certain critical distance from p known as the *focal length* of the lens. If the lens is brought still closer to p *no plane p' can be found at all.*

To make this clearer, it must be realized that p' is not a fixed plane. As the lens moves (with p fixed) the plane p' on which the rays come to a focus also moves. As the lens is moved toward p, the plane p moves farther and farther away to the right. And when the distance of the lens from p becomes equal to the focal length of the lens, the plane p' moves off to infinity. After this, no plane p' can be found.

What is this critical distance, this focal length of the lens, and what does it depend on? Simply on the two surfaces of the lens. If these are spherical surfaces with radii r_1 and r_2, the reciprocal of the focal length is just the sum of the reciprocals of r_1 and r_2. In other words:

$$\frac{1}{\text{focal length}} = \frac{1}{r_1} + \frac{1}{r_2}.$$

We can express all this very simply. The two pictures, the original on p and the *image picture* on p', make the same angles at the center of the lens. If we imagine an observer situated at the center of the lens, he would therefore see the two pictures as having precisely the same size. This means that the image picture is magnified if the lens lies nearer to p than to p', otherwise it is reduced. Figure 2.20 shows that there is an important symmetry between p and p' in the following sense. As the lens moves toward p, the plane p' moves to the right—to

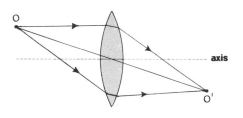

Figure 2.18
When object O is off-axis there will be a defect of focus at O':
coma for objects slightly off-axis, *astigmatism* for those far off-axis.

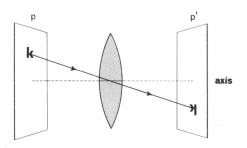

Figure 2.19
Here all points of p (the object) lie in the same plane. Yet there will be some distortion and *field curvature* at the focal plane p'

infinity when the lens reaches its focal length from p. Similarly if p moves off to infinity the distance of the lens from p' becomes equal to its focal length.

It is not difficult to see how this applies to photography. Distant objects we wish to photograph can be thought of as lying on one and the same distant plane, p. Film is placed in the camera on the plane p' and an image is formed with the lens at its focal length from p'. (Reference to Figure 2.19 shows that the image is formed upside down, and that left and right are reversed. But because the negative is transparent it is possible to look through it and to turn it in a way that restores the correct orientation of the original picture.) Now it is well known that nearby objects cannot usually be photographed accurately; some of them will be in focus and some out of focus. This is because we cannot by any stretch of imagination think of nearby three-dimensional objects as lying in a single plane, whereas distant objects can be thought of as doing so—to an adequate degree of accuracy.

In astronomy, we are concerned with observing objects on the distant celestial sphere, and for the most part astronomers are content at any one moment to observe only a tiny portion of the celestial sphere. To an extremely high degree of accuracy, this tiny portion can be thought of as belonging to one and the same very distant plane. With p thus very distant, the image plane p' is spaced from the large main lens of the telescope by an amount equal to the focal length of the lens.

Suppose we place a white screen at p'. *The size of the image on the screen will depend only on the focal length of the lens, and not at all on its diameter.* (This is because the image would appear to an imaginary observer at the center of the lens to have the same size as the original object on p.) Hence if we take a series of lenses of increasing diameter but all with the same focal length, the image on p' will have the same size in each case. But the images will not be equally bright. The lens of largest aperture will give the brightest image, simply because it receives most light from the object plane p; the lens of least diameter will give the faintest image because it receives least light from p.

Here, then, we can see what is the first important function of a telescope. *It must serve as a gatherer of light.* In this connection it may be worth noting that a telescope lens with a diameter of 20 inches gathers 10,000 times as much light as the dark-adapted naked eye.

In principle, we could use the large lens of a telescope as a camera lens for photographing the sky, simply by placing a film on p'. In practice, such a procedure fails because the image on p' is too small. Suppose we wish to photograph a fair-sized portion of the Moon, say the region around Mare Imbrium. The size of the image of Mare Imbrium on p' depends on the focal length of the lens. For a small amateur's telescope, with a focal length of about 3 feet, the image has a diameter of less than a tenth of an inch. Even for a big telescope of focal length about 50 feet, the diameter of the image is still only about an inch. *Hence we must magnify the image on p' before we attempt to make a photograph.*

This is easily done. We simply place a second lens beyond p', as in Figure 2.21. This lens brings the light from p' to a second focus on a second image plane at p''. And provided the second lens is nearer to p' than to p'' the image on p'' will be larger than that on p'. Indeed, we can ensure that the image on p'' will reach a convenient size simply by placing the second lens at a distance from p' that is sufficiently close to its own focal length. By placing film on p'', we can now photograph a small area of the celestial sphere to the required size. In short, we have a telescope with a camera.

We see, then, that a telescope consists essentially of two parts: a light-gatherer which must have a large diameter, and a magnifier which must be adjusted so as to give the final image a convenient size. The light-gatherer is usually referred to as the *objective* of the telescope, and the magnifier as the *eye-piece*.

Instead of making a photograph, we may wish to look through the telescope with the eye. In that case the second image must be formed on the retina of the eye. The situation is then a little more compli-

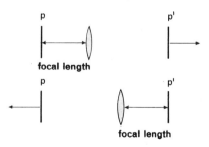

Figure 2.20
When lens is at focal length from p, plane p' moves off to infinity. If p moves to infinity, distance of lens from p' is equal to focal length.

Above: Region of Mare Imbrium as photographed through the 200-inch Hale telescope, with a focal length of 55 feet. Right: Part of the Moon as Galileo drew it after seeing it through a telescope with a very small focal length.

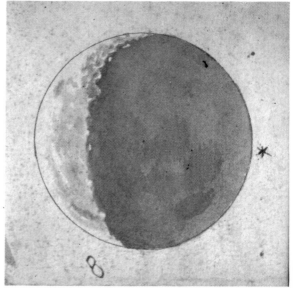

cated, because the eye itself contains a lens, and the eye-lens works together with the eye-piece to produce the focusing of the second image on the retina. Because the eye-muscles can change the focal length of the eye-lens, there is no completely unique combination of eye-lens and eye-piece. In practice, the observer adapts his eye to the position he finds most comfortable, and this position differs from one observer to another, particularly if one is short-sighted and the other long-sighted. This explains why each observer must make his own individual adjustment of the eye-piece.

When we use a telescope with a camera, the image on p'' always appears less bright than the image on p', simply because the second image is spread out over a larger area. Since in astronomical work light is nearly always precious, it is therefore unwise to make the image on p'' any larger than we are absolutely forced to. In the photography of very faint objects the astronomer is usually obliged to accept a compromise. A larger image would provide more detail but it would be fainter and harder to photograph. So in the case of the faintest objects, detail must perforce be sacrificed. But in the case of a brighter object a larger image can profitably be used, thereby allowing more detail to be seen. It is, however, a fact that a limit exists to the amount of detail. One cannot continue indefinitely to increase the detail by taking higher and higher degrees of magnification.

When we look through the telescope with the eye, an apparently different problem arises. In this case, if the second image is made too large, not all of the light from it will enter the eye. Some of the light that could otherwise focus on the retina will be blocked by the opaque front of the eye, as in Figure 2.22. In other words, part of the light collected by

the objective will be lost. To prevent this, the magnification between p' and p'' must not exceed the ratio of the diameter D of the objective to the diameter d of the opening of the eye.

For the purpose of observing the image on p'' in maximum detail it might nevertheless be thought worthwhile to lose some light, especially in the case of a bright object such as the Moon. Actually, it can be proved that this is not so, because the maximum degree of detail, referred to above, has already been reached at precisely the stage at which the light begins to be blocked by the opaque front of the eye. Even so, almost all visual observers do employ magnifications larger than D/d. This is partly because visual observers almost always work on very bright objects where loss of light is not a grave matter; partly because a greater magnification is probably more restful to the eye; and partly because it is easier to deceive oneself as to what is actually seen. There is, too, the better reason that a larger magnification helps to overcome the imperfections of the eye-distortion produced by the eye-lens, and the lack of discrimination caused by the finite size of the rods and cones of the retina. In the case of photography it may sometimes be necessary to exceed the D/d ratio so as to achieve a magnification sufficient to overcome the "graininess" of the film or plate.

A simpler but less convenient arrangement than that of Figure 2.21 is to place the second lens *in front* of p'. In this case the second lens must be concave, as in Figure 2.23. This has the effect of increasing the distance of p' from the objective and of increasing the size of the image. We now have only one image plane, that at p'.

The first astronomical telescope, that of Galileo, was constructed in accordance with Figure 2.23.

Figure 2.21
The objective of a telescope usually gives only a small image at p'. This image is therefore enlarged for photographing at p''.

Figure 2.22
We can look at the enlarged image with the eye. If the image is *too* large, some of the light is blocked by the opaque front of the eye.

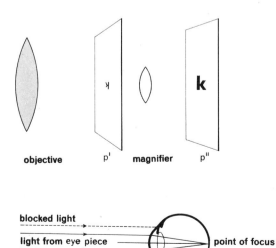

objective   p'   magnifier   p''

blocked light

light from eye piece   point of focus

blocked light   retina

The type of telescope mounting
shown on the opposite page did not
at first give great positional accuracy.
But as mountings improved, star
positions were measured to within
5 seconds of arc. Left is the 4-foot
transit circle of 1806 with which
Groombridge mapped 4000 stars.
The transit telescope above was
used by W. H. Smyth in the 1830s
to observe double stars.

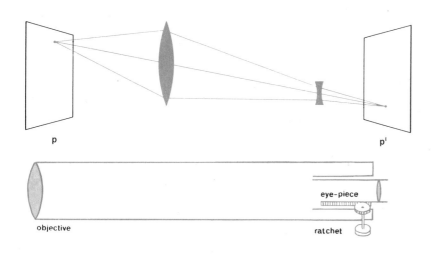

p   p'

Figure 2.23
Principle of Galileo's first
astronomical telescope.

eye-piece

objective

ratchet

Figure 2.24
Usual placing of objective and
adjustable eye-piece.

The far better system of Figure 2.21 was invented by Kepler. Ironically, Kepler referred to himself as dull in observation, awkward in mechanical work!

Figures 2.21 and 2.23 show only idealized telescopes. To make an actual telescope, the lenses must be mounted in some fashion. The usual arrangement is to place the objective at one end of a tube and the eye-piece at the other, as in Figure 2.24. Because it is desirable to adjust the eye-piece to allow for variability in the eye itself, the eye-piece must be capable of motion parallel to the axis of the tube. This is usually achieved with the aid of a ratchet device.

It remains now to mount the telescope. The way to do this is immediately clear from Tycho Brahe's equatorial armillary. In effect, all we need do is replace Tycho Brahe's sighting arm by the telescope. But since the early telescopic observers were much more interested in viewing the Sun, Moon, and planets than they were in positional accuracy, they could dispense with a great deal of the complexity of the equatorial armillary, particularly with its circular metal rings. Today we can still dispense with these rings because we have other and better ways of measuring turning motion. So in the telescope mounting the outer part of the equatorial armillary is replaced by a couple of pillars supporting an axis on which the inner part is mounted. This axis is conveniently orientated parallel to the Earth's rotational axis, exactly as in the armillary. The axis is permitted to turn in bearings fixed to the pillars. A second axis is rigidly fastened at right angles to the first one. The telescope is then mounted at one end of this second axis in such a way that it can turn around it. At the opposite end of the second axis there is usually some kind of counterweight, which serves to balance the turning

moment of the telescope around the first axis.

The direction of pointing of the telescope can be determined from the degree of turning about the two axes. The first axis gives right ascension, the second one gives declination. At first, these measures were cruder than Tycho Brahe's had been. But by the time astronomers again became interested in positional accuracy it was possible to measure the turning motions about the two axes with so great a precision that there was no necessity for returning to Tycho Brahe's system. In any case, positional accuracy could always be obtained with special quadrants fitted with telescopic sights. In Isaac Newton's time, the standard of positional accuracy was gradually pushed from Tycho's one minute of arc to about five seconds of arc. In modern times it has become rather better than one-tenth of a second of arc.

Mirrors and Reflecting Telescopes

The telescope has an important advantage over many other optical instruments. Since the astronomer is not usually concerned with light coming into the objective at more than small angles, the imperfections of spherical aberration, coma, field curvature and distortion can be kept within reasonable bounds. But wherever lenses are employed, as they must be in refracting telescopes, there is one imperfection that is more difficult to overcome. An ordinary lens refracts light of different colors in different ways, and does not therefore bring light of all colors to the same focus.

Even in the early days of the telescope this color aberration was considered a serious defect. In 1636, no more than twenty-five years after Galileo's first telescope, Marin Mersenne, a Minorite friar, proposed the construction of a reflecting telescope. In

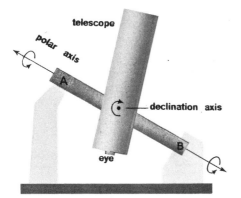

In its simplest form, the equatorial mounting merely dispenses with the metal rings of Tycho Brahe's equatorial armillary and replaces the sighting arm with a telescope.

1663, James Gregory put forward a different design of reflecting telescope, while in the years 1670-72, Isaac Newton and a Frenchman named Cassegrain suggested the most practical arrangements.

The idea of a reflecting telescope is to replace the objective of the refracting telescope by a mirror. That is to say, a mirror is used as the light-gatherer instead of a lens. This has two important advantages. First, while a lens refracts light of different colors in different ways, a mirror reflects all colors in the same way, and thus brings light of all colors from the same object to the same focus. Next, if the mirror is shaped to the form of a paraboloid, light from a distant object lying in the direction of the axis of the paraboloid is brought to a focus without spherical aberration.

But with optical systems perfection in one respect usually implies a serious imperfection in some other respect. The paraboloidal mirror suffers badly from coma, that is the focus becomes bad for objects that do not lie in directions very close to that of the axis. In modern instruments this difficulty is overcome by correcting devices located in the magnifier. Instead of using a single lens as magnifier, we now use a complex optical system, and a prime concern in shaping and positioning the various lenses of the system is to correct errors due to the coma produced by the mirror.

The simplest form of reflecting telescope is shown in Figure 2.25. The mirror brings objects on our distant plane p to a focus on p'. Exactly as before, the picture on p' is then magnified on to p'', where it can either be photographed or viewed by eye. In Newton's time, however, only viewing by eye was possible, and here there was the overriding difficulty that placing the human eye at p'' would have blocked light from reaching the mirror, since the mirrors of those times were small, of course, compared with human dimensions. So the simple device of Figure 2.25 was not then practicable. Yet precisely this system is now employed in the 200-inch reflecting telescope at Mount Palomar. The mirror of the Palomar instrument has so great a diameter that a human being can indeed sit inside the telescope without blocking out very much of the light! The observer does not view the image directly with the eye, however. He rides inside the telescope in order to operate the camera (and other instruments) and to ensure that the image plane p'' is kept in the correct position in relation to the camera.

In many respects the 200-inch telescope is extremely simple in its design. The mounting is more elegant than that shown on page 53. Instead of a simple axis between the bearings on the fixed pillars, there is a cradle, inside which the telescope itself can ride. It again turns on a declination axis which passes through bearings fixed to the cradle. This declination axis is aligned perpendicular to the axis of the cradle. This system dispenses with the need for a counterweight.

When the 200-inch telescope is used in the simple manner of Figure 2.25 it is said to be operated *at the prime focus*. As we shall later see, it can also be used in other ways.

But such a solution of the reflector problem was not possible in the seventeenth century. Gregory

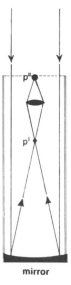

The Hale telescope is so big that an observer can sit inside it without blocking out much light. The arrangement of Figure 2.25 is then a practical proposition. Used in this way the telescope is said to be operated at prime focus.

Figure 2.25
Simplest form of reflecting telescope —impracticable in Newton's time.

mirror

suggested placing a small secondary mirror *behind* the plane *p'*, while Cassegrain proposed a secondary mirror *in front of p'*.

In Gregory's case (illustrated in Figure 2.26) the mirror was an ellipsoidal one with the intersection of the central axis on *p'* as the nearer focus. A second focal plane *p''* is then formed at the farther focus of the secondary mirror. The image on *p''* can now be viewed with a normal eye-piece, a hole in the center of the main mirror being cut away for this purpose. In Cassegrain's case (Figure 2.27) the secondary mirror was hyperboloidal, a second focal plane *p''* being again formed at the outer focus of the secondary mirror. The image on *p'* is not actually formed, as can be seen from Figure 2.27. The image plane *p'* is said to be *virtual* in this case. In the Gregorian telescope, on the other hand, the image on plane *p'* is actually formed, and is said to be *real*.

But neither Gregory nor Cassegrain was able to put his proposal to a practical test. It was left to Newton to construct a working model of a reflecting telescope by the simple device of placing a flat mirror inclined at 45° in front of *p'*, as in Figure 2.28. All light rays coming to *p'* are reflected in the flat mirror and are thereby caused to form an image plane *p''* at right angles to *p'*. The observer views the image on *p''* with a normal eye-piece mounted in the side of the telescope.

The immediate superiority of Newton's device lay in the fact that a flat mirror could easily be made, whereas at that date it was difficult to construct the carefully figured secondary mirrors which

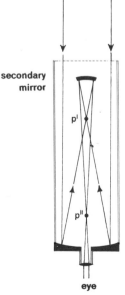

Figure 2.26
Principle of Gregory's proposed reflecting telescope.

A 48-inch Cassegrain reflector erected in Melbourne, Australia, in the 1860s. It had at least one advantage over the Newtonian type. The observer was at the bottom, not perched precariously near the top.

Figure 2.27
Cassegrain reflector. Newton said "Its advantages are none".

Left: Newton's first reflecting telescope, built in 1688. Above: View down open end of telescope, showing both mirrors and also position of eye-piece.

Figure 2.28
Principle of Newtonian telescope.

This 48-inch Newtonian reflector, used in Malta in the 1860s, needed a tower with a kind of sentry box to enable the observer to reach the eye-piece. As it followed a star, the platform carrying the tower had to be rotated.

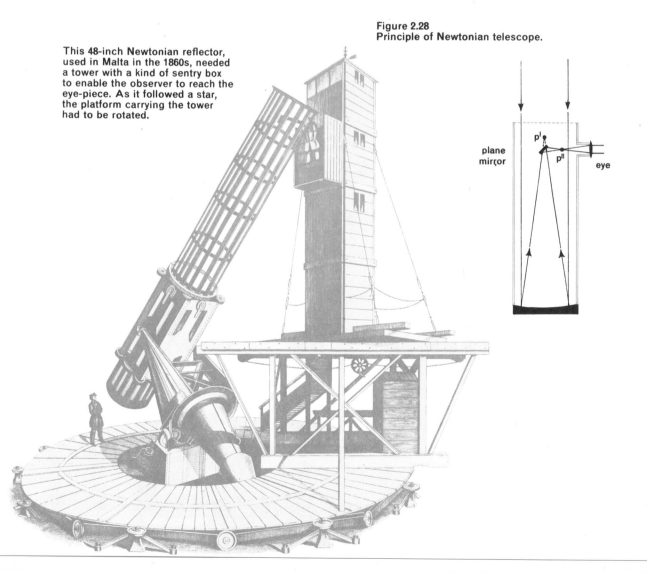

plane mirror

p^I

p^II

eye

the designs of Gregory and Cassegrain demanded. Gregory employed the best available London opticians in an attempt to build his telescope, but results were discouraging. And when confronted by Cassegrain's suggestion, Newton wrote: "The advantages of this device are none, but the disadvantages so great and unavoidable, that I fear it will never be put in practise with good effect. . . ."

Posterity's verdict on Newton's scathing pronouncement is contained in the 200-inch telescope, designed to be capable of operation in the manner of Cassegrain but not in that of Newton! From the modern point of view, the Newtonian system has the grave disadvantage that the observer must climb to the top of the telescope. Moreover he must move his viewing position whenever the telescope moves. This forces him into well-nigh gymnastic contortions which must, of course, be performed in the dark and which can be actively dangerous. In contrast with observation from a Newtonian platform, an observer at the prime focus of the 200-inch telescope sits inside a box that moves with the telescope. He is therefore in no danger of falling—a matter that must be seriously considered at a height of 50 to 100 feet above ground level. With a telescope in its normal working position, pointing nearly toward the zenith, the Cassegrain observer is also placed in comparative safety, since he is situated at the bottom of the telescope.

A better device than that of either Newton or Cassegrain is a combination of the two, shown schematically in Figure 2.29. A flat mirror is used in the manner of Newton, but in front of the plane *p″* of the Cassegrain arrangement. This improvement appears to have been made in the 1840s, by James Nasmyth, the inventor of the steam-hammer.

The remarkable feature of Nasmyth's telescope was that it could be pointed to any object in the heavens without the observer being required to move himself. This operational simplicity was achieved at a serious cost, however, for Nasmyth's mounting was of an altazimuth type, not of the equatorial type shown on page 53. This meant that to compensate for the Earth's rotation it was necessary, in following an object, to make two simultaneous motions of the telescope, one in azimuth, the other in declination.

The equatorial mounting has, of course, the great advantage of requiring only one movement, about the axis parallel to the Earth's rotational axis. One final refinement of Nasmyth's idea will allow the

Above: Part of Nasmyth's 20-inch Cassegrain-Newtonian telescope, showing position of eye-piece in relation to mounting.
Bottom: Nasmyth using the instrument, which could be pointed to any part of the heavens without the observer's having to move.

Figure 2.29 (Right)
Refinement of Nasmyth's idea gives basis of modern coudé system.

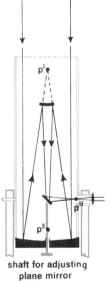

shaft for adjusting plane mirror

observer to remain stationary even when an equatorial mounting is used. The lower flat mirror of Figure 2.29, instead of remaining fixed in relation to the telescope, must be turned by a driving shaft placed through the back of the main mirror. If the drive is adjusted to compensate precisely for the motion of the telescope, the image plane p''' will then always be formed in a fixed direction. This is the basis of the modern coudé system.

Until the middle of last century an important limitation to the design of reflecting telescopes arose from the fact that multiple reflections had to be avoided as far as possible. This was because a good deal of light was lost at each mirror owing to poor reflective efficiency. Even with modern mirrors, multiple reflections must be avoided whenever very faint objects are under investigation. This is exactly why the observer works at the prime focus of the 200-inch telescope (Figure 2.25) whenever he has to deal with extremely faint objects. He must perforce accept the discomfort of sitting inside the telescope, often for many hours on end, rather than use the far more comfortable system of Figure 2.29. The latter is used, of course, whenever comparatively bright objects are under investigation. (A candle at a distance of a hundred miles may be thought of as a bright object.)

Refractors versus Reflectors

The early reflecting telescopes certainly overcame the problem of chromatic aberration but they raised another problem just as grave. The mirrors were solid disks of metallic alloy, and hence were subject to gross changes of form due to temperature fluctuations. So it is not surprising that when, in the mid-eighteenth century, a method was found of overcoming chromatic aberration in the refracting telescope, the reflector fell into immediate disfavor. And interest in the reflector did not revive until about a century later, when Foucault discovered a method of depositing a thin layer of silver on a glass surface.

Before we can understand how refracting telescopes overcame the problem of chromatic aberration we shall need to examine more closely just how the problem arises. In Figure 2.15 we saw that the ratio of the distances AX to DY is always the same for light of a particular color. But this ratio differs slightly with the color of the light. This causes the light that passes through the outer part of a lens to be separated into its constituent colors (Figure 2.30).

It is said to be *dispersed*. In contrast, light of all colors passes straight through the center of the lens, and is therefore neither refracted not dispersed. If the lens has concave, instead of convex faces, the dispersion is simply reversed, as in Figure 2.31.

Thus one method of correcting for dispersion readily suggests itself. It is shown in Figure 2.32. We simply place a concave lens to the right of the convex one.

This explains a point that might otherwise seem puzzling. How was it that astronomers were so disturbed by the chromatic aberration introduced by the objective of a refracting telescope and yet were undisturbed by the chromatic effects of the eye-piece? For even reflecting telescopes make use of lenses in the eye-piece!

The answer is that eye-pieces were made with two lenses even in the time of Newton, the first example being due to Christian Huygens. The two lenses produced something of the effect shown in Figure 2.32, so that chromatic distortions produced in the eye-piece were much less serious than those produced by the objective. The reason why an objective could not readily be corrected by the use of a second lens is that the two lenses, *if made of the same glass*, would need to be very widely spaced—a serious inconvenience. Eye-pieces, on the other hand, being small, permit adequate separation without any such inconvenience arising.

But to come back to the objective of a refracting telescope: how is this to be corrected for chromatic aberration, widely spaced lenses being forbidden? Two quite different considerations are involved: the actual value of the ratio of AX to DY (Figure 2.15) for light of a particular color, and the degree to which that ratio alters when the color is altered. These two factors do not change in exactly the same way when the material of a lens is changed, for example from one type of glass to another. This means that two lenses of different materials can have different ratios of AX to DY in yellow light, but the same degree of dispersion of the ratios with change of color. Then by making a convex lens from the material of larger ratio and a concave lens from the material of smaller ratio, we can produce the desirable situation in which the opposite dispersive effects of the two lenses (Figures 2.30 and 2.31) compensate each other, but in which there is still a net degree of refraction. If, moreover, the lenses are suitably shaped they can be fitted together into a doublet of the form shown in Figure 2.33 which

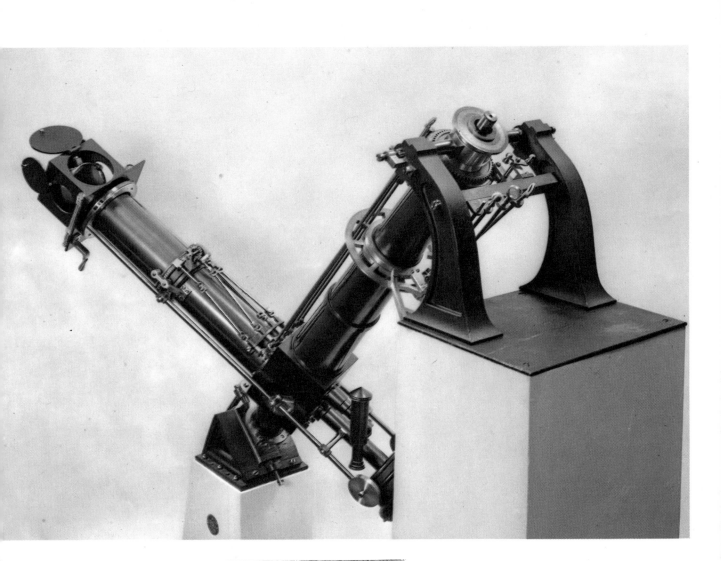

In the coudé system (above)
eye-piece is at upper end of
polar axis, which rotates to make
changes in right ascension.
Changes in declination are made
by the rotation of a plane mirror in
front of the object glass.
A single observer can view any
part of the sky without moving.
Left: Large equatorial coudé
used at the Paris Observatory near
the close of last century.

then gives a focal plane p' that is substantially the same for all colors.

There seems little doubt that the man who discovered this method of making achromatic objectives was Chester Moor Hall, a London barrister whose hobby was making optical experiments. Being by nature a somewhat secretive man, Hall, in 1733, approached two different London opticians, one to grind the convex half of the doublet and the other to grind the concave half. Oddly enough, both of them sub-contracted the work to the same craftsman, George Bass. Discovering that both lenses were destined for the same customer, Bass fitted them together and recognized their achromatic property. Bass was less reticent than Hall, and within the next few years several London opticians were in possession of the new idea and had begun to make achromatic lenses for themselves. Among them was John Dolland, a man of very high reputation in the scientific world, who eventually joined his more commercially-minded son Peter in a business enterprise at *The Sign of the Golden Spectacles and Sea Quadrant* in the Strand.

Peter Dolland persuaded his father to apply for a patent on the new device, and although nobody ever claimed that John Dolland was the inventor, the patent was duly granted. Nevertheless, throughout the remainder of John Dolland's life, other British opticians seem to have gone on making achromatic objectives without let or hindrance. But soon after his father's death, Peter Dolland brought an action against one of them and was successful. Thereupon the London Opticians presented a petition to the Privy Council asking for the patent to be revoked. The legal proceedings which followed were long and complicated, but the upshot was that the Dolland patent was upheld. The court, presided over by Lord Camden, held that Chester Moor Hall, "the person who locked his invention in his scritoire", was not the person who ought to benefit by the patent. The right person to benefit was Dolland "who brought it forth for the benefit of the public."

In fact it is to be doubted whether the granting of such sweeping patent rights is ever an expedient policy, for the interplay of ideas is thereby discouraged, and in the absence of competition the monopolist is apt to become lazy. Certainly, patent rights are hard to justify on moral grounds, for the bigger an idea the less it is patentable. You may make a fortune by patenting a better way of clip-ping an indiarubber to a pencil, but you will not make a cent in patent rights through the discovery of a new scientific theory of the scope and power of Einstein's. Society is well aware that only a king's ransom could pay for a really great scientific idea, so it makes no payment whatever.

At all events, the granting of the Dolland patent had an all but disastrous effect on the course of the optical industry in Britain. With the invention of the achromatic objective the stage was set for the ultimate struggle between the refracting telescope and the reflector. But the British, who had played so large a part in the early development of the reflector and who had produced the first achromatic objective for the refractor, scarcely took any further part in the technological development of the two instruments. The monopoly accorded to the Dollands allowed them, without any great effort, to produce better refracting telescopes than their immediate rivals could produce. Their rivals, discouraged by being debarred from using the correct technique, tended to wither away. Some fifty years after the Dolland case, the government, becoming alarmed by the rapid rise of the German optical industry, at last attempted through the Royal Society to encourage the manufacture of better

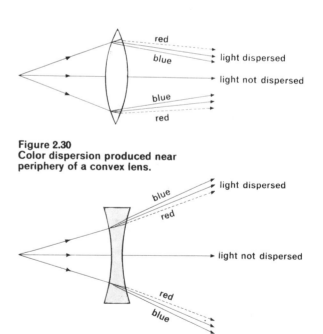

Figure 2.30
Color dispersion produced near periphery of a convex lens.

Figure 2.31
Use of a concave lens merely reverses the dispersion.

optical glass in Britain. But the project failed ignominiously, for by then all really high-grade professional optical work in England was well-nigh destroyed.

In Germany things took a very different course. When, in the early years of the nineteenth century, the Dolland telescopes were critically examined by the young German, Joseph Fraunhofer, it was found that none of the really important problems of the refracting telescope had been solved during the fifty years since Lord Camden's decision. The essential problem of the refracting objective was to choose the material of the lenses and to shape their surfaces in such a way as to give not only chromatic correction but also freedom from spherical aberration and coma in a distant object. This was among the first problems in human history to demand both an accurate mathematical insight and a skilled practical technology. The mathematical insight was available in England but the practical technology was sadly lacking.

The two requirements were combined in the person of Fraunhofer. It is not too much to say that Fraunhofer carried through, essentially by himself, a research program that would nowadays be assigned to a substantial team of scientists. A poor boy, Fraunhofer was trained as a glass technologist. Later, he acquired mathematical knowledge. In an energetic young man of genius the combination proved irresistible. Fraunhofer realized that he must *begin* by measuring the refraction of different kinds of glass in the separate colors, not with light of mixed colors. This led him to the basic technological discovery that one particular kind of glass— flint glass—does not give reproducible results unless the conditions of its manufacture are controlled with extreme care. Impurities produce variations of behavior. Now Fraunhofer's early training, together with a body of information acquired from the Frenchman, Pièrre Louis Guinand, came to his aid. Furnaces were designed and built in which glass disks of stable optical quality could be produced. Fraunhofer's practical skill as a lens grinder and his mathematical knowledge of optics did the rest. The resulting telescopic objectives were sensibly free from chromatic aberration, spherical aberration (distant objects), and coma.

To Fraunhofer it was a simple matter to improve the rigidity and the accuracy of the normal equatorial mounting of the telescope. The final product was of a degree of excellence far surpassing any-

thing that had been seen before. His $9\frac{1}{2}$-inch Dorpat refractor earned him freedom from the taxes of Munich. It did more than that. It shook the complacence of the British government sufficiently for the aforementioned glass-making project to be set under way. But all to no avail. With the failure of the glass-making project the government relapsed once more into technological somnolence.

Throughout most of his short life (he died of tuberculosis at the early age of thirty-nine) Fraunhofer was regarded by the scientific savants as a "mere technologist." He was allowed to attend scientific meetings but not to speak! It is therefore pleasant to record that in the course of his work he made basic discoveries which carried him far beyond the science of his own day, right into the science of the twentieth century. We shall meet his discovery of certain particularly important spectrum lines in a later chapter.

During the era of the Dolland refractors, the reflector was by no means entirely eclipsed. In the last quarter of the eighteenth century, William Herschel, famed for his discovery of the planet Uranus, constructed with consummate skill a series of reflecting telescopes, culminating in one of 48-inch aperture. But although great results were

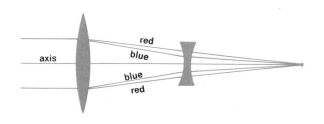

Figure 2.32
Two widely-spaced lenses of same glass can cancel dispersion effect.

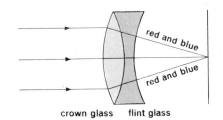

Figure 2.33
By using lenses of different glass need for spacing is avoided.

achieved with these instruments, they all suffered from the defects already remarked on.

The magnificent Fraunhofer refractors transformed the situation. Professional astronomers the world over now had no doubt that refractors were much to be preferred to reflectors. Everybody wanted a Fraunhofer refractor. It was true that reflectors could be made with larger apertures, but because of the inefficiency of reflection at the mirror surfaces, a reflector of given aperture was reckoned to have no greater light-gathering power than a refractor of only half the aperture.

Reflectors were still constructed in England, but now mainly by amateur astronomers such as Nasmyth, whose ingenious instrument we have already seen, and the Earl of Rosse, whose largest reflector had a mirror of 6-foot diameter. Yet Rosse, who saw the reflector as a better instrument than the refractor, was in a small minority. Most astronomers thought that Fraunhofer had brought about the final triumph of the refracting telescope.

Ironically, what Fraunhofer's discoveries had really demonstrated was the ultimate impracticability of the refractor. Fraunhofer's success was based on the superb optical quality of his glass. It had of necessity to be free from bubbles and internal striae. It had to have very precisely defined refracting properties. *And these characteristics are extremely hard to achieve in lenses of appreciable aperture.* The Dorpat refractor, Fraunhofer's masterpiece, had an aperture of only $9\frac{1}{2}$ inches. In spite of the poor reflective efficiency of the mirrors of that time, there was no great difficulty in achieving a greater practical light-gathering power than this with a mirror. If a refractor was to achieve equality with the large Rosse mirror, the aperture would have to be pushed up to about 30 inches. Therefore strenuous efforts were made to increase the diameter of refractor objectives. In fact this was achieved only during the last twenty years of the nineteenth century. During the 1870s two American observatories (Washington and McCormick, Charlottesville) installed 26-inch refractors, while Vienna had one with a 27-inch aperture. In the middle 1880s the Pulkovo Observatory in Russia and the Bischoffstein Observatory in France both had 30-inch instruments. Not until 1888 was a refractor with a still larger objective installed—the 36-inch telescope at Lick Observatory in the U.S.A.

By that time Foucault had discovered how to silver a glass mirror. From then onward, therefore,

reflectors were no longer subject to gross losses of light nor to serious deformations due to temperature changes. The reflector now went rapidly ahead, for it made far less exacting demands upon glass technology than did the refractor.

The glass disk out of which a large mirror is to be made must certainly satisfy the requirements of rigidity and of a low temperature coefficient of expansion, but there is no need for the glass to be of high optical quality. There can even be a plethora of bubbles and striae inside the glass so long as they do not interfere with the grinding of the surface. In contrast, the glass required for a refractor objective must satisfy the most stringent optical requirements. Hence very large mirrors can be made more easily and with less risk of inaccuracy than can very large lenses. For sound technological reasons, therefore, we seem to have reached the ultimate end of the race between refractor and reflector. The world's largest refractor, at present, is the 40-inch instrument at Yerkes, Williams Bay, U.S.A. By way of contrast there are many reflectors with apertures in excess of 50 inches. Some of the largest are listed below.

Observatory	Aperture	Completed
Mount Wilson (U.S.A.)	60 in.	1908
Harvard, Bloemfontein (S. Africa)	60 in.	1933
Bosque Alegre (Argentina)	60 in.	1942
Harvard, Oak Ridge (U.S.A.)	61 in.	1937
Perkins, Delaware (U.S.A.)	70 in.	1932
Dominion, Victoria (Canada)	72 in.	1919
Dunlap, Toronto (Canada)	74 in.	1935
Radcliffe, Pretoria (S. Africa)	74 in.	1948
Mount Stromlo (Australia)	74 in.	1955
Haute-Provence (France)	74 in.	1958
McDonald, Mount Locke (U.S.A.)	82 in.	1939
Mount Wilson (U.S.A.)	100 in.	1917
Lick, Mount Hamilton (U.S.A.)	120 in.	1959
Mount Palomar (U.S.A.)	200 in.	1948

In addition to the fourteen large reflectors listed above, at least half-a-dozen others of comparable size are now either planned or actually under construction in various parts of the world. It is a matter of irony that in the days when reflect-

When refractors gained ascendancy
reflectors were by no means eclipsed.
The Earl of Rosse's 6-foot
reflector, set up near the Bog of
Allen in the 1840s, was known as
the Leviathan of Parsonstown.

Fraunhofer's Dorpat refractor, with
an aperture of 9½ inches, was equal
in light-gathering capacity to a
reflector with an aperture twice
as big. But large lenses are harder
to manufacture than large mirrors.

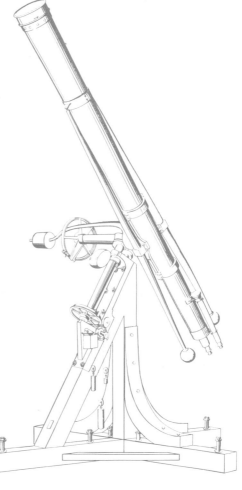

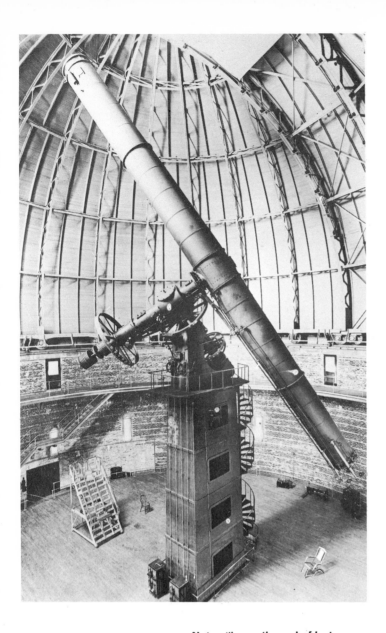

Not until near the end of last century was a telescope equipped with a lens of 3-foot diameter. Today the world's largest refractor is the 40-inch instrument at Yerkes, Williams Bay, shown above.

Here we see first the big lens of the Yerkes refractor and next the main mirror of the Hale reflector. The difference in size is emphasized by the presence of the men in both pictures.

ing telescopes were equipped with metal mirrors, and were hence subject to poor reflectivity and to changes of figure, the largest reflectors were built in England. But since these difficulties were overcome, since it became possible to build a well-nigh perfect reflector, England has not produced a single instrument of large aperture, though it is true that a 98-inch reflector is now being planned. Several contributing reasons for this odd situation can be suggested, including lack of confidence occasioned by the success of Fraunhofer refractors and the bad climatic conditions encountered by the astronomers who used the large Rosse reflector. But a stronger reason is that British astronomers had become almost exclusively interested in the study of the Sun. For this no large reflector was necessary, because there is plenty of light from the Sun! It is probably not an exaggeration to say that the prosecution of general observational astronomy in Britain was all but killed by a grossly lop-sided concentration on solar studies.

There is one final issue concerning the refractor *v.* reflector struggle. Although the reflector was finally established as the more powerful light-gatherer, the traditional paraboloidal reflector suffers more severely from coma than the refractor does. This means that the reflector cannot be usefully employed when the object rays come into the mirror at more than a small angle with the axis of the mirror. In other words, the reflector necessarily has only a small field of view.

This disadvantage would probably have served to keep the refractor "in business" had it not been

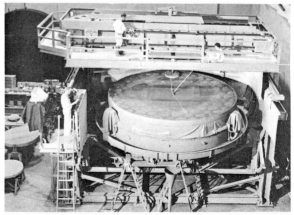

for the invention of a new type of reflector with far less coma than that inherent in the traditional paraboloidal mirror. The optical features of the new system were invented by Kellner in 1910, but the first telescope embodying Kellner's ideas was not constructed until 1930, by Bernhard Schmidt. Such telescopes are now known as Schmidt telescopes.

If rays are admitted through a circular opening on to a spherical mirror, as in Figure 2.34, a change of direction of the object point makes little difference. The rays are brought to a focus without coma, astigmatism, or chromatic aberration. But spherical aberration is now very serious. To overcome this difficulty a correcting plate of good quality optical glass is placed across the circular opening. The surfaces of the glass are carefully figured to give a weak refraction, just sufficient to compensate for the spherical aberration of the mirror. The glass itself introduces optical defects, of course, but these are not serious unless the aperture becomes very large, in which case chromatic aberration raises new difficulties.

A Schmidt telescope is in a sense a cross-breed between the reflector and the refractor. The mirror is borrowed from the reflector, the correcting plate from the refractor. Quite apart from the chromatic difficulty already noted, there is the difficulty at large apertures of obtaining and of shaping a large glass plate of adequate quality. So far, nobody has undertaken the figuring of a plate with a greater diameter than 48 inches. However, it is a less exacting task to shape a plate for only weak refraction than to grind an objective lens of equal aperture.

In recent years, the Schmidt telescope has proved extremely popular. Because of its large field of view it enables the observer to accumulate astronomical material far more rapidly than with a traditional reflector. It was for precisely this reason that the comprehensive sky survey carried out ten years ago by the Mount Wilson and Palomar Observatories was made with the aid of a Schmidt telescope. The instrument is naturally popular with observatories situated in unfavorable climates, for in the rare periods when astronomical conditions happen to be good much more material can be obtained. The Schmidt telescope is also well suited to handling statistical problems involving large numbers of objects, stars or galaxies. Traditional reflectors are better suited to examining particular objects, which they can do in greater detail than the Schmidt.

However, we have already noticed more than once that the resolution of one optical difficulty seems always to raise new ones. So it is with the Schmidt telescope. In practice the apertures of Schmidt telescopes are limited by the difficulties of making correcting plates. To this we must now add that the Schmidt system suffers severely and inherently from field curvature. The focal image is not formed on a plane at all, as it is in the normal telescope, but on a spherical surface. For this reason photographs must be taken on film or on plates that are curved to a spherical form. While this creates no immediate practical difficulty, it makes the Schmidt telescope awkward to use for precise metrical work. Research directed toward overcoming this difficulty is now being actively prosecuted.

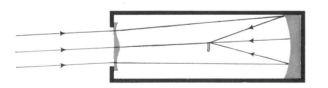

Figure 2.34
Principle of Schmidt telescope, which borrows mirror from reflector and correcting plate from refractor.

The 48-inch Schmidt telescope with which the Mount Wilson and Palomar Observatories made a sky survey published in the 1950s.

Chapter 3   Planetary Motion and Ancient Astronomy

Men of like intelligence to ourselves have been looking out into space for at least twenty-five thousand years. Throughout the five to six thousand years for which written records exist, we know that what they learned at different times and in different places depended partly on the driving interest that underlay their observations, partly on the instruments at their disposal, partly on the care with which they recorded the results of their observations, and partly on the skill and ingenuity with which they interpreted those results.

We can be reasonably sure that until quite recent times there were no really serious attempts to assess the masses or the compositions of heavenly bodies. Without a knowledge of the universal laws of gravitation and without the aid of highly developed optical instruments, any such attempts would have been foredoomed to failure. So early astronomers were interested almost exclusively in noting and in trying to interpret the apparent motions of the Sun, Moon, stars and planets.

The motions of the stars followed a regularly recurring and comparatively simple pattern. Those of the Sun and the Moon, though certainly more complex, were clearly characterized by some fairly regular rhythm. Most baffling of all were the motions of the planets, which fitted into no easily-recognizable and simple pattern. Hence planetary motion formed a major pre-occupation of astronomy in antiquity and, indeed, until long after the close of the Middle Ages.

Much of what follows in this and the next two chapters will therefore be considerably easier to understand if we begin by getting the problem into perspective ourselves.

Three Ways of Viewing the Problem

The motions of the planets are either very simple or very complicated, according to the degree of refinement with which one looks at the problem, and it will be useful to define three stages of refinement. In the least sophisticated stage we may regard the planets as moving in circular orbits around the Sun. The Sun forms the center of each orbit and the planets move with uniform speeds along their respective circles. These circles, moreover, all lie in the same plane.

This very simple point of view is summed up by the entries which appear in Table 1 at the top of page 68.

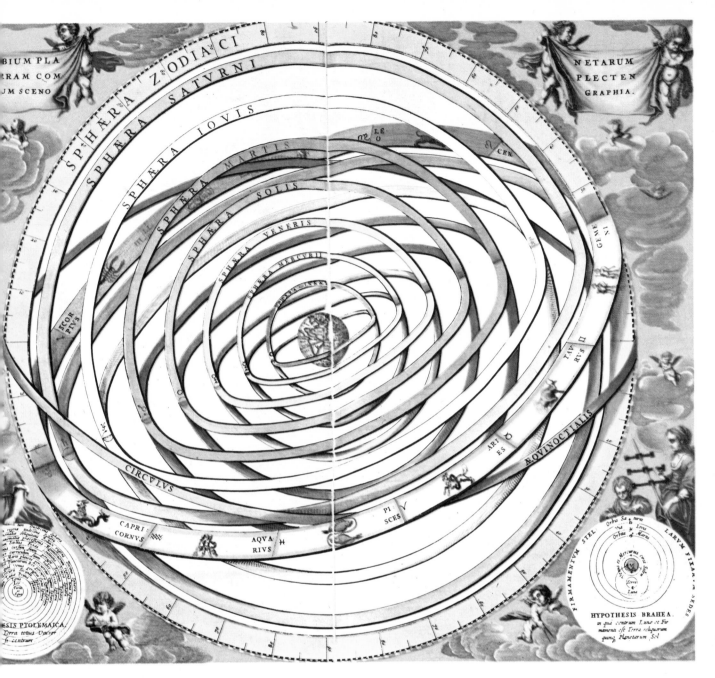

The Babylonians were concerned with listing observed positions of planets. The Greeks thought of the motions of the planets in geometrical terms. Bottom: Part of a Babylonian record of positions of Jupiter during the first and second centuries B.C. Top: Seventeenth-century representation of geometrical picture of the planetary orbits.

Table 1

Planet	Distance from Sun		Sidereal Period	Synodic Period
	Compared with Earth's distance = 1.000	In millions of miles	Years	Days
Mercury	0.387	36.0	0.2408	116
Venus	0.723	67.2	0.6152	584
Earth	1.000	93.0	1.0000	—
Mars	1.524	141.7	1.8808	780
Jupiter	5.203	484	11.862	399
Saturn	9.539	887	29.457	378
Uranus	19.19	1785	84.013	370
Neptune	30.07	2795	164.783	367
Pluto	39.52	3675	248.420	367

Here the full list of planets is given, although, of course, Uranus, Neptune and Pluto were not known to the ancient world. The first two columns give the radii of the circles for the various planets, column one in terms of the radius of the Earth's orbit as unit, and column two in terms of a million miles as unit. The third column states the number of years required for the various planets to complete one circuit of the Sun. After such a complete circuit an imaginary observer *on the Sun* would see the planet as returning to its original position against the background of distant stars. Column four gives the period required for the planets to return to their original positions *as seen by an observer here on the Earth*, a return being again judged to be made when the planet returns to its initial position against the general stellar background.

The last two columns differ because the motion of the Earth has no effect on the so-called *sidereal period* (the period as seen by an observer on the Sun) whereas the *synodic period* (the period as viewed by an observer on the Earth) is, of course, much affected by the Earth's motion. Indeed, the outermost planets appear to complete their movements in little more than a single terrestrial year, though in that time they have scarcely moved at all in their orbits around the Sun. The apparent movement is, of course, caused by the Earth's own motion.

Figure 3.1 indicates what we can explain about the apparent behavior of Venus if we accept the unsophisticated view that all the planets move in circular concentric orbits around the Sun. The figure shows the orbit of Venus and that of the Earth. Because the two planets move around the Sun at different rates, there are moments when the line drawn from the Earth to Venus forms a tangent to the orbit of the latter. Two such cases arise: first when Venus lies to the right of the Sun (tangent EV_1) and second when it lies to the left (EV_2). If we remember that the Earth is spinning about an axis inclined at about 67° to the plane of the orbits shown in Figure 3.1, in the manner indicated by the arrow, it follows that Venus is a morning star when it is at V_1 and an evening star when it is at V_2. In one case Venus precedes the Sun, in the other case it follows the Sun.

In Figure 3.2 we have the situation when the line from the Earth to Venus is in the same direction as the Sun. When at the point V the planet is said to be at inferior conjunction, when at V_1 it is at superior conjunction. Since Venus shines only by reflecting sunlight, as the Moon does, it appears as a thin crescent when near V and as a full disk when near V_1. Evidently, the apparent distance across the horns of the crescent at V will be considerably greater than the apparent diameter of the disk at V_1, simply because V is much nearer to us than V_1.

All this refers to the first stage of sophistication. We have a picture of extreme regularity and simplicity. These qualities begin to disappear, however, when we move on to stage two. In this stage we must take account of the fact that the orbits of the planets are not exact circles but nearly-circular ellipses. The orbit of the Earth, from this second point of view, is shown in Figure 3.3, the ellipticity being exaggerated, however, to show up the new effect. Instead of the Sun lying at the center of a circle, it now lies at one of the foci of the ellipse, marked S. The Earth is nearest to the Sun at the point P, known as the *perihelion* of its orbit, and most distant from the Sun at the *aphelion* point, marked A. If we write a for the radius of the perfect circle postulated at stage one of sophistication, then the distance of the Earth from the Sun at perihelion is less than a by a quantity which we may write as the product $a \times e$. And it is a property of the ellipse that at the aphelion point, the Earth's distance from the Sun exceeds a by precisely the same amount as it falls short of it at the perihelion point, namely by $a \times e$. Thus the distance of the Earth from the Sun always lies between two extremes, an upper extreme $a + ae$ and a lower extreme $a - ae$. For the Earth, the quantity e is equal to 0.0167. In other words, the Earth varies its mean distance from the Sun by approximately one-and-a-half per cent each way.

This means that the Earth is nearer to the Sun at perihelion than it is at aphelion by about 3 per cent.

We saw in Chapter 1 that the plane of the ecliptic cuts the plane of the celestial equator at two points, one of which is the First Point of Aries (Υ). The position of the line pointing from the Sun toward Υ (as it was at the beginning of January, 1920) is shown in Figure 3.3, in relation to the direction from aphelion to perihelion. It will be recalled that at the vernal equinox, the Sun, as seen from the Earth, lies in the direction of Υ whereas it lies in precisely the opposite direction at the autumnal equinox. The positions of the two equinoxes are marked in our figure, and because of the sense of the Earth's motion, summer lies to the left and winter to the right of the line pointing toward Υ.

If the Earth's axis of rotation were exactly at right angles to the plane of its orbit there would, of course, be no seasons of the year. Still thinking in terms of our second stage of sophistication, we may say that the Earth's axis of rotation keeps a constant direction in space, this constant direction being carried round the orbit shown in Figure 3.3. In summer the axis of rotation leans toward the Sun and in winter away from it (summer and winter being here reckoned as experienced in the northern hemisphere). Because of the ellipticity of the Earth's orbit the journey from spring through the point A to autumn takes a little longer than the journey from autumn through the point P back to spring. Thus in the second stage of sophistication we expect a slight inequality in the lengths of the seasons. In point of fact the difference amounts to about seven days, and was easily detected by means of the observational methods used by astronomers of the ancient world. In ancient times, therefore, evidence was already available for the elliptic character of the Earth's orbit, although that evidence was not correctly interpreted.

Also in the second stage of sophistication, we must take account of the fact that the orbits of the other planets are also elliptic. The corresponding values of the eccentricities (e) for all the planets known to antiquity are shown in the first column of Table 2, from which it is seen that the orbit of the Earth is less elliptic than that of any planet other than Venus. Indeed, the fluctuations in distance from the Sun are quite substantial in the case of Mars and even more so in the case of Mercury, amounting roughly to plus or minus 10 per cent and plus or minus 20 per cent respectively.

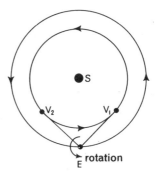

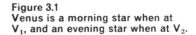

Figure 3.1
Venus is a morning star when at V_1, and an evening star when at V_2.

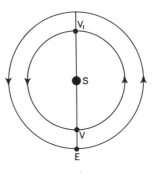

Figure 3.2
V marks position of Venus at inferior conjunction, V_1 marks its position at superior conjunction.

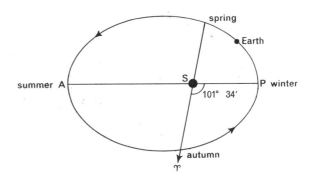

Figure 3.3
Earth's orbit is here an ellipse with the Sun at one of the foci. A is the aphelion point, P perihelion.

Table 2

Planet	Eccentricity of orbit	Longitude of Perihelion	Inclination to Earth's orbit
Mercury	0.2056	76° 13′	7° 0′
Venus	0.0068	130° 27′	3° 24′
Earth	0.0167	101° 34′	——
Mars	0.0933	334° 35′	1° 51′
Jupiter	0.0484	13° 2′	1° 18′
Saturn	0.0558	91° 29′	2° 29′

We see from Figure 3.3 that the perihelion direction of the major axis of the Earth's orbit makes an angle of 101° 34′ with the direction of ♈, the latter direction being judged from the positions of stars in the sky. The corresponding angles for the other planets are given in the second column of Table 2.

A further important point in this second stage of refinement is that the orbits of the different planets do not fall in the same plane. Each orbit defines a separate plane, and the various planes make small angles with each other. The angles which the planes of other planetary orbits make with the plane of the Earth's orbit are shown in the third column of Table 2.

It is clear that there are vital differences between our two stages of refinement. In the first stage we have a simple picture in which the various planets all do essentially the same thing, namely move in circular paths around the Sun with uniform speeds. In the second stage there is nothing uniform about the orbits of the planets. Their eccentricities are all different, the orientations of their major axes are all different, and the planes of the orbits are all different. We therefore pass from uniformity to extreme irregularity.

This irregularity becomes still more marked when we pass to the third stage of refinement. At that stage we have to recognize that the orbits of the planets are not even true ellipses. The orbit of a planet around the Sun would be an ellipse only if all gravitational influences except that of the Sun could be completely neglected. While it is true that the Sun's gravitational influence is much greater than that of the planets themselves, the fact remains that all the planets are pulled by the gravitational fields of the other planets as well as by the powerful field of the Sun. These small effects produce small irregularities in the paths that the planets follow.

Fortunately for the ancient world these fine irregularities in the motions of the planets could not be detected with the observational instruments then

available, otherwise the problem of describing planetary motions in complete detail would have been quite intractable. The irregularities of stage two, however, *were* accessible to the ancient world and this, as we shall see, turned out to be a disadvantage rather than an advantage.

In addition, there were just two facets of the third stage of refinement that also lay within the grasp of ancient astronomers. These were refinements in the motions of the Earth and the Moon. So far nothing has been said about the motion of the Moon, and here again we can describe the situation in three stages. In the first crude stage we can think of the Moon as pursuing a circular orbit with a radius of about a quarter of a million miles with the Earth as its center. We can also think of the plane of the Moon's orbit as coincident with the plane of the Earth's orbit around the Sun. In this simple picture the orbit of the Moon is a tiny circle compared to that of the Earth's circle around the Sun. In fact, the radius of the latter is some 370 times greater than the radius of the Moon's orbit.

In the second stage we must take account of the fact that the Moon's orbit is elliptic, with an eccentricity of 0.0549, and that the plane of that orbit makes an angle of 5° 9′ with the plane of the Earth's orbit.

When we come to stage three of refinement, in which we must take into account more than one gravitational field, we find that this makes a far greater difference to the motion of the Moon than it does to the motions of the planets. The dominating gravitational influence on the Moon comes from the Earth, not from the Sun, simply because the Moon is so close to the Earth. But although the Sun is very much farther away, its large mass produces very serious perturbations in the orbit of the Moon, far more serious than any perturbations which the gravitational field of one planet produces in the orbit of another planet. Thus the perturbations in the orbit of the Moon, that is to say the refinements of stage three, are far more noticeable than the perturbations in the orbits of the planets. Indeed, they are so marked that they lay readily within the grasp of the ancient world.

Turning now to the fine detail in the motion of the Earth, we have spoken of the Earth's axis of rotation as always preserving a constant direction in space. Actually this is not so. The axis moves slowly around a cone with its center at the center of the Earth and with its axis perpendicular to the plane of the Earth's orbit. The half-angle of the cone is just the $23\frac{1}{2}°$ which the Earth's axis always makes with the plane of the orbit. (The situation is shown in Figure 6.1, Chapter 6.) The time required for one rotation of the axis around the cone is about 26,000 years. This means that the poles of the celestial sphere, discussed in Chapter 1, change slowly with time. Moreover, the line in which the plane of the Earth's equator cuts the plane of the Earth's orbit also changes. This causes the line $S\Upsilon$, marked in Figure 3.3, to turn round slowly, making one complete rotation in about 26,000 years.

Because at any given moment the plane of the Earth's equator can be determined with a considerable degree of accuracy, even with the aid of only primitive instruments, the moment in the year when the Sun first lies in the plane of the Earth's equator can also be determined with fair precision. This moment, is, of course, the moment of the vernal equinox. Hence the line $S\Upsilon$ can be determined to within, say, a few minutes of arc. And this can be done in any year. If, now, the line $S\Upsilon$ turns slowly with time, the effect must readily become noticeable as soon as observations are compared over a period of a century or more, for in a century the line $S\Upsilon$ turns by nearly $1\frac{1}{2}°$, and this is much greater than any likely errors of measurement. It is true that the effect is not large over a period of a few centuries, but to a man of the ability of Hipparchus it was readily within the range of observation.

So far we have considered everything from the modern point of view, in which the Sun is taken as the center of the Solar System. But for early astronomers the natural thing to do was to consider the Earth as being the center. The question therefore arises as to what the picture described above looks like if we regard the Earth as being the center from which observations are made. If, for instance, we assume the Earth to be fixed and not the Sun, then in place of Figure 3.3 we must substitute Figure 3.4, where we have the Sun moving in an orbit around the Earth – an orbit of exactly similar shape to that in Figure 3.3 but with reflective symmetry. The matter of reflective symmetry can be understood more clearly with the help of the fantastic example shown in Figure 3.5. Here we have a body E moving around a second body S, the drawing on the left giving the motion of E as determined by an observer situated at S. The question now arises as to how an observer attached to E would regard the apparent motion of S. The answer is shown in the drawing on

the right, where we have an exactly similar curve but with reflective symmetry; that is to say the whole curve is turned through an angle of 180°. This property is general for curves of any shape whatsoever.

When viewed from the Earth the direction of Υ is, of course, the same as it was from the Sun, simply because Υ is a direction associated with the stellar background, and the stars are so far away that they appear to be in the same direction from the Earth as they would do from the Sun.

The point in Figure 3.4 where the Sun is nearest to the Earth is now called *perigee* and the point of greatest distance is called *apogee*. The appropriate seasons of the year are also marked in the figure.

Look now at Figure 3.6, where the orbits of Venus and the Earth are again shown in terms of the heliocentric picture. What does this look like if viewed by an observer on the Earth? For simplicity, we may return to our first stage of sophistication and consider the case where the orbits are taken to be circles. The Sun may then be regarded as pursuing a circular orbit around the Earth, and since Venus is also regarded as moving in a circular orbit

The stone depicted near the bottom of this Greek red-figure vase marked "the navel of the world", at Delphi. To the ancients, who thought of their own locality as the center of the world, it was only natural to think of the Earth, rather than the Sun, as the center of the universe.

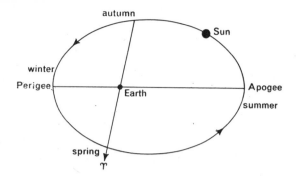

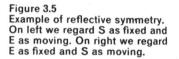

Figure 3.4
If we think of the Earth as center,
Figure 3.3 must be re-drawn with
reflective symmetry, as shown above.
Perigee corresponds with perihelion,
apogee with aphelion.

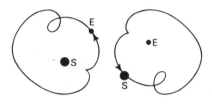

Figure 3.5
Example of reflective symmetry.
On left we regard S as fixed and
E as moving. On right we regard
E as fixed and S as moving.

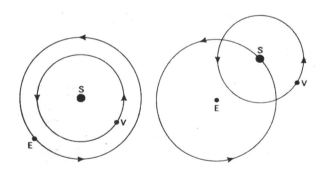

Figure 3.6 (Left)
Orbits of Venus and Earth, with
Sun regarded as fixed center.

Figure 3.7 (Right)
Orbits of Venus and Sun, with
Earth regarded as fixed center.

around the Sun, we must picture it in Figure 3.7 as moving in a circular orbit around the point S. But the point S itself is now moving, and therefore the whole circular orbit of Venus moves with it. So the motion of Venus is made up of two parts: a motion around the circle with center S, and a motion of the center of the circle. Motion of this kind is called epicyclic motion. Both in Figure 3.6 and in Figure 3.7 the heavy dots show the positions of the Earth, the Sun and Venus at a particular moment. The triangles ESV have exactly the same shape in both cases, and corresponding sides of the two triangles are parallel to each other.

So far we have considered only the motion of Venus, a planet nearer to the Sun than our Earth is. What happens if we change over from the heliocentric to the geocentric viewpoint in considering the motion of a planet that is more distant from the Sun than the Earth is? Figure 3.8 shows the orbits of the Earth and an outer planet in terms of the heliocentric picture. The first part of Figure 3.9 shows them in terms of the geocentric picture. The Sun is now traveling around the Earth in a circular orbit, and the outer planet is circling around the moving Sun. Since the first circle has a radius equal to the radius of the Earth's orbit, and the second circle has a radius equal to that of the orbit of the outer planet, it is clear that the second circle is larger than the first one. Both in Figure 3.8 and in Figure 3.9 the heavy dots represent the positions of the Earth, the Sun and a given outer planet at a particular moment. The triangles ESO are similar in both cases; they are of the same size and their corresponding sides are parallel. The type of representation shown in Figure 3.9 is known as an *eccentric circle picture*, that in Figure 3.7 as an *epicycle picture*.

Now it is not hard to see that an eccentric circle picture can be converted into an epicycle picture, and *vice versa*. Take, for example, the case shown in Figure 3.9. Draw a line through E parallel to SO and a line through O parallel to SE, the two new lines intersecting at C. Then $SOCE$ is a parallelogram, as shown in the second part of Figure 3.9. Thus EC is equal to the radius of the orbit of the outer planet and OC is equal to the radius of the Earth's orbit. This allows us to construct an epicycle picture for the motion of an outer planet, as shown in Figure 3.10. We now draw a circle with the Earth as center, the radius of the circle being equal to that of the radius of the orbit of the outer planet, *not* equal to the radius of the Earth's orbit. C is a point on this circle. Now

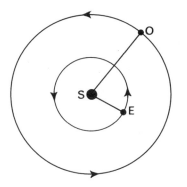

Figure 3.8
Orbits of the Earth and an outer planet with Sun regarded as center.

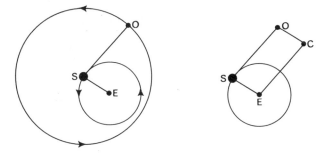

Figure 3.9
Orbit of that same planet if we regard the Earth as center. The small figure hints how to turn the eccentric circle picture of the main figure into an epicycle picture like that of Figure 3.7

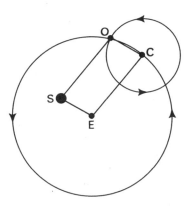

Figure 3.10
Epicycle picture of the orbit of the same outer planet.

with C as its center, draw a second circle with radius equal to that of the Earth's orbit. The motion of the outer planet can now be represented as an epicyclic motion in which C moves around the larger circle in the period of motion of the outer planet around the Sun, and the outer planet itself moves around the small circle not in its own period but in the period of the Earth's motion around the Sun. This follows because in the second part of Figure 3.9 the line EC is parallel to SO, and therefore takes the period of the outer planet in its orbit around the Sun to swing round once, while OC is parallel to SE and therefore swings round once in a year—that is to say, in the period of the Earth's motion around the Sun. The heavy dots in Figure 3.10 show the positions of the Earth, the Sun and the outer planet, and of the epicyclic center C corresponding to the same moment as that in which the planets have the positions shown in Figure 3.9.*

In a similar way the epicycle picture shown for Venus in Figure 3.7 can be replaced by an eccentric circle picture, and the method is exactly the same. Draw a line through E parallel to SV and a line through V parallel to SE, these new lines intersecting at C, as in second part of Figure 3.11. The line EC is equal in length to the radius of the orbit of Venus and swings through a complete rotation in the period of Venus around the Sun. Hence the point C moves around the Earth in a time equal to the motion of Venus around the Sun. This is shown in the other part of Figure 3.11. And the line CV is equal in length to the radius of the Earth's orbit, and therefore makes one complete rotation in precisely a year. Hence the motion of Venus can be represented as being made up of two components: one, a motion around the center C where CV equals the radius of the Earth's orbit, and where the time taken for this motion around C is a year; and two, a motion of C around a smaller circle with radius equal to the radius of the orbit of Venus, this latter

*The reader equipped with modern elementary mathematics will recognize the equivalence of Figures 3.9 and 3.10 as simply the associative law for complex numbers. Let r_E be the radius of the Earth's orbit, and r_O the radius of the orbit of the outer planet; let θ_E and θ_O be the corresponding arguments. Then the position of O in Figure 3.9 is given by $r_E e^{i\theta_E} + r_O e^{i\theta_O}$, while in Figure 3.10 the position of O is $r_O e^{i\theta_O} + r_E e^{i\theta_E}$.

motion taking place in a time equal to the period of Venus. A similar construction obviously applies to the case of the planet Mercury, while constructions similar to those of Figures 3.9 and 3.10 apply to all planets distant beyond the Earth.

This matter has been considered at length because there seems some doubt as to whether the equivalence of the epicycle and the eccentric circle representations was understood by the early astronomers for the cases of Venus and Mercury. It was certainly understood for the outer planets, Ptolemy in particular being quite clear that the two pictures are entirely equivalent. Others were probably much less clear about the point than Ptolemy, and some are said to have favored one picture and some the other without apparently realizing that they are exactly the same thing. There seems to be some doubt as to whether even Ptolemy realized the equivalence for the cases of Venus and Mercury. We shall later see that Ptolemy succeeded by an ingenious construction in modifying the epicycle picture in such a way as to take partial account of the elliptic character of the planetary orbits so far as Mars, Jupiter and Saturn were concerned. The method also worked very well for Venus, but, for a reason explained in the mathematical appendix to this book, it did not work for Mercury. This latter failure arose purely from the use of the epicycle picture. If Ptolemy had carried out an exactly similar construction for Mercury as he did for the other planets, but using the eccentric circle picture instead of the epicyclic one, his method would have been successful for Mercury also.

If the epicycle picture is used in all cases, as in Figure 3.12, then the center C of the epicycle represents the position of the Sun *only for planets interior to the Earth*. For planets exterior to the Earth the Sun lies not at C but on a line through E drawn parallel to CP, and at a distance from E equal to the distance of P from C, that is at the point marked S.

Because of the motion in the epicycle, none of the planets appears to move smoothly round the Earth at a uniform rate. Instead, the appearance as seen by a terrestrial observer takes the form shown in Figure 3.13. This shows that a line drawn from the Earth to a planet does not move smoothly round in an anticlockwise sense. Instead, a planet at X, following the track of Figure 3.13, moves in such a way that the line drawn from it to the Earth swings round in the anticlockwise sense until it reaches the position EA_1, after which it reverses its direction and moves in a clockwise sense back to EA_2. Thereafter the line resumes its anticlockwise rotation until the next loop is reached. Lines such as EA_1 and EA_2 at which the direction of the planet reverses its angular motion are called *stationary directions*. Evidently, the angle A_1EA_2 depends on the radius of the orbit of the planet and on the speed at which it moves around its orbit. In general, the larger the radius of the epicycle in comparison to the radius of the larger circle, the greater is the angle A_1EA_2, the angle through which the planet is said to *retrograde*. This means that the angle is much larger for Mars than it is for Jupiter, and it is greater for Jupiter than it is for Saturn. Similarly, the angle is greater for Venus than it is for Mercury.

Figure 3.11
Here an eccentric circle picture replaces the epicycle picture of the orbit of Venus given in Figure 3.7. Small figure gives basis of change.

Figure 3.12
If we use the epicycle picture for all planets, C represents the Sun only for inner planets. For outer planets S shows Sun's position.

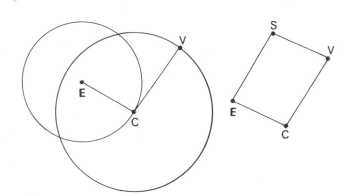

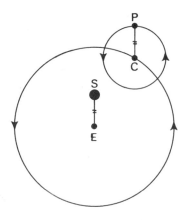

Figure 3.13
Apparent motion of a planet as
seen from the Earth. Planet moves
anticlockwise from X to line EA₁,
then clockwise back to line EA₂.

This photograph was taken in the
Munich planetarium, where the motions
of the planets over a period of
seventeen years are being simulated.
It shows the apparent loops in the
orbits of Mars, Venus and Mercury
and also the retracting motions
of Jupiter and Saturn. The very
complexity of the pattern explains
why planetary motions presented
the astronomers of antiquity with
such a baffling problem.

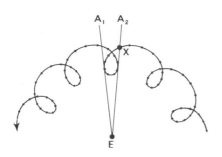

With these introductory remarks in mind we should not only be more able to understand why the problem of planetary motion formed such a dominant theme of early astronomy; we should also be in a better position to appreciate the ingenuity of many attempts that were made to find a satisfactory solution.

Ancient Astronomy in General

Ancient astronomy had two main focal points, one in Mesopotamia and the other in Greece. Although extensive claims have sometimes been made for the development of astronomy in India and in China, much of the work done there was probably derivative from Mesopotamia. The developments in Greece and in Mesopotamia were not contemporary, the latter in its phase of maximum achievement probably preceding the former by as much as five centuries. Certainly Greek astronomy before 1000 B.C. was quite negligible, whereas in the Babylonia of that time astronomy was already a strong development. And even before Babylonian times it is possible that the Sumerians already possessed a considerable body of fairly refined astronomical data.

Because of the difference in their respective moments of greatest achievement, it is well-nigh certain that early Greek astronomy must have been influenced through the importation of ideas from the Near East. In recent years it has indeed been claimed that Hipparchus, as late as 130 B.C., derived certain of his results from the Babylonians, and that they had already anticipated certain others. Neugebauer, for example, has hinted that if credit for early developments could be appropriately apportioned, much that has previously been accorded to the Greeks would need to be transferred to the Babylonians. Although this is probably in some degree true, the present writer tends to feel that the methods of working of the two groups were quite distinct, and that the main features of the Greek mode of thought were not derived from Babylonian astronomers. Indeed it seems likely that Greek ideas from the third century B.C. onward produced considerable repercussions in Mesopotamia, as, for instance, the heliocentric theory of Aristarchus, which was studied by Seleucus, an astronomer from Seleucia on the River Tigris.

My own suspicion is that the work of the Babylonians was largely numerological. In other words, Babylonian astronomers observed the positions of the planets, and more particularly of the Moon, with considerable precision, set out to discover regularities among their observations, and then used the discovered regularities to predict the future positions of the Moon and planets. The regularities were discovered empirically; they were then found to fit various mathematical formulae, and these were used in predicting future positions.

The Greek method was entirely different. Instead of viewing the problem as a species of code-cracking, they conceived the motions of heavenly bodies in terms of a geometrical model. The planets and the Moon were assumed to move along certain geometrical paths, and the effects of their motions along these paths were calculated and then compared with observation. And so the validity of the model they conceived was either confirmed or contradicted. In the latter case they attempted to improve the geometrical picture.

There is a crucial difference between the Babylonian and the Greek methods of approach. If one is seeking only algebraic formulae which will represent the actually observed positions of the planets, then it is quite unnecessary to worry about where the planets are when they cannot be observed, that is, when they are set below the horizon. One does not have to face up to the question of whether the planets and the stars continue their motion below the horizon along paths that take them below the Earth back to points at which they rise. But one cannot even begin to arrive at a sensible geometrical model unless one can answer questions about the whereabouts of stars and planets both when they are above *and* below the horizon.

The opinion that the Greeks were first to think of astronomical problems in terms of a geometrical model is based on logical inference. We know that the early Greeks, in the eighth and seventh centuries B.C., considered that the Sun, Moon, planets and stars did *not* continue their apparent daily circular motions on setting in the west, that they did *not* continue to move in their daily circular

This Egyptian carving on stone, dating from the fifth century B.C., shows Nut, goddess of the sky, arched over the Earth. At right and left of the disk of the Earth are two boats. Egyptian astronomers long believed that the Sun made a hidden journey each night from the western to the eastern horizon in a boat along a river.

paths below the Earth. It was believed, instead, that they changed their motions at the horizon, moving round to the north just below the horizon until they reached the appropriate rising point in the east again. In Egypt the Sun was thought to make this tour from the west to the north and back to the east in a boat along a river'. Now since Egyptian astronomy, mathematics and science were in the main but poor relations of Babylonian astronomy, mathematics and science, it seems clear that the Babylonians themselves had not worried about geometrical models. Similarly, it is difficult to believe that the Greeks of the eighth century B.C. could have entertained similar primitive notions if more refined concepts had been available in Babylonia. And in this connection it must be remembered that the eighth century B.C. was very close to the high point of astronomy in the Near East.

This is not to say that the Babylonians themselves believed any such nonsense as that the Sun was carried around the horizon in a boat. Probably their interests in astronomy were simply not directed toward geometrical notions at all. And there is a very good reason why this should have been so.

It is clear that the motion of the Moon had become wound into the cultural patterns of Mesopotamia and adjacent areas in a very intimate way; and the prediction of the future motion of the Moon, particularly the moments of new moon, was regarded as a matter of the utmost importance. (The Old Testament abounds in references to feasts and rites connected with the new moon, and even at the present day the date of one of the main

Christian festivals, Easter, is decided by the first full moon occurring after the spring equinox.)

Now the case of the Moon is just the one in which a geometrical approach was quite impossible if high accuracy was demanded, for it is just the one in which our third stage of sophistication is needed. Without the modern gravitational theory, the Babylonians could not possibly have determined the orbit of the Moon to the required degree of accuracy. A numerical, empirical approach to the problem was their only hope. And if this was their approach to what they clearly regarded as the most important problem, it is easy to see why the same mode of thought was probably applied to the planets and to the stars. To the Greeks, on the other hand, the Moon was far from being the most important case. It was not necessary to them above all else that the future positions of the Moon be correctly predicted. Indeed, not until comparatively late times did they worry themselves about the intricacies in the motion of the Moon.

It cannot be claimed that this point of view is certainly correct, for the documentary evidence available, even if it could be easily read and deciphered, is insufficient to determine the history of ancient astronomy in great detail, particularly with regard to motives. So far as Mesopotamia is concerned, information is derived from a few thousand tablets obtained from various excavations, and this cannot be regarded as more than a very tiny representation of the thought and activities of a civilization that extended over several thousand years. A different difficulty presents itself in the

case of Greek civilization. Apart from Ptolemy's *Almagest*, very little survives in uncorrupted form of the writings of the great Greek scientists. Existing texts are copied from earlier texts, and these were no doubt already copies of the originals. Following the decline of Greek science in Roman times, the copyists were of lesser intellectual stature than the original Greek scientists and sometimes, indeed, were downright stupid. Hence gross distortions were introduced, and very likely priorities were wrongly distributed. Moreover, only those views of the Greeks that were popular in the early centuries of the Christian era were preserved. Unpopular theories, such as the heliocentric theory of Aristarchus, survive only through casual remarks in the writings of other people. The tantalizing situation therefore arises that those Greek ideas which are of the greatest interest to the modern mind are commonly just the ones about which we have the least certain information. The attempted reconstruction in the remainder of this chapter must therefore be viewed in a cautionary light.

The Seasons and the Calendar

As soon as man passed from his earlier nomadic existence to an agricultural economy a knowledge of the lengths of the seasons became of paramount importance. The correct moment for planting seeds had to be known. One very simple prescription was available, a prescription implicit in the previous chapter. The daily motion of the Sun determines the direction of the south for any observer situated anywhere in the northern hemisphere. Hence the

westerly and easterly directions can also be determined simply by observing the Sun on any one day of the year. There are only two moments in the year when the Sun rises in the due easterly direction and sets in the due westerly direction—the vernal and autumnal equinoxes; and the equinox following winter was the appropriate one for determining the moment of spring sowing.

If the Earth had had no satellite, this method, or some refinement of it, would doubtless have been universally used and mankind would have had little trouble in arriving at a sensible calendar. But through a grotesque set of coincidences the Moon greatly complicated the situation.

The Moon completes a circuit of the Earth in about $27\frac{1}{3}$ days, that is, in $27\frac{1}{3}$ days it returns to essentially the same position when viewed against the background of stars. But the average time between two successive new moons or full moons is about $29\frac{1}{2}$ days. The difference arises because of the motion of the Earth around the Sun. This causes the Moon to have to make rather more than one complete circuit in order to get into a position directly in line with the Sun, which is, of course, the condition that produces new moon or full moon. The latter period of $29\frac{1}{2}$ days is called the synodic month, and the true period of $27\frac{1}{3}$ days is called the sidereal month.

If we speak roughly we can round off the synodic month to 30 days. Then twelve synodic months make 360 days, which is nearly the length of the year. To the modern mind it would seem remarkable if there were any connection between the

Modern photograph of a solar eclipse, with the Moon's disk all but hiding the Sun. To the ancients the fact that Sun and Moon have the same apparent diameter and the fact that the motions of both can be roughly fitted in with the cycle of the seasons, made it seem possible that either could be used as the basis for a calendar.

Little of the Greek geometrical approach to problems of astronomy survived in uncorrupted form in early and medieval Christendom. Over the years copyists introduced errors and distorted priorities. In the fifteenth-century Italian manuscript on the right the artist has confused Ptolemy the astronomer with one of the Ptolemies of Egypt.

Fragment of a Babylonian tablet giving detailed information about positions, phases and eclipses of the Moon during the second century B.C. To the people of Mesopotamia it was a cultural imperative to forecast the Moon's movements accurately. This was just the one problem where a numerological approach gave better results than a geometrical approach.

On this boundary stone of 1100 B.C. the Moon appears between its two "children"—Venus (left) and the Sun (right). So important was the Moon in Mesopotamian culture that it was chosen as the calendrical basis in spite of all the practical difficulties the choice involved.

length of the day, the length of the synodic month, and the length of the year. In fact, the average length of the synodic month is 29 days 12 hours 44 minutes 2.78 seconds, while the length of the year, defined as the interval between successive passages of the Sun across the celestial equator, is 365 days 5 hours 48 minutes 46.0 seconds. But to the ancient mind, without a precise knowledge of these values, there was every reason to fall into the trap of assuming some subtle connection to exist between the Moon and the Sun. When viewed in the sky the Sun and the Moon have almost exactly the same apparent diameter. Today we know that this is a mere coincidence, but to the ancients it must have seemed of the utmost significance. There was a further coincidence between the period of the Moon and women's menstrual period. So when the first crude observations indicated that there were about twelve lunar months in the year, it was entirely natural that this should have been taken as a major regularity in the behavior of the physical world. This assumption, though natural enough, proved disastrous. Not only was it wrong, not only did it lead to a displacement of almost ten days in the computed time of the vernal equinox, but it also put men's minds on a completely wrong track. As we have already seen, it was probably responsible for dictating the course of Mesopotamian astronomy, not merely through centuries, but through millennia. It was a mistake that we have not completely freed ourselves from even to this day. It shows itself, for example, in the computation of the date of Easter, and it shows itself in the division of a circle into 360°.

Agricultural requirements obviously could not tolerate a progressive error of ten days per year in the reckoning of the moment of the vernal equinox. Fortunately the discrepancy was so gross that for practical purposes the seasons of the year simply had to be determined from the apparent motion of the Sun. Thus the Moon lost its importance as a means of determining the seasons; but what it lost in practical importance it gained in mystical significance and in the place it filled in the cultural beliefs of the peoples of the Near East. And for this reason Mesopotamian astronomers were apparently ready to resort to various shifts to continue to use it for calendrical purposes.

Almost certainly the Babylonians discovered the so-called Metonic cycle. It happens that 235 synodic months are very nearly equal to 19 years. This discovery suggests how to operate a lunar calendar with fair accuracy. One must divide the 19 years into two sets: 12 years each with 12 lunar months, and 7 years each with 13 lunar months.

Since both 12 and 7 were numbers of special mystical significance to the ancients, this must have seemed a suggestive feature. A further unfortunate coincidence was that the 19 years of the Metonic cycle fall very close to the 18.6 years required for the turning of the plane of the Moon's orbit. (This will be considered in more detail in Chapter 6.) The existence of the latter period was certainly known to the Babylonians, since it formed an important element in their system for the prediction of eclipses.

It may be appropriate here to add a few words on the construction of a calendar. For practical purposes it is important that a calendar year should contain an integral number of days. This means that a calendar year cannot agree with the astronomical year. Hence dates get further and further out of step from year to year unless the number of days in the calendar year is occasionally varied. Since the astronomical year is nearly $365\frac{1}{4}$ days, the simplest system is clearly to take three calendar years each of 365 days followed by a fourth year in which there are 366 days. This is just the familiar system of the leap year, first introduced by Julius Caesar in 45 B.C.

But of course the astronomical year is not *exactly* $365\frac{1}{4}$ days; it is less than this by 11 minutes and 14 seconds. Although this is not very much it added up persistently over the centuries that followed Caesar's introduction of the so-called Julian calendar, and by A.D. 1582 the progressive discrepancy amounted to about ten days. To deal with the matter, Pope Gregory XIII ordered that the calendar should be corrected by dropping ten days, so that the day following October 4th 1582 should be called the 15th instead of the 5th. This change was immediately adopted by all Catholic countries, but the Greek Church and most Protestant nations refused to recognize the Pope's authority. England did not come into step with most of western Europe until 1752, when, by Act of Parliament, eleven days were dropped from the year, the eleventh day having accumulated since Pope Gregory's proposal.

To ensure that the same difficulty did not arise again, Pope Gregory proposed that certain years which would have been counted as leap years in the system of Julius Caesar should *not* now be counted as leap years. These were the years 1700, 1800,

1900, 2100, 2200, 2300, 2500, etc., the rule being that where the number of the year ends in two zeros it should be counted as a leap year only if the figures preceding the zeros are divisible by four. The new calendar with this extra refinement is known as the Gregorian Calendar.

The Time of Day

Keeping track of the seasons is only one aspect of time-measurement. It is difficult for us today, governed as we are by public and personal time schedules, to realize that the ancient world had no convenient method of measuring the time of day. But at the easier pace of everyday life that existed then this was probably no great hardship. Anyone who accustoms himself to not wearing a watch soon develops a subjective judgment of time that is usually good to within about a quarter of an hour. And in antiquity time-judgment of this kind would have been sufficient for most practical purposes.

Sundials and water-clocks were the practical means for measuring time, as we have already seen. Quite apart from their lack of accuracy by modern standards, these devices did not divide time into equal units. This does not seem to have been deliberate, but to have arisen from an error. The length of shadow cast by a stick changes during the day, but it does not change at a uniform rate. So if one uses the length of the shadow as a measure of time, one has a nonuniform system. The length of the shadow changes more rapidly just after dawn and just before sunset than it does around midday, so if we assess the passing of time according to that rate of change, time passes more quickly in the morning and evening than it does at midday.

It is hard to believe that people were not subjectively aware of this difference. Probably, indeed, they were not only aware of it but even welcomed it, since there may well have been social advantages in having a unit of time that was longer near midday than in the morning and evening. In this connection it is noteworthy that when reasonably reliable water-clocks were invented, great care was taken to ensure that they did *not* measure time in an approximately uniform way, reflecting the pace at which the heavens appear to revolve; instead, they reflected the behavior of the length of a shadow.

Yet the lack of accurate clocks, not only in antiquity but up to and after the time of Newton, did have one grave disadvantage. It meant that longitudes could not be systematically determined, and

SCIPIO TVRAMINVS CRESCENTII FILVIS CV FVERIT MAGISTRATVS BICCHERNÆ
CAMERARIVS TEMPORE OVO GREGORIVS XIII PONTIFEX MAXIMVS ANNO REFORMAVER
IN PERPETVAM HVIVS REI MEMORIAM HANC TABOLA PINGERE FECIT

Because the Earth does not complete its orbit in an integral number of days, an extra day must be added to the year from time to time. By 1582 Julius Caesar's system of leap years had resulted in the calendar being badly out of step with the seasons. Above is the meeting called by Pope Gregory XIII, which inaugurated the Gregorian Calendar we use today.

It was not until 1752 that Britain came into line with most of Europe and adopted the reformed calendar. By then the discrepancy between the old and new calendars amounted to eleven days. This painting by Hogarth shows a rowdy scene at a time when many riots broke out in England. Rioters used the slogan "Give us back our eleven days".

hence that accurate maps could not be drawn. Not until near the end of the eighteenth century, after the invention of reliable chronometers, did maps manifest a dramatic increase in accuracy.

Hipparchus made the ingenious suggestion that the longitudes of a considerable number of places might be established by using a solar eclipse to determine a moment of simultaneity at all of them. The method does not, of course, give strict simultaneity because the eclipse does not start simultaneously at every point along the track of the Moon's shadow. But the method would have given more accurate results than any previously available if only it had been carefully carried out. Unfortunately, the only deliberate attempt to make use of Hipparchus's suggestion seems to have been badly bungled. A substantial error was made and there was no means of discovering it. It was therefore reflected in maps for many years.

The Shape and Size of the Earth

By the time men became concerned with both latitude and longitude, they had already come to believe that the Earth has a spherical, or nearly spherical, shape. But this belief was not universally held throughout Greek times. To the early Greeks the Earth consisted of a circular disk supported by a great ocean, above which was the hemispherical bowl of the sky. Such a picture is clearly revealed by the works of Homer, and was apparently accepted until about the sixth century B.C. This picture clearly poses a problem as to what happens to the stars, the Sun, the Moon and the planets as they set below the western horizon. As we have already seen, the early belief seems to have been that all the heavenly bodies circulated in some fashion around the horizon to the north, later reappearing in the east ready to follow their circular diurnal paths across the sky once more.

The observation that destroyed the flat-Earth concept was simply that the stars visible from different latitudes are not the same. In Egypt, for instance, certain stars were clearly visible that could not be seen at all from Greece. In Greece the constellation of the Great Bear could be seen to complete a circuit around the pole without dipping below the horizon, whereas in Egypt it was found to dip into the sands of the desert. These observations indicated very clearly that the surface of the Earth is curved in some way. The first idea about *how* it might be curved appears to be due to Anaxi-

mander. He had the curious notion that the Earth is curved toward the north and the south but that it goes straight toward the east and the west, forming a surface rather like that of a cylinder. This hypothesis enabled him to account for the changing aspects of the stars between Greece and Egypt, where the difference is essentially one of latitude, and at the same time to preserve the old mythological notion that the region of the dead lay very far away to the west.

According to Theophrastus, a pupil of Socrates, it was Parmenides, a follower of Pythagoras, who first taught that the form of the Earth's surface is spherical. (Later commentators of the early Christian era give the credit for this great step to Pythagoras himself, because by their time the views of the Pythagoreans were very popular and Pythagoras had become an almost legendary hero.) Parmenides lived in the late sixth and early fifth centuries B.C., and his argument for the spherical form of the Earth was a good one. He argued that a body of any other shape than a sphere would fall inwards on itself—that a sphere was the one shape that would remain naturally in equilibrium. No doubt, too, the hemispherical dome of the sky was a great help in arriving at the idea of a spherical Earth. And the idea, once stated, doubtless gained support from the fact that it offered a simple explanation of what happens to stars, Sun, Moon and planets after they set in the west, namely that they continue their circular paths, and reappear again in the east.

Yet the idea of a spherical Earth did not gain general acceptance until the time of Plato, a century or more later. Plato's argument was philosophic and even flimsy: that a sphere was the most perfect shape for a body, that it had the most complete symmetry, and that hence the Earth, at the center of the universe, *must* be a sphere. While such an argument was not as good as the original argument that Parmenides had advanced, Plato's powerful advocacy served to establish the idea. From then onwards no Greek believed that the Earth was anything other than spherical, and when we come to Aristotle, an extremely telling and decisive argument appears. Often when the Sun, Earth and Moon come nearly into line, with the Earth between the Sun and the Moon, the Moon crosses the shadow cast by the Earth. At such times the shadow on the Moon is invariably seen to be circular, and this would not be the case on all occasions unless the Earth were spherical.

With the realization that the Earth is spherical, it became a problem of great practical interest to determine its size, and the most remarkable estimate of antiquity was that made by Eratosthenes, probably about 230 B.C. The method he used is illustrated in Figure 3.14. Eratosthenes stated that at noon on the summer solstice a vertical stick at Syene (Aswan) cast no shadow, thereby indicating that the Sun was vertically overhead. At Alexandria, at the same time, the Sun made an angle with the vertical estimated at 7° 12′, or one fiftieth part of the circumference of a circle. Hence if Alexandria were due north of Syene, which Eratosthenes apparently assumed it to be, the difference in latitude between the two places amounted to 7° 12′, or one fiftieth of the Earth's circumference. The next step was to determine the overland distance from Syene to Alexandria. Fifty times that distance divided by π would then give the Earth's diameter. By this method Eratosthenes arrived at the figure of 7850 miles, a value only about 70 miles less than the modern value of the Earth's diameter. (The precise value depends on one's definition, since the Earth is not *exactly* spherical, the polar diameter being about 7900 miles, the equatorial about 7927.)

Eratosthenes' result was so good that in modern times many people have queried it. For myself I do not see any good reason to doubt its authenticity. In the first place we know that Eratosthenes wrote a book specially about his determination; and although that book has not survived, the very fact that it was written shows that Eratosthenes thought well of the work and had carried it out carefully. In the second place we have independent evidence of the accuracy of Eratosthenes as an observer. He is known to have determined the angle made by the Earth's axis of rotation with the plane of the Earth's orbit around the Sun. The value he arrived at was 23° 51′, whereas at the time of his determination the true value was 23° 43′, which implies an error of only about 0.56 per cent. (The value today is 23° 36′, the change being due to the fine details in our third stage of sophistication discussed above.)

The actual latitude of Syene is 24° 5′. Hence in the time of Eratosthenes the Sun was not strictly overhead there at the summer solstice, but lay out of the vertical by some 22′. On this basis we might expect an error of some five per cent in Eratosthenes' final answer, but by good luck a compensating error was made in the latitude of Alexandria. Thus the actual difference between the latitudes of the two places is 7° 5′, as compared with Eratosthenes' value of 7° 12′. This reduces the error one might expect to about one-and-a-half per cent. It has also been objected that Alexandria does not lie due north of Syene, the difference in longitude being about three degrees. But the error that would arise in this way is only the amount of the difference of the cosine of three degrees from unity, and this is only a little more than 0.1 per cent. Hence the total error arising from the angle determination was about one per cent; Eratosthenes' value should have been too small by this amount. And this, indeed, is just what it was—7850 miles as compared with 7920.

All this, of course, would imply that the distance from Syene to Alexandria had been measured with complete accuracy, and it is here that the main questions have been asked. The unit of distance used was the stade. Unfortunately three different units bearing that name were then in use: the itinerary stade, used in measuring the distance of a journey and equal in length to about 157 meters; the Olympic stade of 185 meters; and the royal Egyptian stade of 210 meters. Pliny states that Eratosthenes used the itinerary stade, and this checks with an independent commentary that Eratosthenes obtained the distance from professional runners—a procedure which seems natural enough, since the transmission of important messages in Egypt must have been maintained through the use of professional runners for upward of two thousand years. It does not seem in the least unlikely that over the centuries specialist runners in a flat country such as Egypt should have established distances to within a margin of one per cent. The alternative point of view (that Eratosthenes used

Figure 3.14
When noon Sun was directly overhead at Syene it made an angle of 7° 12′ with the vertical at Alexandria. If both were on the same meridian, the distance between them was just one-fiftieth of Earth's circumference.

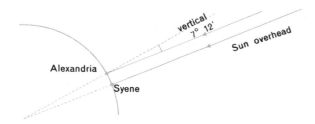

the Olympic stade) would imply that the runners made an error of some 17 per cent in their estimate of the distance, and this seems wildly fantastic.

The Cosmology of the Greeks

The first step to understanding the heavens is probably no more difficult than the first step toward recognizing the Earth's sphericity. It is simply to perceive that the diurnal motion of the stars across the sky arises from the rotation of the Earth. The Greek world as a whole never came to understand this although, as we shall see, there were individual Greeks who did understand it; but these men were never fully able to persuade their contemporaries.

The first step in the right direction was taken by Philolaus, a philosopher of the Pythagorean school. He argued that the main influence in the universe must come from its center, and that since the main influence did not come from the Earth, the Earth could not be at the center. This would suggest that the Earth must be in motion around the center. At first sight one might suppose that this was a step toward a heliocentric theory, but Philolaus did not place the Sun at the center of the system; he thought of it simply as a disk made hot by a rapid passage through the air. Instead, he conceived the center of the system to be a gigantic fire, hidden from us by the body of the Earth. Although this was a fantastic idea according to our modern point of view, Philolaus deserves great credit for two reasons: first for the idea that the center of the system might exert a controlling influence over the whole, and second for realizing that the motion of the Earth around the center would be reflected in a corresponding opposite motion of the stars, which would explain the apparent diurnal rotation of the heavens.

Philolaus was a contemporary of Socrates, and lived shortly before Plato. Plato had no use for his views, being out of sympathy with the Pythagorean school; neither had Aristotle. It is only when we come to the second of the giants of Greek astronomy, Heraclides, that we find the idea being revived and developed. Heraclides dispensed with the fanciful notion of the central fire and simply made the Earth rotate on its axis, as we do today.

Heraclides belonged to the fourth century B.C., and Aristarchus, who did much of his work in the middle of the following century, may well have been influenced by him. Apollonius was the outstanding mathematical astronomer of the third century B.C., Hipparchus of the second century

B.C., and Ptolemy, who lived in the second century A.D., was the last of the great line. Sadly, by the time we come to Hipparchus and Ptolemy, Heraclides' great idea had been dropped, and once again the heavens, rather than the Earth, were assumed to have a diurnal motion. Both Hipparchus and Ptolemy had a reason for rejecting the idea that the Earth rotates, although whether they felt it to be a strong one it is impossible to say. It could have been no more than an excuse for rejecting an idea they did not like. Their ostensible objection was that if the Earth were spinning a body thrown up into the air would simply be left behind.

Perhaps a more valid reason for rejecting the idea that the Earth rotates is that such a theory does not explain the apparent motion of the planets. Reference back to Figure 3.13 shows that as seen from the Earth the planets sometimes reverse their apparent direction of motion. Usually the line from the Earth to a planet turns in an anticlockwise sense, but sometimes it reaches a stationary point and reverses into a clockwise sense; it then continues in that direction until it reaches another stationary point where the anticlockwise motion is once more resumed. The great problem in ascribing any simple geometrical form to the motions of the planets was to give a description of these retrograde motions in terms of the orbits of the planets.

Now it cannot be too strongly stressed that since the Greeks had no physical theory of gravitation, they had no idea of *why* the planets move in orbits. To overcome their physical ignorance they made the bold assumption that all planetary motion is in circles. Combinations of circular motion were permitted in their scheme, as in the epicycles of Figures 3.7 and 3.10, but no motion was admitted that could not be built up from circles. This hypothesis not only veiled the need for a physical theory; it also agreed with the philosophy of symmetry which Plato had expounded for the case of the sphere. Just as a sphere has the greatest degree of symmetry for a three-dimensional body, so a circle has the greatest degree of symmetry for a closed curve.

Without some simple, bold assumption such as Greek astronomers made, the universe would have seemed an entirely lawless place. Although we may now be out of sympathy with such a point of view, we must remember that it persisted until the age of Kepler, and even Kepler finally discarded the notion of circular motion with extreme agony of mind. Perhaps, too, we can have more sympathy with the Greeks if we remember that today's scientists expect physical laws to have elegance and symmetry, even if they no longer expect the material world to manifest those qualities. We have simply replaced the concept of Plato by a similar, but deeper, concept.

The first serious mathematical attempt to understand the complexities of the planetary motions was made by the great Greek mathematician, Eudoxus. It has often been said, somewhat vaguely, that "the Greeks" believed in a system of crystalline spheres: the Moon was believed to be attached to the nearest sphere, then there was a sphere for the Sun, a sphere for each of the planets (in the order Mercury, Venus, Mars, Jupiter and Saturn), and finally a sphere for all the stars. And all these spheres, it is said, were supposed to have their centers at the Earth. This story seems to be a compound between earlier ideas and the theory of Eudoxus, and it is certainly a complete travesty of the theory which Eudoxus actually propounded.

In the theory of Eudoxus only the stars moved on a single sphere. The Moon and the Sun each possessed a nest of three spheres, while the planets each had a nest of four. The outermost sphere of each nest moved in the same way as the sphere of the stars. The second outermost sphere was attached at its poles to the outermost one, and was free to turn around an axis lying between its poles. The third sphere was attached to the second one in a similar way, and so on. Finally, the planet, or the Sun, or the Moon, as the case may be, was attached to the innermost sphere. The polar axes of the various spheres were not parallel to each other, but were chosen in a complicated manner. In this way, highly complex motions of the innermost sphere could be produced.

The situation had some analogy to a compass in gimbals. The mathematical problem was to choose the polar axes, their points of attachment, and the motions of the spheres in such a way as to reproduce the observed motions of the planets, the Sun and the Moon.

How far did Eudoxus succeed? He was, in fact, able to represent the changing directions of the planets, particularly their retrograde motions. Further, his theory automatically required that the directions of the planets did not usually lie in the plane of the Sun's motion around the Earth. In other words, he went some way toward explaining the effect of the tilt of a planet's orbit to the plane of the orbit of the Earth. Unlike the Mesopotamian astronomers before him, and unlike Hipparchus and Ptolemy who came after him, Eudoxus does not seem to have concerned himself with trying to explain the particular motions of heavenly bodies at particular times. Instead, he confined himself to an attempt at explaining the general features of their motions in geometrical terms. And as more details of planetary motions came to light, it be-

Here is a simplified modern diagram of what is sometimes referred to as "the Greek" idea of a system of spheres. In numerical order, spheres shown are propelling sphere (invisible). then spheres of the stars, Saturn, Jupiter, Mars, Sun, Venus, Mercury, the Moon and the Earth.
The theory of Eudoxus was at once more complex and more subtle than this might lead one to imagine. Eudoxus thought of the polar axes of his ideal spheres as not being parallel with each other, yet as being connected with each other in the manner of a compass in gimbals, as indicated above.

came necessary to add more spheres to those which Eudoxus had originally proposed. Thus the nests of spheres were gradually extended, notably by Eudoxus's pupil, Kalippus.

It seems quite clear that Eudoxus never intended his spheres to be thought of as having any actual physical existence. To him they were no more than mathematical devices for representing planetary motions. His theory was produced at about the time that marked the old age of Plato and the early years of Aristotle's maturity, and we find it fully accepted in the writings of Aristotle. But Aristotle made the serious mistake of attaching physical reality to the spheres of Eudoxus, and this mistake compelled him to try to combine the separate nests of spheres for the various planets into one huge mechanical structure. Thus it came about that Aristotle ended his description of the theory with a fantastic total of fifty-five spheres.

After the time of Aristotle, the theory of Eudoxus was discarded. It represented fairly well the changing directions of the planets, but it did not begin to explain why the planets change in brightness, why, for example, Mars is sometimes comparatively bright and sometimes comparatively faint. According to the theory of Eudoxus, Mars is always at the same distance from the Earth and should not therefore change in brightness. Yet plainly Mars must be nearer to the Earth when it appears brightest than when it appears faintest. It was in an endeavor to explain this point that Greek cosmographers arrived at epicyclic pictures of the motions of planets, like those already shown in Figures 3.7 and 3.10.

Working from our present knowledge of the heliocentric theory, we saw above that in Figure 3.10 the radius (OC) of the small circle must equal the radius of the Earth's orbit, and that the radius (CE) of the large circle must equal the radius of the orbit of our outer planet. But this information is not necessary either for understanding the changing directions of, say, Mars, or for understanding the changes in the *relative* distance of Mars. For those purposes, all we need know is the ratio of OC to CE. Then, provided we take the time required to go once round the large circle as being equal to the time that Mars in fact takes to travel once round the Sun, and provided we take the time required to go once round the small circle as being equal to the time that the Earth in fact takes to travel once round the Sun, the epicyclic picture will adequately represent the observed motion of Mars. In other

words, the accuracy of the representation offered by Figure 3.10 is not dependent on the establishment of the true scale of the two circles, but only on the establishment of the ratios of their radii.

Exactly similar considerations apply to Figure 3.7. There the radius of the circle with center at E may be chosen to have any value; it is necessary only that the ratio of the radius of the large circle to the radius of the small circle should be correct.

Thus in drawing Figure 3.7 there was no immediate requirement that the Sun should be the center of the small circle. The essential thing was that the Earth, the Sun and the center of the small circle should be in line, as they are in Figure 3.15. Hence it was not immediately obvious to the men who first used epicycle pictures of planetary motions that the Sun must lie at the center of the epicycle.

Nevertheless, it was clearly suspicious that the points E, S, and C should always have to lie on a straight line. This demanded two coincidences: first that C should move around the Earth in exactly the same period as S, and second that E, S, and C should be lined up initially in the same direction. It is probable that this coincidence suggested to Heraclides that the radius of the solar circle should be taken as equal to the radius of the circle on which the center of the epicycle of Venus moved—that is, that the point S should be taken at the point C, as it is shown in Figure 3.7.

(The difference between Figure 3.15 and Figure 3.7 is, of course, that in Figure 3.15 we are working only from the observations, whereas in Figure 3.7 we were working from an initial knowledge of the heliocentric theory.)

The epicycle picture for Mercury could be amended on the lines Heraclides suggested in just the same way as could the epicycle picture for Venus. But the situation was more awkward for the outer planets. This is clear if we refer back to Figure 3.10. There, unless we set the radius of the solar circle (the distance SE) equal to the radius of the epicycle (OC) then all we can say is that the line SE must be parallel to OC. A crucial feature is lost, namely that the distance from the Sun to the planet (the distance SO) must always be equal to the distance EC, and therefore that the planet maintains a constant distance from the Sun. Hence the discovery of the heliocentric point of view, working simply from the observations, was not so easy in the case of the outer planets as it was in the case of Venus and Mercury.

Yet we have it on the unimpeachable testimony of one of his contemporaries, Archimedes, that Aristarchus did arrive at a heliocentric point of view, probably around the year 260 B.C. We can only speculate as to how he managed to make this remarkable step. Probably he realized the equivalence of the epicycle picture and the eccentric circle picture, discussed early in this chapter. He would then also realize that a representation of the motion of an outer planet such as that in Figure 3.9 could be translated into the kind of representation shown in Figure 3.16. Yet because of lack of knowledge of the true scale of the circles in Figure 3.16, it could still be asserted only that the Sun must lie on the line CE, just as was the case in Figure 3.15. But now it was possible to take the same step as Heraclides had taken in his picture of the motions of the inner planets. It was possible to take the radius of the solar circle as equal to the distance from C to E, so that the Sun fell at the point C, as in Figure 3.9, and so that the planet maintained a constant distance from the Sun.

On this basis, we arrive at a situation in which every planet moves in an orbit around the Sun, and the Sun itself moves in an orbit around the Earth, the situation shown in Figure 3.17. This is the so-called Tychonic picture, the picture which Tycho Brahe accepted almost two thousand years later. But Aristarchus took a step beyond this. He realized that the picture presented in Figure 3.17 could be simplified still further, because the question of whether the Sun moves around the Earth or the Earth around the Sun is a relative one. And if we accept the view that the Earth moves around the Sun, then every planet can be shown as moving around the Sun, just as they are shown in Figure 3.18, opposite.

The remarks of Archimedes also show that Aristarchus took a further remarkable step. He realized that if the Earth does indeed move around the Sun there can be only one explanation of why the background of the stars does not appear to change during the year: the stars must be very far indeed away from us.

At the top of these pages is part of an astronomical papyrus, called "The Teaching of Leptinus" or "The Art of Eudoxus", which was written in Egypt at some time between 331 and 111 B.C. It is noteworthy for the number of simple diagrams which it employs.

Figure 3.15
In an epicycle picture of the motion of Venus, the ancients did not have to make the Sun the center of the small circle. But it had to lie somewhere on the line EC.

Figure 3.16
Similarly, in making an eccentric circle picture of the motion of an outer planet they need not make the Sun the center of the large circle. But again it had to lie on EC.

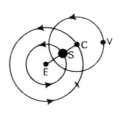

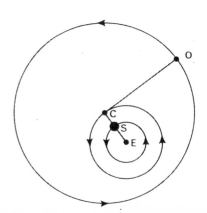

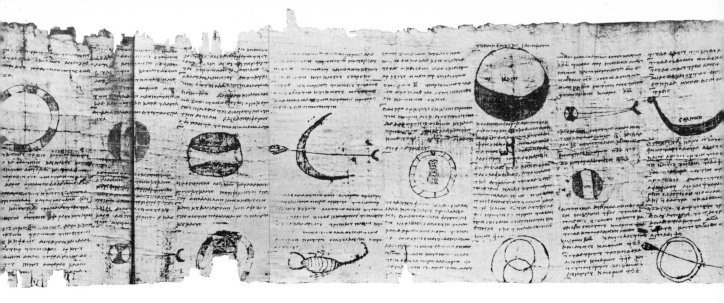

Assessing the Scale of the Solar System

Aristarchus also made a magnificent effort to determine the true scale of the Solar System. He argued that at the moment when the Moon is in quadrature (when, as seen from the Earth, half its surface is lit by the Sun and half is dark) the directions of the Sun and of the Earth, as seen from the Moon, must form a right angle. Thus, at that moment, Sun, Moon and Earth form a right-angled triangle, as shown in Figure 3.19. The angle *SME* is known to be a right angle, the angle *SEM* can be measured, and the angle *MSE* can thus be deduced. A simple calculation then determines the ratio of the distance of the Sun to the distance of the Moon. On measuring the angle *SEM*, Aristarchus found it to be about 87°, and his calculation, based on this measurement, showed the Sun to be about twenty times as far away as the Moon is. We shall later see that this estimate was grossly deficient, but Aristarchus was not aware of this. Thus it seemed to him that if he could establish the Moon's absolute distance he could easily establish that of the Sun.

Establishing the distance of the Moon was comparatively easy. For example, it could be done at a time of an eclipse of the Moon. We have already noticed that the edge of the Earth's shadow as it sweeps across the Moon is always circular in shape. By comparing the apparent radius of this circle with the apparent radius of the Moon one can discover the ratio of the radius of the Earth to the radius of the Moon. Knowing this, and knowing the Moon's apparent angular diameter, it is easy to calculate the distance of the Moon in terms of the radius of the Earth. A surprisingly accurate value can be obtained in this way, and about a hundred years later Hipparchus obtained a value that was

Figure 3.17
Since epicycle picture and eccentric circle picture are equivalent, we can make an epicycle picture for all the planets. If we take ES as equal to EC we then have the so-called Tychonic picture of the planets.

Figure 3.18
The question of whether the Sun moves around the Earth or the Earth around the Sun is a relative one. If we accept the latter view we can simplify Figure 3.17 and get the heliocentric representation below.

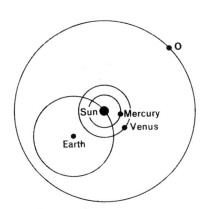

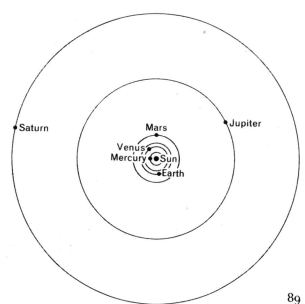

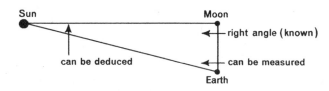

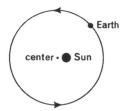

Figure 3.19
When the Moon is in quadrature we know one angle of the triangle formed by Sun, Moon and Earth and we can measure another. Aristarchus used this information to determine the ratio of the Sun's distance to the Moon's distance.

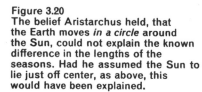

Figure 3.20
The belief Aristarchus held, that the Earth moves *in a circle* around the Sun, could not explain the known difference in the lengths of the seasons. Had he assumed the Sun to lie just off center, as above, this would have been explained.

within about one per cent of the correct value. Earlier determinations were less accurate, but they were sufficient for Aristarchus's purpose.

Knowing the distance of the Moon in terms of the radius of the Earth, he then also knew the distance of the Sun. Further, it was possible to calculate the radii of the orbits of all the known planets in terms of the distance of the Sun from the Earth. Hence Aristarchus made possible the first determination of the scale of the Solar System.

Using Eratosthenes' estimate of the Earth's radius, or even earlier and less accurate estimates, Aristarchus calculated the Sun's distance to be some four or five million miles. Although this was far short of the true value, it was remarkably useful in establishing something of the general order of magnitude of the Solar System. The snag in the method Aristarchus employed lies, of course, in the difficulty of judging the precise moment of quadrature of the Moon. This is rendered difficult because

the Moon is not strictly spherical in shape. If the moment of quadrature is not correctly judged, then the angle measured at E is wrong, and here even a slight error makes a very large difference to the result. For example, if the measured angle had been 89° instead of 87°, the calculated distance of the Sun would have been tripled; and if it had been about 89 5/6°, Aristarchus's result would have been almost correct.

Aristarchus seems to have propounded his heliocentric theory only in a tentative fashion. He did not set out his arguments comprehensively in a book, and we may well ask why. Probably it was because he was well aware that his theory, as it stood, simply did not fit the observed facts. We have already noticed that the seasons of the year are of uneven length. Why should this be so if the Earth moved around the Sun in a circular path? This difference in the length of the seasons could be explained by supposing that the Earth moves not around the Sun but around a point slightly displaced from the Sun, as in Figure 3.20. But such an assumption would already mar the beautiful simplicity of the heliocentric picture. Further, Aristarchus must have known that the directions of the planets do not in general lie in the plane of the Earth's orbit, and the simplicity of his theory would also be partially destroyed by the requirement that the planes of the orbits of the various planets are not coincident.

At the outset of this chapter we saw that irregularities arise as soon as we move from the first stage of sophistication to the second, and this is just what Aristarchus was up against. His picture was admirably suited to the first stage of sophistication, but it was not suited to the second stage. For this, it would have been necessary to break with the idea of circular motion and to go over to elliptic motion. And this was a step the Greeks were not capable of making. It is true that so far as the planets are concerned, the effects arising in the second stage of sophistication are comparatively small ones, or could have been regarded as so in Greek times. But this is not true of the Moon. Even in ancient times it was comparatively easy to see that the Moon could not be represented as moving around the Earth uniformly along a circular path. But its motion could be reasonably well represented by an epicyclic picture, since the epicycle can be made to mock the effects of elliptic motion in a first order of approximation. Hence it looked to the Greeks as if the Moon *must* be allowed to move in an epicycle, and if one were obliged to assume epicyclic motion for the Moon, then why not also for the planets? These, then, seem to have been the considerations that restrained Aristarchus from pressing his heliocentric views. Certainly they were among the main reasons that prevented such men as Hipparchus and Ptolemy from accepting that viewpoint.

It is remarkable that following Aristarchus we have two quite contrary trends. On the practical side, the appreciation of the observational situation became more and more refined, and Greek astronomy passed into the second stage of sophistication. But on the theoretical side, the ideas of the Greeks moved steadily further and further away from the correct picture.

We noticed earlier that Hipparchus and Ptolemy discarded Heraclides' great idea of a rotating Earth in favor of the old idea of a diurnal rotation of the heavens; and we have now seen why the heliocentric theory of Aristarchus found no favor with the astronomers who followed him.

Here we have a remarkable example to show that it does not always pay to know too much about the facts of a situation. No theory ever proposed has been found ultimately to fit *all* the facts, and even the most profitable theory will be rejected if the discordant facts are known at too early a stage. This must not be construed as a plea that facts should be ignored. All one can hope is that discordant facts will not appear until worthwhile theories have had a chance to establish themselves. If Greek astronomy had remained in the first stage of sophistication for five hundred years or so after the time of Aristarchus, so that the heliocentric theory could have become firmly established, then the history of astronomy from the beginning of the Christian era to modern times might have been entirely different.

From the point of view of astronomy it has proved almost disastrous that our Earth possesses a satellite. If there had been no Moon astronomy would have developed far more easily. In the very early stages there would have been no problem of trying to reconcile a solar calendar with a lunar calendar; in Greek times divergences from simple circular motion would not have been so glaringly obvious; and the modern astronomer, in his turn, would not have been forced to carry through all his most delicate work during the half of the month when the Moon is not visible in the sky.

After the time of Aristarchus, Greek astronomy developed along lines that might be called the geometrical equivalent of the numerology of the Babylonians. The reason for this development is quite clear. The Greeks, like the Babylonians before them, were attempting to represent phenomena that were far too complicated for them. In the event, the world had to wait almost two thousand years before Kepler succeeded in realizing that the complexities of the second stage of sophistication demanded no more than a representation of elliptic motion. And Kepler had the advantage of living at a time when the value of the heliocentric theory had recently been strongly re-emphasized by Nicolaus Copernicus.

Before ending the present chapter we should take at least a brief look at the work of Hipparchus and Ptolemy. This work proceeded on the basic assumption that all motions must be compounded out of circular motions—essentially the same assumption as Eudoxus had made three centuries or so earlier. Subject to this condition being satisfied, mounting degrees of complexity were allowed. Planets were still required to move around circular epicycles, and the centers of the epicycles were still required to move around circles, but it was not demanded that the centers of the latter circles must coincide exactly with the Earth. Moreover, there was no requirement that the centers of the epicycles should move around their circles with uniform speed. With these additional degrees of freedom Ptolemy, in particular, was able to reproduce many of the features of elliptic motion.

Even though we now know that he had set his course along a wrong path, the ingenuity of his constructions cannot fail to excite our admiration provided we understand what they really mean. Unfortunately those constructions are usually described in a way that makes them look arbitrary and unattractive. This is simply because they are described against an inadequate mathematical background. Here they are dealt with in an appendix at the end of the book, where the main construction, in terms of circular motion, is compared mathematically with the real situation, namely with the situation for elliptic motion. Since Ptolemy's *conclusions* will be stated simply in the next chapter, the nonmathematical reader can pass over this appendix without feeling that he has missed anything essential to an understanding of the remaining chapters of this book.

Chapter 4 Copernicus and Kepler

Luther: The fool would overturn all of astronomy. In the Holy Scriptures we read that Joshua ordained the Sun to stand still, not the Earth.
Copernicus: To attack me by twisting a passage from Scripture is the resort of one who claims judgment upon things he does not understand.

Probably nothing would have surprised the Greek, Ptolemy, more than to have been told that no significant advance in astronomy beyond his own *Almagest* would be forthcoming for some fourteen hundred years.

The reasons for the long delay are not hard to find. The growing cleavage between eastern and western Europe which marked the decline and fall of the Roman Empire, coupled with the rise of Christianity, resulted in an almost complete obliteration of Greek science in the west. The Hebrew people, whose writings made up the bulk of the Christian Scriptures, had never been much interested in astronomy, and as a consequence these writings, and particularly the Book of Genesis, consisted of astronomically naïve borrowings from other peoples. The heavens were a firmament separating the waters above from those below.

Such statements did the Hebrews themselves no particular harm, but in the hands of the early Church, they came nigh to destroying science completely. For the Bible now had to be interpreted literally; there really *had* to be a firmament that separated the waters above from those below. In other words, above the sky there had to be another ocean which, at a moment's notice, could pour through a hole in the sky and deluge the Earth as it had done in the time of Noah. Such notions were easier to accept on the basis that the Earth is flat. So we find commentators such as Lactantius and Kosmas pouring scorn on the idea of a spherical Earth and thus denying the first great discovery of the Greeks. Indeed, we find a return to the crude notion that the stars and the Sun, after setting in the west, proceed to change their course, passing round to the north just below the horizon until they are in a position to emerge again in the east.

It is true that the less prejudiced members of the Church, such as St. Augustine of Hippo, living in the fourth and early fifth centuries, did not treat Greek science with contempt; but unfortunate phrases in the Bible, such as "the firmament and the waters above it," made it impossible for them

Astronomically naïve Hebrew writings
incorporated in the Christian Bible
long imposed strange views of the
universe on western Christendom.
Piero di Puccio's picture of the
universe, made in the fourteenth
century, is typical of its period.
Not until the time of Copernicus
did Europe make any advance on the
cosmologies of the Greeks.

to accept any sensible system of cosmology. Over the centuries things slowly improved. Soon after the close of the seventh century the Venerable Bede was willing to consider the idea that the Earth might be a sphere. He mentions the zones of the Earth, saying that only two of them are inhabitable but that no assent should be given to fables about the Antipodes, since nobody had ever heard or read of anyone having crossed the torrid zone and found human beings dwelling beyond it. But for the fact that history, as well as science, had been largely obliterated, this would have been an astonishing statement in view of the circumnavigation of Africa, by Phoenicians in the service of King Necho of Egypt, completed more than a thousand years earlier.

By about the ninth century the sphericity of the Earth and the Greek views of planetary motions had once again become largely accepted by the liberal section of Church opinion. The later Greek writers, particularly Ptolemy, were once again being read, albeit only through the medium of Arabic translations. It must be emphasized, however, that because a few men had familiarized themselves with the general outline of Greek astronomy, this was not true of the population at large. In the popular imagination the notion that the Earth was flat continued to survive until the fifteenth century and even beyond. Moreover, there was little or no appreciation of anything beyond the crude facts of astronomy. The refined details that had so tormented the Greeks were unknown in medieval Europe, nor was Europe in any mental condition to determine such detailed facts for itself. Such was the price of accepting the Scriptures literally and *in toto*.

Meanwhile the spirit of astronomy was being kept alive by other peoples. The torch had been passed first to the Hindus, and probably from them to the Arabs who became avid observers of the sky. In this they were probably aided and encouraged by the clarity of a desert climate. By the beginning of the present millennium the Arabs had become deeply interested in the finer details of planetary motions. They had learnt the intricate theories of Ptolemy and they had found that the theories did not fit the facts as they found them.

Here a word of explanation may be necessary. Ptolemy's theory was constructed to enable astronomers, starting from a known situation, to work out where the planets would be found at some later

time, and provided the predictions were not made too far in advance, it worked pretty well. But as time went on, predictions became increasingly inaccurate, and over a century, if not over a year or two, the inadequacy of the theory became clearly apparent. Over the time that separated Ptolemy from the Arabic astronomers, it was quite incapable of yielding accurate predictions.

Now the Arabs pursued both the theoretical and the practical aspects of astronomy. On the theoretical side they attempted to improve the theory of Ptolemy, but in this they were quite unsuccessful in spite of the great complexity of the systems of circles and spheres that they employed. Their observational work was both a help and a hindrance to the further development of astronomy. It was a help because Arabic influence in Spain did much to kindle European interest in observational astronomy. It was a hindrance because, at a later date, Copernicus placed too great a reliance on its accuracy, as we shall see below.

It is fascinating to speculate on the causes of the great scientific outburst in Europe soon after 1500, an outburst in which Copernicus played so conspicuous a part. It is probable that the political diversity of Europe and, after the Reformation, its religious diversity, helped to bring it about. Although Copernicus was obliged to proceed with caution within his own Church, he was not afraid to deal sharply with Luther. Indeed, but for the existence of Protestantism in Germany, it is probable that the great work of Copernicus would never have been published at all. The advantage of religious diversity lay in the fact that the suppression of an idea by the religious authorities in one place did not imply the suppression of that idea by other authorities in another place.

But, of course, the scientific revolution in Europe came largely as a result of a long period during which Greek ideas were gradually reintroduced into western Europe, and astronomy was naturally only one facet of Greek learning to excite scholastic attention. With the rediscovery of the Greek authors, particularly in the original Greek, interest soon became focused on the works of Aristotle. Already in the thirteenth century Aristotle was lifted to pre-eminence among philosophers through the writings of St. Thomas Aquinas. It will be recalled that Aristotle, who lived before the discovery of the epicyclic theory of planetary motions, was a believer in the spheres of Eudoxus. The

During the Middle Ages astronomy flourished mainly in Moslem lands. The figure on the right above is Ulagh Beg, an outstanding observer of fifteenth-century Samarkand.

Astronomers of Istanbul Observatory. Men such as these had learnt the theories of Ptolemy. They had also realized that those theories did not fit the facts as they found them.

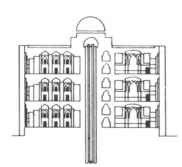

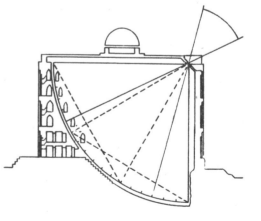

Reconstructions of the observatory at Samarkand. Left: General view. Center: View showing placing and size of the great mural quadrant. Right: Full view of quadrant.

Thorn, the birthplace of Copernicus,
as it was toward the close of
the Middle Ages.

Copernicus and (right) the uncle who
did so much for his advancement
and education, Lucas Waczenrode.

reverence that developed for the works of Aristotle in the years preceding A.D. 1500 meant that, in addition to the theory of Ptolemy, a different theory, that of homocentric spheres, now became canvassed. This may have helped to weaken the long-established authority of Ptolemy and to set men searching for yet another theory, different from both the known theories of antiquity.

Within the Church itself there were signs of incipient revolution. Men such as the English Franciscan friar, Roger Bacon, were clearly seeking to break away from the old ideas, although Bacon himself was too isolated to make the great step that had lain open to everyone since the time of Aristarchus. Nevertheless, Bacon—one of the founders of experimental science—is perhaps the best example of the general mental unrest and ferment that were developing among thinking men in the thirteenth and fourteenth centuries.

By the middle of the fifteenth century, astronomers such as Johann Müller, better known as Regiomontanus, had familiarized themselves with the finer details of the Ptolemaic system, taken now from the Greek, not from corrupt translations. Books were written setting out the Greek ideas and making them more widely accessible. So it was that by the close of the fifteenth century the original Greek ideas had been largely or completely recovered. They also became widely diffused through a number of countries with differing political and religious affiliations. These factors, together with a greatly improved physical sense, seem to have provided the foundations on which the extraordinary scientific developments of the following centuries were based.

It is clearly evident when one turns to the works of Copernicus that he possessed a far better developed physical sense than had his Greek forerunners. Ptolemy had rejected the notion of a rotating Earth on the ground that if the Earth were rotating then bodies thrown upward from it would be found to lag behind. Copernicus dismissed this objection, arguing correctly that a body thrown up into the air possesses two essentially independent motions, a circular motion due to the rotation of the Earth, and a motion up and down. Because we ourselves also possess the circular motion, we do not recognize it in the body; we recognize only the up and down motion. To the argument that the Earth would fly asunder if it were spinning round, Copernicus answered by saying how much more certainly must the sphere of the stars burst asunder if it were spinning around; for the distant stars would have to move at far greater speeds than the Earth in order to make a complete revolution in twenty-four hours.

Although, unfortunately, we have no precise records telling us about the evolution of his ideas,

CLARISSIMUS ET DOCTISSIMUS DOC
TOR NICOLAUS COPERNICUS TORU
NENSIS CANONICUS WARMIENSIS
ASTRONOMUS INCOMPARABILIS 1575

it seems to be a fair presumption that Copernicus started from precisely this point, that it was physically more reasonable to suppose that the Earth is in rotation than to suppose that the rest of the universe is. And it was probably from this beginning that he was led bit by bit toward his great theory of planetary motions.

Where did this crucial physical intuition come from? Certainly Copernicus was an unusual man, but there had been remarkable men among the Greeks, too. Very likely the Europeans of the fifteenth and sixteenth centuries possessed a better-developed physical sense than the ancient Greeks simply because of the very wide variety of small practical problems that had been solved in Europe during the intervening centuries. As an example, the building of the great medieval cathedrals must have presented a host of practical problems that were almost certainly more severe than those which faced Greek builders. Further, during the Middle Ages mechanical devices such as windmills and watermills had become of great practical and economic importance, while to the Greeks they had been little more than toys. Such devices demanded the widespread use of simple mathematical calculations, and this need led to the beginnings of mathematical tables. For example, in the fifteenth century fairly detailed tables of trigonometrical functions were constructed. Without such tables

the observational work of the sixteenth century would have been greatly impeded. Tycho Brahe, the greatest observational astronomer of that century, did not have to depend on a crude system of measuring instruments as Ptolemy had had to do!

Nicolaus Koppernigk, known to posterity as Copernicus, was born at Thorn on the Vistula on February 19th, 1473. In 1491 he entered the University of Cracow where he was taught astronomy and mathematics by Albert Brudzewski. As befitted a young man of means, he proceeded some five years later to one of Europe's chief centers of learning, the University of Bologna, where he worked for some time under the direction of Maria da Novara, from whom he learnt the elements of practical astronomy. In 1500 he traveled to Rome, then in 1501 he made a brief return to northeastern Europe—to Frauenberg, where he was installed as a canon due to the good offices of his uncle Lucas Waczenrode, Bishop of Ermland.

Plainly Copernicus must have found the intellectual atmosphere of Italy extremely congenial, for within a few months of being installed in his canonry he was traveling hot-foot to Italy, this time to Padua, and he remained in Italy for a further five years. During the total of some ten years which he spent there he studied law, theology, medicine, mathematics, astronomy, and the classics. Study of the classics was of vital importance since it enabled him to read the works of the great Greek astronomers in their own language.

We know little of the precise steps by which Copernicus arrived at the great ideas set forth in his *De Revolutionibus Orbium Coelestium*. We have already noticed that he was impressed with how much easier it is to suppose that the Earth is turning around than to suppose that the whole sphere of stars rotates daily around the heavens. It seems as if he may have started from the feeling that it was entirely implausible to suppose that the Earth is the only body in the universe that does not move. Once the idea of a motion of the Earth was admitted, the strange part played by the Sun in the theory of Ptolemy must surely have made a deep impression. According to Ptolemy the outer planets move in their epicycles in the same period as the Sun moves around the Earth. But why? Again, according to Ptolemy, the Sun is nearly the center of the epicycles of Mercury and Venus. But why?

Copernicus must have seen that these questions were immediately answered if he assumed that the Earth moves around the Sun, for then these strange features become simply a reflection of the Earth's motion. Moreover, by placing the Earth third in the sequence of planetary distances from the Sun it was possible to divide the planets into two groups: Mercury and Venus lying closer to the Sun than the Earth does, and Mars, Jupiter and Saturn lying farther away. It was then easy to see why the two groups had to be treated differently in the theory of Ptolemy. Most important, the retrograde motions of the planets were easily explained.

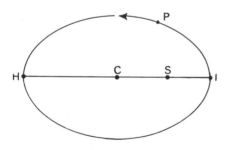

Figure 4.1
Modern picture of the orbit of a planet, with ellipticity greatly exaggerated. C marks the center, S the Sun's position. The fraction by which the length of CI must be multiplied to give the length of CS is the eccentricity of the orbit.

Very likely these ideas, or the germ of them, had already occurred to Copernicus during his student days. Only so does it seem possible to understand why he left his congenial environment in Italy in 1506 and went first to Heilsberg and later back to Frauenberg, essentially to lead the life of an intellectual hermit for the rest of his days. Almost certainly he understood that a description of the planetary orbits in terms of simple circles with the Sun at their centers would have been even less satisfactory to his contemporaries than it had been in the days of Aristarchus. In order to be acceptable, any new heliocentric theory would have to satisfy the demands of what, in the previous chapter, was called the second stage of sophistication; further, it would have to achieve at least as much as the theory of Ptolemy. And for this huge task Copernicus needed a life free from distraction, free from the incessant interruptions that must have accompanied life in the intellectual center of the world.

From what has been said it will be realized that the commonly-held ideas concerning the work of Copernicus are a wild travesty of the facts. Copernicus did *not* produce a simple circular picture of the planetary motions. He was not an innocent who was unaware of the difficulties which had faced Aristarchus and which had caused the heliocentric theory to be abandoned in favor of the epicyclic theory. The task he set himself was to produce a picture of planetary motions both simpler in form than that of Ptolemy and in better accord with the observed facts. If he had done no more than to postulate a simple system of circular motion, he would scarcely have deserved the enormous credit that must be accorded to him.

Copernicus was quite certainly aware of the opinions of such men as Heraclides and Aristarchus, and indeed he was greatly encouraged to find that others before him had seriously entertained the idea that the Earth itself might move. His greatness lies in the fact that he faced up to the difficulties that had caused Hipparchus and Ptolemy to turn away from the heliocentric theory. Not only did he succeed in this but, as we shall see, he came within a hair's breadth of producing a system that would have been in almost perfect accord with observation at the standards of accuracy available in his own day. But for sheer bad luck he would have come very close indeed to anticipating Kepler.

In order to appreciate how Copernicus improved on the simple-circle picture of planetary motions,

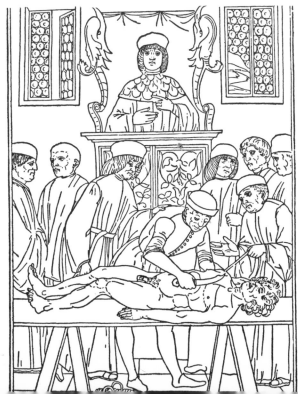

Above: The Geometry Room at Cracow, where Copernicus pursued his early study of astronomy and mathematics at about the time when Columbus first set foot in the New World. Many traditional Euclidean diagrams permanently covered the walls. Left: An anatomical lecture at Padua shortly before the time when Copernicus studied medicine there.

we may well begin by looking at the modern picture of the orbit of a planet. In Figure 4.1 we have a planet P pursuing its orbit around the Sun. Neglecting the influence of other planets, the orbit is an ellipse with the Sun, S, at one of the foci. The point I represents the position of the planet when it is nearest to the Sun and the point H the position when it is farthest from the Sun. C is the center of the ellipse. If a is the length of the line from C to I, and $a \times e$ is the distance from C to the Sun, then e is called the eccentricity of the orbit. Values of e for the orbits of all the planets known in the time of Copernicus are tabulated in the previous chapter. Reference to the table will show that all the values are much smaller than one. The eccentricity is largest for Mercury (0.2056) and next largest for Mars (0.0933); then come Saturn and Jupiter, with eccentricities close to 0.05, then the Earth with 0.0167, and finally Venus with 0.0068.

The fact that all the values of e are much smaller than one means that all the planetary orbits are rather similar to circles. Indeed, as a first crude approximation they can be considered as circles, just as we consider them when we erroneously refer to the Copernican picture. But we need not go the *whole way* of regarding them as circles. In our calculations it is possible to include all terms that contain the quantity $\cdot e$ but to neglect all that contain e^2, e^3, etc. In words we can then say that the calculation is made to the first order in the eccentricity, but that second and higher order terms are neglected. This gives a much closer approximation

to the true orbit than the use of a simple circular picture. To regard the orbit of Mars as a circle would be to achieve only about 10 per cent accuracy, whereas to include terms in the eccentricity but not in its square means that we work to better than one per cent accuracy—actually to about a quarter of one per cent. Looked at from the modern point of view, the geometrical constructions of both Ptolemy and Copernicus did just this. They included the effects of the first order terms in the eccentricity but not those of the second order terms.

In Figure 4.2 we have the construction of Ptolemy, which is mentioned in the previous chapter and more fully explained in the mathematical appendix at the end of the book. The planet P is taken as moving around a circle of radius a and with center C. The distance from C to the Sun, S, is again the product $a \times e$. The distance from C to S is equal to the distance from C to the point A. The significance of the point A is that a straight line drawn from A to P turns around at a uniform rate, while a line from C to P does not. A is Ptolemy's *punctum aequans*. Of course, Figure 4.2 is here drawn on the basis of a heliocentric picture. In Ptolemy's theory the point S was not taken as the Sun but as the Earth. Nevertheless, Figure 4.2 is still the essential construction of Ptolemy.

In Figure 4.3 we have what appears to be a quite different construction. S is again the position of the Sun, but the distance of S from K (the center of the large circle) is now half as great again as was the distance from C to S in Figure 4.2. That is to say, it

Figure 4.2
Ptolemy's construction of planetary orbit. Here the distance C to S (center to Sun) is the product of the radius (a) and the eccentricity.

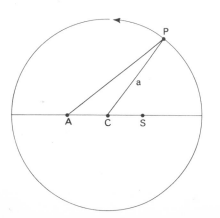

Figure 4.3
Corresponding Copernican construction. Here L moves around K at same rate as AP turns in Figure 4.2. LP turns at twice the rate of LK.

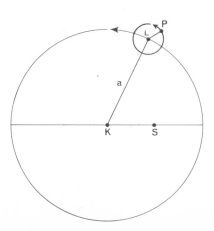

is one-and-a-half times the product $a \times e$. The distance from K to L is again a. L now moves at a uniform rate around the circle with center K— indeed at exactly the same rate that the line A to P turns in Figure 4.2. But L is not now the position of the planet. P, the planet, moves on a small epicycle with center at L, the radius L to P being one half of the product $a \times e$; and the line L to P turns round at twice the rate at which the line L to K turns round. Thus the planet P completes two revolutions of the epicycle in the time required for L to complete one revolution around the main circle. (Rotations are referred to fixed directions, these being determined by the direction of some particular star.)

Figure 4.3 is the essential construction of Copernicus. From a mathematical point of view it is exactly equivalent to Figure 4.2, the construction of Ptolemy. Both constructions are equivalent to the elliptic motion of Figure 4.1 provided second and higher order terms in the eccentricity are neglected.

Copernicus preferred Figure 4.3 to Figure 4.2 because he appears to have felt it unnatural that the radius C to P of Figure 4.2 should not turn round at a uniform rate. (In Figure 4.3 both of the radii, K to L and L to P, turn uniformly.) As things turned out, Copernicus paid dearly for his preference for the more complex construction. Had he preferred the construction of Figure 4.2, as Kepler later did, it is likely that the two errors in his theory might have been avoided.

Nevertheless, if Copernicus had used the construction of Figure 4.3 consistently for *all* planets,

Copernicus knew that to produce a heliocentric theory consistent with observation demanded freedom from distraction. Above is his quiet study, below, the sleepy town of Frauenberg.

he would have obtained a theory fitting perfectly with the observations available in his day. All he need have done was to use the observations to determine the slightly different planes of the orbits of the planets, to find the point K for each orbit and the length of the radius K to L for each orbit. This would have given him his complete theory. His only error would have lain in the neglect of the second order terms in the eccentricity.

The essential feature of the theory is that the point S is the same for all the planets. The point K is different for each planet and must be determined from observation: and the same thing is true of the radius of the circle, K to L. The distance from L to P does not require separate determination since this distance is one third of the distance from K to S. One further detail needed fixing from observation, namely the particular position of each planet at one particular moment of time. Exactly where in the construction was the point P on some specified date? When this had been fixed for each planet the theory could be used to work out future positions.

As we have just noticed, the point S must be the same for all the planetary orbits, and it must be the Sun. Copernicus realized the importance of the first of these requirements, but he made an astonishing error over the second. Instead of taking S to be the Sun, he made the mistake in all cases except that of the Earth of assuming it to be the point K for the Earth's orbit. That is to say, he found the point K for the Earth's orbit and regarded the point S for all the other orbits as being coincident with that point. This error was an astonishing one because in all other respects Copernicus seems to have been quite clear in his mind that the Earth must be deposed from having any importance as a center; yet here he was attaching a special significance to a particular geometrical point associated with the Earth's orbit. Here, however, was almost the only mistake for which Copernicus might reasonably be blamed, while the mistakes of Kepler, nearly a century later, were many.

It is possible that the remarkable error just noted sprang in some way from a second error. In the special case of the Earth, Copernicus omitted the epicycle of Figure 4.3 and it is not very difficult to trace the probable reasons why he did so. In breaking away from a two-thousand-year-old prejudice that the Earth possessed no motion at all he had already attributed several motions to it: first a diurnal rotation, second an annual rotation about a

center K, and third a motion needed to account for the phenomenon of precession. Copernicus visualized the motion round the circle with center K as being rather like that of a bob held by a string and suspended from a fixed point, as in Figure 4.4. N is the fixed point and E_1, E_2, E_3, E_4 and E_5 are a set of points on the Earth's orbit. The effect of the motion was to cause the Earth's axis of diurnal rotation to point always toward the fixed point N. Thus when the Earth was at E_1 the axis of rotation would tend to point along the line E_1N, when at E_2 the axis would point along the line E_2N, and so on; and because the point N was not as far away as the stars, the Earth's polar axis would point in different directions relative to the stellar background at different moments of the year. Now this did not agree with observation. Hence Copernicus held that the Earth's axis of rotation must possess a counter-motion that compensated for the effect shown in Figure 4.4. Then came the crux of the argument. Perhaps the counter-motion did not *exactly* compensate for the swinging shown in Figure 4.4. If this were so, then the heavens would appear to possess a very slow rotation, and this was precisely the phenomenon of precession.

Subsequent writers have criticized Copernicus for the artificiality of introducing this counter-motion. Why not simply postulate a slow motion of the Earth's axis of rotation by itself to account for precession? Why introduce two large, opposed annual motions? The answer may lie in the incredible slowness of the precession. It takes the

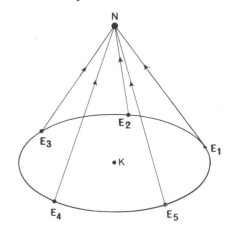

Figure 4.4
Copernicus thought of the Earth (E) as moving around a center K in the manner of a pendulum bob suspended from the point N.

First right is an extract from the preliminary account of the Copernican theory which Rheticus wrote. Next is the title page of Book VI of the work of Copernicus himself.

Earth's axis some 26,000 years to complete one circuit. Copernicus probably felt this slow motion to be so much at variance with the rapidity of the Earth's diurnal rotation and of its annual motion, that he thought it could be more plausibly represented as a slight difference between two comparatively rapid motions. Given the change in direction of the Earth's axis shown in Figure 4.4 together with a compensating motion, one could properly ask why the two motions should exactly compensate each other. Copernicus would probably have answered that they did not *quite* compensate each other, and that the lack of precise compensation accounted for the phenomenon of precession.

There were certain other long-term problems connected with the Earth's orbit that Copernicus felt obliged to face. If we apply Figure 4.3 to the case of the Earth, we have to recognize that the line from S to K is not strictly of fixed direction. It turns steadily around. That is to say, the line I to H of Figure 4.1 turns steadily around, due to the influence of the other planets. Such an effect had already been detected by comparing the observations of the Greeks with those of Arabic astronomers, and this caused Copernicus to give a slow motion to the point K for the Earth's orbit.

Now comes the stroke of sheer bad luck. In addition to this perfectly correct inference from a comparison of Greek and Arabic observations, other long-term effects were also deduced. These were illusory, and arose simply from observational errors, particularly errors in Arabic observations.

Thus the plane of the Earth's orbit was thought to undergo oscillations, and even the phenomenon of precession was thought not to be steady. These errors forced Copernicus to introduce a variety of slow trepidations into his picture of the Earth's orbit. His picture of the motion of the Earth therefore amounted to this: a diurnal rotation; an annual motion around the circle with center K (Figure 4.3); a third motion to account for precession; a slow change in the direction of the line from K to S; and various trepidations in the orbit, such as changes in the orbital plane.

All these motions were forced on him by observation. It is easy to see that he felt them to be so complex that he hesitated to add yet another motion for theoretical reasons, namely the motion in the little epicycle with center at L. It seems a safe guess that it was for this reason that the correct epicyclic representation of the Earth's motion was not introduced; and given this omission it became necessary to add complications to the motions of Mercury and Venus. Thus we find the point K being given complicated and unnecessary motions in the cases of the two latter planets. These could have been avoided if Figure 4.3 had been adopted *in total* for the case of the Earth. If we wish to indulge in being wise after the event we can say that what Copernicus should have done was to forget about the trepidations, to forget about precession, and to use the construction of Figure 4.3 uniformly for all the planets, making the point S the same in each case, namely the position of the Sun.

Even so, Copernicus produced a better theory than that of Ptolemy. Not only was it simpler in its geometrical construction, but also it agreed better with the facts. Particularly did it agree better with the facts when the slight differences between the orbital planes of the different planets were taken into account. In Ptolemy's theory the planes of the orbits all passed through the Earth. In the Copernican theory they all passed through the point K of the Earth's orbit. In fact, they should all pass through the Sun. But although Copernicus was wrong, he was only slightly wrong. For in the case of the Earth the distance from K to S (Figure 4.3) is only about one fortieth of the distance from K to L. So the error in the Copernican system was only about two per cent as great as that in the Ptolemaic.

These, then, were the considerations that occupied Copernicus after his return to Frauenberg. The practical problem he had to face was to determine the point K for the Earth's orbit and then to substitute the point so determined for the point S of Figure 4.3, treating that point as the fixed reference point for all the other planetary orbits. This left him with the determination of K for the other planets, and also with the determination of the length of the line K to L in each case. All estimates of distance, such as that from K to L or from S to K or from L to P, were made in terms of the distance from K to L in the case of the Earth—that is, in terms of the mean radius of the Earth's orbit.

Absolute distances could not be found at this stage.

The observations of Ptolemy and of the Arabs were not sufficiently complete for Copernicus's purposes and he was therefore obliged to make some observations of his own. Some commentators have criticized these observations as fragmentary and incomplete. Actually they were precisely what Copernicus needed. They were carried out with great economy of effort, and their accuracy can be judged by comparing the values Copernicus arrived at for the distances K to L of each planetary orbit with the modern values. The two sets of values are given in the following table.

Planet	Mean Radius of Orbit (Compared with mean radius of Earth's orbit $(= 1.0000)$)	
	Copernican Value	Modern Value
Mercury	0.3763	0.3871
Venus	0.7193	0.7233
Earth	1.0000	1.0000
Mars	1.5198	1.5237
Jupiter	5.2192	5.2028
Saturn	9.1743	9.5388

When we consider that this was the first time the relative scales of the planetary orbits had been given, Copernicus's achievement was a most remarkable one. It is true that Ptolemy might have obtained similar results if he had made the hypothesis that all circles, whether epicycles or deferent

Left: Planetary orbits as Copernicus depicted them in his great work, *De Revolutionibus Orbium Coelestium*. Below: Giese, the Protestant bishop to whom the work was first sent.

circles, that were traversed in the annual period, possessed the same radii. But the fact that it did not occur to Ptolemy to make this step—a natural one for Copernicus—is a measure of the improvement of the Copernican theory on that of the Greeks.

In time rumors of the new theory made their way to the south, and without Copernicus himself being in any way involved, heated discussions based on inadequate information took place. At Wittenberg a young professor, Joachim Rheticus, became keenly interested in the theory. After giving a course of lectures in which he attempted to disprove it, Rheticus apparently found himself in a position where he could see the advantages of the simple heliocentric picture but could not understand the details. So in 1539 we find him traveling to Frauenberg. There he was welcomed by Copernicus who at once gave him leave to study the new work. By the following year Rheticus had understood it and had written a preliminary account of it, the *Prima Narratio de Libris Revolutionum Copernici*. This account produced a great sensation, and now Copernicus, at the age of 67, was pressed on all sides to publish his theory.

To the modern mind it seems surprising that Copernicus was willing to work for upward of thirty years without attempting to receive recognition for his great discoveries. Although we have no clear-cut evidence as to why he apparently decided against publication, it is not difficult to see that the decision must have arisen from a clear and accurate appraisal of the religious temper of the age in which he lived.

The fragmentary evidence we do have shows Copernicus as a man of swift and determined decisions. Yet although a man of incisive character he was prepared to make a compromise with life. Just as he was prepared to sacrifice the conviviality of the Italian scene for the intellectual freedom and simplicity of life in Frauenberg, so, it seems, he was willing to sacrifice the publication of his life work rather than face persecution by his own Church. It is likely that he saw clearly what course publication would have set him on—much more clearly than Galileo was to do—and that it was a course that led almost certainly to the Inquisition. Doubtless, too, he knew himself well enough to realize that once he had embarked on a course of action he was not lightly to be dissuaded from it.

In the event, publication did occur in the very last year of Copernicus's life. Probably as a result of

AD LECTOREM DE HYPO.
THESIBVS HVIVS OPERIS.

ON dubito, quin eruditi quidam, uulgata iam de nouitate hypotheseon huius operis fama, quòd terram mobilem, Solem uero in medio uniuersi immobilē constituit, uehementer sint offensi, putētq́ disciplinas liberales rectè iam olim constitutas, turbari nō oportere. Verum si rem exactè perpendere uolent, inueniēt authorem huius operis, nihil quod reprehendi mereatur cōmisisse. Est enim Astronomi proprium, historiam motuum cœlestium diligenti & artificiosa obseruatione colligere. Deinde causas earundem, seu hypotheses, cum ueras assequi nulla ratione possit, qualescunq́ excogitare & confingere, quibus suppositis, ríjdem motus, ex Geometriæ principíjs, tam in futurū, quàm in præteritū rectè possint calculari. Horū autē utrunq́ egregie præstitit hic artifex. Neq́ enim necesse est, eas hypotheses esse ueras, imò ne uerisimiles quidem, sed sufficit hoc unum, si calculum obseruationibus congruentem exhibeant. ni si fortè quis Geometriæ & Optices usq́adeo sit ignarus, ut epicyclium Veneris pro uerisimili habeat, seu in causa esse credat, quod ea quadraginta partibus, & eo amplius, Solē interdum præcedat, interdū sequatur. Quis enim nō uidet, hoc posito, necessario sequi, diametrum stellæ in περιγίω plusq́ quadruplo, corpus autem ipsum plusq́ sedecuplo, maiora, quàm in ἀπογίω apparere, cui tamen omnis æui experientia refragatur? Sunt & alia in hac disciplina non minus absurda, quæ in præsentiarum excutere, nihil est necesse. Satis enim patet, apparentiū inæqualium motuū causas, hanc artē penitus & simpliciter ignorare. Et si quas fingēdo excogitat, ut certe quàplurimas excogitat, nequaquā tamen in hoc excogitat, ut ita esse cuiquam persuadeat, sed tantum, ut calculum rectè instituant. Cum autem unus & eiusdem motus, uarie interdum hypotheses sese offerant(ut in motu Solis, eccentricitas, & epicyclium) Astronomus eam potissimum arripiet, quæ compræhensu sit quàm facillima. Philosophus fortasse, ueri similitudinem magis re-

Opening page of the damaging preface which Osiander added to the work. (Translation of part is given below.) Since it was unsigned most people assumed Copernicus had written it until Kepler undeceived them in 1609.

Note To The Reader Concerning the Hypotheses Put Forward in This Work.

No doubt there are learned men who have been shocked by the rumor that has already spread abroad touching the strange new hypotheses put forward in this work: for it states that the Earth is in motion and that it is the Sun that holds a fixed position at the center of the universe. These men imagine that the liberal sciences were correctly established a great while ago and ought not to be altered. But if they are willing to examine the question thoroughly, they will find that the author has done nothing which deserves reproach. For it is the astronomer's duty to collect the records of the movements of the heavenly bodies with diligent and skilful observation. Then, if he has no means of finding the true causes or hypotheses underlying this information, he must conceive and work out such hypotheses as, once assumed, will enable him to calculate those same movements correctly from the first principles of Geometry—for the future as well as for the past. Now the author of this work has fully discharged each of these duties. These hypotheses are not necessarily true or even probable, but if they provide us with a method of calculation which is consistent with observation, this alone is enough.

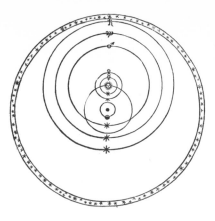

The Copernican theory stimulated observation, and during the sixteenth century Europe produced its first really great observer, Tycho Brahe. On the left is the man and above is his own picture of the universe. Opposite is the room at Uraniborg, Denmark, that held his great quadrant. On the walls are pictures of Tycho and some of his instruments.

the visit of Rheticus, he entrusted the publication of his great book to the Protestants, sending it to Giese, the Bishop of Kulm. Giese immediately entrusted the publication to Rheticus, who arranged for the printing to take place in Nürnberg. Unfortunately, before the printing was completed Rheticus left Nürnberg to take up a new professorship at Leipzig, and handed over the supervision of the printing to one Andreas Osiander, a Lutheran theologian of Nürnberg. Osiander took the opportunity to add a preface of his own writing but without signing it, thereby making it seem as if the opinions it expressed had come from Copernicus himself. The preface says that while the hypothesis of the motion of the Earth may appear to fit the facts, this does not necessarily mean that that hypothesis is true or even probable. In this way Osiander attempted to devalue to the maximum degree within his power the greatest scientific work that had emerged since Greek times.

Those immediately connected with the publication, Giese and Rheticus, knew full well that the preface did not come from Copernicus, but the world at large believed it did for almost three-quarters of a century. Then Kepler found out the real author's name from a learned colleague in Nürnberg, and announced it on the title page of his own book on Mars issued in 1609.

Copernicus died in the year 1543 at the age of seventy. By turning his back on the world, he had forced the world to come to him. The following century was filled with intense controversy over the Copernican theory. Excepting merely prejudiced discussions, of which there were more than plenty, the issue now was whether the new theory was capable of representing the observations of planetary motions to a still greater degree of accuracy. Thus theory gave a new impetus to observation and in the last quarter of the sixteenth century the first really outstanding European observational astronomer had arisen in Denmark—Tycho Brahe. Just as Copernicus was the first European since Greek times to rise to the stature of Aristarchus and Ptolemy in theoretical matters; so Tycho Brahe was the first to rise to the stature of Hipparchus as an observational astronomer.

Tycho was unaffectedly opposed to the Copernican theory. His objections do not appear to have arisen through religious bigotry. Rather, it seems, they sprang from a characteristic that marks almost all great observers: that the world as they see it has a more immediate emotional reality than it does for an ordinary person, and very much more than it does for the theoretician. This mystical relationship between observer and object seems to arise only as a result of light actually entering the telescope or the eye, and does not exist, for instance, when one is looking at a photograph of a celestial object. This psychological trait leads the observer to doubt the reality of situations in which he cannot establish the same physical contact. For example, we have no immediately direct awareness of the Earth's motion.

EFFIGIES TYCHONIS BRAHE O.F.
ÆDIFICII ET INSTRUMENTORUM
ASTRONOMICORUM STRUCTORIS.
A°. DOMINI 1587, ÆTATIS SUÆ 40.

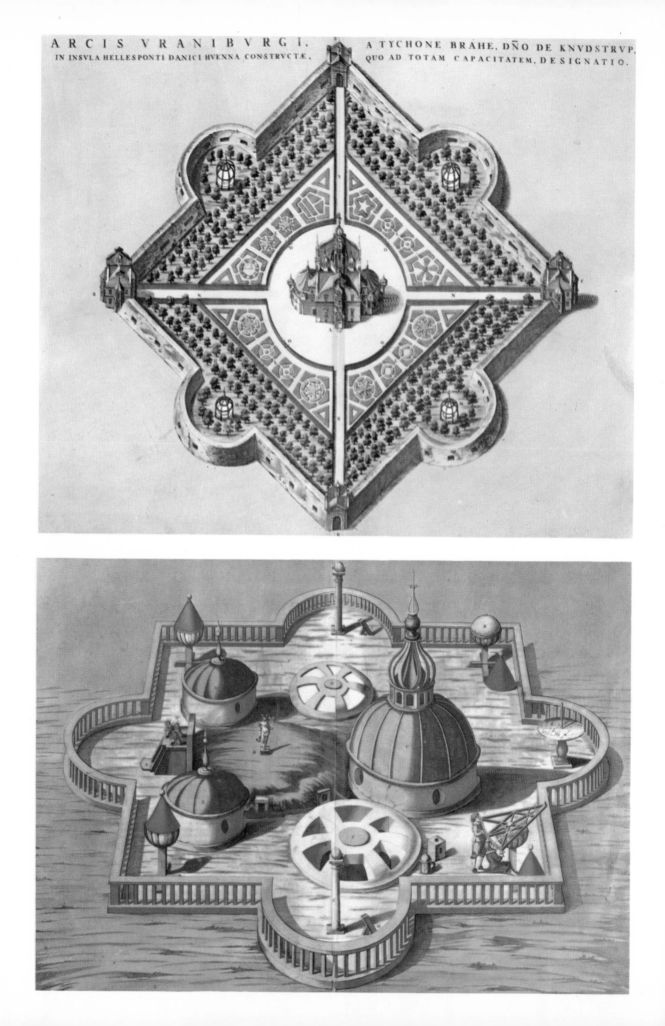

Tycho Brahe's Observatory

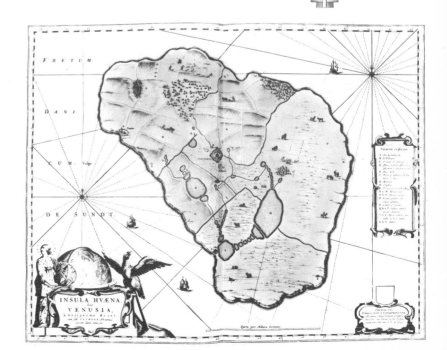

At the top left is the observatory at Uraniborg, built for Tycho Brahe by a German architect and said to be epoch-making in the history of Scandinavian architecture. At the bottom left is the Stjerneborg, a kind of annexe that Tycho built when his fame brought him many assistants Most of it was underground so as to protect instruments from the wind. The cross section of the Uraniborg observatory (top right) shows where most of the important instruments were housed. Under the arch near the left is Tycho's largest celestial sphere. The cross section just above shows the placing of the main instruments in the Stjerneborg. On the right is a map of the island of Hveen.

Indeed, our senses seem to indicate that the Earth is still and the universe outside in motion.

This, then, was the probable cause of Tycho Brahe's objections to the Copernican theory, and to satisfy his prejudices it was necessary to establish a theory that the Earth did not move. He found that such a theory could be built up by letting all the planets except the Earth move around the Sun exactly as in the Copernican theory, but by making the Sun itself move around the Earth. To the end of his life he was incapable of seeing that this so-called new theory was exactly the same as the Copernican theory. To the mathematician the transformation from one system to another is trifling.

Yet although Tycho was undoubtedly quite naïve in this sense, his observational work forms a great monument of human endeavor. It was on this observational work that the decisive steps taken by Kepler were based. Quite apart from his observations of the planets, Tycho settled a number of issues that otherwise might have caused great trouble in the seventeenth century. He showed, for instance, that the trepidations which had so worried Copernicus had no real existence, but were due to inaccuracies of observation; the plane of the Earth's orbit is not subjected to the variations that worried Copernicus, nor is the rate of precession irregular. From his observations of the comet of 1577 Tycho made the first suggestion that an astronomical body might move along a curve that was not compounded out of a number of simple circular motions. His observations of the new star (supernova) of 1572 were so accurate that they have yielded valuable information even in modern times.

Johann Kepler, whose work owes so much to Tycho Brahe, was born in Würtemberg on December 27th, 1571, almost a century later than Copernicus. At the age of eighteen he entered the University of Tübingen where, through the lectures of Mästlin, he became acquainted with the Copernican theory. He was instantly delighted by it and decided to devote his life's work to astronomy. His first work, the *Mysterium Cosmographicum*, which appeared in 1596, is interesting on two major counts. First, it gives a very clear exposition of the Copernican theory, showing its advantages over the Ptolemaic theory; second, it reveals something of the strange questing nature of Kepler's mental make-up. As regards the first of these, it was probably at about this time that Kepler realized the equivalence of the constructions shown in Figures

Below this portrait of Kepler is his abortive attempt to associate the planetary orbits with a system of regular solids inscribed in spheres.

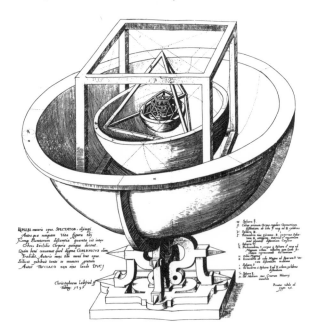

4.2 and 4.3. As regards the second, it will be as well to explain Kepler's ideas in detail, since, fantastic as they now seem, they held Kepler's attention throughout his life and undoubtedly provided the driving force toward his great discoveries.

We have already noticed, in this and in the previous chapter, the values of the mean radii and the values of the eccentricities of the planetary orbits. To the modern mind these values have no special significance, except insofar as they reflect the manner in which the planets were originally formed and in which they have evolved by slow dynamical changes over thousands of millions of years. But Kepler felt he must give some cogent explanation of *why* the radii and eccentricities had those particular values and no others. There had to be a unique theory. His attempt to grapple with this quite unnecessary problem was most remarkable.

Imagine a cube inscribed inside a sphere. Now inscribe a sphere inside the cube. Next inscribe a second cube inside the second sphere. Then keep on repeating the process, inscribing a third sphere inside the second cube, and so on. In this way a series of spheres of different radii will be found. Suppose, now, that the radii of these spheres turn out to have the same relation to each other as do the radii of the planetary orbits. We shall then have a weird and mysterious explanation of why the radii of the planetary orbits have the particular values they do in fact have. Such was the basis of Kepler's idea. Let us see where it led.

The sequence of spheres calculated in this manner did not agree at all with the radii of the planetary orbits. This forced Kepler to change the idea in detail, though not in principle. Instead of inscribing a second cube inside the second sphere, inscribe a tetrahedron in its place. Then inside the tetrahedron inscribe a third sphere. Next inscribe a dodecahedron inside the third sphere. Now a fourth sphere goes inside the dodecahedron, and inside this fourth sphere comes an icosahedron. A fifth sphere is added inside the icosahedron, and then comes an octahedron inside this fifth sphere. Finally comes a sphere inside the octahedron, although Kepler found it better to cheat at this last stage and to place a mere circle inside the octahedron. How do the radii of all these spheres compare with the relative radii of the planetary orbits on this basis? Standardized to the case of the Earth, they take the values shown in the first column of the table on page 113.

Cross section through Kepler's original system of cubes inscribed in spheres. It gave poor comparative values of the planetary orbits.

Kepler's own diagram of the spheres and inscribed regular solids. This gave results just good enough to encourage Kepler to try once more.

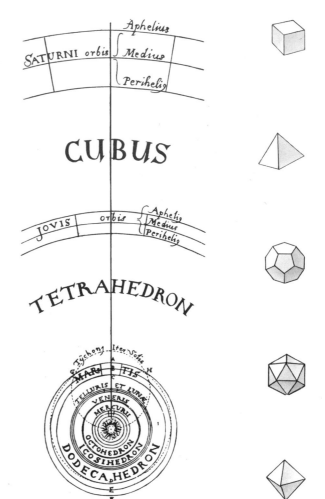

TABULÆ
RUDOLPHI
ASTRONO
MICÆ

COPER
NICUS.

TYCHO
BRAHE.

MYSTER COS
ASTR.P.OPTICA
COM MARTIS.
EPITAST.COP

INSVLA. HVENNA. DANIÆ.

Planet	Kepler's Value	Copernican Value
Mercury	0.56	0.38
Venus	0.79	0.72
Earth	1.00	1.00
Mars	1.26	1.52
Jupiter	3.77	5.22
Saturn	6.54	9.17

The agreement, while not good, was sufficient to encourage the indefatigable Kepler. His next step was to replace each of the spheres by two spheres. That is, he took two spheres for each planet, the smaller one representing the least value of the distance of the planet from the center, and the larger one corresponding to the greatest distance of the planet from the center. In this picture we have two spheres for Saturn, then a cube inside the innermost of the two spheres; next come two spheres for Jupiter, with a tetrahedron inside the innermost of Jupiter's spheres, and so on. By this device the eccentricities and the radii of the planetary orbits are connected together through the agencies of the various regular solids, the cube, the tetrahedron, etc. Although agreement with observation was still far from perfect, Kepler was not discouraged. He asked himself the question what was the center? Was it really the center of the Earth's orbit, as Copernicus had supposed it to be, or could the center really be the Sun?

Here we have a typical example of Kepler's methods. He had hit on a capital notion for entirely the wrong reasons. Throughout his life he was to make at least three mistakes for every correct step he took, but the correct steps were so tremendous that they vastly outweigh the mistakes. To these remarks concerning Kepler's way of thinking, we must now add a further vital characteristic. He was never satisfied by a moderate agreement between theory and observation. The theory had to fit exactly, or at any rate to within the range of accuracy of the observation, otherwise some new possibility had to be tried. However much time and effort had gone into the previous calculations, they had to be scrapped. Just as Kepler's successes outweighed his mistakes, so this characteristic of always deferring to the observations outweighed the strange products of his peculiar imagination.

Still following his idea of solids and spheres, he noticed that Copernicus had treated the case of the Earth differently from that of the other planets. It struck Kepler that if Copernicus had erred here,

Tycho Brahe's tomb in Prague, the top panel of which declares "Nor power nor wealth but the rule of art alone endures". Kepler, whose temperament clashed badly with that of Tycho, was nevertheless always ready to defer to observation, and he learned much by working as assistant to Tycho during the last two years of the master-observer's life. In gratitude, Kepler dedicated his *Rudolphine Tables* to Tycho's memory. In the frontispiece, shown opposite, Kepler insisted that prominence was given to Copernicus, to Uraniborg and to his old master.

It is through his determination of the true orbit of Mars that Kepler emerges as a great discoverer in his own right. Above are two of several hundred pages of calculations that this important work entailed.

and if the Earth should in fact be treated in the same way as all the other planets, his own weird theory could be brought into better consonance with observation. So we now find Kepler resolved on a determination of the correct orbit of the Earth. For this he needed the most accurate observations, so he decided to make himself assistant to Tycho Brahe. The great distance from Graz, where Kepler lived, to Denmark might have prevented him from joining Tycho, but fortunately Tycho had quarreled with many people in Denmark, and fearing that his instruments might be taken from him, he left Denmark in 1597 and settled in Bohemia toward the close of the sixteenth century. Kepler, meanwhile, had been driven from Graz by religious persecution and had arrived in Prague in January 1600. So it became easy for Kepler to join Tycho— easy, that is, from a geographical point of view. But the association could not have been easy to Kepler from a human point of view, for, as he himself remarks, Tycho was a man with whom one could not live without exposing oneself to the greatest insults. Perhaps there is no more fitting testimony to the character of Kepler than that some twenty-five years later he dedicated his great planetary tables, the *Tabuli Rudolphinae*, to Tycho Brahe's memory.

Kepler did not have to swallow the insults for very long, for Tycho died in 1601 leaving the rich harvest of his observations in Kepler's hands. Without these observations Kepler could scarcely have determined the true nature of the planetary orbits. On his death-bed Tycho implored Kepler not to forget the system that he himself had advocated, that the Sun moves around the Earth, and that all the other planets move around the Sun. Kepler promised that he would not forget, and although he was well aware that this system was only trivially different from the Copernican system, he faithfully kept to his promise in his subsequent works.

So it came about that Kepler set himself the task of determining the true orbit of the Earth with respect to the Sun. To do this he made one crucial assumption which fortunately is very nearly satisfied: namely, that whenever a planet is in the same direction from the Sun (as judged with reference to the background of stars) then it is always at the same distance from the Sun. This assumption is very nearly true over limited lengths of time, such as that spanned by Tycho Brahe's observations. In Figure 4.5, S represents the Sun and M the position of Mars. We choose a set of moments when the direction from S to M is always the same, and we then say that the *distance* from S to M is always the same. Now because the time required for the Earth to move round in its orbit is different from the time required for Mars to move round its orbit, the Earth will not in general be in the same position on occasions when Mars is in the same position. Thus we get a set of positions E_1, E_2, E_3, etc., for the Earth. When the Earth is at the position E_1, observations give both the angle between MS and SE_1, and also the angle between ME_1 and E_1S. Hence the angles of the triangle are known, so that the ratio of the distances from S to M and from S to E_1 can be computed. By doing this for each of the Earth's positions E_1, E_2, E_3, etc., Kepler obtained the corresponding values of the Earth's distance from the Sun at various points along its orbit, that is, the distances from S to E_1, from S to E_2, and so on. In this way he was able to map the orbit of the Earth to within the accuracy of the observations. He found that the Earth follows the construction of Ptolemy given in Figure 4.2.

It will be recalled that this construction is correct to terms of the first order in the eccentricity. Because the eccentricity of the Earth's orbit is very small, terms of the second order (terms involving the square of e) were too minute to be revealed by Tycho's observations. Hence it appeared to Kepler that the Earth followed Ptolemy's construction exactly. Since Ptolemy's construction, as we have seen, is exactly equivalent to Copernicus's construction of Figure 4.3, it followed that Copernicus had been wrong in not giving to the Earth the small epicycle of Figure 4.3. Hence Kepler's hunch that Copernicus had erred here was shown to be correct.

Now if the Earth's orbit followed Ptolemy's construction, then perhaps those of all the planets did, too. Kepler's next step, therefore, was to use the construction of Figure 4.2 for all the planets, but of course with different directions for the line from S to C, and with different values for the eccentricity of the orbits (that is to say, with different values for the ratio of the distance CS to the distance CP). The situation now was that Kepler had rectified the two mistakes of Copernicus. He had added the epicycle to the Earth's motion and he had correctly established the Sun, rather than the center of the Earth's main circle, as the center of all the planetary orbits.

When one considers that Ptolemy's theory had stood for almost fourteen hundred years and that the Copernican theory had stood for close on a century, this new picture might have been expected to persist for quite some time. What Kepler had done, in effect, was to recover the elliptic motions of the planets correct to the first order in the eccentricity, and one might have expected this to be a major landmark in astronomy. Yet by the irony of fate the new picture did not last for more than a single year. The very observations of Tycho Brahe that had enabled Kepler to correct the Copernican theory, themselves revealed that Kepler's picture did not accurately represent the motion of Mars in its orbit. In the case of Mars the distance from C to S is almost 10 per cent of the distance from C to P. Now as we have seen, Figures 4.1 and 4.2 are *not* identical when quantities involving the square of the eccentricity are considered; and the term involving the square of the eccentricity of Mars amounted to about one part in four hundred. This means that Kepler's theory gave the position of Mars incorrectly by anything up to about a quarter of one per cent. Thus the actual position of Mars could differ from its calculated position by about eight minutes of arc, and this difference was well within the range of Tycho Brahe's observations.

Of course Mars was not always out of its calculated position. At the points I and H of Figure 4.1, for example, the error was quite different from

what it was when Mars lay in the intermediate parts of its orbit. In fact the calculations sometimes gave the positions of Mars almost exactly, but on other occasions the discrepancy of eight minutes would show itself again. Probably to most men such a discrepancy would not have mattered very much. They would have been content with the fact that the theory gave very nearly the correct predictions. (Indeed for all the other planets the situation was much better, except in the case of Mercury, and there the observations were not very complete.) But Kepler was not the man to permit such errors. Just as he had determined to find the true orbit of the Earth, he now determined to find the true orbit of Mars. And it was through this determination that Kepler emerges as a great discoverer in his own right, and not merely as a corrector of two errors in the work of Copernicus.

Before we look at Kepler in this role, it will be as well to say a little more about the construction shown in Figure 4.5. How was it possible to know that the line from S to M always pointed in a fixed direction for each of the points E_1, E_2, E_3, etc.? Simply by knowing the revolution period of Mars, and by making sure that the points E_1, E_2, E_3, etc. were taken at a definite number of Martian years apart. Next, how were the angles in the triangle

Figure 4.5
Kepler chose a set of moments when the direction S to M (Sun to Mars) was the same. At each moment chosen the position of the Earth (E) was different. The positions E_1, E_2, etc., thus mark part of the Earth's orbit.

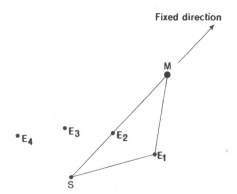

SME measured? The angle *SEM* was given by direct observation. The angle *SME* could also be determined by direct observation, provided that the star to which the line *SM* pointed was known in advance; all that need be done was to measure that angle between the stars in the direction from *E* to *M* and those in the direction from *S* to *M*. The required information, namely the direction toward which the line *SM* pointed, could be obtained provided one of the points E_1, E_2, E_3, etc., lay on the line *SM*, that is to say, provided one of the points was taken at an opposition of Mars.

We come now to Kepler's determination of the true orbit of Mars. The method employed was rather complex in its details; but its principle was simply to carry out the work indicated in Figure 4.5 *for a number of directions of the line S to M*. The orbit of the Earth had to be the same for all cases, and this allowed the distances from *S* to *M* (the distances of Mars from the Sun at different times) to be directly compared in the various cases. The result showed that the orbit of Mars took the form of a symmetrical oval of the kind shown in Figure 4.1, with the Sun lying on the long axis of the oval. A circle could be circumscribed about the oval in the manner shown in Figure 4.6, and for any point *P* on the oval a corresponding point *Q* could be found on the circle. If we take the line through *P* perpendicular to the long axis of the oval, *Q* is simply the point at which this perpendicular line cuts the circumscribed circle.

After many trials and false starts, Kepler at length made the remarkable discovery that the distance from the Sun, *S*, to the planet, *P*, was always given, no matter where the planet was in its orbit, by the following simple relation. The distance *SP* was always equal to the distance *CI* minus the product of *CI* and a constant number which we may denote as *e*, and of the cosine of the angle *QCI*. We may write this more briefly in the form $SP = CI - e.CI.cos(QCI)$. Now this is the relation for a point on an ellipse with the Sun, *S*, as one of its foci. The great problem had at last been solved. The planets move in ellipses with the Sun as one of their foci. The principle of motion in circles had at last been abandoned.

Perhaps in taking this crucial step, Kepler had been helped by Tycho's observations of the comet of 1577, for as we have already noted, Tycho had himself suggested that the comet seemed to be moving along a path that was not compounded from simple circular motions.

To set the physical discoveries of Galileo and his followers in a correct light, it will be as well to end

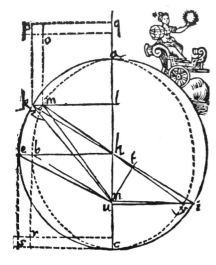

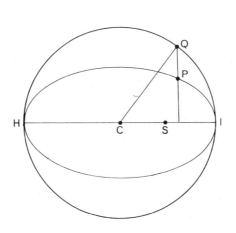

Figure 4.6 (Below)
The ellipse represents a planetary orbit. Around it a circle is escribed. S marks the Sun's position, P the planet's position. Kepler discovered that the distance SP is always equal to CI—e.CI.cos(QCI).

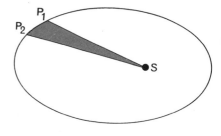

Figure 4.7 (Above)
As a planet moves from P_1 to P_2 it sweeps out the area P_1SP_2. In spite of two errors in working out, Kepler arrived at the correct result—that the area is proportional to the time taken to move from P_1 to P_2.

Left: The observatory at Prague where Kepler did much of his work. Above: Kepler's demonstration of the orbit of Mars. The broken line marks the orbit. The Sun lies at *n*, one of the foci of the ellipse.

the present chapter by mentioning some of the stranger notions that Kepler held. To explain why the planets move around the Sun, he held that the Sun radiated some sort of influence, the radiation being after the manner of the spokes of a wheel. Because of the rotation of the Sun, the spokes impinged on the planets, pushing them around in their nearly circular orbits. Hence Kepler believed that the planetary motions were caused by forces essentially at right angles to the direction from the Sun to the planet in question. In the following chapter we shall see that the true physical explanation of the motion of the planets depends on a force not transverse to the direction from the Sun to the planet, but along that direction. Moreover, Kepler believed the Sun to radiate its influence not equally in all directions, but only along the planes of the planetary orbits. This led him to believe that the influence of the Sun decreased with increasing distance simply as the inverse of the distance. The gravitational theory, of course, requires the force exercised by the Sun to fall off as the inverse *square* of the distance.

It is a curious anomaly that working from this incorrect notion, Kepler nevertheless arrived at an entirely correct result, namely that the planets describe equal areas in equal times. In Figure 4.7 the points P_1 and P_2 represent two positions of a planet, and the shaded area has the lines SP_1, SP_2, and the arc P_1 to P_2 of the planetary orbit as its boundaries. Then the shaded area is simply proportional to the time taken for the planet to move from P_1 to P_2. Double this area, and the time doubles.

The reason why Kepler arrived at this correct conclusion was that he combined the physical error of supposing that planetary velocities decreased inversely with their distance from the Sun with a mathematical error in estimating the area shown in Figure 4.7. The two errors just compensated each other. Kepler did, in fact, discover his mathematical error but strangely enough he did not realize that this implied some second error. To the end of his days he believed that the planetary velocities decreased inversely with their distance from the Sun. The strange thing about this conclusion was that it could not apply from planet to planet, but only for the same planet when taken at different distances from the Sun. The fact that the periods of revolution of the planets around the Sun did not depend on the squares of their distances, should have shown Kepler that his idea could not be correct. Indeed Kepler discovered a most important relation between the periods of revolution of the planets and their mean distances from the Sun. It took the very simple form that the squares of the periods were proportional to the cubes of the distances.

Another distinctly odd notion of Kepler's was that the period of revolution of Mercury around the Sun must bear the same relation to the Sun's rate of rotation as the period of revolution of the Moon around the Earth bears to the Earth's rate of rotation. This would mean that the Sun must rotate in about one twenty-seventh of the period of revolution of Mercury, which is about 88 days; thus the Sun was supposed to rotate around an axis of rotation in about three days. Galileo's discovery of

6   *JOANNIS KEPPLERI*

de tempore eundi, quàm Luna ab orientis partibus ceperit deficere : quæ vbi tota luxerit, nobis adhuc in itinere hærentibus : irrita redditur noftra profectio. ⁶⁴ Tàm præceps occafio efficit, vt paucos ex humana gente, nec alios, nifi noftri obfervantifsimos comites habeamus. ⁶⁵ Ergò hominem aliquem hujus modi agminatim invadimus, omnesque fubtus nitentes, in altum eum tollimus. ⁶⁶ Prima quæq; molitio duriffima ipfi accidit.⁶⁷ Nec enim aliter torquetur ac fi pulvere Bombardico excuffus, mõtes & maria tranaret. ⁶⁸ Propterea Narcoticis & Opiatis, ftatim in principio fopiendus eft, & ⁶⁹ membratim explicandus, ne corpus à podice, caput à corpore geftetur, fed vt violentia in fingula membra dividatur.⁷⁰ Tunc excipit nova difficultas, ingens frigus, &⁷¹ prohibita refpiratio,⁷² quorũ illi, ingenita nobis vi,⁷³ huic verò, fpongijs humectis ad nares admotis, obviam imus. ⁷⁴ Confectâ primâ parte itineris,

Right: The range of sounds that Kepler ascribed to the planets, based on their speeds and the eccentricities of their orbits.

Left: Extract from Kepler's *Somnium*, the earliest, or one of the earliest, works of science fiction. In this passage Kepler describes the hazards of a flight into space. A man would be thrown upward, he says, as if by an explosion of gunpowder. He would therefore first have to be dazed by opiates, and his limbs protected to prevent them being torn from him.

sunspots, which led to the first determination of the Sun's rate of rotation, immediately showed that this curious notion was very far from correct.

Kepler never entirely lost interest in his idea about a cube, a tetrahedron, etc., but he developed an odd new theory that seemed to fit the facts far better. He suggested that the planets emit some sort of harmony analogous to musical notes, the pitch of the note being proportional to the speed of the planet. By using the known size of the orbits of the planets, their eccentricities and their periods, he obtained the system of notes illustrated below. The two planets Mars and Mercury have a large range of notes simply because their eccentricities are comparatively large. This means that they have comparatively large variations in their distance from the Sun, and hence, according to Kepler, large variations in their velocity and in their emitted notes. Venus, on the other hand, has only a very tiny eccentricity, so it hardly changes its distance from the Sun at all. Hence Venus emits only the same note. Of course it was not the case that the calculated notes agreed precisely in frequency with the musical notes here shown. Could this be due to errors of observation? Suppose we make the notes come out exactly as they should be on a properly tempered scale, and suppose we then infer from this the maximum and minimum distances of the planets from the Sun. How will the results compare with observation? The answer is shown in the following table, where values of the aphelion (maximum distance) and perihelion (minimum distance) are compared, first as inferred from the harmonic

theory, and next as given by the actual observations that Tycho Brahe had made.

Planet	Harmony		Tycho Brahe	
	Aphelion Distance	Perihelion Distance	Aphelion Distance	Perihelion Distance
(Mean distance of Earth from Sun is taken as 1.000)				
Mercury	0.476	0.308	0.470	0.307
Venus	0.726	0.716	0.729	0.719
Earth	1.017	0.983	1.018	0.982
Mars	1.661	1.384	1.665	1.382
Jupiter	5.464	4.948	5.451	4.949
Saturn	10.118	8.994	10.052	8.968

The agreement is frighteningly good—frightening because the idea has no physical relevance whatever. One wonders how many modern scientists faced by a similar situation in their work would fail to be impressed by such remarkable numerical coincidences.

Quite apart from his scientific activities, Kepler's life is a matter of absorbing interest. We have already noticed the strange combination of meticulous deference to observation with the wildest speculative fancies. It is fair to say that Kepler had a far greater respect for the facts than the average scientist has, and that he was also a good deal more crazy than the average scientist. To these remarkable characteristics can be added a highly eventful life—wife troubles, religious persecution, the defending of a mother accused of witchcraft, and the writing of what may very well have been the first science-fiction story. These qualities have made Kepler an almost ideal study for the biographer.

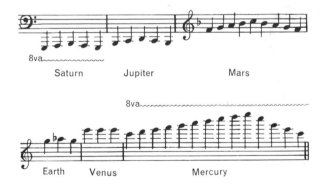

8va

Saturn   Jupiter   Mars

8va

Earth   Venus   Mercury

Kepler marked the end of an era. A forerunner of modern astronomers, he was also in the long line of astrologers. He cast this horoscope for the great adventurer Wallenstein, but he did so with the warning that the predictions of astrology should not be accepted without taking into account the character of the man.

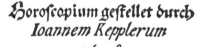

Horoscopium gestellet durch
Ioannem Kepplerum
1608.

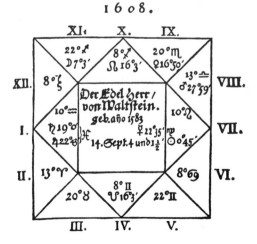

Chapter 5   The Theory of Gravitation

Kepler's great work on the planetary orbits was carried out during the first five years of the seventeenth century. Newton's great work on the theory of the planetary motions was carried out some eighty years later. A vast range of human thought separates Newton from Kepler, a range of thought even greater than that which separated Kepler from Ptolemy.

Up to the time of Kepler, men had set themselves the comparatively modest goal of describing accurately how the planets move. They had been satisfied by a geometrical description of the orbits of the planets. But *why* do the planets move in such orbits? Particularly, why does a planet move in an elliptical orbit and not along some other type of curve? This is the problem that Newton solved in his great book, the *Principia*. The difference between the kind of problem that Kepler tackled and the kind that Newton tackled is the difference between kinematics and dynamics. In kinematics we simply describe the paths along which bodies move. In dynamics our aim is to explain why the bodies move along their paths.

The subject of dynamics had been far too difficult for even the Greeks to make any progress in it.

The basic difficulty lay in giving a precise statement of what one means by a force. A vague qualitative concept of force does, of course, arise in everyday life. We use the word force frequently in common speech, but exactly when does a force operate and when does it not?

Aristotle gave an answer that, while plausible, was entirely wrong. He said that a force operated whenever a body moved. As soon as the force ceased to operate the body ceased its motion. The apparent truth of this statement can be seen by attempting to push an automobile along a level road. As soon as the push stops, the automobile stops. But how about the flight of an arrow? Aristotle supposed that the continuing motion of the arrow was caused by the air following along behind it and constantly pushing it. This curious notion did not find favor in Europe even as early as the thirteenth century. Suppose the arrow were fired against the wind, what then? Later, with the advent of cannons, another question could be posed: is a cannon ball also pushed along by the wind?

Questions such as these, while highly pertinent, did not of themselves solve the problem, but they did supply a climate of thought that was to lead

Less than a century separated the work of Newton from that of Kepler, but in that time the intellectual climate had changed enormously. The man primarily responsible was Galileo Galilei. Beside his portrait is a model made from his drawing of a pendulum clock. Above is a picture of seventeenth-century observers using a Galilean telescope. Galileo's work on the pendulum led to the beginnings of dynamics. The way in which he developed and used the telescope opened up vast new possibilities of observation.

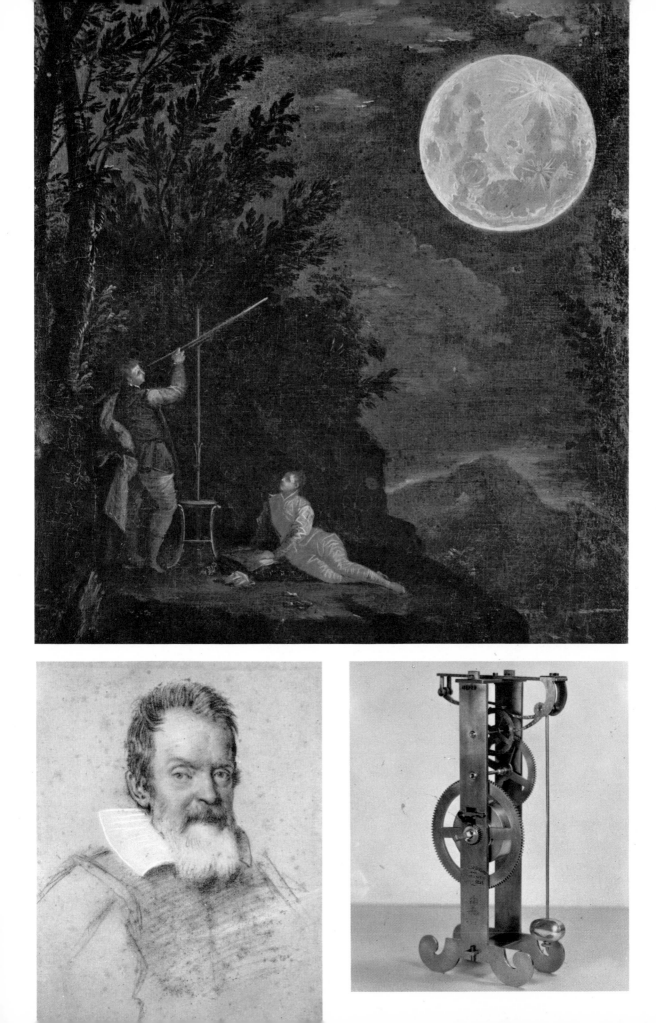

eventually to its solution in the seventeenth century. We have already noticed the wide gulf between the semi-mystical notions of Kepler and the physical assurance of scientists some seventy or eighty years later. Insofar as this great change can be attributed to one man, it must be credited to Galileo Galilei.

When we compare the work of the two men it is difficult to believe that Galileo and Kepler were contemporaries. Indeed, Galileo was Kepler's senior by seven years, being born in Pisa in 1564. Galileo's work was essentially modern in its style, whereas in many respects Kepler's was essentially medieval. Kepler may be said to have closed an era while Galileo started a new one. The differences between the two men arose from a different cast of mind, well recognized in modern times but not so commonly distinguished at the beginning of the seventeenth century. Galileo was in his instincts an experimental physicist whereas Kepler was a mathematical theoretician. The difference shows itself very clearly in their respective attitudes to the invention of the telescope by a Dutch spectacle-maker. Galileo's immediate reaction was to construct a telescope for himself, without worrying too much about the way it worked, and to point his instrument at the sky to find out what the Sun, Moon, planets and stars looked like. Kepler, on the other hand, proceeded to work out the optical theory of the telescope; but he did not build one,

being, as he said himself, unhandy in such matters. The difference is all the more striking when we consider that before the invention of the telescope Kepler had attached himself as assistant to Tycho Brahe.

All this is not to say that Kepler had less respect for observation than Galileo. In fact, he had more. Galileo could never bring himself to believe the finer observational points on which Kepler's deduction of the elliptical orbits of the planets rested. The difference between a theoretician and an experimentalist is very far from being a difference in the degree of their respect for observations. In fact it is quite common to find theoreticians more respectful than the observers themselves, just as in Kepler's case. The difference is one of instinct. Kepler's instinct was to understand how a telescope works; Galileo's was to make one.

Both methods of approach are essential for the progress of science but at the beginning of the seventeenth century Galileo's method was particularly necessary. Science had become ripe for the emergence of the experimental physicist. This was the field in which progress could be made most easily. Kepler's speculations on the orbits of the planets, on the causes of their motions around the Sun, and on their relative spacings, were unprofitable because at that stage physics had not developed sufficiently to enable the theoretician to grapple successfully with these problems. Indeed, half a

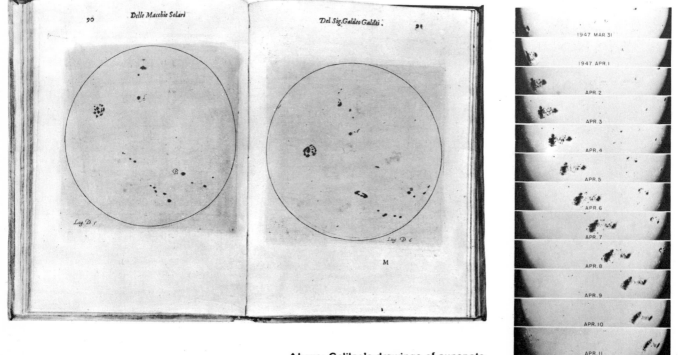

Above: Galileo's drawings of sunspots, from his work *Delle Macchie Solari*. Right: A series of photographs, taken at Mount Wilson Observatory in 1947, showing how the Sun's rotation carries spots across the solar disk.

century of progress in physics was needed before this could be achieved.

A single example will suffice. Kepler had a theory that the ratio of the period of rotation of the Earth to the period of revolution of the Moon about the Earth was the same as the ratio of the period of rotation of the Sun to the period of revolution of Mercury about the Sun. According to this theory the period of rotation of the Sun worked out at about three days. With his telescope Galileo found that the Sun in fact rotates not in three days, but in about twenty-seven days. This he did by observing sunspots, which appear to move from the western limb of the Sun to its eastern limb as the Sun turns on its axis of rotation.

(The discovery of sunspots, by the way, was first announced not by Galileo but by Father Scheiner. The reason for this was that Galileo held back the announcement of his observation of sunspots for about two years, probably because he wished to make absolutely sure that the spots really were associated with the Sun and were not simply small bodies that had interposed themselves between the Sun and the Earth. From time immemorial, very large spots must have been seen on the disk of the Sun by naked eye, so the telescopic discovery of sunspots was not really their first discovery; but the naked-eye observations had always been attributed to the passage of bodies in front of the Sun. In one recorded case, it was thought that the planet Mercury had come between the Earth and the Sun.)

The use that Galileo made of his observations of sunspots easily surpasses that of all his contemporaries. Not only did he use them to determine the period of rotation of the Sun, but he also noticed that they are not absolutely dark. They only appear dark in comparison with the brightness of surrounding regions of the solar disk. He also noticed that the spots are confined to an equatorial zone of the Sun, being rarely found at latitudes greater than 30°. Galileo even noticed that the axis of rotation of the Sun is not exactly perpendicular to the plane of the Earth's orbit.

Galileo's life's work and his personal character can perhaps best be exemplified by describing one of his experiments. According to Aristotelian physics bodies that fall down possess weight, and those that do not fall down do not possess weight. Since the air does not fall down it therefore has no weight. Galileo dealt with this matter in an extremely simple way. He pumped air into a bladder, sealed the bladder and weighed it. Then he punctured it, so that air escaped, and weighed it again. The weight at the second reading was less than at the first, thus proving that the air which had escaped possessed weight.

Throughout his life Galileo was a puncturer of mental balloons and bladders. It seems clear that

Scheiner announced the discovery of sunspots before the more cautious Galileo. Here we see how he used a telescope to give an inverted image of the Sun on an opaque screen.

SIDEREVS
NVNCIVS
MAGNA, LONGEQVE ADMIRABILIA
Spectacula pandens, suspiciendáque proponens
vnicuique, præsertim verò
PHILOSOPHIS, atý ASTRONOMIS, quæ à
GALILEO GALILEO
PATRITIO FLORENTINO
Patauini Gymnasi Publico Mathematico
PERSPICILLI
Nuper à se reperti beneficio sunt obseruata in LVNÆ FACIE, FIXIS IN-
NVMERIS, LACTEO CIRCVLO, STELLIS NEBVLOSIS,
Apprime verò in
QVATVOR PLANETIS
Circa IOVIS Stellam disparibus interuallis, atque periodis, celeri-
tate mirabili circumuolutis; quos, nemini in hanc vsque
diem cognitos, nouissimè Author depræ-
hendit primus; atque
MEDICEA SIDERA
NVNCVPANDOS DECREVIT.

VENETIIS, Apud Thomam Baglionum. M DC X.
Superiorum Permissu, & Priuilegio.
,2,

THE
STARRY MESSENGER

Revealing great, unusual, and remarkable spectacles, opening these
to the consideration of every man,
and especially of philosophers and
astronomers ;
as observed by Galileo Galilei
Gentleman of Florence
Professor of Mathematics in the
University of Padua,
With the Aid of a
Spyglass
lately invented by him,
In the surface of the Moon, in innumerable
Fixed Stars, in Nebulae, and above all
in Four Planets
swiftly revolving about Jupiter at
differing distances and periods,
and known to no one before the
Author recently perceived them
and decided that they should
be named
The Medicean stars

Venice
1610

Title page, together with translation,
of Galileo's *Sidereus Nuncius*.
Published in 1610, it announced the
first impact of the telescope on
the exploration of the heavens.

he must have decided as a matter of policy that almost all that had been said in previous generations
about the physical world was wrong. His technique
was to take any widely-held belief, to doubt its
validity, and to plan an experiment to test it. The
motive for adopting this technique was probably
that Galileo positively enjoyed the shocks and sur-
prises that his discoveries caused. Clearly he was
much happier when an experiment disproved an
old-established notion than when it confirmed one.
Heavy bodies were supposed to fall to the ground
faster than light ones. Galileo simply dropped
several objects of different weight from a height on
to the ground in front of the noses of his colleagues.
They all hit the ground at very nearly the same
instant. The slight differences which did exist
Galileo correctly ascribed to the differing effects of
the resistance of the air to the downward passage
of the various objects.

Here we have an experiment, probably started
with the motive of "taking a rise" out of the complacent schoolmen around him, which led Galileo
to a discovery of first-class importance, the discovery that all bodies started in motion in the same
way in the same gravitational field pursue identical
orbits, irrespective of their different masses. This
discovery was to have an important place in the

Newtonian theory of gravitation, and about four
centuries later it was to form the cornerstone of
Einstein's general theory of relativity.

Galileo's triple policy of doubt, experiment and
derision naturally made him extremely unpopular
among his academic colleagues at the University
of Padua, but it made him extremely popular with
the students. While his colleagues could scrape together little more than a quorum of students, Galileo
lectured in the largest available auditorium. This
would be sufficient in a university atmosphere to
make many enemies, even if Galileo had been mild-
mannered and gentle, but he was neither. He
was forthright and outspoken, irritable and deri-
sory, and above all he could not suffer fools.

When Galileo received news of the invention of
the telescope he probably sensed the possibility of
escaping from the tension of the university atmosphere in Padua to a larger life outside. He turned
his first simple instrument not only on the Sun but
also on the Moon, planets and stars. He found that
the Moon was not a smooth sphere, as the philosophers had claimed it to be. There were mountains
and valleys there, just as there are on the Earth, and
there were also round-walled craters. He saw the
shadows cast by the Sun, and from these he was
able to calculate the height of the mountains, and

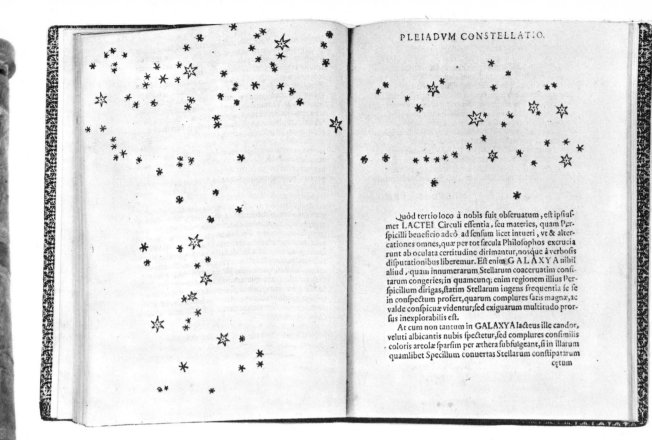

These pages from Galileo's booklet show the many "new" stars which the early telescope revealed. Before 1610 the belt and sword of Orion (left) appeared as a group of only nine stars, the Pleiades (right) as a group of only seven stars. On the left is a replica of one of Galileo's telescopes.

to show that they compared with those on the Earth. He found that the planet Jupiter had four small satellites that move in orbits around the central massive planet just as the planets themselves move in orbits around the Sun. He found that Venus showed phases like the Moon.

These discoveries were announced in the book *Sidereus Nuncius*, published in Venice in March 1610. The book created a major sensation. It lifted Galileo out of the comparatively narrow atmosphere of university life to a position where he could talk on terms of equality, or near equality, to princes and cardinals, and from which he could even ask for and be granted numerous audiences with the Pope. In the same year that his book was published he took up residence in Florence where he lectured to a brilliant audience from all parts of Europe.

An interesting idea which Galileo developed at this time arose out of his observations of the satellites of Jupiter. As these satellites move around their parent planet their positions change from day to day. Galileo suggested that their positions might be worked out in advance, just as the positions of the planets themselves as they move around the Sun can be worked out in advance. Since Jupiter is so far away from the Earth the aspects of the satellites would look the same from all parts of the Earth. Hence, wherever one was on the Earth, one could measure time by comparing the observed disposition of the satellites with a catalog of their predicted positions and thus establish one's longitude. The idea was a good one. The whole issue boiled down to whether the future positions of the satellites could be worked out with sufficient precision. The problem was referred to Kepler who decided that they could not. Galileo disagreed, but here we have a theoretical problem, not an observational one, and Kepler's judgment turned out to be right.

Galileo was overwhelmingly impressed by the frequent points of contact between his telescopic observations and the Copernican theory of the motions of the planets. The satellite system of Jupiter and the phases of Venus were cases in point. Moreover Galileo's experimental work had shown him how completely unfounded were the previous objections to the motion of the Earth—the objection that such a motion would show itself on falling bodies, for example. Tycho Brahe had believed that if a heavy body were released from a tower, the path along which it fell to the ground would be affected if the Earth were in motion. Galileo disposed of this objection by pointing out that no such effect arises if a body is dropped from the mast of a ship moving smoothly through the water. (In actual fact, the motion of the Earth *does* produce a very small effect on the path along which a falling body travels, but this effect was too small to be noticed at the beginning of the seventeenth century. It arises from the fact that the Earth is turning around, so that a place on the Earth's surface is not in strict rectilinear motion, but is moving along a curved path.) Here Galileo had the germ of another great physical discovery, that uniform rectilinear motion of a laboratory has no effect on the events that take place inside the laboratory. This is the cornerstone of the special theory of relativity. The modern physicist still refers to *Galilean systems of reference*, any uniformly-moving laboratory constituting such a system of reference.

From his now exalted position Galileo set himself the task of establishing the Copernican system in Italy, and in the Catholic world in general. His failure to do so is too well known to need any extensive description here. He began well, however, by sensing a hesitation in the attitude of the Church. On the one hand common sense and rationality suggested acceptance of the Copernican system, but on the other hand the Protestant Reformation had almost certainly made the Papal authorities feel that unless the Church asserted itself firmly, the whole Catholic world might fall rapidly to pieces. And in this instance the method of asserting itself was to insist on adherence to strict dogma which plainly demanded the rejection of the Copernican theory. One has the impression that the authorities arrived at this conclusion with regret, but Galileo, being a scientist, could not accept such a conclusion at all. He believed that one's position is never weakened by acceptance of the truth, and so his disastrous campaign began.

At first he was warned in a friendly manner that he must not teach or advocate the idea of the movement of the Earth; he was free to consider it as a hypothesis, but he must not say that the Earth actually moves. For ten years Galileo fretted under this restriction, for such a nicety of argument was not to his taste. Then, when he was almost sixty years old, a new Pope was elected, Urban VIII, who, as Cardinal Barberini, had been friendlily disposed toward him. Galileo immediately went to Rome, and in a series of audiences with the Pope he pleaded for acceptance of the Copernican theory. The Pope pointed out that the Copernican doctrine had not officially been declared heretical; it was rather that the Church considered it to be not proven. This encouraged Galileo to go back to Florence and to set about proving it. This he attempted to do in his famous book *Dialogue on the Chief Systems of the World*.

Actually Galileo did not possess any proof at all. We have already noticed in the previous chapter that the theory of Tycho Brahe, in which all the planets except the Earth move around the Sun and in which the Sun itself moves around the Earth, is really entirely equivalent, so far as the apparent motions of the planets are concerned, to the Copernican system. Proof of the Copernican theory can be given, but not along the lines followed by Galileo. In a later chapter we shall come to consider Bradley's discovery of the phenomenon of aberration. This demands that we adopt the Copernican picture and not the Tychonic picture. (In accordance with the theory of relativity it is, of course, always possible to regard the Earth as being at rest provided we are prepared to depart from simple Euclidean geometry. But if we stick to Euclidean geometry, then it can be demonstrated from the phenomenon of aberration that the Earth must move around the Sun, and not *vice versa*.)

Galileo was so impressed with the simplicity and elegance of the Copernican picture as compared with the complexity of the Ptolemaic picture that he felt emotionally that it must be true; and in the absence of a convincing physical argument, his method of discussion really amounted to little more than ridiculing the complexities of the Ptolemaic system. It was natural enough that the Church should object to this ridicule. Indeed, Galileo completely misjudged the considerations that were then influencing the innermost councils of the Church. When it was first published, the *Dialogue* received quite general approval. It was supported by the Jesuits and by the Pope's own secretary, as well as by the wider public who could all appreciate the common sense on which the whole discussion was based. But the situation was that common sense was at that time opposed to the policy of the Church.

Moreover, Galileo had written his book in an entirely uncompromising style. The situation could therefore not be ignored.

It was fortunate for Galileo that his case was investigated by a special commission rather than by the Holy Office, but it was unfortunate that the warning delivered to him seventeen years earlier had been officially minuted. Now, to his consternation, it was produced in evidence against him. Clearly he had no logical defense, except, of course, to deny the authority of the Church in such matters. Instead he prevaricated. He claimed that his book did not advocate the idea that the Earth moves. In this it is quite probable that when he re-examined his own arguments, he saw that they really did not

On the 7th of January 1610 Jupiter was seen in my telescope with 3 fixed stars thus: east **O * west. These were invisible without the telescope. On the 8th they appeared thus: O***.

They were therefore direct and not retrograde, as previously calculated. On the 9th it was cloudy. On the 10th I saw them again, like this: **O. The most westerly seemed to be occulted. On the 11th they were arranged thus: ** O, and the nearest star to Jupiter was half the size of the other and close to it; whereas on other nights they appeared of equal size and equidistant.

From this it appears there are 3 wandering stars around Jupiter, previously invisible to everyone.

Below is a page from the notes that Galileo made on the satellites of Jupiter. Above is a translation of the first few lines.

Frontispiece to an early edition of the *Dialogue*, representing Aristotle, Ptolemy and Copernicus. It was in this work that Galileo backed the Copernican theory and so came into conflict with the Church.

In 1600 Giordano Bruno had died a martyr's death, refusing to repent of his own heretical views on the universe. Galileo thus knew he must either recant or suffer martyrdom.

prove the motion of the Earth, and this may have suggested to him a possible line of defense. But his book had been so plainly written with an emotional bias toward the Copernican theory that such a defense stood little chance of succeeding, and Galileo was privately warned that this was so. The only course now open to him if he wished to avoid torture, condemnation, and death was to admit error and to plead for mercy, and it is common knowledge that this is the course he took.

Much has been written both for and against Galileo over this decision. It seems to me that those of us who have never been threatened by immediate torture are in no position to pass judgment. It is, moreover, doubtful whether anything would have been achieved by taking the martyr's course, the course which Giordano Bruno had taken some years earlier.

We can assess the quality of Bruno by comparing some of his ideas with those of Kepler. Kepler believed that all the stars were confined to a distant shell only two miles thick; Bruno suggested that they were bodies like the Sun and were hence at enormous distances away from us. He extended this concept to infinity, suggesting that space might be infinite, and that the universe might be eternal, without beginning and without end. Such remarkably modern ideas led him to the stake. He was burnt in Rome in February 1600. His final remark at his trial was "I await your sentence with less fear than you pass it. The time will come when all will see as I see." The time has come indeed, but Bruno's martyrdom probably did little to bring about the result. It can also be said that a rational mode of thought ought to be able to triumph of itself without the need for martyrdom. Martyrdom implies the matching of emotion by emotion, and this is not the essence of rational thought.

The outcome of the trial was that Galileo was forced to deny the Copernican doctrine and was placed under house arrest, in his own country house near Florence, for the rest of his life. He was allowed visitors and many people made pilgrimages from abroad to see him. During the last year of his eight-year confinement his sight failed, but never his questing mind.

In the most important sense of all, the story of Galileo may be said to start rather than to finish with the period of his house arrest. If the Church had accepted his *Dialogue*, Galileo would certainly have gone down in history as an outstanding scientist but

hardly as one of the very greatest. He had established the experimental method but he had not
initiated it; others before him had used experiments
to test ideas. He had made important astronomical
discoveries, but they were of a qualitative kind, and
once their wonder was passed they had left no great
body of precise data on which theories could be

Galileo chose to recant. On the right
is part of the document in which he
abjured and cursed his false opinions,
and below is a translation of it.
Whatever view one takes of Galileo's
decision, it is doubtful whether he
could have achieved much through
martyrdom. Recanting gave him eight
years of life, which he employed in
laying the foundations of dynamics.

"I, Galileo, son of the late Vincenzo Galilei, Florentine,
aged seventy years, arraigned personally before this
tribunal and kneeling before you, Most Eminent and
Reverend Lord Cardinals Inquisitors-General against
heretical pravity throughout the entire Christian com-
monwealth, having before my eyes and touching with my
hands the Holy Gospels, swear that I have always believed,
do believe, and by God's help will in the future believe all
that is held, preached, and taught by the Holy Catholic
and Apostolic Church. But, whereas—after an injunction
had been judicially intimated to me by this Holy Office
to the effect that I must altogether abandon the false
opinion that the Sun is the center of the world and immovable and that the Earth is not the center of the world
and moves and that I must not hold, defend, or teach in
any way whatsoever, verbally or in writing, the said false
doctrine, and after it had been notified to me that the said
doctrine was contrary to Holy Scripture—I wrote and
printed a book in which I discuss this new doctrine already
condemned and adduce arguments of great cogency in its
favor without presenting any solution of these, I have
been pronounced by the Holy Office to be vehemently
suspected of heresy, that is to say, of having held and
believed that the Sun is the center of the world and
immovable and that the Earth is not the center and moves:
    Therefore, desiring to remove from the minds of your
Eminences, and of all faithful Christians, this vehement
suspicion justly conceived against me, with sincere heart
and unfeigned faith I abjure, curse, and detest the aforesaid
errors and heresies and generally every other error,
heresy, and sect whatsoever contrary to the Holy Church,
and I swear that in future I will never again say or assert,
verbally or in writing, anything that might furnish occasion
for a similar suspicion regarding me; but, should I know
any heretic or person suspected of heresy, I will denounce
him to this Holy Office or to the Inquisitor or Ordinary
of the place where I may be. Further, I swear and promise
to fulfil and observe in their integrity all penances that have
been, or that shall be, imposed upon me by this Holy
Office. And, in the event of my contravening (which God
forbid!) any of these my promises and oaths, I submit
myself to all the pains and penalties imposed and promul-
gated in the sacred canons and other constitutions, general
and particular, against such delinquents. So help me God
and these His Holy Gospels, which I touch with my hands."

founded, as had the observations of Tycho Brahe. Galileo had missed the actual invention of the telescope, even though his use of it had given decisive momentum to its development as a scientific instrument. He had also missed Kepler's great discovery of the elliptic orbits of the planets. It is true that Tycho Brahe's observations were available only to Kepler, but even if Galileo had been the man to have access to them he was almost certainly not the man to undertake the meticulous, backbreaking calculations which Kepler carried out. Galileo had, indeed, made two great discoveries in embryo—the relativity of uniform motion, and the fact that bodies started in motion in similar ways in the same gravitational field have identical orbits; but the importance of these two discoveries was not immediately apparent. They would very likely have been forgotten and rediscovered at some later date, but for the final tremendous discovery which Galileo made during his term of house arrest.

Galileo had always been interested in the pendulum. At Padua, as a young man, he had discovered that the time required for a pendulum to swing through one complete oscillation is independent of the angle of swing, provided only that the angle is small. This had suggested to him that a pendulum might provide an excellent method of measuring time. Unfortunately, however, the amplitudes of swing became gradually less and less owing to air resistance, and Galileo could find no satisfactory way of keeping the pendulum swinging against this resistance. He thought of swinging the pendulum in a vacuum, but this was beyond the

range of his experimental technique, and the problem of keeping the pendulum swinging was not solved in an elegant way until some seventy years later, by Robert Hooke, in England.

Now, in his last years, Galileo again turned his attention to the pendulum. He noticed that provided the speed of the pendulum bob at the bottom of its oscillation remained unchanged, the height to which the bob rose was always the same, irrespective of the length of string that attached it to a fixed point. For instance, if at the moment when the string was vertical he took hold of it at some point between the original fixed point and the bob, the bob would still rise to the same height. This suggested that the backward and forward movement of the pendulum bob was really quite independent of the existence of the string. A ball rolling backward and forward without slipping inside a bowl shaped like part of a sphere would possess exactly the same property. That is to say, it would go on rolling backward and forward, rising always to the same height, until friction and air resistance gradually damped out the motion.

Suppose, now, that the bowl is not made as a portion of the inner surface of a sphere; suppose it is steeper on one side than on the other. Does the ball rise to the same height on both sides? Galileo found that it did. Let us think for a moment only of the less steep side. If we make this side even less steep, the ball will still continue to rise to the same height as before, but because of the decrease in steepness it will travel a greater actual distance in doing so than it did before. If we go on decreasing the steepness, then the ball will roll farther and farther in the horizontal sense before it attains the required height. What happens if we decrease the steepness to zero? The answer is that the ball will go on rolling indefinitely, always trying to rise to the required height, which, of course, it will not be able to do.

The last link in the chain of reasoning that Galileo forged is to forget about the bowl and to ask what happens if we simply start the ball rolling along a horizontal table. In fact the conditions are the same as before, so the ball will roll on indefinitely. One last refinement is needed. In everyday life we can think of a horizontal plane in which the pull of the Earth's gravitational field is everywhere perpendicular to the plane. But this obviously holds good only if the plane is of very limited extent. We cannot consider distances on the plane

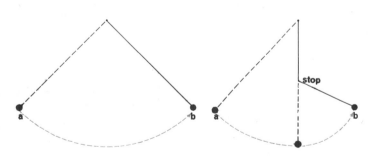

Galileo found that if the speed of a pendulum bob at the bottom of its swing remains unchanged, the height to which the bob rises is not affected by changing the length of the string. This suggested that the behavior of the bob does not depend on the existence of the string.

at all comparable with the radius of the Earth, otherwise it would no longer be true that the gravitational force was everywhere perpendicular to the plane. Thus Galileo's result only held in planes of limited size, in relation to which the curvature of the Earth could be neglected. But the essential point had been made. So long as all forces were normal to the plane—perpendicular to it—the ball would go on rolling for ever.

We have already removed the pendulum string and the bowl from the problem. We can now remove the Earth and consider in the abstract a plane along which a ball is set rolling. Then provided no forces act on the ball in the direction of its motion, provided there are no forces at all, or provided there are only forces acting perpendicular to the plane, the ball will go on rolling for ever; and it will do so at a constant speed. The last stage of abstraction is to remove the plane. Consider a particle projected into a region of space where there are no forces at all. What will happen? The particle will go on moving with a uniform speed in its original direction of motion.

Notice the developing stages of abstraction in arriving at this result. Start with the pendulum, then remove the string and replace it by a bowl. Then change the shape of the bowl, and next replace the bowl by a horizontal plane. Then remove the Earth, and finally remove the plane. This at last gives the result that a body in motion under no forces moves with a constant velocity in a constant direction.

From this we can give an answer to the question posed almost at the beginning of this chapter: exactly when does a force operate on a body? The answer is whenever the body does not move with constant speed along a straight line. This defines the *presence* of the force. The degree to which the motion of the body departs from simple constancy along a straight line *measures* the force acting on the body. This great discovery, which Galileo made during the term of his house arrest, was one for which the world had waited two thousand years. From now on the science of dynamics could make progress at break-neck speed.

The reason why it had taken so long to arrive at this apparently simple result is that in nature we just do not see bodies in rectilinear motion. This is because all the bodies we see *are* subject to forces, bodies at rest as well as bodies in motion. If you stop pushing your car and the car stops, there are

still forces acting on it. To us nowadays this seems obvious, but it was not at all obvious until Galileo made his discovery. And until one could define the state in which there was zero force, it was impossible to define and measure forces in any quantitative way. Hence it was impossible to arrive at any reasoned system of dynamics.

Galileo had also been right in his estimate of the importance of the Copernican issue, not only to science but also to Italy and to the whole Catholic world. By its decision, the Church effectively stemmed the advance of science wherever it was strong enough to enforce its decrees; and with the decline of science there was a failure to follow up the rapidly developing technologies of the seventeenth and eighteenth centuries. Hence those countries such as Italy and Spain, which had hitherto played an important part in enlarging the field of human knowledge, became poor and backward. The development of science was in very large measure handed over to the Protestant world. (France was an important exception but only to the extent that Catholicism did not wield complete power there.) For this reason we find the next great scientific developments taking place not in Italy, hitherto the center of intellectual advance, but in a remote island off the European continent, in England.

Before we pass to the Newtonian revolution it will be as well to look at an important step taken by Huygens. We have just seen that the force acting on a body is to be measured by the degree to which the body departs from rectilinear motion at fixed speed. Let us take a special and important case, that of a

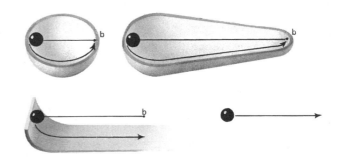

A ball rolling without slipping in a bowl behaves in the same way. However much the two sides of the bowl differ in steepness, it always tries to reach the same height on both sides. If one "side" becomes horizontal, the ball therefore rolls on indefinitely in the same direction.

body moving in a circle. What force must act on it? A very simple experiment brings us to grips with the problem. Tie a heavy bob to one end of a piece of string and whirl the bob round in a circle, making the other end of the string the center of the circle. Here we have a body moving in a circle under the influence of a force transmitted along the string. Now a taut string can transmit a force only along its length, not transverse to itself. Hence at any given moment the force acting on the bob must always be directed along the string, that is, toward the center of the circle.

Huygens found that the magnitude of the force increases as the square of the velocity of the bob, and that it decreases inversely as the length of the piece of string. Furthermore, if the quantity of material in the bob is changed, the force is changed in a similar proportion. If, for instance, we double the quantity of material in the bob, then the force required to keep it moving in a circle of the same radius at the same speed is just twice as great as before. Taking these three results together, the force can be written as $\dfrac{mV^2}{r}$ where V is the speed of the bob along the circle, r is the radius of the circle, and m is the measure of the amount of material in the bob.

What happens if we remove the string and place a very massive body at the center of the circle? Provided the massive central body pulls the bob

The force acting on a body is to be measured by the degree to which the body departs from rectilinear motion at fixed speed. It was Huygens (above) who discovered how to measure the force needed to keep a body moving in a circle. It is the same whether the force is transmitted along a string or, like gravity, through space.

The rule is that the force is equal to the mass of the body times the square of its velocity divided by the radius of the circle.

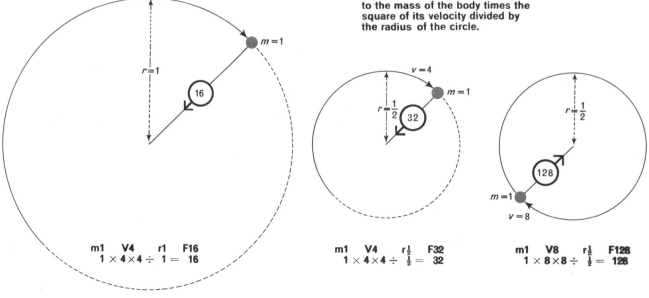

m1   V4   r1   F16
1 × 4 × 4 ÷ 1 = 16

m1   V4   r½   F32
1 × 4 × 4 ÷ ½ = 32

m1   V8   r½   F128
1 × 8 × 8 ÷ ½ = 128

toward itself with a force F which equals $\dfrac{mV^2}{r}$ the bob will continue to move around the central attracting body exactly as it did while it was attached to the end of the string. The force F, which we now describe as the gravitational force, takes the place of the tension previously developed in the string.

To the equation $F=\dfrac{mV^2}{r}$.we can add a second equation. The length of the circumference of the circle described by the bob is $2\pi r$, and the time required for the bob to move once around this circle is $\dfrac{2\pi r}{V}$. If we call this length of time the period, P, we can write $P=\dfrac{2\pi r}{V}$. From these two equations we can derive a third one, in which the velocity, V, is eliminated. This equation can be written in the form $P^2=\dfrac{4\pi^2 m r}{F}$.

At this stage we recall Kepler's third law, namely that the square of P is proportional to the cube of r. We then see that the quantity F, the gravitational force, must be proportional to $\dfrac{1}{r^2}$. If we also take account of Galileo's result that the orbit of a body moving in a gravitational field does not depend on the mass of the body but only on the way it is started off, then we see that the period P cannot depend on the mass m of the bob. Hence the force F must itself contain a factor m. Combining these two requirements we can write $F=\dfrac{Am}{r^2}$ where the quantity A may contain some as yet undetermined factors.

Next consider the gravitational force between two particles of equal status—not the case of one body being very large compared to the other, but the case of two particles of comparable mass. Call their respective masses m_1 and m_2, and let them be spaced apart by a distance r. From what we have just said the gravitational force exerted by m_1 on m_2 can be written $A \times m_2 \div r^2$ or $\dfrac{Am_2}{r^2}$. If we now make the sensible requirement that both m_1 and m_2 must appear in the expression for F on equal terms, then clearly A must contain the factor m_1. That is to say A can be written as the product $G \times m_1$, the expression for F now taking the form $G \times m_1 \times m_2 \div r^2$, where the quantity G is retained so as to allow for any other still undetermined factor.

Now let us go back to our formula for P^2, returning to the case of a large central massive body. Write m for the mass of the bob and M for the mass of the central body. From what we have just said the force F is equal to $G \times m \times M \div r^2$. Inserting this in the expression for P^2 gives $P^2=\dfrac{4\pi^2 r^3}{GM}$. This now is Kepler's third law applicable to planets moving

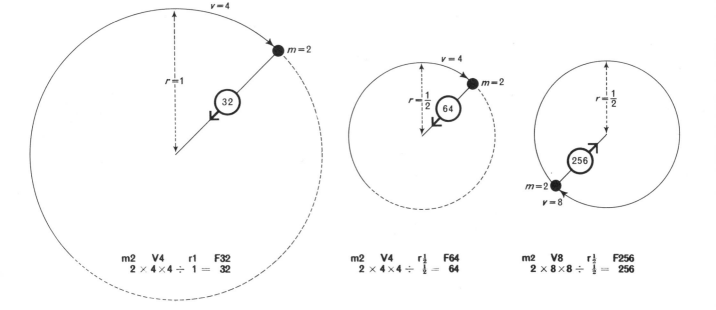

$$\begin{array}{ccccc} m2 & V4 & r1 & F32 \\ 2 \times 4 \times 4 & \div & 1 & = & 32 \end{array}$$

$$\begin{array}{ccccc} m2 & V4 & r\tfrac{1}{2} & F64 \\ 2 \times 4 \times 4 & \div & \tfrac{1}{2} & = & 64 \end{array}$$

$$\begin{array}{ccccc} m2 & V8 & r\tfrac{1}{2} & F256 \\ 2 \times 8 \times 8 & \div & \tfrac{1}{2} & = & 256 \end{array}$$

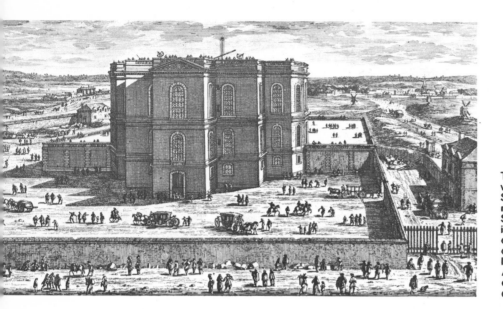

The picture at right shows Louis XIV visiting the French Academy of Sciences which he founded in the middle of the seventeenth century. Seen through the right-hand window is the Paris Observatory, then in course of erection. (A print of the completed observatory is shown on the left.) Members of the newly-founded Academy made the first sensibly correct determinations of the distances of Mars and the Sun,

in circular orbits. It is also approximately true for the actual planets moving in not-quite-circular orbits. It will also serve for the satellites of the planets—for example, for the case of the Moon.

Evidently if the quantities P and r are determined by observation in a particular case, then the product $G \times M$ can be determined from our equation. And if in some way the quantity G could be found, then the mass M of the central attracting body could be immediately obtained. Suppose for the moment that G is known, and consider the determinations of P and r for the planets.

The period P had, of course, been known with tolerable accuracy since the time of the Greeks. It was known with comparatively high accuracy to Tycho Brahe, but only the ratios of the radii of the planetary orbits were known, not their absolute values, represented in our equations by r. We saw in Chapter 3 that Aristarchus's determination of the distance of the Sun, while a remarkable step in its time, gave a result that was far too small. Kepler realized this fact, but even so he still set the distance of the Sun much too small himself. His value was about 15 million miles as compared to the true value of about 93 million miles. It must be said, however, that Kepler gave his value as a lower limit. He said that the Sun must be *at least* 15 million miles away.

The first sensibly correct estimate of the true scale of the Solar System was obtained by members of the French Academy of Sciences, founded by

Louis XIV in the middle of the seventeenth century. They determined the distance of Mars by straight-forward triangulation, one of the sides of the triangle being the line between Paris and Cayenne. The distance between the two towns was measured as were the directions of Mars from each end of the base line, the observations of Mars being made at essentially the same moment. It was then a simple matter of trigonometry to determine the distance of Mars from the Earth. The method could not give an extremely accurate answer because the distance from Paris to Cayenne was very small compared to the distance of Mars. This meant that the angles had to be measured with high precision, and slight errors here led to appreciable errors in the distance of Mars. Nevertheless, the value obtained was correct to within about ten per cent.

Let us now rewrite our equation connecting P, r and M in the form $GM = \dfrac{4\pi^2 r^3}{P^2}$ Knowing r and P, the right-hand side of this equation could be computed, and hence the product $G \times M$ could be determined. Thus if G were known, the mass M of the Sun was easily obtained. Actually the quantity G was not known in the seventeenth century, so all that this argument gave at that time was the product $G \times M$. But what could be done was to carry through an exactly similar argument for the case of the Earth and the Moon. Now M in our equation represents the mass of the Earth; P represents the period of revolution of the Moon around the Earth;

and r represents the radius of the orbit of the Moon. The period P was known, and the determination of r was much easier than it was for the case of the planets. Indeed r was known to within an accuracy of about one per cent to Hipparchus. So the product $G \times M$ could be determined for the case of the Earth. If, now, the quantity G is the same in both cases, then a simple division of the product $G \times M$ for the Sun by the product $G \times M$ for the Earth cancels out the unknown G and leaves the ratio of the mass of the Sun to the mass of the Earth as a known number. The calculation showed the mass of the Sun to be about 300,000 times as great as that of the Earth.

The determination of the value of G demanded a different type of experiment. Let us go back to our two particles of mass m_1 and m_2. The force of attraction between the two particles is the product $G \times m_1 \times m_2 \div r^2$ where r is the distance apart. Suppose we set up an experiment in which the force of attraction is actually measured for two particles of known mass and known distance apart. Then by equating the measured value of the force to our formula, the hitherto unknown quantity, G, will be determined. In fact, such an experiment could not be carried out in the seventeenth century. It had to wait until almost the beginning of the nineteenth century when it was carried through by Henry Cavendish.

So far we have thought only about the simple case of a planet or a satellite moving in a circular orbit around its primary. But need the orbit necessarily be circular? Could it be that the case of a circular orbit arises only if the planet or the satellite is initially set in motion in an appropriate way, and that if it is set in motion in some other way the orbit will not be a circle? Let us formulate the

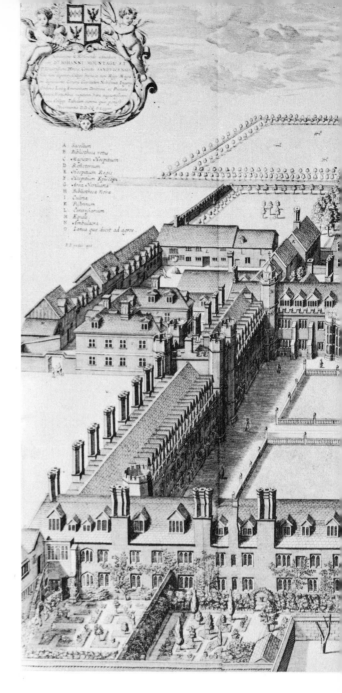

Newton (right) not only formulated the law of universal gravitation; he also showed that a flattened elliptical orbit satisfies the law of gravitation just as well as a circular one.

Newton's diagram demonstrating how a projectile launched at different speeds from a great height above the Earth follows different tracks. Launched from the right height at the right speed, it circles the Earth in the manner of a sputnik.

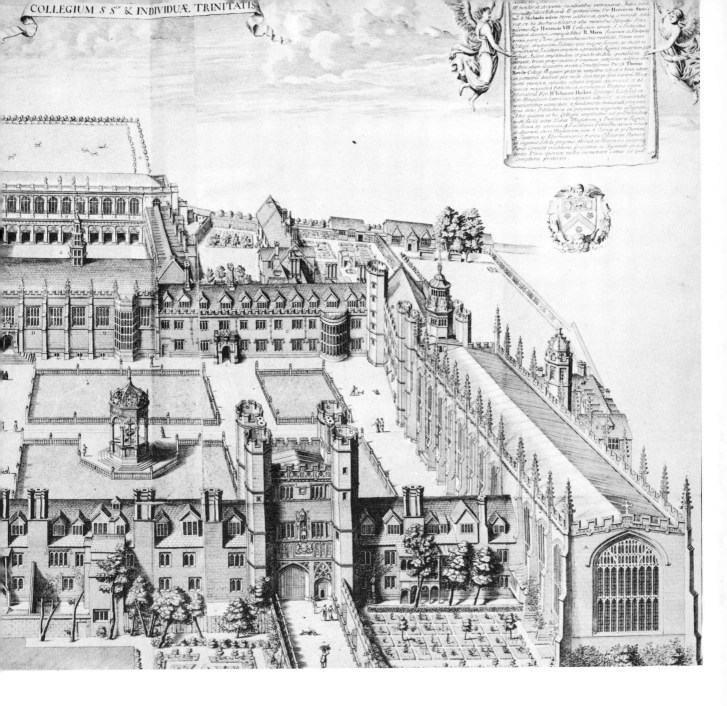

Right: Woolsthorpe Manor, where
Newton began his work on gravitation
at the time of the Great Plague.
Above: Trinity College, Cambridge,
where his mathematical genius
first showed itself. His living
quarters and the highly formal
garden so eloquent of his character
appear in the right foreground.

problem a little more precisely. We have a body of large mass which we shall denote by M, and a body of small mass which we shall denote by m. Given that the force acting on the small body is directed toward the large body and is of magnitude $G \times M \times m \div r^2$, where r is the distance apart of the two bodies at the moment in question, and given, also, that G is a constant number, what will be the orbit of the mass m when it is set in motion initially in some particular specified way? Before we attempt to answer the question it is worth noting the steps in reasoning that led up to it. First we used the simple case of circular orbits in order to guess a formula for the gravitational force. Then, equipped with this formula, we have turned the whole question around to ask what is the general nature of the orbit of a planet or satellite acted on by the gravitational force.

Equipped with the appropriate mathematical technique, namely the differential and integral calculus, probably one person in about a thousand or even one in a hundred, could answer for themselves the question we have just posed. But in the seventeenth century, before this technique was available, not more than perhaps one person in a hundred million, or even one in a thousand million, was capable of supplying the answer. It is often said that mathematics and science become harder and harder as more is known. This is a misreading of the situation, for although the problems themselves may become more complex, the techniques with which scientists are equipped to solve them become more and more effective.

In the seventeenth century, then, there were perhaps two men who were capable of answering our question—Newton and Leibniz. Leibniz was a mathematician not primarily interested in astronomy, and so far as is known he made no attempt to solve the problem. Some time between 1680 and 1685 it was solved by Newton. The answer he gave consisted of two parts. If the body m were projected with a sufficiently high speed it would swing around the massive body and eventually recede to a very large distance—to infinity—from it, along a path known as a hyperbola. But if the speed of projection of m were not as large as this, then the body would pursue a closed orbit that was an ellipse; moreover, the massive body M would lie at one of the foci of the ellipse. Finally, the small body m would sweep out equal areas of its orbit in equal times. Newton thus demonstrated that the laws which Kepler had

discovered empirically could also be arrived at deductively by precise mathematical argument from the law of gravitational force obtained from the simple case of the circular orbit.

Since Newton's answer to our problem specifies only that the planetary orbits should be elliptical, we may well ask why the planets do in fact move along paths which are very nearly circular ellipses. The answer must be because they were set in motion initially in a special way, in the special way required to make them move along nearly circular orbits. The slight deviations from circular motion also depend on the manner in which the system was started, and not at all on such mystical considerations as those which Kepler envisaged.

It was natural, following Newton's discovery, to pursue the question still further. Equipped with the means of calculating the motions of the planets, could not one work backward in time, instead of forward, and so deduce the manner in which the planets originated? After considering the problem, Newton decided that such an enormous calculation could not, in fact, be carried through, and subsequent experience has confirmed his judgment. Nowadays we do have ideas on how the planets originated, but these arise from entirely different considerations, as we shall see in a later chapter.

Are there any celestial bodies whose orbits are not nearly circular? The answer is yes, the comets. Newton found that the comet observed in 1680 followed a highly flattened elliptical orbit. This demonstrated that a highly flattened elliptical orbit satisfies the law of gravitation just as well as an almost circular one. The degree of ellipticity of the orbit simply depends on how the body was initially set in motion.

In Chapter 3 we saw that a description of planetary orbits can be given in three stages of sophistication. In the first stage the orbits can be regarded

Before Newton's time the motions of comets were thought to be quite unpredictable. Part of the Bayeux Tapestry, shown opposite, records how King Harold regarded the appearance of a strange star only as an omen of misfortune. In 1682 Halley saw the same comet, calculated its orbit, and almost correctly predicted its return. The top picture shows its next appearance, as seen from London in 1759. The diagram shows the extreme ellipticity of the orbit of Halley's Comet compared with the almost circular orbits of the planets.

orbit of Pluto

orbit of Neptune

orbit of Halley's Comet

orbit of Earth

as simple circles. In the second stage the deviations from the circles are of such a nature that the planetary orbits can be considered as nearly circular ellipses. In the third stage, in which the mutual influences of the planets on each other are taken into account as well as the major influence of the Sun, the planetary orbits must be regarded as changing minutely all the time. We now see what light the Newtonian theory shed on the orbits postulated at each stage of sophistication. The first arose from the manner in which the planets were initially set in motion; the second was a natural consequence of the law of gravitation; the third Newton set himself the task of investigating by calculation.

In particular he set himself to examine the case of the motion of the Moon, for in this case the third stage of sophistication, which takes account of more than one gravitational field, is extremely important, as we already saw in Chapter 3. Newton took into account not only the gravitational force acting on the Moon from the Earth, but also that acting on it from the Sun. He found that almost all the irregularities in the motion of the Moon that had so troubled the astronomers of antiquity could be explained in a natural way by the new theory. There were still a few small discrepancies between observation and calculation,

and these we shall refer to again in the next chapter. Suffice it, for the moment, that the major part of the hitherto intractable problem of the motion of the Moon had been solved.

Several times in previous chapters we have had occasion to refer to the phenomenon of precession. The Earth's axis of rotation is not perpendicular to the plane of the Earth's orbit. Taken over a few years, the direction of the axis of rotation can be regarded as sensibly constant, but over a long period of time we have to recognize that the axis moves around a conical surface. The axis of the cone is taken perpendicular to the plane of the Earth's orbit, and the half-angle of the cone is $23\frac{1}{2}°$. As time proceeds the Earth's axis of rotation moves around the cone in such a way that it always passes through the vertex. It completes one circuit of the cone in about 26,000 years. It is this motion of the axis that constitutes the phenomenon of precession. Newton discovered that the effect is caused by the fact that the Earth is not strictly a uniform sphere. It is an oblate spheroid, the diameter through the poles being some 27 miles less than the diameter through the equator. Because of the Earth's strictly non-spherical shape, the gravitational force which the Moon and the Sun exert on it produces a very slight twist. And it is this twist that causes the Earth's axis of rotation to move around its cone.

Newton, indeed, calculated the time required for the motion around the cone and obtained almost exactly the correct answer.

Let us move back from this third stage of sophistication to the simple case of a planet moving around the Sun in an almost circular orbit. The surprising thing is that no transverse force along the circumference of the circle is needed to keep the planet moving. The gravitational theory showed that the only force entering into the problem is a radial one, directed from the planet toward the Sun. The idea that some force was needed to keep pushing the planets along their orbits—the idea that had been entertained by continental mathematicians of the caliber of Huygens—could now be completely dispensed with.

One detail remains to be discussed, that of taking the quantity G to be the same in all cases, of regarding it as a constant. Newton had already tested this link in the chain of argument when, at the age of 23, he returned from Cambridge to his native village of Woolsthorpe in Lincolnshire at the outbreak of the Great Plague. The formula $G \times M \times m \div r^2$ could not only be used for determining the period of revolution of the Moon around the Earth in the manner described above; it could also be used for finding the speed with which a vertically falling body drops to the surface of the Earth. The quantity M would represent the mass of the Earth in both cases. The quantity r would, however, be different in the two cases. In the first case it would represent the radius of the orbit of the Moon, and in the second case it would represent the radius of the Earth itself. (The mass m would also be different in the two cases, but this did not matter since m canceled out of both calculations. We have already noticed Galileo's great discovery that the orbit followed by a body in a gravitational field is independent of the mass of the body.)

From this it followed that if the ratio of the values of r in the two cases were known, then the period of revolution of the Moon around the Earth and the speed with which a falling body dropped from a known height reaches the surface of the Earth would give the values of the product $G \times M$ for the two cases. Since the product was found to be the same in both cases, then the quantity G *must* be the same, since the mass of the Earth, M, was certainly the same. Besides testing the constancy of

the value of G this ingenious argument also showed very clearly that the Moon is held in its orbit by a radial force and not by a transverse one, since it was plainly a radial force that caused bodies to fall vertically to the ground.

This was in the year 1665. Twenty-two years later, in 1687, Newton's great work, the *Philosophiae Naturalis Principia Mathematica*, was seen through the press by Samuel Pepys. What Newton had done for the first time was to show that the phenomena of the physical world were accessible to precise calculation. If one knew how a system was started off then its subsequent behavior could be calculated. This was the science of dynamics. While it is true that Newton did not show that all natural phenomena were accessible to mathematical investigation, the range of phenomena he did consider was sufficiently wide to convince mankind of the general proposition that if one knows the present state of affairs completely, one can calculate the future.

With certain reservations relating to modern developments in quantum theory, all subsequent scientific experience has confirmed this tremendous idea. The apparently impenetrable undergrowth in which scientists had hitherto been laboring was suddenly cleared away, and a new path was opened before them.

Right: Title page of the *Principia*. Left: Extract from a minute recording the presentation of the manuscript to the Royal Society. In this work Newton showed for the first time that the phenomena of the physical world are accessible to precise calculation. From that time onward astronomy moved into a new era.

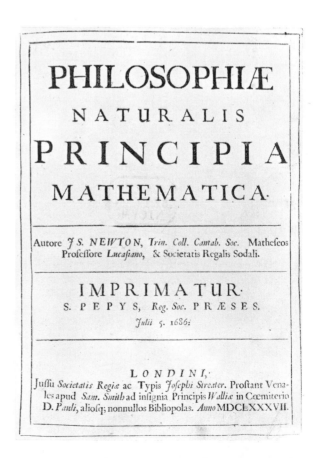

PHILOSOPHIÆ
NATURALIS
PRINCIPIA
MATHEMATICA.

Autore JS. NEWTON, Trin. Coll. Cantab. Soc. Matheseos Professore Lucasiano, & Societatis Regalis Sodali.

IMPRIMATUR.
S. PEPYS, Reg. Soc. PRÆSES.
Julii 5. 1686.

LONDINI,
Jussu Societatis Regiæ ac Typis Josephi Streater. Prostant Venales apud Sam. Smith ad insignia Principis Walliæ in Coemiterio D. Pauli, aliosq; nonnullos Bibliopolas. Anno MDCLXXXVII.

Chapter 6   The Post-Newtonian Era

So great were the advances in mathematics and the physical sciences during the Newtonian Age that it took astronomers something like a century and a half to exploit them at all fully. Their achievements during this period, which lasted from the early eighteenth century to about the middle of the nineteenth century, can conveniently be divided into three parts. First, they attained far greater accuracy than ever before in measuring the positions of stars and planets. Next they employed the Newtonian mathematical theory of gravitation to explain not merely the broad features of planetary motion but also many of the intricate details of motions within the Solar System. Finally, they began to reach out beyond the Solar System into the larger universe outside. It is simplest to consider each of these major developments in turn.

The Positions of Stars and Planets

The Post-Newtonian era began with a strong emphasis on the practical applications of astronomy. In 1714, British sea captains presented a petition to the House of Commons asking for a solution to the problem of determining longitude at sea. As we saw in Chapter 2, determining latitude is comparatively easy; all one need do is to observe the elevation of the sun at midday. But the determination of longitude is more difficult.

If you were dropped by parachute on to some remote, and to you unknown, point on the Earth's surface, you would find it quite impossible to work out your longitude unless you had a record of the time being kept at some standard meridian on the Earth, say the meridian of Greenwich Observatory. But if you did have that information, it would be just as easy to determine your longitude as your latitude. You would merely have to find the moment of midday at your own position and compare it with the time then being registered at Greenwich. Each difference of one hour between the two times corresponds to a difference of 15° of longitude. For example, suppose that at your noon Greenwich time was 9 o'clock in the morning, you would know you were placed three hours east of Greenwich. In other words, your longitude would be 45° East. The difficulty lies only in how you are to know the time at Greenwich.

Today, provided you had a radio receiver, you could easily pick up one of the frequent transmissions of Greenwich Mean Time, but in the

A pressing practical problem at the beginning of the eighteenth century was to find a way of determining longitude at sea. Eventually the best solution was provided by Harrison's marine chronometer. (Above is his first model of 1735 and below is Kendal's replica of his fourth model of 1759, together with Captain Cook's comment on its reliability.) But until the advent of chronometers the longitude problem gave a great impetus to the closer study of the motions of the Moon, the planets, and their satellites.

eighteenth century no such easy means was available. True, there were pendulum clocks, but the rolling and pitching of a ship subjected them to such gross errors that they could not be relied upon to show the same time as the home-port clocks by which they were set at the beginning of a voyage. So it was natural that people should turn their attention to using the movements of the planets and their satellites—which can be viewed simultaneously from many parts of the Earth—as a means of fixing the time at some standard meridian.

Already, almost a hundred years earlier, Galileo had been thinking along the same lines. Galileo's idea was to use the moons of Jupiter. If one could work out in advance precisely what positions these moons would be in, hour by hour, for many months ahead, then it would be possible to provide seamen with an almanac tabulated in terms of some standard time, say the time at Greenwich or the time at Genoa. A seaman would then be able to observe the position of the moons, search the almanac until he found the same position, and read off the standard time. One drawback to the scheme was that the positions of heavenly bodies cannot be observed when skies are cloudy, but the project failed for two even more cogent reasons. First, it was next to impossible to make the necessary observations from the deck of a rolling ship; next, it proved incredibly difficult to do the calculations which such an almanac demanded.

When the problem was put to Newton he thought of a similar but simpler idea. Our own Moon moves constantly against the background of the stars. If one could work out in advance just where the Moon was going to be hour by hour, then an almanac of the Moon's motions could be provided. In this case the seaman would have to observe the stars that lay near the Moon and then, by consulting the almanac, he could infer the standard time. The second of the difficulties which applied to Galileo's idea applied also to Newton's, and for this reason some forty years were to elapse before anything came of it. Newton himself tried to work out the future motion of the Moon, but found it so difficult that he declared it to be the only problem that ever made his head ache. Indeed, it was not until after Euler invented new mathematical techniques that reasonably accurate calculations of the Moon's future motions became practicable. Such calculations were actually carried through by Tobias Mayer, who published his tables in a form suitable for the determination of longitude at sea in the year 1752.

By an odd trick of fate, just as it became possible to use the Moon as an astronomical clock, a mechanical invention made the whole method obsolete. An English inventor, John Harrison, produced a chronometer, not regulated by a pendulum, which proved itself capable of keeping accurate time at sea over a long period. Tobias

In theory longitude can be found by observing the positions of the moons of Jupiter and consulting a table listing the times of those positions at a known place. Up to the eighteenth century, however, it was hard both to work out the table and to make the observation from a rolling ship.

AUGUST 1767. [89]

Configurations of the SATELLITES of JUPITER

at 9 o' th' Clock in the Evening.

Mayer's Moon clock and Harrison's marine chronometer were both tested out by the Astronomer Royal of the time, Nevil Maskelyne, who found that Harrison's chronometer gave the better results. With the Moon clock it was possible to determine longitude correctly to within four minutes of arc; with the chronometer the margin of error was only about one minute of arc.

Maskelyne was faced with a somewhat delicate human problem. The British government had offered a prize of £20,000 to anyone who solved the longitude problem, and Maskelyne was left to decide how the money should be apportioned. His decision was that it should be shared equally between the two methods. This was fair. The only questionable point was that of the half-prize paid for the Moon clock, Euler received very little. But since most of the half-share for the Moon clock was received by Mayer's widow, there is, perhaps, little to complain about.

At the time of the seamen's petition, some forty years earlier, the problem of the Moon clock had been referred to the newly-established Greenwich Observatory. The first Astronomer Royal, John Flamsteed, then felt that he could best assist the project by plotting accurately the background of stars against which the Moon moves. To this end he determined the positions of nearly 3,000 stars to within an accuracy of about ten seconds of arc—about six times closer than the one minute of arc

that Tycho Brahe had achieved. This work which Flamsteed started as something merely ancillary to the Moon clock project turned out to be of surpassing astronomical importance; for in pursuing the program of accurate position measurement, the third Astronomer Royal, James Bradley, made a remarkable discovery which greatly assisted the emergence of modern astronomy.

To appreciate the importance of Bradley's discovery we must take a second look at the problem of defining positions on the celestial sphere, which we met with in Chapter 1. We saw there that in one system we can regard the polar axis of the celestial sphere as an extension of the Earth's axis of rotation, and the equator of the celestial sphere as lying in a plane at right angles to that axis. Before we can state the longitude of a star, we must then decide on some arbitrary point on the celestial equator from which to measure. In the equatorial system the arbitrary point chosen is the First Point of Aries (Υ), one of the two points at which the plane of the Earth's orbit around the Sun (the ecliptic) cuts the celestial equator.

In all our previous discussion we regarded the direction of the Earth's axis of rotation as being fixed with respect to very distant objects in the universe. But is this actually the case? The answer is that it is not.

The direction of the Earth's polar axis is constantly changing. This means that the celestial

equator is changing too. Even the First Point of Aries is constantly changing, a fact which the great Greek astronomer, Hipparchus, realized. Hipparchus probably established this by comparing his own observations of the equinoxes, made with the help of the Hipparchus ring described in Chapter 2, with the records made earlier by Babylonian astronomers. Unless he made the rash assumption that the older the observations the less they could be relied on, there was only one conclusion to be drawn. The comparison disclosed that the position of the Sun at the equinoxes, against the background of stars, had changed considerably over a period of about 2,000 years.

The length of this time scale is significant. If we are not concerned with observations made over long periods of time, and if we are not concerned with extreme accuracy, then it is satisfactory to ignore the changing direction of the Earth's polar axis. But if we are to achieve modern standards of accuracy the slight change of direction from year to year must quite certainly be taken into account.

For many centuries after the time of Hipparchus no one could explain *why* the direction of the Earth's polar axis changes. Newton's theory of gravitation gives a complete explanation of the phenomenon. Consider the situation shown in Figure 6.1. The line *OA* is drawn perpendicular to the ecliptic, which is the plane of the Earth's motion around the Sun. The Earth's axis of rotation makes an angle of approximately $23\frac{1}{2}°$ with this line, and this angle is maintained to a close approximation throughout the *motion* of the axis of rotation. That is to say, the axis of rotation precesses about *OA* in much the same way as the axis of spin of a top precesses around the vertical direction.

This precessional motion arises because the Earth is not a perfect sphere. The Earth's polar diameter is some 27 miles less than its equatorial diameter. This causes the gravitational pull of both the Sun and the Moon to put a twist on the Earth, and it is this twist, or torque, that causes precessional motion. Despite its far smaller mass, the Moon plays a greater part than the Sun in producing this twist, simply because it is much closer to us.

The time taken for one complete precession of the Earth's axis is about 26,000 years, so from year to year the motion is obviously very slight. In fact, the axis of rotation moves in a year through an angle of only some twenty seconds of arc. But once we become concerned with positional accuracies of the order of ten seconds or better, as Flamsteed and Bradley were, we must take account of the changing standard of reference. Because the main effect of precession is quite smooth from year to year, there is no difficulty in making a proper correction to allow for it.

However, in addition to this smooth precession there is a much smaller motion which varies from year to year. If the plane of the Moon's motion around the Earth were the same as the plane of the Earth's motion around the Sun, this latter complication would not exist. But the Moon's orbit is slightly inclined to the ecliptic and does not stay fixed with respect to the Earth and the ecliptic. Indeed, the Moon moves only approximately in a plane—a plane that slews round with respect to the axis *OA* of Figure 6.1.

The situation is illustrated in Figure 6.2, where the line *OB* is drawn perpendicular to the plane of the Moon's orbit, and *OA* is again drawn perpendicular to the ecliptic. Over a period of a few months the Moon can be considered to move in the orbit shown in our figure. But over a longer period we have to take into account the fact that the line *OB* precesses about *OA*, the period of the precession being 18.6 years.

Evidently, then, the plane of the Moon's orbit presents a different aspect from year to year and this causes the effect of the Moon's pull on the Earth to change from year to year as well. Because of this variability there are corresponding fluctuations in the rate of precession of the Earth's axis, and each complete cycle of these fluctuations takes 18.6 years. It was Bradley who first discovered this effect and who referred to it as a *nutation*.

We have seen that precession arises because the Earth is not a perfect sphere. The realization of the importance of the deviation of the Earth from perfect spherical form stimulated great interest in geodesy. In particular, the whole problem of the shape of the Earth was taken up by the French Academy of Sciences, and in the years following 1735 measurements of unprecedented accuracy were made in places as widely separated as Peru and Lapland; and for the first time in human history it became possible to give a tolerably correct assessment of the shape of the Earth.

Before leaving the question of precession it is worth noting that over a long period of time it

PROSPECTUS INTRA CAMERAM STELLATAM

Top: The Octagon Room at Greenwich, now a museum, as it is today. Below: The same room as it was in the time of Flamsteed. It was here that Flamsteed set out to assist the Moon clock project by plotting the background of stars against which the Moon moves. On the left is a star map from his *Atlas Coelestis*. Flamsteed plotted the positions of nearly three thousand stars to an accuracy within ten seconds.

147

gives rise to gross changes of the seasons. The Earth's axis of rotation completes half of a precessional cycle in 13,000 years, and in that time summer and winter are completely interchanged. That is to say, the part of the Earth's orbit where the northern hemisphere now experiences summer and the southern hemisphere winter will, in 13,000 years' time, be the part where the northern hemisphere experiences winter and the southern hemisphere summer.

In his pursuit of accuracy in measuring the positions of stars and planets, Bradley made another discovery which was to have far-reaching consequences—the discovery of the phenomenon of aberration.

In Figure 6.3 light from a star is admitted through a slit, S_1. The question now arises: where must a second slit, S_2, be placed so that the light passes through S_2 also, remembering that light travels in straight lines? The obvious answer is on the line joining S_1 to the star, so that the star and both slits lie on the same straight line. This answer is correct if the slits are at rest, but if they are in motion in a direction transverse to the direction of the star, the situation is altered. It is altered because the light takes a definite period of time to travel from S_1 to S_2, and during that time S_2 has moved relative to S_1. In that case we have to place the slit S_2 *off* the straight line joining S_1 to the star, as shown in Figure 6.4.

The situation is made clearer by the two parts of Figure 6.5. In the first part we have a pulse of light just passing through the slit S_1. In the second part the pulse of light has now reached the slit S_2, and in the time interval between the two parts of the figure, the slits S_1 and S_2 have moved as shown.

Returning now to Figure 6.4, we see that the line joining S_1 and S_2 makes a slight angle to the direction that joins S_1 to the star. This result is of importance when we consider the problem of

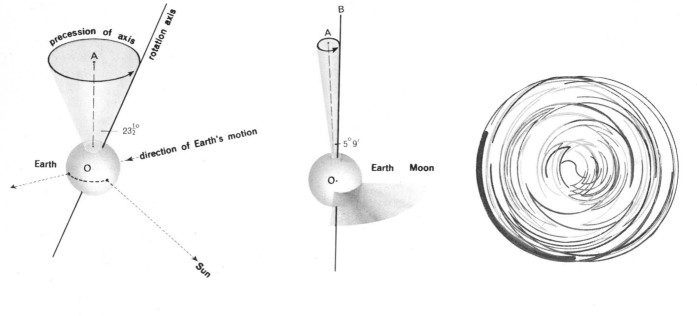

Figure 6.1
OA is perpendicular to the ecliptic. The Earth's axis of rotation precesses about OA just as the axis of spin of a top precesses about the vertical direction. Time for one complete motion is about 26,000 years.

Figure 6.2
OB is perpendicular to the plane of the Moon's orbit, OA perpendicular to the ecliptic. OB precesses about OA, the period being 18.6 years. Thus the plane of the Moon's orbit (and the effect of the Moon's pull on the Earth) varies. This causes fluctuations (nutation) in the rate of the precession of Figure 6.1.

Precession causes a slow migration of the center about which the stars appear to rotate. Here two sets of star trails, one of 1907, the other of 1941, are superimposed. Note how the centers of the two sets differ.

star

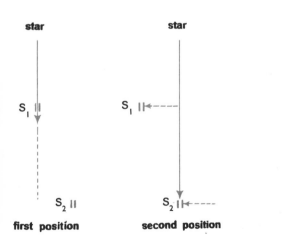

Figure 6.3
Placing two slits, S_1 and S_2, so that
light from star passes through both.
If slits have no motion transverse
to direction of star, S_2 must lie
on straight line joining S_1 to star.

star

$$\text{angle} = \frac{\text{velocity of motion}}{\text{velocity of light}}$$

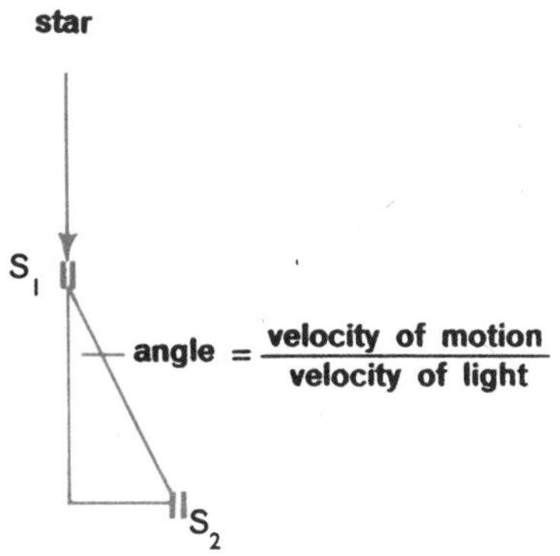

Figure 6.4
If slits *do* move in a direction
transverse to that of star, S_2 must
lie *off* that line by an amount to
be measured by the above formula.

star   **star**

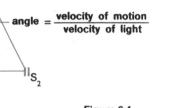

first position   **second position**

Figure 6.5
Light and both slits move at finite
speeds. S_2 must be so placed that
it takes same time to move from first
to second position above as light
takes to travel the distance S_1 to S_2.

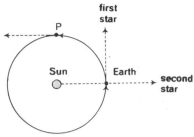

Figure 6.6
Figures 6.4 and 6.5 explain why the
axis of a telescope must commonly be
offset when observing a star. But the
degree of offset varies. When the
Earth is in the position shown, it will
be maximal for the second star and
zero for the first. When the Earth is
at P, the reverse is true.

pointing a telescope at a star. We can think of S_1 as being the objective of the telescope and S_2 as being the eyepiece. The line from S_1 to S_2 then represents the axis of the telescope, and we see that this axis must be slightly offset in order to observe the star from the direction which would be appropriate if there were no motion of the telescope.

If the degree of offset were always the same for all stars, this aberration effect would be of no practical importance, but this is not so, as we can see from Figure 6.6. Here we have the Earth at a particular point in its orbit around the Sun. If we point the telescope toward the first star, which lies in the direction of the Earth's motion, there is no motion of the telescope transverse to the direction of the star. There will therefore be no aberration effect. Now suppose we point the telescope at the second star. In this case the motion of the Earth, and therefore the motion of the telescope, is wholly transverse to the direction of the star, and the effect of aberration is at a maximum. In fact, the degree of offset required to observe the second star would be about twenty seconds of arc. We see, therefore, that aberration does not distort the directions of the stars in any uniform way.

The situation is made even more complicated by the changing direction of the Earth's motion. For instance, after a quarter of a year, when the Earth has moved to the point P of Figure 6.6, the situation is precisely reversed. The motion of the Earth,

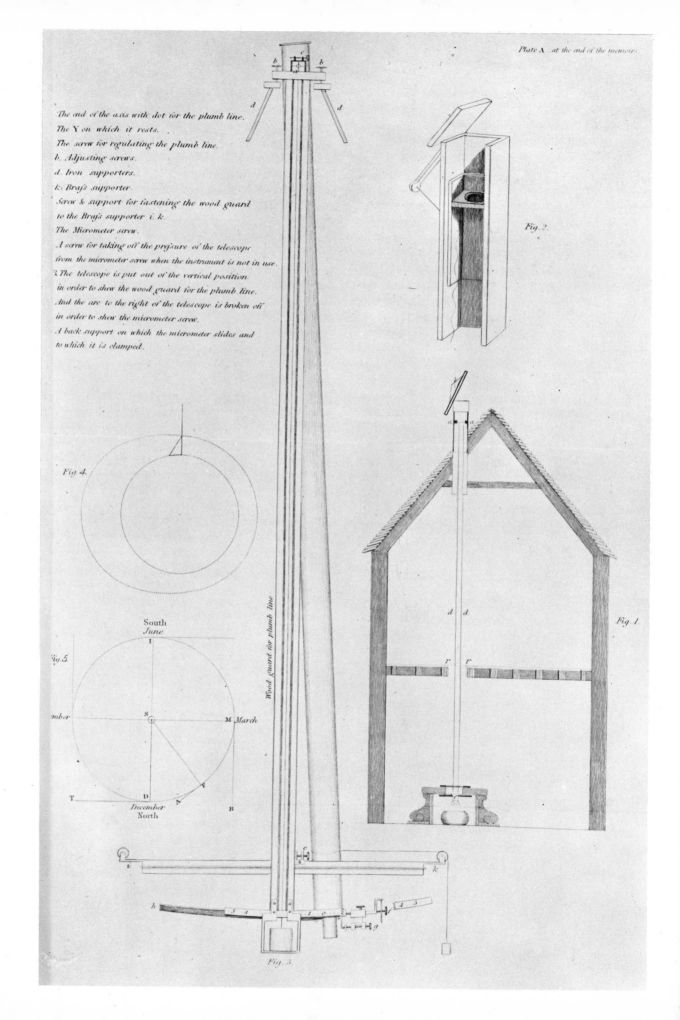

The end of the axis with dot for the plumb line.

The Y on which it rests.

The screw for regulating the plumb line.

b. Adjusting screws.

d. Iron supporters.

k. Brass supporter.

Screw & support for fastening the wood guard
  to the Brass supporter i. k.

The Micrometer screw.

A screw for taking off the pressure of the telescope
  from the micrometer screw when the instrument is not in use.

The telescope is put out of the vertical position
  in order to shew the wood guard for the plumb line.

And the arc to the right of the telescope is broken off
  in order to shew the micrometer screw.

A back support on which the micrometer slides and
  to which it is clamped.

Fig. 2.

Fig. 4.

Fig. 1.

Fig. 5.

South
June

December
North

Wood guard for plumb line

Fig. 3.

and therefore the motion of the telescope, will then be transverse to the direction of the first star and this will be subject to aberration; on the other hand, the motion is now along the direction of the second star and this will accordingly be free from aberration. So for every star the distortion varies throughout the year. For stars that lie in the plane of the Earth's orbit aberration is sometimes absent; at other times it is at a maximum. For stars that do not lie in the plane of the Earth's orbit aberration is never absent. Consider, for example, a star lying in a direction perpendicular to the plane of the Earth's orbit. When a telescope is pointed at such a star, the direction of the Earth's motion must necessarily be transverse to it at all times of the year.

To summarize, then, the motion of the Earth distorts the pattern of the stars on the sky. The distortion varies throughout the year, and also according to the angle that the line of sight to a star makes with the plane of the Earth's orbit; and the general order of the distortion is about twenty seconds of arc. This was the remarkable discovery which Bradley made.

If we stick to a simple form of geometry, avoiding the complications mentioned at the outset, in Chapter 1, then the phenomenon of aberration offers convincing evidence that the Earth moves

Left: Page from an early nineteenth-century book showing the zenith instrument which James Bradley used for many of his observations.
Right: Photograph of part of the instrument (preserved at Greenwich), and notes made during the course of one of Bradley's observations.

around the Sun—the kind of evidence for which Galileo sought in vain. We have seen in an earlier chapter that in the absence of such evidence, the system of Tycho Brahe, in which the Sun is assumed to move around the Earth and the other planets around the Sun, gives just as good a description of the planetary motions as does the system of Copernicus. But Tycho Brahe's system cannot explain the aberrations which Bradley observed. For that, we must follow the system of Copernicus.

As an aside, however, it may be mentioned that the modern theory of relativity still allows us to regard the Earth as the center of things, provided we are willing to dispense with simple Euclidean geometry. But if we persist in regarding the Earth as fixed, we have to go far beyond the complexities of the Ptolemaic picture or of the Tychonic picture in order to explain the phenomenon of aberration.

It is clear that the phenomenon would not arise if light traveled at infinite speed, because the light would then travel from slit S_1 to slit S_2 of Figure 6.3 before the slits themselves had time to move. Aberration is, therefore, a phenomenon that depends on the finite speed of light. Indeed, the angle of distortion shown in Figure 6.4 is simply the ratio of the speed of transverse motion of the slits to the speed of light itself. This raises the immediate question: what *is* the speed of light? The classic determination is due to the Danish astronomer Olaf, or Olaus, Römer who, in the year 1675, obtained a value whose principal

uncertainty arose from an inaccurate knowledge of the true size of the Earth's orbit. Here is a description of Römer's method.

Figure 6.7 shows the orbit of Io, the innermost of the four large satellites of Jupiter which Galileo first discovered. Its distance from the planet is closely similar to the distance of the Moon from the Earth. We are able to see Io because of the sunlight reflected from its surface, but at times it passes into the shadow cast by Jupiter itself, and we cannot observe it when it lies in this shadow. Suppose, now, that we wish to determine the length of time that Io takes to move once round its orbit. The obvious method would be to make a note of the moment at which Io moves into eclipse. Then we might say that the time interval between successive moments of eclipse determines the time taken to complete one circuit. But is this *exactly* right? To examine whether it is or not, we must consider a little more closely just what happens when we make our observations.

At the moment the satellite passes into the shadow, light ceases to be reflected from its surface. The change from light being reflected to light not being reflected travels across space from Jupiter to the Earth, so that the cessation of light is recognizable on the Earth only some time after it has actually taken place. But how long after? The answer depends on how far away the Earth is from Jupiter. In fact, the delay is simply the distance of the Earth divided by the speed of light. Provided the delay

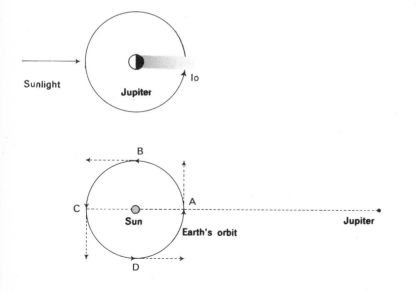

Figure 6.7
The obvious way to find how long Io takes to move once round its orbit is to measure the interval between two successive occasions when it moves into eclipse.

Figure 6.8
When the Earth is at D the distance between Earth and Jupiter shortens between successive eclipses of Io. Light, moving at finite speed, takes less time to reach us, and we thus underestimate the time between two eclipses. When the Earth is at B, precisely the reverse applies.

In 1675 Olaus Römer made use of the lengthening and shortening of the apparent periods of the satellites of Jupiter to deduce the speed of light. The picture shows Römer at his meridian instrument in 1689.

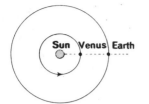

Figure 6.9
Because the plane of the orbit of
Venus is not identical with that of
the Earth's orbit, it is only rarely
that Earth, Sun and Venus lie almost
on a straight line. Such occasions
give the opportunity of measuring
the distance of Venus from the Earth.

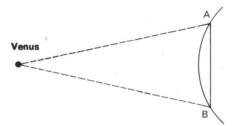

Figure 6.10
An easier way is to find the angles
at which the planet is sighted from
two stations at a measured distance
apart *at the same instant*, and make
a simple trigonometrical calculation.
But in the eighteenth century it was
hard to establish simultaneity.

is precisely the same at two successive moments of
eclipse—that is, provided the distance of the Earth
from Jupiter is precisely the same—then our method
of measuring the time which Io takes to complete
one circuit will be correct. But if the distance
between the Earth and Jupiter changes between
one eclipse and the next, our method will quite
clearly be incorrect, because the amount of delay
will be different in the two cases.

The question therefore arises as to whether the
distance of the Earth from Jupiter does or does not
change during the time interval between two
successive eclipses; and the answer is that it must
change if the Earth is moving toward or away from
Jupiter. Reference to Figure 6.8 shows that the
situation in this respect changes throughout the
year. At the points A and C of the Earth's orbit,
the Earth is moving transversely to the direction
of Jupiter, and the distance of the Earth from
Jupiter does not then change appreciably between
two successive eclipses of Io. But when the Earth
is at D the distance shortens steadily, which means
that we shall underestimate the time between
successive eclipses. When the Earth is at B the
reverse applies: the distance then lengthens
steadily, which means that we shall overestimate
the time between successive eclipses.

Edmund Halley laid elaborate plans
for observing the transit of Venus
of 1761 and using the observations
to establish the absolute dimensions
of the Solar System.

What Römer found was that the apparent periods of motion of Jupiter's satellites do in fact shorten when the Earth is moving toward Jupiter and lengthen when it is moving away. And, indeed, from the amount of the shortening and lengthening he was able to deduce the speed with which light moves. In fact, the fractional changing of the orbital period of the satellite is simply the ratio of the speed of the Earth's motion to the speed of light. Römer measured the fractional shortening of the period of the satellite and, since he knew approximately the speed of the Earth's motion, was able to deduce the speed of light. In this way he demonstrated its enormous value—about 186,000 miles per second. His contemporaries were sceptical about the result, and indeed it did not become widely accepted until after Bradley's discovery of the phenomenon of aberration. But that phenomenon gave an independent measure of the speed of light which closely corroborated Römer's findings. We can see how this independent measure came into operation by referring again to Figure 6.4. The angle of aberration shown there is determined by exactly the same ratio as the fractional shortening of the period of orbital motion of the satellites of Jupiter, namely the velocity of the Earth's motion to the velocity of light.

The Mathematics of the Solar System

Today we can reasonably expect any intelligent young student to know that the distance from the Earth to the Sun is about 93 million miles; but even the greatest astronomers of classical times had no knowledge of that important fact. Right up to Newton's day the distance was known only to within about 30 per cent. So the whole long controversy between the Copernican and the Ptolemaic schools, like the work of Kepler, Galileo and Newton, was concerned with the shapes and the *relative* sizes of the planetary orbits rather than with their absolute sizes. Yet further progress toward understanding many of the fine details of the Solar System depended essentially on determining absolute sizes. And it was to this problem that the second Astronomer Royal, Edmund Halley, addressed himself during his term of office, from 1720 until his death in 1742.

The method of determining the scale of the Solar System which Halley invented is illustrated

British men of science, 1807-08.
The signatures, grouped as the men,
include those of Cavendish, Maskelyne,
Joseph Banks and William Herschel,
all of whom played a notable part
in the development of astronomy.

The Transit of Venus, 1769

Plans for observations of transits
of Venus were carried out in 1761
and in 1769. In the latter year
Sir Joseph Banks and Captain Cook
made observations from Tahiti. Above
are Cook's ships in Matavie Bay.
The map of the bay, on the right,
marks Fort Venus and Point Venus.

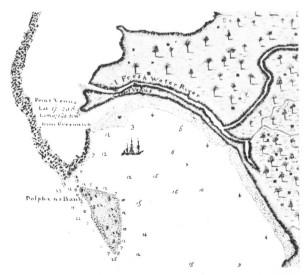

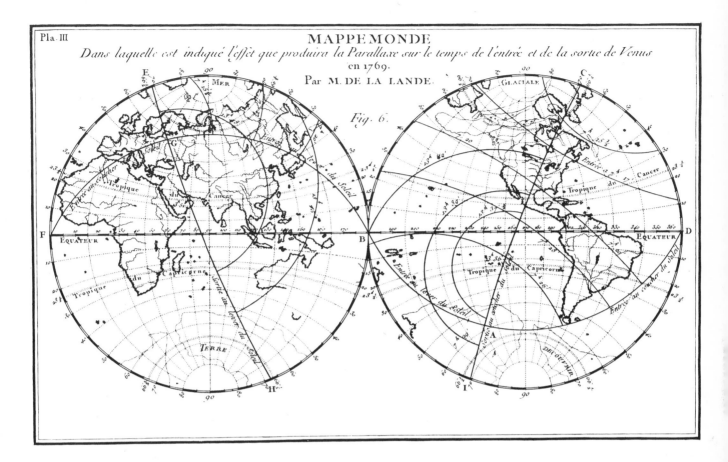

MAPPEMONDE

Dans laquelle est indiqué l'effet que produira la Parallaxe sur le temps de l'entrée et de la sortie de Venus en 1769.

Par M. DE LA LANDE.

Fig. 6.

Top: Lalande's map, made before the earlier transit, showed the effect which would be produced by parallax on the times of the planet's ingress and egress at the transit of 1769.
Right: Main observation points, 1769.
Below: Sir Joseph Banks showing a telescope to natives of Tahiti, as an artist imagined the scene.
Bottom right: The camp at Fort Venus.

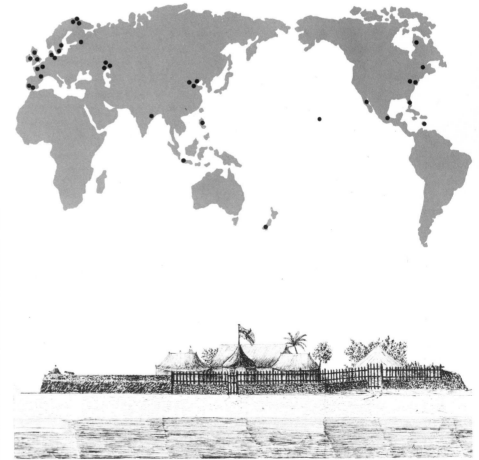

in Figure 6.9. Here we have the orbits of Venus and the Earth. Because Venus moves more rapidly round its orbit than the Earth does, a situation often arises when the Sun, Venus and the Earth lie more or less in a straight line. The collinearity of the center of the Sun with the centers of the two planets is never perfect, however, because the plane of Venus's orbit is not identical with the plane of the Earth's orbit. In each circuit of its orbit Venus crosses the plane of the Earth's orbit twice. If on either of these occasions the Earth happens to be at the appropriate point of its orbit, there can be a good approximation to collinearity. On such rare occasions Venus is projected as a dark blob against the bright background of the Sun's disk. An observer on the Earth therefore sees a dark spot move across the face of the Sun, the motion arising, of course, from the progress of the Earth and Venus along their orbits. Now it was known in Halley's time that such a rare combination of circumstances would occur in 1761.

Halley's idea sprang from the circumstance that the path of Venus across the Sun is not the same for different terrestrial observers. Thus two observers at different terrestrial latitudes will see Venus sweep across the Sun along two different chords, the amount of the difference depending on the size of the Earth itself, on the particular geographical positions of the observers, and on the true scale of the Solar System. The first two of these factors can be considered known. Hence the third factor—the true scale of the Solar System—can be deduced, if the difference between the chords can be measured with adequate accuracy.

Halley's plans for observing the transit of Venus from various terrestrial stations were carried through in 1761, and also at a later favorable transit in 1769. As a result, the absolute scale of the Solar System was established to within an accuracy of about 5 per cent—a considerable improvement on the previous 20 to 30 per cent.

Further attempts to employ this method had to wait until the nineteenth century, when elaborate preparations were made to observe the favorable transits of 1874 and 1882. The preparations were carried through by the Astronomer Royal of the day, George Airy, in consultation with the Royal Astronomical Society, but in spite of all the careful precautions taken, the results of these observations were disappointing. Trouble arose from the atmosphere of Venus, which prevented the position of the planet on the Sun from being defined with sufficient sharpness.

Before leaving the Venus transit method, it is interesting to ask why the geometrically far simpler system illustrated in Figure 6.10 was not much to be preferred. With the angle at A and the angle at B both known by observing Venus at the same moment, and with the distance between the two terrestrial stations A and B accurately measured, the other dimensions of the triangle could easily be calculated. This very simple method could, moreover, be carried out at any time. There would be no reason to wait for a transit of Venus,

The asteroids shown on this time-exposure appear as elongated blobs. Through a telescope they appear as mere points of light. Telescopes can thus be lined up on them without ambiguity. This enables observers to make very accurate estimates of the absolute scale of the Solar System.

If we know the sizes of the Earth's orbit around the Sun and the Moon's orbit around the Earth, Newton's law of universal gravitation enables us to work out how the mass of the Sun compares with the mass of the Earth. To work out these masses in absolute terms, we must first establish the gravitational pull of some standard chunk of material. The first man to do so was Henry Cavendish (opposite). With the apparatus on the right he measured the deflection of the small hanging pellets (x) toward the large known weights marked W.

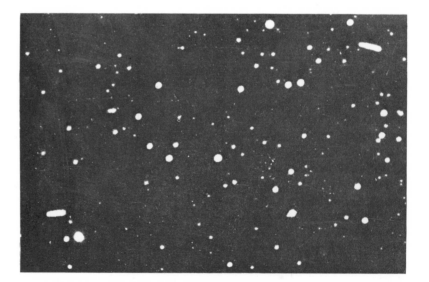

and indeed the presence of the Sun would be a disadvantage rather than an advantage in this method.

The reason for neglecting the simpler method was that in Halley's day there was no means of defining simultaneity for the observers at *A* and *B*, and unless this could be done with great accuracy, errors due to the motions of the Earth and Venus vitiated the method. But with the invention of reliable mechanical clocks the situation was quite changed. The simple trigonometrical method of Figure 6.10 could then be used. Not only was the great inconvenience of waiting for a transit of Venus dispensed with, but Mars could be used perfectly well instead of Venus; and this provided two further advantages. When at its nearest to us (at a distance of about 35 million miles) Mars lies in a night sky, whereas Venus at its nearest lies close to the bright Sun itself, and is therefore much more difficult to observe. Moreover, Mars is not a cloud-covered planet, and it is therefore easier to specify a definite point on the surface of Mars toward which the different observers should direct their telescopes in making the measurements of the angles.

So far nothing has been said of the minor planets and asteroids. The largest minor planet is very much smaller than the Moon, while the smallest asteroids are no more than tiny chunks of rock. Most of them move in orbits lying between those of Mars and Jupiter, but some move outside this range, and a few come quite close to the Earth.

It turns out that those which come close to the Earth provide the best opportunity for determining the scale of the Solar System. For this purpose the asteroids have one great advantage over the planets. Because of their small size they appear as mere points of light, so that there is no possible ambiguity in the lining up of the telescopes of the several observers. In modern times, by observation of the asteroids, the distance of the Sun has been determined to an accuracy of somewhat better than 0.1 per cent.

By comparing the scale of the Earth's orbit around the Sun with the scale of the Moon's orbit around the Earth it is possible, by relying on Newton's law of universal gravitation, to estimate without difficulty the ratio of the mass of the Sun to the mass of the Earth. It turns out that the mass of the Sun is about one-third of a million times greater than that of the Earth. Suppose we wish to go further, and compare the mass of the Sun with that of a chunk of material of a size that can be handled in a laboratory. Before we can make such a comparison, we must be able to measure the gravitational pull, or gravitating power, of our small piece of material. Such a measurement was first made by Henry Cavendish, at the close of the eighteenth century. This made it possible to compare the gravitating power of a standard chunk of material with the gravitating power of the Sun; and since gravitating power is directly proportional to mass, we can also compare the mass of the Sun with the mass of some standard

It is said that Frederick the Great thought everything of importance had already been discovered in science. In view of the great advances of the post-Newtonian era, few astronomers of the time would have disagreed. It thus came as a bombshell when William Herschel (left) discovered a new planet. A detail from Herschel's portrait (right) is a reminder of his wish to name his discovery after his patron, George III. His notes for March 1781 show that he at first thought he had found a "curious Nebulous star or perhaps a Comet."

piece of material, say a piece weighing one kilogram. In this way it was established that the Sun's mass is close to two million million million million million kilograms.

We can determine the mass of a planet by a similar method to that just described, provided it has at least one satellite. That is, if we know the size and the shape of the satellite's orbit and the time it takes to move around that orbit, we can calculate the mass of the planet from Newton's theory of gravitation. Two of the three items of information we need, namely the shape of the orbit and the time the satellite takes to move around it, can be determined by direct observation. But in order to determine the absolute size of the orbit we must also know the distance of the planet from the Earth. And this, again, demands a knowledge of the absolute scale of the Solar System. It follows therefore, that not only the determination of the mass of the Sun, but also the determinations of the masses of all the planets with satellites, depend on the fixing of the absolute scale of the Solar System.

With this absolute scale firmly established, astronomers were able to calculate the masses of the five planets with satellites. Jupiter has a mass nearly 320 times greater than that of the Earth, Saturn some 95 times greater, Uranus nearly 15 times greater, and Neptune a little above 17 times greater; in contrast with these large planets Mars has a mass equal to about 11 per cent of that of the Earth. The following table gives the information that can be obtained by combining direct observation of the planets with the determination of the absolute scale of the Solar System.

Name	Mass (Earth = 1)
Mars	0.11
Jupiter	318.35
Saturn	95.30
Uranus	14.58
Neptune	17.26

More than once in the above discussion we have referred to the fine details of the Solar System. What are these fine details? In earlier chapters we have thought of the orbits of planets as being determined solely by the gravitational field of the Sun. We saw that these orbits are ellipses and that the Sun lies at one of the foci. But the planets do not, in fact, move in the *isolated* gravitational field of the Sun. They are also subjected to the gravitational influences of the other planets. It is true that the mass of the Sun is so great compared with that of all the planets that the gravitational field of the Sun does dominate the motions of the planets, and it is true that their orbits are very nearly true ellipses. Yet they are not exactly so. In fact, after a circuit of the Sun the orbit does not exactly close up on itself.

The problem of determining planetary orbits with great precision is evidently one of surpassing difficulty, for all the planets are moving all the time, and they are moving in different ways, so that their

The Georgian Planet with its Satellites.

Tuesday March 13

*Pollux is follow'd by 3 small stars at abt 2'
and 3'. distance.*

as usual. ♂ ♄

*in the quartile near ζ Tauri the lowest of two is a
curious either Nebulous star or perhaps a Comet.*

*preceding the star that precedes ν Geminorum double
about 30".*

a small star follows the Comet at ⅔ of the field's

combined gravitational field is constantly altering and never exactly reproduces itself. The perturbations of the orbits produced by these small complicated effects belong to the fine details of the Solar System. Evidently, if these fine details can be worked out mathematically, and can be shown to agree with observation, we shall have a subtle and far-reaching confirmation of Newton's theory of gravitation. This was the great problem of celestial mechanics to which mathematicians of the latter half of the eighteenth century and the first half of the nineteenth century directed their attention. The name of Euler has already been mentioned. To it must be added the names of two great French mathematicians, Lagrange and Laplace. Very largely as an outcome of the work of these men, the problem was brilliantly solved. Observation showed that in fact the planets do not move strictly along elliptical paths. They follow more complicated paths which can be logically inferred from Newton's law of gravitation.

It is here that we should note a crucial difference between the outlook of modern science and the geometrical thinking of classical times. Plato thought that all motion must be made up of circles and straight lines, because these geometrical forms have a natural simplicity and elegance. The Ptolemaic and even the Copernican descriptions of planetary motions were entirely in terms of circles. Even to Kepler it was a shock to find curves as complicated as ellipses turning up in the analyses of his observational material. And now, when we consider the fine details of planetary motions, all semblance of simplicity and elegance is gone. Yet so far from being disturbed by the increased complication, scientists of the eighteenth and nineteenth centuries were delighted to find the complexities of their calculations reflected in nature.

In modern science we have no thought that the motion of matter should be simple and elegant, but what we do hope for and expect is that it should obey simple and elegant laws. It was therefore a tremendous satisfaction to find that the many complexities of planetary orbits could all be explained in terms of a very simple law of gravitation, namely the inverse square law, discussed in Chapter 5.

In the above table of planetary masses no value was given for the mass of Mercury or of Venus. Neither of these planets has a satellite, so that the simple method of determining mass described above cannot be applied. It must be determined instead by analysing the gravitational effects which these planets exercise on each other, or on the Earth. For example, Venus produces slight perturbations in the orbit of Mercury, the amount of the perturbations being, of course, dependent on the mass of Venus. If, now, we observe very accurately the orbit of Mercury or of the Earth, and if we make full allowance for the effects produced by all the planets of known mass, such as Jupiter and Saturn, then the perturbations that still remain can be attributed to Venus. Hence, the mass of Venus itself can be determined. From such calculations

Above: Herschel's house at Datchet, near Windsor, and the telescope he used for many of his explorative sweeps of the heavens during the early 1780s. This twenty-feet-long reflector had a twelve-inch aperture.
Right: Extracts from the journal of Caroline Herschel, outlining how she and her brother worked at this time.

28
1782

my Journal N°.1, I see that I began Aug.ᵗ 22, 1782 to write Down and describe all remarkable appearances I saw in my Sweeps (which were horizontal.) But it was not till the last two months of the same year before I felt the least encouragement for spending the starlight nights on a grass-plot covered by dew or hoar frost without a human being near enough to be within call; for I knew too little of the real heavens to be able to point out every object for finding it again without losing too much time by consulting the Atlas. But all these troubles were removed when I knew my Brother to be at no great distance making observations with his various Instruments on D. Stars, planets &c. and could have his assistance immediately when I found a Nebula or cluster of Stars, of which I intended to give a Catalogue (but at the end of 1783 I had only 14. when my Sweeping was interrupted by being employed with writing down my Brothers observations with the large 20 feet.)

I had besides the comfort to see that my Brother was satisfied with my endeavours in assisting him when he wanted another person, either to run to the Clocks.

it has been established that the mass of Venus is about 82 per cent of that of the Earth, and the mass of Mercury about 5 per cent.

The Moon has a mass about one-eightieth as great as the Earth's. This is determined from the manner and extent to which the Moon influences the Earth's motion. We have already considered one such important influence, namely the fluctuations produced in the rate of precession of the Earth's axis of rotation. Only in one other case can a similar method be used to determine the mass of a satellite—the case of Neptune. In all other instances the satellite masses are so small in comparison with the masses of the parent planets that any such influences are not readily observable. Here, perturbation methods must be used. This is possible in the case of Jupiter and Saturn, because both these planets possess many satellites. The method is to study the gravitational influence of one satellite on the orbits of the others, and the calculations involved are among the most difficult in the theory of gravitation. But not even this method will determine all the satellite masses, for some of the satellites are too tiny to produce any appreciable perturbation effects. An interesting feature of this work is that there are only six other satellites in the whole Solar System at all comparable with the Moon in mass. Jupiter has four of the six—the four which Galileo discovered. Saturn has one and Neptune one.

Two of the planets which figure in our table of planetary masses, Uranus and Neptune, were not known at all in Newton's time. The story of their discovery is one of the great highlights of the post-Newtonian era.

Frederick the Great is said to have remarked that everything of real importance had already been discovered in science, and toward the end of the eighteenth century this did indeed seem to be so. The law of gravitation had been discovered. Men had learned how to calculate the intricate motions of planets and their satellites. Their calculations were found to agree with the ways of nature herself. So it is little wonder that the discovery of a new planet in the year 1781 burst like a bombshell on a complacent scientific world.

The discoverer was William Herschel, music master at Bath. His life there was a busy one, playing the organ for the main church services, giving recitals, and conducting oratorios with what at that time was a huge orchestra and chorus. At night he read books on mathematics and astronomy, and observed the heavens, at first using only a small telescope which he bought. Soon, however, he was building the first of a series of telescopes that was to culminate in the great 48-inch reflector, an enormous aperture by the standards of the eighteenth century. Herschel's penchant for doing things in a big way showed both in the size of his orchestras and in the size of his telescopes.

writing down a memorandum fetching and carring instruments, or measuring the ground with poles &c. &c. of which something of the kind every moment would occur. For, the eagerness with which the measurments on the diameter of the G. Sidus, and observations of other Planets. D. Stars &c. &c. were made was incredible which may be seen by the various papers that were given to the Royl. Soc. in 1783. Which papers were written in the day time or when cloudy nights interfered, besides this the 12 inch speculum was perfected before the spring, and many hours were spent at the turning bench, as not a night clear enough for observing ever passed but that some improvements were planed for perfecting the mounting and motions of the various instruments then in use, and some trials of new constructed eye-pieces to be made which mostly all were to be made by my Brothers own hands. Though wishing to save his time he began to have some work of that kind executed by a watchmaker who had retired from business (and lived on Datshed common) but the work was so bad and the charges so unreasonable that he could not be employed. And it was not till some time after that

1783

29

The discovery of Uranus did not demand a particularly large telescope, however. Herschel's achievement was due less to his instruments than to his method of working and his attitude of mind. Whereas other astronomers pointed their telescopes at known and predetermined objects, usually with the view to measuring their positions, Herschel was an explorer. He searched the heavens systematically for whatever he could find there. He surveyed all objects without preconceived preferences. The main theme of his astronomical life was to survey the skies with bigger and still bigger telescopes; and it is a fitting coincidence that the most detailed modern survey of the sky was made with an instrument of an aperture identical to that of the largest of Herschel's telescopes, namely the 48-inch Schmidt telescope on Palomar Mountain.

On March 13, 1781, while he was sweeping the heavens with a 7-inch reflector, Herschel came across an unusual object. It was certainly not a star, for it presented a definite disk-like appearance. Never dreaming it to be a new planet, Herschel thought that he had found some new, strange form of comet. Its planetary nature was, in fact, demonstrated by Lexell, at St. Petersburg, about a year later, when he found by calculation that the new object lies beyond Saturn and that it moves in an almost circular orbit around the Sun. Herschel was immediately honored by the Royal Society of London. The King became his patron, granting a pension which enabled Herschel to devote himself to astronomy. In return for this munificence Herschel named the new planet Georgium Sidus, a name that naturally found no favor with astronomers the world over, who preferred the name Uranus, suggested by Bode.

That Herschel's success arose out of his method of working is made clear by the fact that other astronomers had observed Uranus on a number of occasions without noticing its exceptional character. Several such observations had been made by the French astronomer, Lemonnier. These former observations were of great value in calculating the orbit of the new planet, from which it was possible to predict its future positions. Various tables giving these future positions were soon drawn up, notably by an Italian astronomer, Barnabas Oriani. So by the end of the eighteenth century the situation was that a new planet had been discovered, its orbit was known, and the path along which it was expected to move had been calculated.

But during the second quarter of the nineteenth century suspicion gradually hardened to certainty that Uranus was not moving along its assigned path. Admittedly the deviations were small, but they were well outside the range that might be accounted for by errors in carefully-made calculations. The deviation of Uranus from its expected position amounted, in fact, to about twenty seconds of arc.

What was the cause of these perturbations? Perhaps Uranus was not the outermost planet of the Solar System. Perhaps there was some still more distant planet whose gravitational effect on the orbit of Uranus was producing the observed discrepancies. The discovery of Uranus itself had opened men's minds to the possibility that the confines of the Solar System had not yet been reached, and such speculation was therefore natural. But only two mathematicians tackled the following problem which such speculation posed. Given the deflections in the orbit of Uranus, find purely by theoretical calculation the mass and the position of the hypothetical new planet; then, from the deduced theoretical position, actually discover the planet with a telescope.

The two men concerned were John Couch Adams, a young graduate of St. John's College, Cambridge, and a French astronomer, Urbain Jean Leverrier. Adams was the first to start his calculations and the first to finish. He communicated his results to the British astronomical authorities, notably to Sir George Airy, the Astronomer Royal, and to the Reverend J. Challis, the director of the Cambridge Observatory. These men were sceptical

Memoranda.
1841. July 3. Formed a design, in the beginning of this week, of investigating, as soon as possible after taking my degree, the irregularities in the motion of Uranus, wh. are yet unaccounted for; in order to find whether they may be attributed to the action of an undiscovered planet beyond it; and if possible thence to determine the elements of its orbit, &c. approximately, wh. wd. probably lead to its discovery.

of the value and accuracy of Adams's work, and were consequently slow and dilatory in their search for the new planet.

Leverrier managed things with much greater efficiency. Whereas Adams took some five years over his calculations, Leverrier completed his in two. He then sent them to J. G. Galle of the Berlin Observatory. Galle picked up the new planet almost immediately, on September 23, 1846, and instantly sent news of his discovery to Leverrier. Galle suggested the name Janus for the new planet, but Leverrier preferred to call it Neptune, and its discovery, under that name, was announced in Paris without delay.

Only after that announcement was the work of Adams made known to the scientific world. To the French, the claims made for Adams smacked strongly of plagiarism. Why had there been no mention of the work in any reputable scientific journal? Even a letter in the press would have been sufficient to establish the genuineness of Adams's claims, or rather of the claims made by his supporters, notably by Sir John Herschel, son of the discoverer of Uranus. For Adams himself took no part in the discussions that followed.

Much has been written about this unhappy affair. The blame, if blame there be, is not easy to place, for a strange compound of human values and scientific values were involved. There were elements of strong conservatism and even of conceit in the attitudes of Airy and of Challis; Adams himself was reticent to a fault; and the opinion of Airy and of many other astronomers that the problem itself was mathematically insoluble, was

very nearly true. If the incident had occurred 75 years earlier, or 75 years later, the problem would indeed have been insoluble. By a great stroke of luck Neptune then happened to be in the one part of its orbit that permitted of a solution of the problem; otherwise the efforts of both Adams and Leverrier would have been doomed to failure.

Both men in fact made a very doubtful assumption throughout their calculations. They assumed that Neptune obeyed an empirical rule known as Bode's Law. The rule is expressed by the following simple formula. For each planet first write a four, then add a number that varies from planet to planet: for Mercury, the innermost planet, the number is zero; for Venus, next nearest to the Sun, it is three. After Venus the number is simply doubled each time. For the Earth it is six, for Mars twelve, and so on. The numbers obtained in this way run in the series, 4, 7, 10, 16, 28, 52, 100, 196 and 388. If the actual mean radii of the planetary orbits are measured by a scale on which ten units represent the radius of the Earth's orbit, then the planetary orbits run in the sequence 3.9, 7.2, 10, 15.2, and so on. These figures lie strikingly close to the series suggested by Bode's Law.

Nowadays, astronomers are divided in their opinions as to whether this near-agreement is a mere coincidence or whether it has some deeper physical significance. The sceptics point out that given any limited sequence of numbers it is always possible to find some rule that fits the sequence tolerably well. But in the time of Adams and Leverrier nobody doubted the significance of Bode's Law. Indeed, there were two apparently

	Mercury	Venus	Earth	Mars	*Ceres*	Jupiter	Saturn	Uranus	*Neptune*
	4	4	4	4	4	4	4	4	4
	0	3	6	12	24	48	96	192	384
Law	4	7	10	16	28	52	100	196	388
Observation	3.9	7.2	10.0	15.2	27.7	52.0	95.4	191.9	300.7

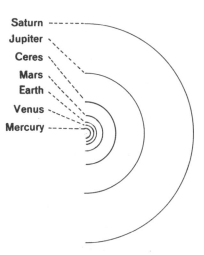

The memorandum opposite states that it was the unexpected perturbations in the orbit of Uranus that spurred Adams to seek another planet. The third horizontal row of figures in our table shows the comparative orbits of planets as expected from Bode's Law. The bottom row of figures shows the comparative orbits as established by actual observation (and as depicted in the diagram). When it was first suspected that yet another planet might lie beyond Uranus, scientists expected its orbit to be nearly as Bode's Law suggests. In fact it proved much smaller.

George III granted a total of £4,000 toward the cost of building this 48-inch reflector—the largest of Herschel's telescopes. The king took pleasure in taking people through the instrument. To the Archbishop of Canterbury he said " Come, my Lord Bishop, and I will show you the way to Heaven." Herschel employed the instrument in surveying the sky in greater detail, and in reaching out to a study of the Milky Way.

On the right is a modern photograph of the North America Nebula in Cygnus, showing certain dark regions which appear to be almost starless. Herschel noticed that the Milky Way in the region between Scorpio and Cygnus appears to be split into two branches. This arises because many of the stars are hidden from us by a comparatively close cloud of dust. But to Herschel the gap seemed like a window opening on distant space.

very good reasons for accepting its validity. When the German astronomer Johann Elert Bode first proposed this law, in 1772, the planet Uranus was unknown. Nine years later, when it was discovered, it turned out to fit surprisingly well into the place beyond Saturn which Bode's figures would assign to it. The predicted size of the orbit was 196 units, whereas observations gave a figure of 191.9 units. Perhaps even more telling was the entry in the table between Mars and Jupiter. In Bode's time there appeared to be a genuine gap in the table, for no planet was then known to lie in this position. But in 1801 the observational discovery by Piazzi of the minor planet Ceres filled the gap almost to perfection, for the orbit of Ceres turned out to be 27.7 of our units, compared with Bode's hypothetical 28 units.

To both Adams and Leverrier it therefore seemed entirely natural to assume that their new planet would also obey Bode's Law. In fact the orbit of Neptune has a value of 300.7 units, very markedly less than the 388 which Bode's Law would lead one to expect.

By a lucky chance this error did not affect the positions of Neptune calculated by Adams and Leverrier for the particular year 1846. But their calculations of its orbit and future positions turned out to be entirely wrong. In a recent very interesting paper, R. A. Lyttleton has pointed out that if, instead of relying on Bode's Law, Adams and Leverrier had assumed that the orbit of Neptune was circular, their calculations could have been carried through far more simply and with a far greater degree of accuracy.

Subsequent to the Neptune incident, Adams and Leverrier were again involved in controversy over fine details in the orbit of the Moon. This time the main body of French scientists supported Adams, who indeed turned out to be right.

The controversy was in effect only one stage of a much greater debate which began in the time of Newton and continued into our own century. First Newton's discussion of the motion of the Moon led Edmund Halley to suspect that the period of revolution of the Moon around the Earth had changed since Babylonian times. The suspicion arose that Newton's law of gravitation might not be precisely correct, since it offered no explanation of any such change. The second stage of the debate is associated with the name of Laplace, who reworked the problem in greater detail. In fact, Laplace's calculations closed the gap between theory and observation, indicating that the law of gravitation was not at fault.

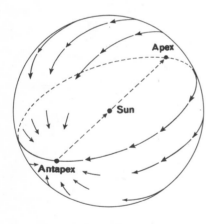

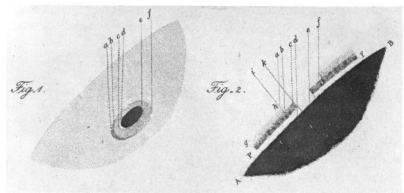

Maskelyne and Lalande measured the apparent motion of the stars which arises because of the real motion of the Solar System through space. Using those measurements, Herschel was able to infer the direction of this motion with surprising accuracy. In the diagram the Sun's motion is toward the Apex. The stars thus appear to move to the Antapex.

By contrast, Herschel's views about the Sun were very naïve. In this diagram he showed the main bulk of the Sun (AB) as solid rock, which was surrounded by an outer envelope of fire (PF). He thought of a sunspot (de) as a hole in the fiery envelope through which the possibly inhabited rocky interior could be seen.

Adams came on the scene in 1853, when he published a paper claiming that Laplace's discussion of the problem was incomplete, and that a careful re-examination resuscitated the disagreement between observation and theory. The following remarks by Delaunay in 1864 comment on the resulting Leverrier-Adams controversy. "The publication of Adams's paper truly marks a memorable step forward, an entire revolution in this branch of theoretical astronomy. His result has therefore been strongly attacked . . . But of all the arguments put forward against Adams's paper not a single one was right, and the insistence with which they were presented and maintained produced an entirely opposite effect to what was intended." Delaunay concludes by saying that Adams's analysis, which was declared fallacious and incorrect, had been recognized as exact.

The last stage of the story came in our own century, when it was first realized, notably as a result of the work of Sir Geoffrey Taylor, that the difficulty arose out of the neglect of the frictional effects of the lunar tides. At first it was thought that the oceanic tides, as they impinge on the continents of the Earth, constitute the whole effect. Now, however, it is known that tidal effects produced not merely on the waters of the oceans but also on the interior material of the Earth play an important role in the resolution of this old discrepancy.

By the middle of the nineteenth century the great surge of scientific development which Newton initiated had largely expended itself, but the ingredients of a new revolution in astronomy had already come into being. These ingredients were of three distinct kinds, and to a scientist of the nineteenth century it would have seemed highly unlikely that they could usefully be brought together. First, there was a reaching out from the Solar System, to be described in the last section of the present chapter; second, there were remarkable discoveries in the field of electricity and magnetism, which will be discussed in some detail in Chapter 7; third, there was further work on fine details of planetary motion, which we may well look at now.

We have already noticed that since Venus has no satellite, the only practicable way to determine its mass is to observe the effects which it produces in the orbits of the Earth, of Mars and of Mercury. Nineteenth-century astronomers were faced by the disconcerting fact that the mass of Venus inferred from the perturbations of the orbits of Mars and the Earth is not quite the same as the value inferred from the perturbation of the orbit of Mercury. Because the values derived from Mars and the Earth are in sensible agreement, it is reasonable to regard these estimates as essentially correct and to face up to the strange circumstance that the value inferred from the orbit of Mercury is wrong for some reason. This means that after the gravitational effects of all the planets on the orbit of Mercury have been allowed for (accepting the mass of Venus given by the effect of Venus on the Earth and Mars) there still remains an unexplained perturbation in the orbit of Mercury. Leverrier thought that this remaining perturbation arose from a still-undiscovered planet situated within the orbit of Mercury. Strenuous efforts to detect such a planet failed. Toward the end of the nineteenth century, a thorough discussion of the whole problem by the American astronomer, Simon Newcomb, demonstrated that the discrepancy is undoubtedly real. It remained unexplained until Einstein's general theory of relativity showed that indeed Newton's law of gravitation is not strictly correct. Thus, arising out of the fine details of the Solar System, came a decisive confirmation of a new theory which drastically changed our outlook concerning space and time, and which today enables us to grapple with the complexities of the largest features of the universe.

Reaching Out from the Solar System

Herschel's main object in constructing larger and larger telescopes was to survey the sky in ever greater detail. He counted the stars in different areas of the sky, demonstrating quantitatively that they are concentrated toward a plane, namely the plane of the Milky Way.

Of particular interest were the clusters of stars and the nebulae. The nebulae are amorphous masses of light. Herschel first thought them to be star clusters at such great distances that their individual stellar components could not be resolved in his telescope. Later he abandoned this idea, when it became clear that nebulae and star clusters show a marked difference in distribution. Whereas star clusters are concentrated toward the Milky Way, Herschel's counts of nebulae in different parts of the sky indicated that nebulae tend to avoid the Milky Way. Moreover, he found that certain of the nebulae are clearly associated with a definite

Pleiades

North Celestial Pole
(Pole Star)

Galaxy in Andromeda

Vega

Ophiuchus
(Asras Alhague)

Ar

Panoramic photographic map of the
Milky Way, built up from a large
number of separate photographs.
Dark gaps of the kind that Herschel
regarded as windows on space are
common, particularly in the region
of the plane of the Milky Way.
The co-ordinates used on the map
are galactic latitude and longitude
(those of Case (4) in Chapter 1.)

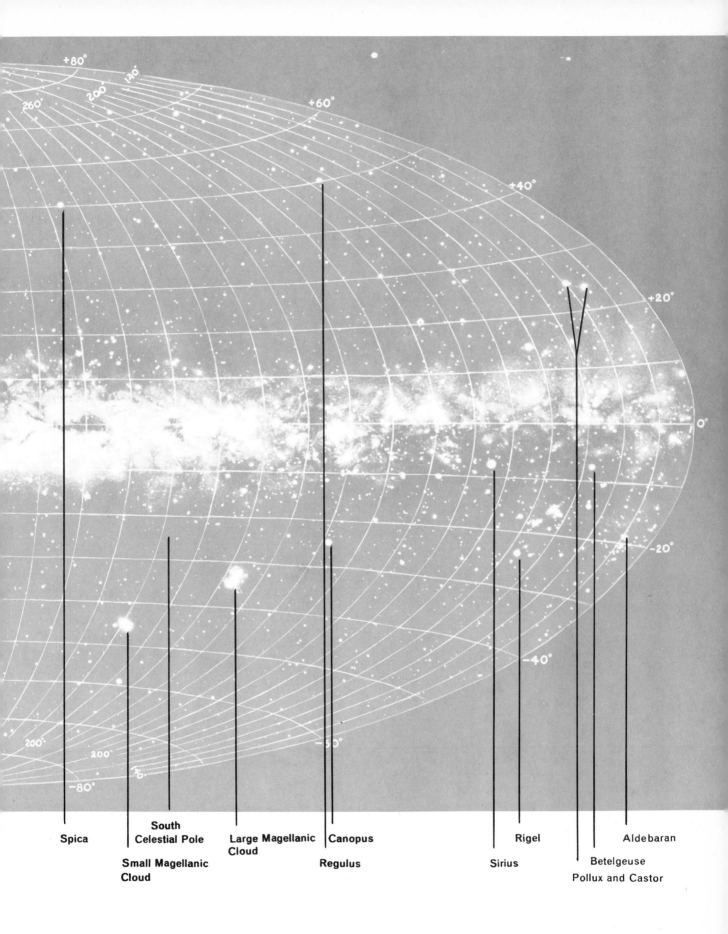

Spica

South
Celestial Pole

Small Magellanic
Cloud

Large Magellanic
Cloud

Canopus

Regulus

Sirius

Rigel

Pollux and Castor

Betelgeuse

Aldebaran

central star. This suggested that the nebulae were not stars at all, but consisted of a bright fluid immersed in the spaces between stars. If this were so, there was no need to think of them as being particularly far away after all.

We now know that both these ideas about the nature of nebulae were partially correct. Some of them are indeed bright clouds of gas situated not very far away from us. Others, on the other hand, are large groups of very distant stars.

A most remarkable prophecy concerning the nature of these distant groups was made by J. H. Lambert, a mathematician especially interested in light, toward the middle of the eighteenth century. Lambert presented a surprisingly penetrating qualitative picture of the structure of the universe. He suggested that the stars of the Milky Way constitute one large cluster and that these stars are in motion around a common center, so that the Sun and the planets together move around a center just as the planets themselves move around the Sun. Lambert went on to suggest that the nebulae are similar huge aggregations of stars lying far outside the confines of the Milky Way.

For very many of the nebulae this is a correct picture, but it is one that most professional

astronomers refused to accept until the second or even the third decade of the twentieth century. The grounds for scepticism arose from Herschel's observation that for the most part the nebulae avoid the plane of the Milky Way. Why should this be so if they lie far outside the Milky Way?

The answer is that clouds of fine dust particles are concentrated near the plane of the Milky Way, and these clouds act as a fog, obscuring all distant objects lying directly beyond them. Herschel had noticed that the Milky Way in the region between the constellations of Scorpio and Cygnus appears to be split into two branches. This split is not genuine; it arises from a comparatively close cloud of dust which obscures many of the stars that lie beyond. But to Herschel the gap appeared as a genuine hole in the Milky Way, and he believed that he was looking out through a window into distant space.

Looking back we can see that such mistakes and uncertainties arose from a lack of physical knowledge. In the year 1800 men had an accurate and precise knowledge of the phenomenon of gravitation, but their ideas concerning certain other branches of physics were entirely rudimentary. We can see a remarkable contrast between sophistication and naïveté in two other aspects of Herschel's work. Tobias Mayer had already pointed out that if the Sun is in motion there must be a systematic *apparent* motion of the stars in the sky: stars lying in the same direction as the Sun's motion must appear to be slowly moving apart from each other, whereas those lying in the opposite direction must appear to be slowly converging. The expected motion from year to year was, of course, very small, but Mayer thought that it might just be measurable. Measurements were in fact made by Maskelyne and Lalande, and using these measurements Herschel was able to infer the direction of the Sun's motion with surprising accuracy. At the opposite extreme, however, Herschel held beliefs about the Sun that now seem to be wildly fantastic

Because of the Earth's annual motion around the Sun, the nearby stars appear to execute a small annual oscillation against the fixed background of distant stars. If we can isolate and measure this oscillation we can calculate the distance of a nearby star. In 1838 Friedrich Wilhelm Bessel became the first man to make such a calculation.

nonsense. He thought that the inside of the Sun was cold, and that the sunspots were places where an outer fiery envelope was pulled away enabling us to see deep into a dark rocky interior. Most ludicrous of all, he believed the cooler regions to be inhabited by living creatures.

One thing at least was certain once astronomers began to study the stars in bulk. It was vitally necessary to construct a catalog accurately describing the positions of vast numbers of stars, otherwise it was impossible for two astronomers to know when they were speaking about the same one. In his pioneering work, Flamsteed had measured the positions of almost 3,000. Friedrich Argelander now undertook a far more ambitious task. In his famous *Bonner Durchmusterung*, published between 1852 and 1862, he catalogued over 300,000 stars of the northern hemisphere, and this work forms the basis of the catalogs still used by modern astronomers. The magnitude of Argelander's achievement is increased by the fact that it was carried through without the aid of photography.

The idea of making a photographic map of the sky was first proposed by David Gill, in 1886. The project took about half a century of continuous work and was completed with the aid of a large number of observatories scattered over the whole Earth. The result was a celestial map containing about 100 million stars, accompanied by an actual catalog of the six million brightest ones.

One of Herschel's greatest achievements was that in reaching farther out into space he demonstrated that Newton's law of gravitation operates outside the Solar System. He found far more cases where a pair of stars lie close together on the sky than could reasonably be explained on the ground of mere coincidence. This suggested that many such pairs must consist of stars genuinely associated with each other, in which case one would expect that the two components of a pair would move in orbits around each other, in much the way that the Earth moves around the Sun.

Herschel set himself the task of discovering whether or not such a motion actually takes place. To do this it is necessary to observe whether the positions of the two stars change from year to year in relation to the background formed by more distant stars. Castor, the brightest star in the constellation of Gemini, resolves in even a small telescope into two moderately bright stars. By comparing his observations of these two stars with the observations previously made by Bradley, Herschel was able to show that the two stars do indeed move around each other in orbits of the expected character. The time required for a complete circuit of the orbits could be calculated, and Herschel's value of 342 years is not very much different from the modern value.

About a quarter of a century later, the systematic study of double stars, as they were called, was initated by Friedrich Wilhelm Struve, the founder of the great Pulkovo Observatory near Leningrad. As an outcome of this work it was firmly established that the law of gravitation operating inside our own Solar System is indeed a universal law. It also became clear that so far from being rarities, double stars, and indeed systems containing more than two stars, are quite common.

The post-Newtonian reaching-out into space raised in an acute form a crucial problem that had plagued astronomers for over two thousand years: how far away are the stars? Among other reasons, the Greek astronomer Hipparchus rejected the heliocentric ideas of Aristarchus of Samos on the grounds that if the Earth moved around the Sun there should be an annual variation in the positions of the stars. He argued that since no such variation was detectable Aristarchus was wrong. With the revival of Aristarchus's ideas by Copernicus, the belief grew that such a variation must, indeed, exist but that it is not easy to observe because the stars are very far away from us. With the development of more and more accurate instruments, astronomers were always hoping that the stage had been reached where the annual variation could be detected. If one could only measure this variation for a star, the distance of that star could readily be calculated.

Much of the work of the second half of the eighteenth century was motivated by the hope that this parallax effect, as it was called, might at last prove measurable. The work of James Bradley was initially started in this hope. It was while he was trying to measure the parallax effect that he discovered the important effects of nutation and aberration, for until these effects had been discovered the harder parallax problem could scarcely have been tackled with much hope of success.

The problem can be formulated as follows. Sufficiently distant objects can be regarded as presenting a virtually unchanging background. Against this background a comparatively nearby star will appear to move, and this for three reasons. First, because the Sun itself is moving; next, because the star in question is moving; and last, because of the Earth's motion around the Sun. If the third of these effects can be disentangled from the other two, then the distance of the star can easily be determined by trigonometrical calculation.

To make such a separation we notice that the first two effects are systematic, that is to say, they cause the star to drift along a fixed course with respect to the distant background. The motion of the Earth, on the other hand, causes the position of the star to execute an annual oscillation. So we have an oscillation superposed on a steady drift, and our problem is to separate out the oscillation. In modern times we should simply take photographs of the star against its background at different times during the year. The photographs could then be measured at leisure and the oscillatory motion separated out.

But before the advent of photography all measurements had of necessity to be made at the telescope. Because the measurements were delicate, they could not be made quickly. This meant that the telescope had to be turned so as to compensate very precisely for the rotation of the Earth, otherwise the star and its background would simply drift out of the field of the telescope. Hence the first requirement was for a smooth, accurate drive of the telescope. Next it was necessary to measure the angles between the star in question and a number of fixed points in the background. This demanded mounting illuminated threads in the focal plane of the telescope, and these threads had to be movable with the aid of a micrometer thread. All this was very difficult, and was not done successfully until nearly the middle of the nineteenth century.

Stellar distances were first measured with the aid of an ingenious instrument known as the heliometer, so-called because it was originally designed in relation to problems concerning the Sun. A heliometer is a refracting telescope with a split objective. It is possible to move the two halves of the object lens as shown in Figure 6.11. This motion causes a double image to appear in the focal plane, one being produced by the upper half of the objective, and the other by the lower half. That is, each star produces

a double image separated by a distance depending on the extent to which the two halves of the objective have been moved. Suppose, now, that we wish to measure the angle between a certain definite star and some fixed reference point in the background. By changing from position (i) to position (ii) we split the image of our star into two distinct separated points of light; and by setting the two halves of the objective appropriately, we can arrange that our two images are separated by exactly the same distance as are the star and the reference point. It can then easily be shown that our required angle is simply the distance of separation of the two halves of the objective divided by the focal length of the telescope we use.

With the aid of this device the German astronomer Friedrich Wilhelm Bessel obtained the first measured stellar distance in the year 1838. The star was 61 Cygni, and its distance turned out to be about 11 light-years, or the distance which light travels in about 11 years, namely some 66 million, million miles. The following year Thomas Henderson at the Cape Observatory obtained the distance of one of the brightest stars of the southern hemisphere. It was the brightest star in the constellation of Centaurus. Its distance was less than that of Bessel's star, namely about 4 light-years. Almost immediately after that, Struve, at the Pulkovo Observatory, measured the distance of the star Vega.

In the years that followed, astronomers measured the distances of a number of other stars by the parallax method. But the method can be applied only to comparatively nearby stars. Quite new techniques had to be discovered before vastly greater distances could be determined.

Having served its purpose, the heliometer quickly became obsolete. Soon telescopes could be accurately driven; soon photography was to become available; soon, indeed, astronomy was to enter the modern era, when the scale of the Milky Way itself would be determined. But in order to understand the instruments used in modern astronomy it is necessary that we should first look at what scientists learned about the nature of light from the Newtonian age onward, and how their ever-growing knowledge of the subject has been applied.

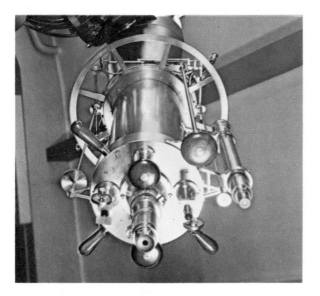

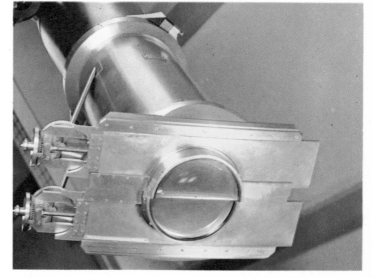

The instrument first used to measure star distances was the heliometer. On the left is a general view of the heliometer installed at the Oxford Observatory in 1848. To the right are close-ups of the eyepiece and the split objective.

Figure 6.11
How the split objective is used to produce two images of the same star.

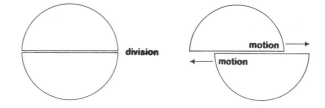

Chapter 7   Instruments and the Nature of Light

The somewhat surprising fact is that the design of several important optical instruments, including the camera, the telescope and the microscope, calls for very little knowledge of the nature of light. Provided one is conversant with the laws of reflection and refraction, it is sufficient to think of light as a collection of fast-moving bullets that travel in straight lines. This is, in fact, how Newton pictured light, but both he and others who accepted this picture recognized that it posed several awkward problems.

Take first the laws of reflection and refraction. In Figure 7.1 we see a ray of light incident on the surface of a block of glass. Two things happen: some of the light is reflected back into the air, but some also continues into the block of glass, so we have a reflected ray and a transmitted ray. How can we explain this simple experimental result on the basis of the Newtonian picture? We can say that the incident ray is a collection of bullets which move through the air and strike the glass interface, whereupon some bounce back into the air along the direction of the reflected ray while others enter the glass and move along the direction of the transmitted ray. But now we are faced with

a far more perplexing question. What decides whether a particular bullet is going to be reflected or transmitted?

Newton answered this conundrum in a wholly remarkable way. He suggested that the bullets worked by fits, so that a bullet would sometimes bounce back into the air while on other occasions, under identical circumstances, it would continue on into the glass. This idea that in identical circumstances a particle could sometimes do one thing and at other times something quite different was curiously prophetic of the point of view of modern quantum theory. Newton's immediate successors, however, were not to know this; and throughout the eighteenth century and into the nineteenth century they became more and more impressed by the steadily-mounting difficulties that confronted the bullet picture.

One of these difficulties arises when we consider how light travels from a distant source. All the light rays from such a source move essentially parallel to each other, as in Figure 7.2. Some of the light is made to pass through a hole AB in an otherwise opaque sheet and travel on toward a viewing screen. The light that just misses the edge

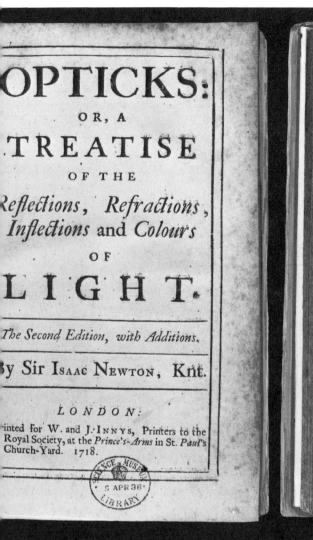

Newton was content to picture light as a collection of bullets that move in straight lines. But as we see in the definition above, he also assumed that the bullets worked by fits.

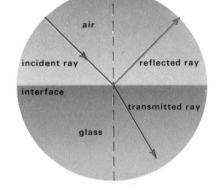

Figure 7.1
Without some such assumption it is hard to explain why some bullets of this incident ray travel on into the glass while others bounce off it.

of the hole at A reaches the screen at C, and the light which just misses the edge of the hole at B reaches the screen at D. So we see an area extending from C to D illuminated on the screen. All this can be understood very simply in terms of the Newtonian picture. We can say that the bullets which just miss striking the opaque part of the sheet at A continue to move in a straight line until they hit the screen at C, while those which just miss striking the sheet at B continue in a straight line until they hit the screen at D.

But supposing we decrease the size of the hole AB; what happens? We have already seen the answer in the diagrams on page 13. So long as the hole remains fairly big the size of the spot of light CD on the screen decreases exactly as we might expect on the basis of the Newtonian picture. But if the diameter of the hole is reduced to a small fraction of a millimeter something quite different happens. The spot of light on the screen then begins to increase again, so that we have the apparently paradoxical result that as the hole in the opaque sheet becomes still smaller, the area of light on the screen becomes larger. We might attempt to explain this by saying that somehow the light has managed to turn a corner, but this is something that our bullets are not allowed to do, for the Newtonian picture postulates that they move *consistently* in straight lines.

Bullets or Waves?

While we cannot concede to bullets the possibility of turning corners, we can do so to waves. Figure 7.3 shows a succession of waves advancing on a breakwater which has a vertical slit at the point P. As the waves reach the breakwater a disturbance goes through the slit. New waves travel outward from the point P on the far side of the breakwater, and they travel outward *radially*. That is, they have just the same sort of appearance as the ripples that are produced by dropping a stone into still water. This means that if there is a second obstacle beyond the breakwater—a wall, say—the disturbance from P will reach that obstacle over a large area and will not be simply confined to a central spot at C directly opposite to P. In other words, the waves have succeeded in turning a corner.

Thus the way in which light travels through very small apertures, coupled with what they knew about ordinary water waves, suggested to many of Newton's successors that some form of wave motion

may be associated with the nature of light, and that the bullet idea might be completely wrong. The thing to do was to put the matter to further experimental test.

Before looking at the kind of test needed, let us think a bit more about water waves. Suppose we make two vertical slits in the breakwater, at P and Q, as in Figure 7.4. Each point on the far side of the breakwater will now receive disturbances from both P and Q. What happens at a particular point depends on the timing of the waves. If the crests of the two waves arrive at the same moment there will be a particularly high wave; but if a crest of the waves from P arrives simultaneously with a trough of the waves from Q, then the crest and the trough will tend to cancel each other out and there will be little or no disturbance.

The situation is illustrated in Figure 7.5. It is assumed that P and Q are entirely similar slits in the breakwater and the point O is exactly midway between them. From O a number of radiating lines can be drawn, one of them, OC, being along the direction of the original wave motion. At any point along OC the peaks of the waves from P and Q arrive simultaneously. The troughs of the waves also arrive simultaneously. So at all points along OC there are particularly high crests and particularly low troughs. Exactly the same is true along the other heavily marked lines radiating outward from O. But lying between these lines are other lines, marked lightly. Along these, the peaks of the waves from one slit in the breakwater arrive simultaneously with the troughs of the waves from the other slit, so that there is no disturbance at all. These are the lines of still water. To complete the picture, suppose now that we have a sea wall inside the breakwater, as shown in Figure 7.6. Then, at the points A, C and E, where the heavy lines meet the sea wall, the waves will rise high and fall low; but between those points, at B and D, the water will remain still.

Experiment shows that an entirely analogous phenomenon occurs in the case of light. In fact, we can replace the original water waves to the left of Figure 7.6 by light incident from a distant source. We can also replace the breakwater by an opaque sheet in which two parallel slits are cut at the points P and Q, and we can replace the sea wall by a viewing screen. On the viewing screen we then find that we obtain a series of bright bands or fringes, as shown in Figure 7.7.

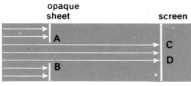
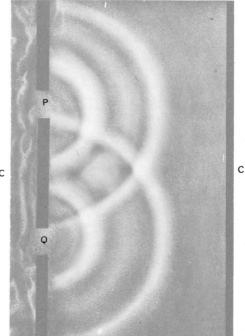
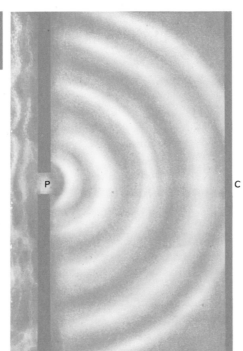

Figure 7.2 (Above)
Bullet picture explanation of how
light behaves on passing through a
small hole. But the bullet picture
cannot explain how light can turn
corners, as in diagram on page 13.

Figure 7.3 (Adjoining)
We can, however, explain how *waves*
turn a corner on passing through a
narrow slit in a breakwater.

Figure 7.4 (Extreme Right)
If there are two slits, crests will
reinforce crests in some directions,
troughs will cancel crests in others.

Figure 7.5
Along OC and the other heavy lines,
reinforcement produces high crests
and low troughs. Along lightly marked
lines, cancellation produces the
effect of almost still water.

Figure 7.6
This cross section through part of
Figure 7.5 shows that at points
A, C and E on a sea wall inside the
breakwater, waves rise high and fall
low. At B and D water is almost still.

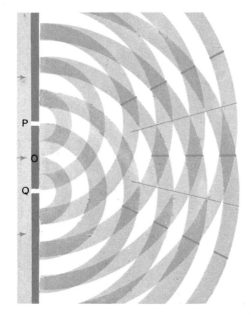

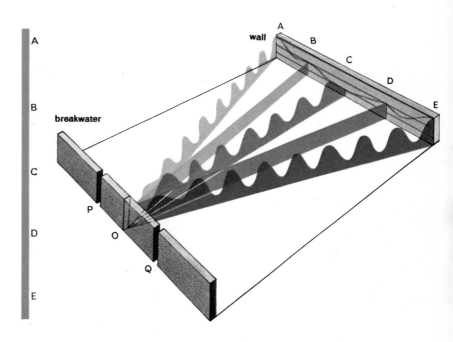

But we must be cautious in at least one respect in applying our water wave analogy. The length of the fringes in Figure 7.7 is not produced by the rise and fall of the waves. It is simply due to the size of the slits at *P* and *Q*. If these were made longer, then the fringes would be longer. It is the *brightness* on the screen which is the true analogue of the rise and fall of the water waves. Points on the viewing screen at which the waves rise and fall by a large amount appear bright; points where the waves cancel each other out—where a trough from one slit arrives simultaneously with a crest from the other—appear dark. So each point of a bright fringe is a place where the waves are rising high and falling low, while each point of a dark region is a place where the waves are interfering with each other and tending to cancel each other out.

Let us return for a moment to the behavior of water waves as shown in Figure 7.6. If the distances between the wave crests of the original waves to the left of the breakwater are changed, then the points *A*, *B*, *C*, *D*, and *E* on the sea wall will change also. The wider the spacing of the original waves, the greater will be the distance from *A* to *B* to *C*, etc. In fact, by carefully measuring the distance between the slits in the breakwater, the distance separating the sea wall from the breakwater, and the distances between the points *A* and *B*, *B* and *C*, etc., we can calculate the spacing of the original waves. In this way an observer on the sea wall can determine the distance between successive crests of the original waves without bothering to look outside the breakwater.

What is the analogue of this in the case of light, and what, especially, is the analogue of the distance between the crests of the original waves to the left of the breakwater? The answer is color. Each pure color consists of a train of waves with the same definite fixed distance from one wave crest to the next. This distance is different for different colors. For blue light it is about 1/3000 part of a millimeter, for yellow light approximately 1/2000 part of a millimeter, and for red light about 1/1600 part of a millimeter. In order to make light turn corners it is necessary for the width of the slit in the opaque sheet to be not much greater than the distance between the wave crests of the light. In fact, as we have already seen in Chapter 1, it must not be much more than 1/100 part of a millimeter. By everyday standards this would obviously be a quite extraordinarily thin slit, which explains why we are not used to seeing light turn corners.

In the case of a pure color, the fixed distance between the wave crests is called by the obvious name of *wavelength*. Ordinary white light, as we call it, is a mixture of pure colors. It consists of a whole set of different waves with different wavelengths. These different waves can easily be separated, however, by making use of a point we noticed in Chapter 2. The angle through which a ray of light is bent as it enters a glass plate depends both on the nature of the glass itself and on the color of the light. In particular, blue light is bent more than red light, as we can see from Figure 7.8. If a ray of light containing mixed colors is allowed to hit a glass prism, the various colors as they pass through the prism are refracted

Figure 7.7
If we pass light through fine slits on to a screen we also get points of reinforcement (showing bright) and of cancellation (showing dark).

Figure 7.8
The angle at which a ray of light is bent on entering a given plate of glass depends on the color of the light—that is, on its wavelength.

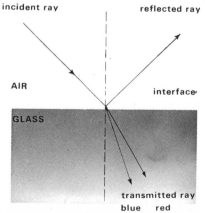

differently, and in such a way that they can be separated out as they emerge from the far side of the prism. This is shown in Figure 7.9, where by using a viewing screen the separated colors may be observed. Blue light appears at one extremity and red light at the other, the remaining colors of the spectrum lying between the two extremes. So with this simple device we can separate ordinary white light into the colors of the rainbow. Indeed, in the phenomenon of the rainbow water drops in the atmosphere perform a function similar to that of the prism in our diagram, separating the ordinary white light from the Sun into its constituent colors.

If we are interested only in separating one particular color from all the other constituent colors of white light, then a still simpler method is available. All we need do is to pass the light through a filter. For example, if we want to obtain the yellow light only, we simply pass the original white light through a piece of yellow glass. The yellow glass allows only the yellow light to pass through, and absorbs all the remaining colors.

Just as the distance between the points A and B, B and C, etc., in Figure 7.6 depends on the wavelength of the original water waves outside the breakwater, so the distance between the fringes in Figure 7.7 depends on the wavelength of the light. The longer that wavelength, the wider apart are the fringes. All this can be easily demonstrated by the simple experiment shown in Figure 7.10. The lamp L has a cylindrical source marked S. Because the lamp does not emit light of a pure color, a filter F must be used. (In practice, no filter gives completely pure color. A small dispersion of wavelengths still remains after passage through the filter, but the remaining wavelengths are sufficiently similar to each other for the purposes of our experiment.) The " breakwater," marked D, consists of an ordinary photographic plate on which slits, spaced about half a millimeter apart, have been ruled with a knife-edge. The interference fringes can be viewed directly by placing the eye immediately behind this photographic plate. Just as our observer on the sea wall could tell the wavelength of the original waves outside the breakwater from the positions of the points A, B, C, etc., in Figure 7.6, so we can here calculate the wavelength of the light by measuring the distance between adjacent fringes. By changing from a blue filter to a red one, the distance between the fringes can be changed. The fringes are more widely spaced for red light than for blue light.

What would happen if we repeated this experiment without using a filter? We should then have fringes formed for the whole range of colors emitted by the lamp; and because fringes for different colors fall in different places, the bright fringes from one color could fall in the dark gaps belonging to another color. So instead of obtaining a series of clearly defined bright bands as in Figure 7.7 we should tend to get a continuous strip of light. But the strip would evidently not be uniformly colored. The places where the blue fringes fell would tend to appear blue and the places where the red fringes fell would tend to appear red. This means that the two slits in our breakwater would have served to separate the colors present in the original light emitted by the lamp.

Figure 7.9
For this reason we can use a glass prism to separate light of mixed colors, projecting the separate colors on to a viewing screen.

Figure 7.10
In Figure 7.7 distance between bright and dark fringes depends on wavelength of light. Here filter allows only light of a certain wavelength to pass. Breakwater screen enables us to measure distance between fringes and so to calculate the wavelength.

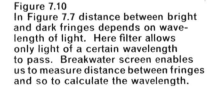

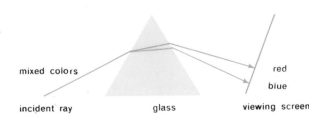

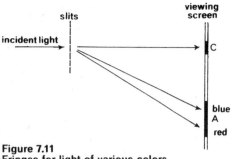

Figure 7.11
Fringes for light of various colors
fall in different places. By ruling
many fine slits close together in
the breakwater screen, we can produce narrow bright bands for each
color, adjacent to each other, without
entirely filling up the dark gaps.

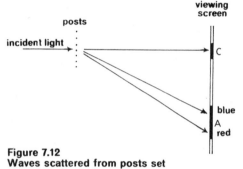

Figure 7.12
Waves scattered from posts set
close together behave like waves
passing through closely spaced slits.

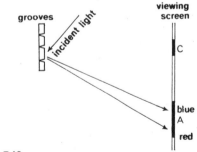

Figure 7.13
A diffraction grating is based on the
principle exemplified in Figure 7.12,
evenly spaced grooves on glass serving
as "posts". Instead of shining light
through the posts, we shine it from
the side on to the glass plate,
thus efficiently separating colors.

This result offers us a challenge. Is it possible, by
a suitable arrangement of slits in the breakwater, to
separate the different colors emitted by the lamp in
a systematic way, so that the fringes from the various
colors fall into an orderly sequence instead of overlapping with each other in a confused jumble? If we
can do so, we shall have succeeded in separating the
light into its constituent colors, just as in the case of
the prism shown in Figure 7.9. In fact, we shall
have succeeded in producing the kind of instrument
known as a diffraction grating.

Think for the moment of the fringes produced by
one particular color. If we can make the gaps between successive fringes become large compared to
the widths of the fringes themselves, then clearly it
will be much easier to lay sets of fringes from different colors side by side without running the risk of
their overlapping. Both experiment and calculation
show that there is a simple prescription for increasing the distances between successive fringes. To do
so we need only rule the two slits in our breakwater
closer together than they were before. Unfortunately,
however, this also has the effect of increasing the
width of the fringes themselves, so that there is still
a risk of overlapping.

The solution to the problem turns out to be that
we must not only cut the slits very close together,
but we must also have a very large number of slits
in our breakwater, as shown in Figure 7.11. Although
more complicated, the situation is exactly the same
in principle as it was before. Now, however, we have
waves spreading out from a whole multitude of slits.
In some directions the waves from all the slits augment each other, just as they did in the case of two
slits, and where these directions impinge on our
viewing screen we again have bright bands. In other
directions the waves interfere with each other, because crests of some arrive simultaneously with
troughs of others, and where these directions impinge
on our viewing screen we have dark bands. But it
happens that the bright bands are much narrower
than the dark spaces between them. This is just the
condition we set out to achieve. If we now take light
made up of a range of colors, instead of light of one
particular wavelength, the bright bands for the
different wavelengths can be made to fall adjacent
to each other without entirely filling up the dark
gaps. This result is more clearly observable by taking
the bright bands which fall on the outskirts of the
screen, say near *A* in Figure 7.11, rather than
those near the center, at *C*.

Color dispersion by the arrangement shown in Figure 7.11 is more complicated both to understand and to produce experimentally than the simple prism dispersion shown in Figure 7.9. It may be wondered, therefore, why the astronomer prefers to use a diffraction grating rather than a simple prism for obtaining a spectrum. The reason is that the diffraction grating does the job of separating colors far more efficiently than the prism.

Suppose we wish to separate light of two different colors. Provided they are of widely different wavelengths the job of separation is easy, but as the wavelengths become more and more similar the problem becomes increasingly difficult. Indeed, every known method of separating light fails sooner or later as the wavelengths become too close. The prism is a comparatively crude method of separation, and it fails long before the diffraction grating does. With a prism it is possible to separate two wavelengths differing from each other by about one part in 10,000; with a diffraction grating wavelengths differing by as little as one part in 100,000 can be separated. To separate wavelengths with even smaller differences—as little as one part in a million —it is necessary to use highly specialized equipment which need not here concern us.

Before we leave the subject of diffraction gratings it is worth noticing that a similar phenomenon arises if instead of a breakwater with many slits in it we utilize a series of posts, as shown in Figure 7.12. Waves are scattered by the posts and interfere with or reinforce each other in exactly the same way as we have already considered. This fact greatly assists the practical construction of a diffraction grating. The method of making one is to rule on a plane glass surface a very large number of equally spaced lines, the rulings being cut in the glass with a diamond or some other hard point. Great care must be taken to ensure that the rulings are spaced at precisely equal distances apart. They then act like the posts of Figure 7.12, but now, instead of shining the light *through* the posts, it is possible to shine it from the side on to the glass plate, as shown in Figure 7.13. The grooves in the glass plate now scatter the light waves just as they did in Figure 7.12, and the scattered waves reinforce each other in certain directions just as in Figure 7.11. By viewing the light scattered in these particular directions a spectrum is obtained; we have at our disposal the essential feature of an instrument called the *spectroscope*, which plays a vital part in modern astronomy.

Above: Early ruling engine, designed to ensure equal spacing of lines on grating. Below: 5000-lines-per-inch grating as seen under microscope. Bottom: Diffraction grating separates colors more efficiently than a prism.

The accurate ruling of diffraction gratings is a technical problem of very considerable difficulty, and the outstanding pioneer work in this field was done by H. A. Rowland, who in 1882 successfully constructed a ruling engine capable of making almost 15,000 lines per inch on the surface of speculum metal, a hard alloy of copper and tin. As we have seen, the chief requirement of a good grating is that the lines should, as nearly as possible, be equally spaced. To get such a result it is necessary that after each groove has been ruled the machine should lift the diamond point and move it forward by a fixed distance determined by a small rotation of a screw. The screw must clearly be of almost perfect construction, and it was Rowland who first achieved such near-perfection.

In modern times gratings are ruled on aluminized glass surfaces instead of on speculum metal. The presence of the aluminum causes the grooves to produce a much stronger scattering, so that far less light is lost in the process than would be lost by a grating ruled on an untreated glass surface. This is a point of great importance when very faint astronomical objects are under observation.

We may now profitably compare the wave picture of light with the Newtonian bullet picture. We have seen that the wave picture offers a reasonable explanation of how light turns corners and how a diffraction grating works—explanations which the bullet picture does not offer. On the other hand, we have seen in Chapter 2 that the bullet picture offers a satisfactory explanation of the construction and operation of the telescope. Can we explain the focusing property of a telescope, or even of a single lens, within the framework of the wave picture? If so, then all the conclusions drawn in Chapter 2 still hold good, and the wave theory clearly offers a wider range of necessary explanations than the Newtonian bullet theory does.

Let us look first at Figure 7.14, where a train of light rays traveling in the direction of the arrows encounters a convex lens. We make the very important assumption that the wave travels more slowly through glass than it does through air. Since some parts of the wave must travel farther through glass than other parts, and are therefore slowed down longer, the wave crests will be curved when they emerge from the lens, instead of being ranged in parallel planes as they were before entering it. Provided we make the lens correctly, we can delay the central part of the wave just sufficiently to ensure

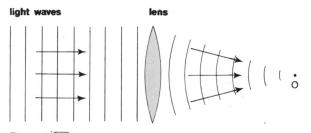

Figure 7.14
If we assume that waves travel more slowly through glass than through air, the wave theory can explain the focusing property of a convex lens.

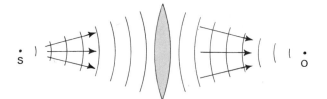

Figure 7.15
It can also explain how such a lens brings light from S to a focus at O.

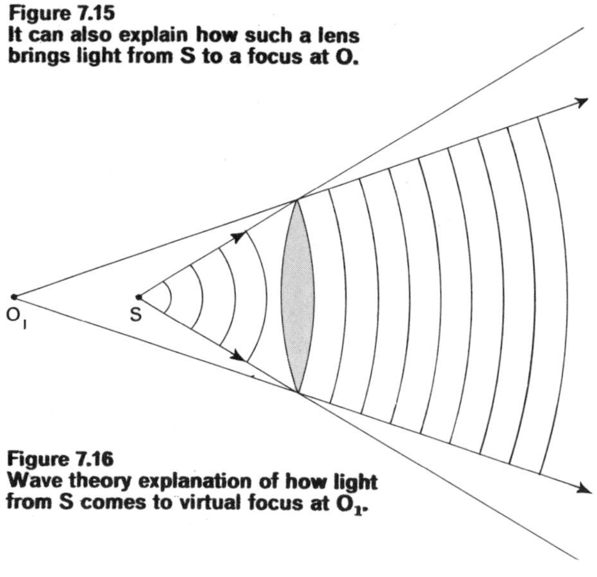

Figure 7.16
Wave theory explanation of how light from S comes to virtual focus at O₁.

Figure 7.17
Concave lens accentuates spherical form of wave from S. Thus center of emergent wave is seen at O₁.

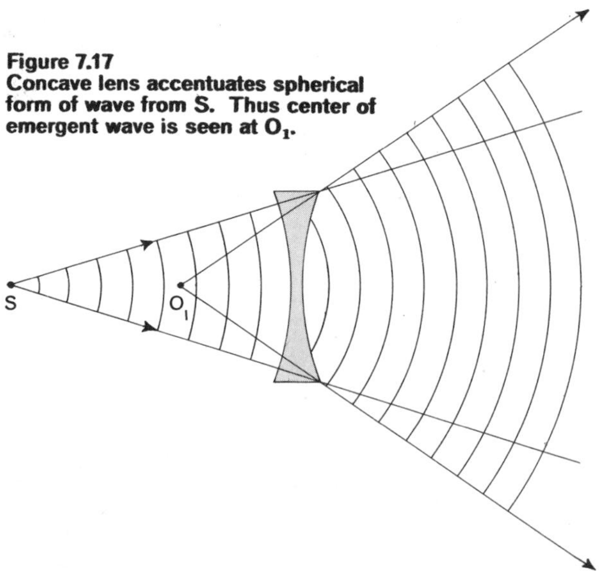

that on emerging to the right of the lens the wave takes on a convergent spherical form. This is very easily understood by recalling how water waves spread out in concentric circles from a stone dropped into water. Here we have exactly the opposite situation: in this case, instead of spreading out, the waves converge. According to the wave picture, it is just this convergence which constitutes the focal property of the lens.

It is noteworthy that the wave picture brings out very clearly the necessity for a correct shaping of the lens. If the lens were made unevenly the waves would emerge in some non-spherical form, in which case they would not converge to a point. The wave picture also explains the necessity for making the lens of perfect optical glass, because it is necessary that there shall be no uncontrolled variations in the speed at which the wave travels through the glass, such as would happen, for example, if the glass contained bubbles of air.

In an exactly similar way we can understand the focusing of light from a source S, shown in Figure 7.15. The light wave from S moves radially outward until it encounters the lens. Because of the delay through the central portion of the lens, the shape of the wave is altered as it emerges to the right. So long as the delay at the center of the lens is large enough compared with the delay at the periphery, the emergent wave will be changed into a convergent form, as shown. If, however, the delay were insufficient for this and a wave were to emerge in a modified but still spherical form, the light would not be brought to a real focus. We should then have the situation shown in Figure 7.16. In this case, the center of the spherical emergent wave lies to the left of S, and is said to be a virtual focus at the point O_1.

Similarly, too, the wave picture enables us to understand the operation of concave lenses. These result in more delay at the periphery of the lens than at the center, and this causes the original spherical form of the wave from S in Figure 7.17 to be accentuated. The center of the diverging spherical wave to the right of the lens must therefore lie nearer to the lens than the point S—at O_1 in the figure. It is clear, therefore, that all the essential features of the operation of lenses can be just as well explained within the framework of the wave picture as within the framework of the bullet picture, provided that light travels more slowly in glass than in air.

An interesting point now arises. If we look again at Figure 7.14 we may reasonably ask whether the wave produces any disturbance at points near O. We can decide this question by using a simplification first discovered by Huygens. The effect of the wave at future times can be decided first by taking the position of the wave at the present moment, and second by considering subsidiary waves to spread out from all points of the present wave front. In Figure 7.18 we have a spherical wave emerging from a lens. This is to be the "present" state of affairs. To calculate the "future", we imagine new wavelets to spread out as shown. If we now wish to find what disturbance occurs at some point P close to O we must work out how all these subsidiary wavelets affect each other when they reach P. All the subsidiary wavelets add together, by the way, when they reach O, the focal point, so clearly they will all augment each other at O. Calculation shows that the subsidiary wavelets will all cancel each other out at the point P when the distance from O to P is given by the formula $OP = 1.22 \lambda \frac{F}{D}$, where λ is the wavelength of the light in question, F is the distance of O from the lens, and D is the diameter of the lens. In other words, there will be no disturbance at P if the distance OP is greater than the wavelength of the light multiplied by the ratio of the distance F to the diameter D, and multiplied again by the number 1.22, which is close to unity. We can write this result in a slightly different but equivalent way. Join the point P to the center of the lens. The angle between this line and the axis of the lens is closely equal to the ratio of OP to F, and by our formula this is just equal to the ratio of the wavelength of the light divided by the diameter of the lens and multiplied by the number 1.22.

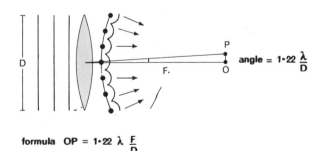

formula $OP = 1.22 \lambda \frac{F}{D}$

Figure 7.18
At focal point O all wavelets augment each other. They cancel each other out at P if the distance OP is as given by the formula.

This complication is worth grappling with because it has an interesting application to the resolving power of the telescope. Suppose a telescope is pointed toward a distant star. According to the Newtonian picture, the image of the star is formed precisely at a particular point of the focal plane—the point O in Figure 7.18. According to the wave picture, if we place a screen at the focal plane of the telescope, we will obtain not a mere point of light but a circular disk of light. Indeed, not until we reach a distance equal to OP from the center of this circle of light, will the screen appear to be dark. Next suppose that there is a second star lying quite close to the first one. The image of the second star on the focal plane will also be a circle of light. Unless this second circle is well distinguished from the first one the telescope will not tell us that there is a second star there at all, for the two images will be fused together. In order that the two circles of light shall be well separated from each other, it is essential that the center of the second shall be distant from the center of the first by a distance equal to or greater than the distance from P to O. This, in turn, means that the angle between the directions of the two stars must be at least equal to the angle marked in Figure 7.18, namely 1.22 times the wavelength divided by the aperture of the telescope. If two stars are separated by an angle smaller than this their images will be blurred together, and we shall have no certain indication of their separate existence.

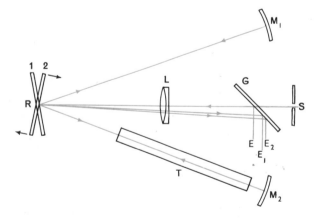

Figure 7.19
The wave theory of light is tenable only if light travels more slowly through a medium such as glass or water than it does through air. Here is the equipment Foucault used in proving that it actually does so.

Here are a few instances of what this fact implies. The same applies to the human eye as to the telescope. In the case of the eye, the diameter D is very small—under normal conditions only about 2 millimeters. Remembering that the wavelength of light is only about 1/2000 part of a millimeter, it is easy to calculate that under normal conditions the human eye is unable to distinguish between two objects that are separated by an angle of less than about one minute of arc. This is about the order of accuracy achieved by the best observers in the days before the telescope. It will be recalled from Chapter 2 that Tycho Brahe was able to estimate the positions of the stars to about the same order of accuracy —one minute of arc. But using a telescope with an aperture of 20 inches, it is theoretically possible to distinguish between two stars separated by an angle of as little as a quarter of a second of arc. And with a telescope as large as the one at Palomar Mountain, with an aperture of 200 inches, the theoretical resolution is about one-fortieth of a second of arc. In point of fact, the twinkling of stars caused by the passage of light through the Earth's atmosphere, and which is always present to some degree, even on the clearest and steadiest nights, prevents the theoretical resolving powers of large telescopes from ever being achieved in practice.

These considerations sharply remind us that a telescope is not merely a collector of light. It also overcomes the inherent handicap of the human eye —that it cannot, unaided, distinguish between two objects lying nearly in the same direction.

The Conflict Between Two Theories

So great was the prestige of Newton that many people still refused to accept the evidence for the wave nature of light, even after it had been demonstrated by the experiments of such men as Fresnel and Thomas Young, experiments that followed along lines similar to those we have just considered. Because of this, attempts were made to find a crucial experiment that would finally decide between the relative merits of the Newtonian picture and the wave picture.

Such an experiment was indeed found. We have seen that the wave theory is tenable only if it is true that waves of light travel more slowly through a medium such as glass than they do through air. The Newtonian picture, on the other hand, can be valid only if light travels faster through glass than through air. It will be recalled that when light which has passed through air is incident on to a glass surface, the transmitted ray in the glass is bent nearer to the normal than was the original incident ray. Newton explained this fact by supposing that his particles, or bullets, gained speed as they entered the glass. The argument was that glass attracted the particles, so for light striking a plane glass surface there was an increase of speed and, moreover, the increase was entirely in the direction normal to the surface. It is easy to see that this would cause the direction of motion of the bullets to become nearer to the normal than it was during their passage through the air. The thing to do, clearly, was to measure the speed of light through a solid or liquid medium, and to compare it with the speed through air. According to the Newtonian picture the speed should be greater in the denser medium; according to the wave picture, it should be greater in air.

The experiment was actually carried out by Foucault in 1850. The equipment he used is shown schematically in Figure 7.19. Light from a source S passes through a small hole. Part of it then traverses a half-silvered mirror, G. Next it is focused through a lens L on to a plane mirror at R. When R is in the position 1, the light is reflected on to the mirror M_1 which serves to return the light immediately back to R. The mirror R is rotating rapidly, however, so that although the light takes very little time to travel from R to M_1 and back again, by the time the light has made this double journey R is not quite in the same position as it was before. That is to say, it is not quite in the position 1. Hence R returns the light through the lens L along a slightly different path. Part of this light strikes the half-silvered mirror G and is reflected now into the eye at the point E_1. The experiment is repeated, but now with the rotating mirror R started in the position 2. In this case the light is sent toward the mirror M_2 instead of toward M_1. The distance from R to M_2 is exactly the same as the distance from R to M_1 but between R and M_2 is a tank (T) filled with water, so that the light has to traverse the water in order to pass from R to M_2 and also in order to return from M_2 to R. The mirror R is rotating at exactly the same speed as in the first experiment, and because of this the light is returned to the lens L again along a track slightly different from the one it originally traversed on its journey from the source to R. Again light is reflected from the mirror G into the eye, but this time at E_2.

Here we come to the crux of the matter. If light travels more rapidly through water than it does through air, as the Newtonian picture requires, then the point E_2 will lie to the left of E_1. But if light travels more slowly through water, as the wave picture requires, then the point E_2 will lie to the right of E_1. Foucault established that E_2 does, in fact, lie to the right of E_1, thus vindicating the wave theory. Thenceforward, for the rest of the nineteenth century, nobody gave any very serious credence to the Newtonian picture. As we shall see later, the developments of the twentieth century have forced us to think again, at any rate in part, in terms of the Newtonian picture, but let us first follow the wave picture still further, to the moment of its greatest triumph.

We may begin by trying to understand a little more clearly just what a wave is. A water wave has three basic properties. First, at each point there is an oscillation—the water moves up and down. This is easily shown by putting a float on top of the water. Second, there is a spatial correlation between the up-and-down motions at different points. This is illustrated in Figure 7.20. A peak at A is followed by a trough at B, and that trough is then followed by another peak at C, and so on. Not only is there an oscillation at each point taken by itself, but also different points have an orderly relation with respect to each other. If at one point the wave is up, then at an adjacent point it will be down, and so forth. This spatial ordering is measured by the wavelength (λ), the distance between two adjacent wave crests, or two adjacent wave troughs. As time proceeds, the whole spatial pattern moves along as shown in Figure 7.21. The effect of this motion is to produce the oscillation at each separate point. At one moment, at a given place, the wave is up, and at a later moment it is down. The time required to complete the oscillation at each point is simply the time required by the wave to travel through a distance equal to the wavelength. If the speed of travel of the wave is V, then the time required for the wave to move through the distance λ is simply $\lambda \div V$. This is the time that a float placed on the water takes to move from its highest to its lowest position and back again.

The third feature of water waves is that the effect of the motion of the waves can cause the whole train to move through the water, as it does when we drop a stone into a still pond. Waves spread outward—they actually *travel* outward through the water. At

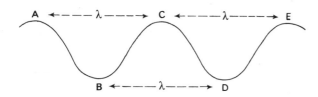

Figure 7.20
At every point of wave there is an oscillation; λ denotes wavelength.

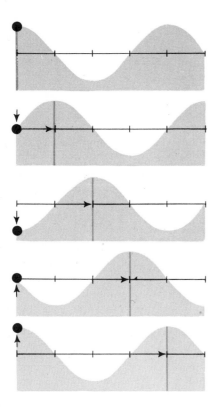

Figure 7.21
Movement of float shows that the oscillation at any one point is completed in the same time that the whole wave takes to move through a distance equal to the wavelength.

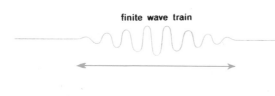

finite wave train

Figure 7.22
Wave trains are always of finite length. Height of waves decreases toward edges of wave train.

one moment waves have not yet reached a post. At a later moment they have traveled outward beyond it. In practice, wave trains are always of finite length. The height of the waves gradually dies away at the edges of the train, as in Figure 7.22.

So the three basic properties of waves are these: at each point there must be something that oscillates (in the case of water waves it is the up-and-down motion of the water); then there is a correlation between the state of this oscillation at different points, a regular sequence of peaks and troughs; thirdly, as time proceeds the whole spatial pattern moves along, causing a finite train of waves to propagate itself. Before we decide to accept the wave picture of light it is reasonable to ask whether light possesses these same three properties.

Let us take them in the reverse order. Light certainly has the ability to propagate itself. A light signal emitted from some source certainly travels outward from that source in such a way that it can be received a moment later by a distant observer. Over small distances we are not very conscious of the time required for a light signal to reach us, simply because light moves so fast; but light emitted by a distant star may take thousands of years to travel across space to us. Light also exhibits the second property of our waves, a spatial correlation expressed in a sequence of regularly arranged peaks and troughs, as depicted in Figure 7.20. But does light exhibit an oscillation at each separate point, and if so, what is it that oscillates?

Here there is a crucial difference. In the case of water the thing which oscillates is the water itself; it actually moves up and down. But the motion of the water itself and the motion of the wave are not at all alike. The wave is a structure, an organization, that moves forward. The water itself does *not* move forward, it simply moves up and down. The material particles of the water have to move in this way in order to express the oscillation. Since light can travel through regions where there are virtually no material particles, any oscillatory movement it may have *cannot* be carried in this fashion. But the movement of material particles is not an essential condition for the existence of a wave. It is quite possible to have something that oscillates at each point without any displacement of particles being involved at all. Once this is understood, it becomes comparatively easy to see just how a light wave differs from a water wave. To make the point clearer, let us look at a somewhat fantastic parable.

In a certain country the cities were built at equal intervals along a long straight road. A new cinema film was supplied each day to the first city on the road. On Mondays the film supplied was very good, and the attendances at the cinemas were therefore greatest. On Tuesdays the film was not quite as good, and attendances were a little lower. On Wednesdays it was definitely poor and the attendances were lower still, while on Thursdays the film was so execrable that hardly anybody went to the cinema that day. On Fridays, however, there was an improvement, and this improvement continued on Saturday and Sunday until by Monday night a really excellent film was again being shown. So things continued week by week. In this way an oscillation was produced in the number of people attending the cinemas each day. On Mondays the attendance was up, on Thursdays it was down. So, too, was the amount of money taken at the box offices.

Now from day to day the films which had been shown at the first city were passed along the road by a messenger, so that the film shown in the first city on Monday became available in the second city on Tuesday. This meant that at the second city there was also an oscillation in cinema attendances. There the peak was on Tuesday and the trough on Friday, everything occurring one day later than at the first city. And after carrying the films to the second city, the messenger continued the following day to carry them to the third city. So in the third city the best films were shown on Wednesdays and the worst on Saturdays. And so it continued from city to city, with a delay of one day between each city and the next one along the road.

Clearly, then, the first city, the eighth city, the fifteenth city, and so on, all showed the best films on Mondays, while the second city, the ninth city, the sixteenth city, and so on, showed them on Tuesdays. Thus the first city, the eighth city, and so on, had peak attendances on Mondays and trough attendances on Thursdays. The second city, the ninth city, and so on, had peak attendances on Tuesdays, and trough attendances on Fridays.

The wave of this parable clearly shows the second and third basic properties of the water wave. The distance from the first city to the eighth city determines the wavelength of the system, while the wave itself travels a distance equal to that between any two neighboring cities in a time of one day. This wave of our fantasy also has the first property of a water wave, in the sense that there is *something* that

Below: James Clerk Maxwell, the man who showed that the quantity which oscillates in a light wave is the electric field. Above: Diagram of lines of force in a disturbed field taken from Maxwell's *Treatise on Electricity and Magnetism.*

Much pioneer work on magnetism and electricity had to be done before the nature of light waves could be understood. The eighteenth-century print above shows an experiment to demonstrate the attractive effect of electricity generated by friction. Below is the type of torsion balance Coulomb used in formulating the law of force between electric charges.

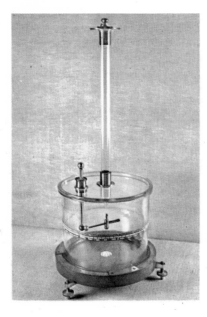

oscillates in each of the cities. But here it is certainly not material particles in the sense of a water wave that carry the oscillation; what oscillates is the number of people attending the cinema day by day. In short, a wave is simply a moving structural organization, an organization from point to point of some oscillatory property, quite irrespective of what the oscillatory property may be.

Today we have freed ourselves from the necessity of thinking of an oscillation as the displacement of a particle or particles, but scientists of the nineteenth century had not done so. They were obsessed with the idea that any oscillation necessarily involves the displacement of particles, as in the case of the water wave. Yet they were well aware that light can travel through space, where there are insufficient particles to carry such an oscillation. How could this be reconciled with the wave picture of light?

So confused were even the greatest scientists about this point that they postulated the existence of an ideal solid filling the whole of space. It was obviously not a solid in the accepted sense, and they held it to be a solid not perceivable by any of the senses. It existed in all ordinary matter as well as in vacuum. They even gave it a name—"æther". Light was thought to consist of an oscillation of this elastic solid, and the calculations of the oscillation of the solid were handled in much the same way as we handle the calculations in the case of an ordinary solid. The greatest mathematicians of the nineteenth century all worked along these lines. Gauss, Couchy and Riemann all attempted to solve the problem in this way. But whenever calculations revealed some new result which could be checked against experiment, it nearly always turned out to be wrong. Even so, scientists and mathematicians still clung to the notion of the æther, so hag-ridden were they by the notion that a wave oscillation necessarily entails the displacement of particles.

Ironically, James Clerk Maxwell, the man who solved the puzzle in the third quarter of the nineteenth century, could not really accept the implications of his own work. Although he had obtained the correct answer, an answer that required no æther at all, he tried right to the end of his days to interpret his theory in terms of the æther. Indeed, he felt it to be a defect of the theory that it could not be satisfactorily adapted to the æther concept. It was Einstein who finally dispelled the notion of the æther, a notion which had merely served to confuse men for upward of a century.

An intriguing historical question now arises. How was Maxwell able to arrive at the correct answer even though he was himself prejudiced in favor of an erroneous concept? The answer is that Maxwell worked on the results of experiments instead of developing a purely mathematical concept as did Gauss, Riemann and Couchy. Maxwell took the results of a whole host of experiments and translated them into mathematical form.

So far we have done no more than show that an oscillation does not demand the movement of particles; we have *not* shown what the oscillatory character of light consists of. Before we go on to examine Maxwell's solution it will be necessary to retrace our steps and look at developments which had been going on in other branches of science.

In the eighteenth century it was already known that there are two sorts of electricity. Nowadays we know that these two forms of electricity arise from the two different types of charge carried by the basic kinds of particles of which matter is constructed. Electrons carry one form and protons the other. When two material surfaces are rubbed together, one is often found to have acquired an excess of one type of charge, and, of course, the other surface will have an excess of the other type. This is easily observed in quite a number of commonplace experiences. For example, if you comb your hair in a dry atmosphere, the comb will become charged with an excess of one type of particle and your hair will be left with an excess of the other type. The same kind of thing sometimes happens if you pull a nylon shirt off your back very quickly.

The two different types of charge attract each other. That is to say, having been separated by some process or other they try to come together again and mix, so that one type alternates with the other, instead of both remaining in separate bunches. Perhaps the most dramatic form of mixing we can observe on the Earth is that which takes place in a lightning stroke. What happens in a storm cloud is this. Drops of water carry an excess of one type of charge, while the air around them carries an excess of the other type, so that to begin with the two types of charge are tolerably well mixed. But then the water drops start to fall to the ground as rain, carrying their charges with them as they do so. This leaves the cloud as a whole with an enormous excess of one type of charge. This excess continues to build up until the electric forces between the cloud and the ground become so great as to produce the lightning

The most dramatic form of the mixing of opposite charges observable on Earth, seen in action over Moscow.

Oersted first showed that while any charge produces an electric field only a *moving* charge will produce a magnetic field. Above is a model of the apparatus he used to show the effect that a direct current has on a compass needle pivoted below the wire which carries it.

stroke. This is simply an extremely rapid transfer of charge between the cloud and the ground which enables the two different types of charge to become well mixed once more.

The law of force between electric charges was discovered by Coulomb toward the end of the eighteenth century. It can best be understood in terms of a new concept—the electric field. As its name implies, an electric field can exist in a region of space quite regardless of whether the region contains any matter or not. Electric fields may be thought of as something that push electric charges and try to start them moving. The strength of the push depends on the strength of the field, and the direction of the push depends on the direction of the field. Both of these in general vary from one point to another.

Charges produce electric fields, and it was Coulomb who discovered the way in which they do so. We can think of the reaction between two different charges in the following way. The first charge produces an electric field in accordance with Coulomb's law, and this field produces a mechanical reaction on the second charge. Equally, we could say that the second charge produces an electric field which reacts on the first charge. In this way we obtain a mechanical force acting on both the charges. If the two charges are of similar type the mechanical forces tend to push them apart, whereas if they are of opposite type the mechanical forces tend to make them come together. Coulomb's law can be stated in precise mathematical form, and this was in fact done by Gauss.

Because charges placed in an electric field are subject to a mechanical force they will start to move unless they are held fixed in some way, and a collection of moving charges is called an electric current. This is just what happens when a current flows in a wire. Inside the wire there is an electric field which produces a flow of electrons along the wire. This electric field lies in a direction parallel to the wire, and if it is steady and constant the electrons attain a steady flow along the wire. We have what we call a direct current (D.C.)

But what about the alternating currents (A.C.) with which we are perhaps even more familiar in everyday life? An alternating current is one in which the electrons flow alternately in one direction then in the opposite direction along the wire. To produce such an oscillation in the direction of motion of the electrons, it is necessary for the electric field to oscillate at each point inside the wire. At any given point we may think of the electric field as pointing strongly toward the right to begin with. As time goes on, the field weakens but still points to the right, and the weakening continues until eventually there is no electric field at all at the point. With a further passage of time, a weak electric field builds up, pointing to the left, and the leftward field continues to grow until it becomes just as strong as the former rightward field. Thereafter, the leftward field starts to weaken and goes on weakening until it, too, falls to zero, after which another rightward-pointing field starts and continues to grow until it attains to the same strength as the original rightward-pointing field. At this stage one cycle—one oscillation of the electric field—has been completed.

In the case of alternating currents such as those that are derived in Britain from the national grid, there are fifty such cycles every second; in the United States the standard frequency is sixty cycles per second.

Here we have a concept of an oscillation very different from that involved in the propagation of water waves. We have an oscillation of a field at a point, not the displacement of material particles as in the case of water waves. This gives us the beginning of an insight into Maxwell's solution to the problem of the nature of light, for the quantity that oscillates in a light wave, or rather one of the quantities, is the electric field.

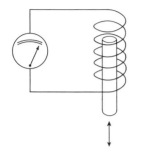

The picture shows one of the rooms of Faraday's laboratory. It was Faraday who showed that an electric field can be produced from a magnetic field provided the magnetic field changes with time. *The magnet must move.*

But this was a concept that could not be easily grasped a hundred years ago when oscillating currents were not yet a feature of everyday life. Indeed, the electric currents which scientists investigated in the first part of the nineteenth century were all of the steady D.C. type. Around 1820 Oersted discovered that such steady direct currents produce *magnetic* fields. Magnetic fields were not new to science, but before Oersted's discovery they were thought to arise only from magnets. Oersted showed that while a charge produces an electric field quite regardless of whether or not the charge is moving, it will produce a magnetic field *only* if it is moving. Ampère followed up Oersted's discovery with an important set of experiments which enabled Maxwell to determine a mathematical equation whereby the magnetic field produced by a steady current could be precisely calculated. In fact, Maxwell succeeded in doing for steady currents and magnetic fields what Gauss had already done for charges and electric fields.

It was now easy to see that starting with an electric field it is possible to produce a magnetic field; for the electric field acting on charges could cause them to move, and the moving charges, or current, would produce a magnetic field. But could this work in reverse? Could one start with a magnetic field and produce an electric field? The solution of this problem was Faraday's crowning achievement. It

was a solution not easily arrived at because Faraday, like everyone else at that time, started with an erroneous assumption. Because in the case of D.C. currents a steady electric field produces a steady magnetic field, everyone tried to reverse the situation. That is, they tried to produce a steady electric field from a steady magnetic field, and the problem simply would not yield to solution that way. An electric field can be produced from a magnetic field only if that magnetic field changes with time. If you have a magnet and a loop of wire you will never make a current flow in the wire by maintaining wire and magnet in a constant relation to each other. Yet that is just what everybody was trying to do until Faraday had the idea of moving the magnet. In that way an electric field is, indeed, produced in the wire and a current is thereby made to flow. This was Faraday's principle of induction.

When Maxwell looked at Faraday's work from a mathematical point of view, he discovered a relation between the electric field and the magnetic field quite independent of the immediate presence of either magnet or loop of wire. This was something that had to apply at *every* point, whether or not there happened to be a piece of wire or a magnet at that point. In this sense the new relation resembled Gauss's generalization of Coulomb's experiments; it also resembled Maxwell's own expression of the results of Oersted and Ampère. Where

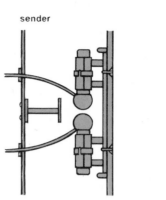

sender   receiver

Once it was shown that the quantity
that oscillates in a light wave is
the electric field or the magnetic
field, Heinrich Hertz artificially
produced waves of different wavelength from those of visible light.
Above are his oscillator, or sender,
and his resonator, or receiver.

the new relation differed from the old ones was that
changes with time now became of paramount importance. Maxwell had found a relation not directly
between the electric field and the magnetic field at
a point, but between the way in which the electric
field varies from point to point of space and the rate
at which the magnetic field varies from moment to
moment of time.

The introduction of the time variation was quite
new. It showed that the electric field and the magnetic field are not separate, independent entities. It
is only when everything is steady and nothing is
changing with time that the two fields appear to be
independent of each other, but when things do
change with time the two fields are seen to be in-
extricably linked together. It is impossible for a
magnetic field to change with time without giving
rise to a corresponding electric field.

So the situation was this. Maxwell had at his
command three different mathematical results.
That of Gauss enabled him to determine the electric field produced by a set of charges; his own
equation enabled him to determine the magnetic
field produced by a flow of current; and the new
equation derived from Faraday's results expressed
the relation between the electric field and the time-
dependence of the magnetic field. When Maxwell
took these three results together, he found they were
not in every case mathematically consistent with
each other. The electric field determined by the

first equation (Gauss's equation) and the magnetic field determined by the second equation, did
not in all cases fit in with the third equation, the
one derived from Faraday's experiments. Now a
mathematical inconsistency could not, of course, be
tolerated, so Maxwell set out to modify the equations in such a way as to achieve consistency. This
had to be done subject to the condition that anything new introduced into the equations must not
mar their agreement with the experiments of
Coulomb, Oersted and Ampere, or of Faraday.

Maxwell found that he could achieve consistency
within the framework of this vital condition by introducing a new term into the second of the equations, the one whereby he had himself represented
the experiments of Oersted and Ampère. Originally
this equation had done no more than connect the
magnetic field with the flow of a steady D.C. current. Maxwell now saw that he must introduce into
it a term that depended on the rate of change of the
electric field with respect to time. The situation now
had a satisfying symmetry. The second equation
now connected the magnetic field with the time
variation of the electric field, whereas the third
equation, derived from Faraday's results, connected
the electric field with the time variation of the magnetic field. Moreover, the new term simply vanished,
giving no contribution, under steady conditions,
and therefore did not mar the agreement with the
experiments of Oersted and Ampère.

Now came a result which enabled scientists finally to discard the troublesome æther which had for so long bogged down their thinking. When the new equations were applied to a vacuum, where there was neither charge nor current, it was found that the electric field and the magnetic field were, in fact, carried in waves, and that these waves had all the properties of light so far discovered by experiment. Here, then, was the answer to the quest for an understanding of the nature of light. The quantity that oscillates in a light wave is the electric field, or, if you prefer it, the magnetic field. You can choose either, because if you know one you can determine the other from Maxwell's equations.

The thing which oscillates in a light wave is, in fact, the ability to push electric charges, namely the electric field; and Maxwell's equation showed that the electric field has the full structural organization of a wave. At a particular moment of time there are analogues of wave crests and wave troughs, and these are interlinked with each other along the direction of travel of the light. By saying that at a particular moment the wave has a peak at a particular point, we simply mean that the electric field has its maximum strength in a particular direction, say to the right; by saying that it has a trough, we mean that the electric field has its maximum strength the opposite way, say to the left. There is no up-and-down motion as in the water wave, and there is certainly no oscillation of an idealized æther.

At first sight it might be thought that a theory of light ought to account for the limited range of wavelengths which we find light to have. Why is light confined to a range of wavelengths between approximately 1/3000 and 1/1500 part of a millimeter? Maxwell's theory gives no answer to such a question. There is nothing in the theory which precludes the possibility of the existence of waves of any length whatsoever. So if we accept the Maxwell theory we have also to accept that a virtually limitless range of wavelengths can exist in nature, and that the only reason why what we call light appears to be confined to a certain very narrow range is that this happens to be the only range of wavelengths to which our eyes are sensitive.

At the time when Maxwell produced his theory neither very long wavelengths nor very short ones were known to exist in nature. The question immediately arose whether new wavelengths not previously experienced could be produced artificially in the laboratory. For technical reasons it was at first

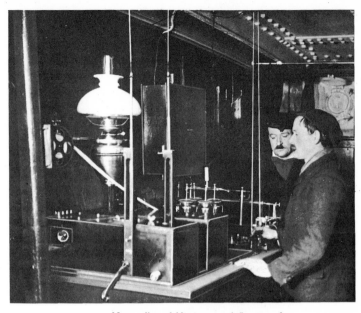

Maxwell and Hertz paved the way for radio. This photograph, taken near the turn of the century, shows an early Marconi wireless installation.

found easier to produce long waves rather than short ones, and indeed, a few years after Maxwell's work long wavelengths were produced by Heinrich Hertz. The theoretical discoveries of Maxwell and the pioneer work of Hertz together formed the basis of modern radio technology.

In succeeding years shorter wavelengths were also found. Toward the end of the nineteenth century X-rays were discovered, having wavelengths 100 to 1000 times shorter than that of blue light, and in recent times we have become only too familiar with gamma rays produced in the explosions of atomic weapons. These rays are simply radiation with wavelengths about a million times smaller than those of ordinary light. So we see that Maxwell succeeded not only in explaining the nature of light, but also in predicting the existence of a host of new radiations not then known to science.

Throughout the history of man it is probable that no more momentous prediction has ever been made.

The Quantum Theory of Light

It is ironical that flaws should have become apparent in the wave picture at the moment of its greatest triumph; for it quickly appeared that the wave theory alone offers no explanation of what happens when light is absorbed.

Consider the situation shown in Figure 7.23, where white light is dispersed by a prism into its constituent colors. These are incident on a screen

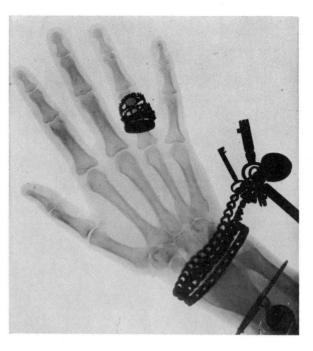

At first long waves proved easier to produce than short waves. But before the nineteenth century ended X-rays were discovered—waves a hundred to a thousand times shorter than those of blue light. This X-ray plate was made in 1897. Today we are all too familiar with the far shorter gamma rays of atomic explosions.

Figure 7.23
White light is dispersed by prism, and only light of a particular color passes through slit S on to metal foil. Metal reflects part of light and absorbs part. Absorption causes electrons to be thrown out of metal. Speed at which electrons are emitted depends only on color of light, and not on its intensity.

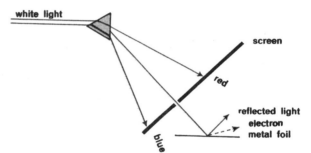

Figure 7.24
White light is again dispersed but this time light of different colors falls on different parts of the foil. If electrons produced by absorption of each color can be kept separate, streams of electrons for each color can be made to impinge at different points on a detecting film or plate.

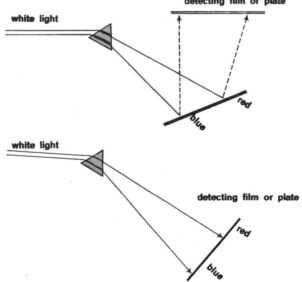

Figure 7.25
This arrangement, by which dispersed light falls directly on a detecting film, is simpler; but an arrangement like that of Figure 7.24 could be made many times more sensitive. A 30-inch telescope utilising the arrangement of Figure 7.24 would be potentially equal to a 300-inch instrument using the simpler device.

which has a slit at S so arranged that only light of a particular color passes through to the far side of the screen. This light falls on metal foil where part of it is reflected by the metal and part absorbed. It can be proved by experiment that the effect of the absorption is to cause charged particles to be thrown out of the metal. These particles are electrons. (It will be recalled that in all normal atoms there is a comparatively extensive cloud of electrons surrounding a small, weighty nucleus. It is these cloud-particles that are ejected from the metal when it absorbs light.)

The surprising thing is that the speed with which the electrons are emitted depends only on the color of the light and not on its intensity. This is a strong indication that "white" light is made up of discrete units and that the units are different for light of different colors. We now call these units *quanta*, and we describe the absorption of light in discrete terms. We say that an atom of the metal absorbs a quantum and that as a result of the absorption it emits an electron outward from its surface. Faint light consists of only a few quanta, strong light of many quanta; but provided the color of the light is the same, the individual quanta are indistinguishable. Hence for light of a pure color, since the emission of each electron is an individual process concerning only one quantum, the electrons are always emitted with the same speed and energy.

The energy of emission of the electrons does change, however, when the color of the light is altered, being greater for blue light than for red light. We therefore say that the quanta which make up blue light all have individually more energy than the quanta which make up red light. Similarly, the quanta that make up red light have individually more energy than those that make up infrared light. Those that make up ultraviolet light have more energy than those that make up blue light while those that make up X-rays have still more. The quanta that make up gamma rays have the greatest energies of all. At the other extreme, radio-wave quanta have the smallest energies.

In brief, quantum energy plays the same role in the quantum theory of light as wavelength plays in the wave picture: the shorter the wavelength the greater the quantum energy. It is because the quanta that constitute X-rays and gamma rays have such great energies that they are so damaging to biological tissues; radio-wave quanta are comparatively harmless because of their small energies.

The quantum theory has a direct bearing on the design and construction of modern astronomical instruments. Many of the celestial objects that astronomers wish to study are so intrinsically faint that the eye cannot be used to detect the light from them which telescopes collect. For the most part the photographic plate is used, but in recent years there has been an increasing tendency to work with the electrons produced by some process such as that shown in Figure 7.23. The amount of light being received from a faint cosmic object can then be accurately measured by actually counting the number of electrons emitted from the metal surface. Alternatively, instead of counting the electrons individually, we may take them as a whole. As they come off the metal foil, or *cathode*, as it is usually called, they can be channeled in the same direction to form an electric current, and the strength of that current can be measured with great precision. It is in this way that astronomers nowadays measure the apparent brightnesses of the stars.

The arrangement shown in Figure 7.23 also opens up other possibilities. By varying the position of the slit we can arrange that light of different colors falls on the cathode, so that the brightness of a star with respect to one particular color can be measured. In this way it is possible to say precisely how blue, or how red, stars are, and the astronomer can deduce a great deal of information from such measurements, as we shall see in a later chapter.

Research is now proceeding on a more ambitious device. If we dispense with the slit and allow the whole of the light to fall on the cathode, as in Figure 7.24, electrons will be knocked out of the cathode by light of all the various colors. If we can somehow prevent all these electrons from getting mixed together—if we can keep the electrons from the blue light separate from those from the red light and so on—we can then arrange that the separate streams impinge at different points on a detecting film. In this way we could obtain a picture on the film through the agency of the electrons and *not* directly through the light.

The point of all this is that such a device would enable us to work with much weaker light. In fact, a device of the kind shown in Figure 7.24 could be made about a hundred times more sensitive than one using a straightforward detecting film, as in Figure 7.25. This means that a telescope with an aperture of only 30 inches would be potentially equal to a telescope of 300 inches.

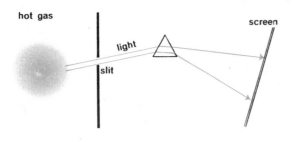

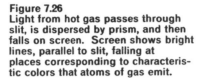

Figure 7.26
Light from hot gas passes through slit, is dispersed by prism, and then falls on screen. Screen shows bright lines, parallel to slit, falling at places corresponding to characteristic colors that atoms of gas emit.

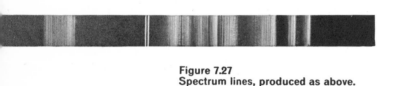

Figure 7.27
Spectrum lines, produced as above.

Part of spectrum produced by hot sodium vapor. The two strong lines (yellow) are the so-called D lines.

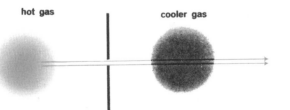

Figure 7.28
Here hot gas containing free-moving electrons as well as atoms emits light with a continuous color-range. On passing through cooler gas some of this light is absorbed. Light so absorbed has same discrete colors as cooler gas would have emitted under conditions of Figure 7.26. On emerging, the light is therefore deficient at those particular colors.

So far we have thought only about the absorption of light. What happens when matter emits light? Consider the simple case of a hot gas in which the individual atoms are widely separated from each other except at brief moments of collision. Often, when such collisions occur, the atoms behave like billiard balls: they bounce off each other in new directions and no energy is lost from their motions. In other cases, however, energy *is* lost from the motions of colliding atoms. The atoms are activated or excited by the collisions and the excited atoms then emit one or more quanta of light.

A particular type of atom is able to emit only quanta of certain colors that are characteristic of it. With the right apparatus we can use this fact to determine what kinds of atoms are emitting light.

In Figure 7.26 light from a hot gas is passed through a slit and then dispersed by a prism into its constituent colors. Thereafter the light is allowed to fall on a screen. There we observe not a smooth, continuous gradation of color, but a number of bright lines, parallel to the slit, falling at places corresponding to the particular colors that the atoms of hot gas emit. These lines are known as *spectrum lines* (Figure 7.27). The next photograph shows part of the spectrum produced by hot sodium vapor. It has two particularly strong lines. These are the so-called D lines, and their color is yellow. This explains why a handful of common salt (sodium chloride) thrown into a hot fire emits yellow light. Some of the sodium atoms in the salt are vaporized and after colliding with each other and with other vaporized atoms they emit the strong yellow D lines.

Since each type of atom has its own characteristic bright lines, the study of these lines provides an excellent method of chemical analysis. If we wish to know what atoms are contained in a given chemical sample, all we need do is to heat the sample, vaporize it, and examine the light emitted by the hot gas. By carefully studying the bright lines produced we can tell exactly what atoms were contained in the original sample. This method of analysis has two disadvantages, however. By vaporizing the sample we destroy its original structure, so though our analysis will tell us what types of atoms it contained, we shall learn nothing at all about the way in which those atoms were combined to form compounds. Secondly, in spectrum analysis it is difficult, though not impossible, to infer the relative proportions of the different types of atom.

We have seen how different types of atom emit only their own characteristic colors. It remains to see how it is possible for matter to emit light with a continuous range of color. If a gas is made hot enough, electrons will be stripped off some, or perhaps all, of the atoms, so that there will be collisions not only between atoms and atoms, but also between electrons and atoms. It is in these latter collisions that light with a continuous range of color is emitted, and it is in this way that light with a continuous range of color is emitted from the surfaces of the stars.

At the left of Figure 7.28 we have a hot gas containing free-moving electrons as well as atoms. The light with a continuous range of color which it emits is allowed to pass through a cooler gas consisting simply of atoms. Some of the light is absorbed by the atoms of the cooler gas. Now the light so absorbed has exactly the same discrete colors as this cooler gas would have emitted if it had been subjected to the experiment shown in Figure 7.26. This clearly means that after emergence from the cooler gas, the light will be deficient at exactly these particular colors. If this light is now dispersed through a prism and allowed to fall on a screen, we shall therefore have the situation depicted in Figure 7.29. Against a continuous *bright background* we shall have a number of *dark lines*, the dark lines occurring at places corresponding to the particular colors that were absorbed by the atoms of the cooler gas. Thus Figures 7.27 and 7.29 correspond to opposite situations. In the first figure we have the emission of bright spectrum lines by a hot gas, whereas in the second we have dark spectrum lines caused by a process of absorption.

The dark-line spectrum of Figure 7.29 has a special interest. It is the spectrum of sunlight. This means that the situation shown in Figure 7.28 actually occurs in the Sun. The ordinary surface of the Sun, known as the photosphere, emits light of all colors, but lying above the photosphere are layers of cooler gas, and in order to escape out into space the light from the photosphere must pass through them. It is this passage through the cooler gas that produces the dark spectrum lines.

What we have seen about the emission and absorption of light by matter constitutes overwhelming evidence that this takes place through the agency of individual discrete units known as quanta. Here, then, we have some measure of return to the Newtonian bullet picture, but this does not mean that we must abandon the wave picture entirely and return wholeheartedly to the Newtonian picture, for quanta are not localized bullets in the simple Newtonian sense. Rather we should think of each quantum as being a separate little wavelet. We can then conceive of light in bulk as being made up of a multitude of individual wavelets. When an atom emits a quantum it increases by one the number of wavelets that go to make up the light; conversely, when an atom absorbs a quantum of light it decreases the number of wavelets by one.

The essential point is this. When we consider ordinary light we have to deal with a large number of quanta. Each of these is a separate wavelet and all these individual wavelets add together in such a way as to reproduce the properties of the wave picture of light. So although Newton was right in supposing that light has a discrete structure he was not right in his idea of how the individual units fit together. They are not separate and more or less disconnected bullets. They are wavelets, fitting together in a highly subtle manner. To understand exactly how this fitting together takes place one must penetrate deeply into modern physics—an exercise which lies beyond the purview of this book.

Figure 7.29
If emerging light of Figure 7.28 is dispersed and falls on a screen, it produces bright background and dark lines. The lines correspond to colors absorbed by atoms of cooler gas.

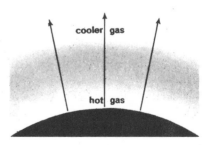

Light emitted from Sun's surface goes through same process as that shown in Figure 7.28. Figure 7.29 is in fact the spectrum of sunlight.

Here we need only note the final result—that the gross properties of the wave picture, as determined by Maxwell, are reproduced whenever the number of quanta with which we are dealing is very large.

Radio Astronomy

Because the structure of a radio wave is exactly the same as that of a light wave, the logical problem of designing a radio telescope is similar to that of designing an ordinary optical telescope. There are, however, practical differences. When radio waves pass through materials they do not behave in the same way as light does. It is extraordinarily difficult to construct a refracting lens for radio waves, for instance, because there is no simple material which has exactly the same kind of effect on radio waves as glass has on light. But though there are as yet no refracting radio telescopes, any metal can give a surface which will *reflect* radio waves. This means that mirrors and reflecting telescopes can be built for radio waves. In such telescopes the mirrors serve to focus the radio waves in essentially the same way as optical mirrors focus light.

Radio telescopes have at least one great advantage from the constructional viewpoint. The mirrors need not be made nearly as accurately as the mirrors for optical telescopes. To have good focal properties an optical mirror must be made to within a tolerance of about 1/10,000 of a millimeter. In contrast, a radio mirror will give a comparable accuracy of focus with a tolerance as large as an inch or two. Thus radio mirrors can be made enormously bigger than optical mirrors without any great risk of exceeding the required tolerance. The mirror of the radio telescope at Jodrell Bank has fifteen times the diameter of the largest optical mirror, and plans already exist for making even larger ones. But there are no plans for making optical mirrors substantially larger than that at Palomar Mountain.

The enormously larger size and weight of radio mirrors raises mechanical problems of a different order and type from those encountered in the design of optical telescopes. The great weights involved may cause the designer of a radio telescope to prefer a style of mounting for his mirror which the designer of an optical telescope would never contemplate. For example, the equatorial mounting that is so convenient for optical telescopes raises difficult problems of weight distribution in the case of the radio instrument. These problems were in fact solved in the case of the 90-foot mirrors used by the radio astronomers at the California Institute of Technology, but the technique they employed would be difficult for appreciably larger mirrors such as that at Jodrell Bank. For such large mirrors as these it is preferable to use an altazimuth type of mounting.

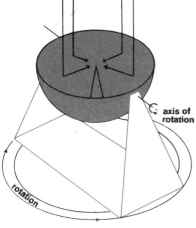

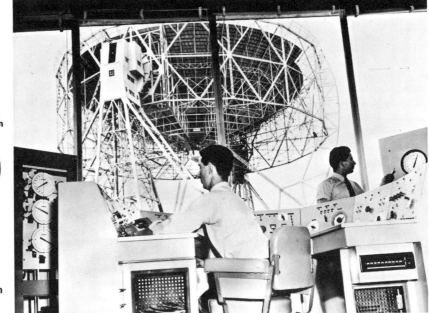

axis of
rotation

rotation

Left: View of the 250-foot mirror of
the Jodrell Bank radio telescope.
Above: Diagrammatic representation
of its altazimuth mounting.
Right: View from control room.

It will be recalled from Chapter 2 that with an altazimuth mounting it is necessary for the telescope to be moved continuously about both a vertical axis and a horizontal axis in order to compensate for the rotation of the Earth. With an equatorial mounting, on the other hand, motion about only one axis is required. Moreover, the motion necessary for an equatorial mounting is the same at all observatories, irrespective of the latitude, whereas the motions required for an altazimuth mounting depend on the position of the observer and differ from one latitude to another. So the whole problem of moving an altazimuth telescope is much more complicated than that of moving an equatorial telescope. There is, moreover, the further difficulty that in the catalogs the positions of all astronomical objects are given in the equatorial system, and any observer who uses the altazimuth arrangement must make a rather cumbersome arithmetical conversion in order to find the direction in which he must point his telescope to pick up a specified object at a specified time.

The situation is saved in the case of the large altazimuth radio telescopes by the use of an automatic computer which performs the necessary arithmetical computations very quickly, and by the provision of automatic servomechanisms which direct the telescope in its complicated double motion, the one about a vertical axis, the other about a horizontal.

It is only the existence of these modern devices that makes the design of the large altazimuth telescope feasible. Similar devices could, of course, be provided for optical telescopes, but because there is no special difficulty about building equatorial mountings for them, nobody has thought it worth while.

We have seen that a radio telescope focuses radio waves in much the same way as an optical telescope focuses light. But what happens to the radio waves after they have been brought to a focus? Obviously they cannot be viewed directly with the eye, nor can they be photographed with a camera. The answer is that they are picked up on a small aerial placed at the focus and are led either by pipes or by cables to a radio receiver. The receiver amplifies the radio signal, delivering a voltage directly proportional to the signal, which is then used to activate some recording device—in most cases a simple pen recorder. This technique, which the radio astronomer must perforce adopt, unfortunately gives much less information than optical photography. In the radio telescope the whole of the waves focused by the mirror are directed into the receiver, where they produce one single output voltage. It is as though an optical telescope, instead of giving a photograph of an area of the sky, were to take all the light and focus it into one single bright spot. This would tell us nothing except the total brightness of all the objects lying within the field of view of the telescope. It would not enable us to judge whether the field of view contained just one bright object, two less bright objects, or a great many dim ones. And this is just the state of uncertainty in which the radio telescope leaves us. It simply gives us the total radio brightness of all the objects in its field of view.

By pointing it to different parts of the sky, different fields of view can be examined, and their radio brightnesses compared, and that is the most that a single radio telescope can do. Once the sky has been completely surveyed with a given instrument, it is possible to construct a radio map showing the relative radio brightness of different areas, but only to a degree of accuracy determined by the field of view of the telescope. To obtain a more refined map it is necessary to build a new instrument giving a smaller field of view. This means constructing a telescope with a still larger mirror, since the field of view is determined by the size of the mirror—the larger the mirror, the smaller the field of view.

All this refers only to the operation of a radio telescope at one particular wavelength. Now a radio mirror will serve to bring to a focus *all* radio waves, irrespective of their wavelength, just as an optical mirror brings light to a focus irrespective of its color. So what determines the wavelength on which a radio telescope is operated? The answer is the par-

ticular aerial and receiver used to pick up the radio waves. If these are changed, the wavelength on which the telescope operates will be correspondingly changed; and if the pick-up aerial and receiver are arranged to accept a shorter wavelength, the field of view of the telescope is reduced. The telescope then gives more information about the distribution of radio intensity over the sky at the new wavelength than it did at the old, longer wavelength.

So there are two ways in which the radio astronomer can gain more information about the sky. He can build telescopes with larger and larger mirrors or he can use shorter and shorter wavelengths. Unfortunately, it isn't very easy to do both, because the shorter the wavelength used, the more accurately must the mirror be made, and, of course, the larger the mirror the harder it is to make it within the required tolerance. Moreover, the intrinsic radio brightness of the sky decreases everywhere as the wavelength becomes shorter, so at shorter and shorter wavelengths it becomes necessary to measure weaker and weaker signals. For these reasons a mere reduction of wavelength is no simple solution to the radio astronomer's problems.

At the time of writing, there are two schools of thought among radio astronomers. There are those who believe that more detail about the sky will best be observed by building huge mirrors, and there are those who believe that the best policy is to use shorter wavelengths. Among those who prefer larger mirrors, there is again a divergence of views. Some prefer a reflecting telescope of orthodox design, such as the one at Jodrell Bank, the one now being constructed in Australia, or the one with a mirror of 600-feet diameter to be constructed by the U.S. Navy. Others, particularly the radio astronomers at

These photographs of the Mullard Observatory, Cambridge, show first a giant mobile aerial mounted on 1000 feet of railway track running north to south, and next a fixed aerial, 1450 feet long, running east to west. With equipment of this kind nebulae 5000 million light years away have been observed.

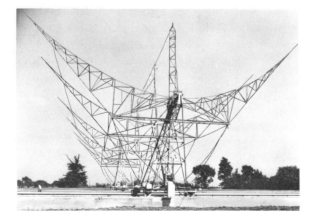

Cambridge, believe that it will never be possible to build an orthodox moving telescope having a mirror with a diameter of more than about 500 to 1000 feet. They prefer telescopes of a less orthodox design, a design which sacrifices entirely free movement but which in return is able to obtain an effective diameter of almost fantastically large dimensions.

It might be thought that the solution to these problems lies in inventing some sort of radio photography, but this is not so, for the difficulty the radio astronomer faces is one not of technique but of principle. From our discussion of the optical telescope it will be recalled that there is an inherent limitation to the resolving power of the telescope. It is impossible to distinguish two objects when the angle between their directions is less than a certain calculable quantity, given as 1.22 times the wavelength (λ) divided by the diameter of the aperture of the telescope. Exactly the same limitation applies in the case of a radio telescope, and because the wavelength is so very much greater in that case than in the optical case, the limitation is vastly more stringent. Consider, for instance, the radio telescope with an aperture of 200 feet operating at a wavelength of about 3 meters. Our formula shows that with such a telescope two objects must be separated by an angle of more than 3° in order for them to be distinguishable. And it is this limitation which decides the effective field of view of the radio telescope. Clearly, it is not merely technical ignorance that prevents us from determining the details of what lies within the field of view of the radio telescope. We are prevented from doing so by the inherent structure of the radio waves themselves.

The radio astronomer can measure and map the radio brightnesses of different parts of the sky at any given wavelength. In the map below, contours denote strength of radio emission at a frequency of 160 megacycles (wavelength 1.875 metres) in an area of sky visible from Cambridge.

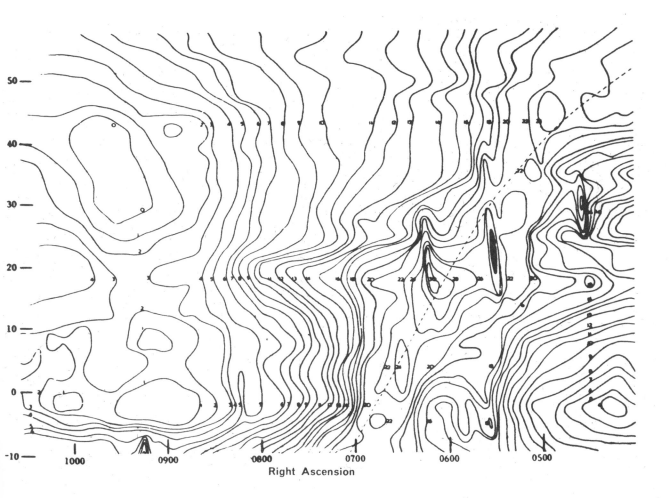

Right Ascension

Chapter 8   The Birth of Modern Astronomy

Until about a century ago astronomers were concerned only with the positions, the motions and the masses of celestial bodies. Of the physical make-up of stars they knew little or nothing and had no means of finding out. Yet today that is one of the prime concerns of astronomy. This revolutionary change is due in large measure to two results of man's ever-growing knowledge of the nature of light: the ability to make spectroscopes capable of breaking down light from a distant source into its component wavelengths, and the recognition that each different type of atom emits lines only at its own characteristic wavelengths.

When the slit of a spectroscope is illuminated by sunlight the solar spectrum can readily be observed or photographed. It consists of a continuous bright background of colors ranging from red for the longest visible wavelengths to violet for the shortest. This bright background is crossed by many transverse narrow dark lines, called Fraunhofer lines in honor of the great German scientist Fraunhofer, who first discovered them.

Wavelengths are commonly measured in units called angstroms, named after the Swedish physicist Anders Ångström. The angstrom is a unit of length equal to 1/10,000,000 of a millimeter. Blue light has wavelengths around 4,000 angstroms, yellow light around 5,000, and red light around 6,000. The human eye is sensitive only to wavelengths ranging from about 4,000 to 8,000 angstroms, and this is more likely due to biological adaptation than to accident, for most of the light emitted by the Sun falls within a similar range. In fact, the solar spectrum that can be photographed with normal astronomical equipment is limited to a range of between about 3,000 and 10,000 angstroms.

This limitation is due to a variety of causes. The Sun actually does emit most of its radiation within this range, with the maximum emission occurring in the yellow part of the spectrum, near wavelength 5,000 angstroms; but it also emits some radiation at wavelengths shorter than 3,000 angstroms and some at wavelengths longer than 10,000 angstroms. The short-wave radiation entirely fails to reach our telescopes because it is absorbed by the gases of the Earth's atmosphere. Long-wave radiation in the region of 10,000 angstroms also finds it difficult to penetrate the atmosphere; some of it does get through, however, but photographic plates fail in sensitivity in the region of 10,000 angstroms and

It was through the work of the early spectroscopists that man gained his first insight into the compositions of the stars. In the 1860s William Huggins of London used this 8-inch refractor fitted with a spectroscope (in circle) to obtain star spectra. Comparison with spectra actually produced in the observatory showed that the stars possess many elements in common with our own Earth.

therefore do not enable us to detect it. Special equipment of a photoelectric character can be used to extend the range of sensitivity beyond 10,000 angstroms, but up to now such equipment is far less convenient in practical use than the photographic plate.

A portion of the spectrum of the Sun is shown in Figure 7.29 (page 199). We saw that the bright continuous background is produced by collisions of electrons with atoms in the photospheric regions of the Sun, while the dark lines are produced by individual atoms lying in the cooler gases above the photosphere. These atoms absorb radiation at their own characteristic wavelengths, and the absorptive power varies from one kind of atom to another; it also varies with the temperature, and between one characteristic wavelength and another for the same atom. It is because of all these variations that the dark lines of the solar spectrum vary so much in width. When the absorptive power of a particular atom is weak the corresponding line appears narrow; when it is strong the corresponding line appears wide. Two of the lines of the solar spectrum are particularly wide. These are lines produced by calcium atoms that have lost one of their electrons. Such atoms have an enormous absorptive power at these particular wavelengths.

What Spectrum Lines Tell

Just as we can obtain the spectrum of the Sun, so we can obtain the spectra of stars. Their study forms a major branch of modern astronomy and provides three broad streams of information. First, it tells us a great deal about the physical conditions at the surfaces of stars—about the temperature and density of the gaseous material that produces the spectrum lines. Second, it tells us about the chemistry of the stars, for since different atoms have different characteristic lines, we can infer the existence of those atoms by detecting those particular lines. Third, a careful study of the wavelengths at which the lines are found gives important clues about the motions of the stars.

Let us look at the last point first. Consider a source of light that moves toward the observer, remembering that the light is a succession of crests and troughs. As successive crests reach the observer they will be slightly closer together than if the source were stationary. That is, the wavelength of the light will be a little less than it would otherwise be. It will appear slightly bluer to the observer.

To see this, we first notice that the time required for a particular wave-crest to travel from the source to the observer is simply the distance between the source and the observer divided by the speed of light. But when the source is moving toward the observer that distance decreases from one crest to the next. Hence the time delay between emission at the source and reception at the observer also decreases from one crest to the next. This means that the crests reach the observer with progressively shorter time

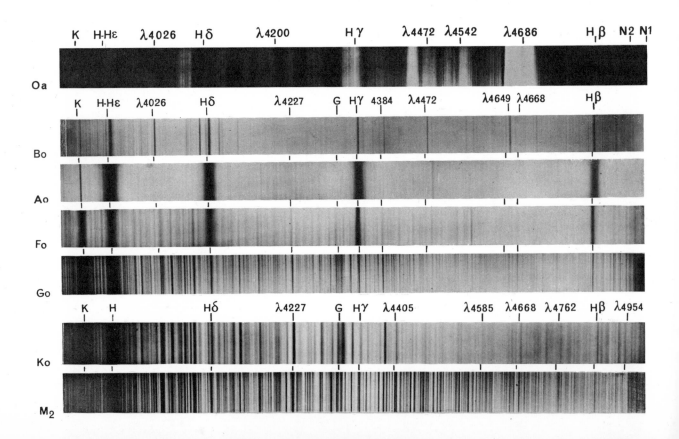

delays. In other words, the time interval between the arrival of successive crests is less than the time interval between the emission of successive waves from the source. Since the waves always pass the observer at the standard fixed speed of light, it follows that the distance between the wave-crests must be less than it would be if the source were stationary. The light therefore appears bluer to the observer than it would do to anyone who happened to move with the source.

We can derive a simple mathematical formula from these considerations. Suppose that V is the speed at which the source moves toward the observer and t is the time between the emission of successive wave-crests at the source. Then in the time t the source moves a distance equal to $V \times t$ toward the observer. Hence the second wave-crest takes less time to reach the observer than the first one by an amount equal to $V \times t \div c$ where c represents the speed of light.

If the source of light were stationary, successive wave-crests would also take a time t to pass the observer, but when there is the motion V that time is reduced by $V \times t \div c$. That is to say, it is *proportionately* reduced by $V \div c$, and this is just the amount by which the wavelength is proportionately reduced. Suppose that the unshifted wavelength is λ and that the shifted wavelength is $\lambda - \Delta\lambda$; then the proportionate shift of the wavelength is just $\Delta\lambda \div \lambda$, and this must be equal to $V \div c$. We thus obtain the simple equation $\dfrac{\Delta\lambda}{\lambda} = \dfrac{V}{c}$.

From this simple equation we derive much of our knowledge of the motions of the stars and of the structure of our own galaxy, and our ideas about the universe in the large also make use of it. Yet the derivation of the equation depends only on the concept of wave motion. It could equally well be derived from a knowledge of water waves or sound waves and would equally well apply to them. It is a matter of common experience that the pitch of a train whistle is raised when the train is moving toward the observer. The degree to which the pitch of the whistle is raised depends precisely on our equation.

One detail remains to be mentioned. Exactly similar considerations apply when the source of light (or sound) is moving away from the observer. The situation is then reversed. Instead of the wavelength decreasing, it is increasing, and it is increasing by an amount given by an exactly similar equation. So when a source of light is moving away from the observer we get a shift toward the red end of the spectrum.

Leaving aside this question of wavelength shift, which is now important in the study of the motions of galaxies, there were two other kinds of information which the pioneers of modern spectroscopy hoped to gain by studying the spectra of the stars. First they hoped to be able to determine the physical conditions at the surfaces of the stars, particularly the temperature and the density of the material in which the spectrum lines are formed. Next they hoped to determine the chemical composition of the material itself. This was a difficult and ambitious program, and astronomers have only come near to carrying it out in recent years.

At an early stage it became clear that the spectra of stars can be classified into several broad groups, according to which lines dominate them. There is a group in which the lines of the simplest element of all, hydrogen, form the dominating feature. Such stars are known as A type stars. There are other stars in which the second simplest element, helium, provides the dominant lines of the spectrum. These stars can be subdivided into two groups, according to whether the lines of the ordinary neutral form of the helium atom dominate, or whether the dominant lines come from helium atoms that have lost one of their two electrons. These two groups are called B and O type stars respectively.

Left: Spectra of O, B, A, F, G, K and M stars. In each case the number beside the letter denotes subtype. Shorter wavelengths show at left and longer wavelengths at right of all spectra. In the sequence shown, this system of classification is also a guide to surface temperatures of stars, ranging from O (hottest) to M (coolest).

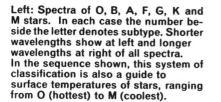

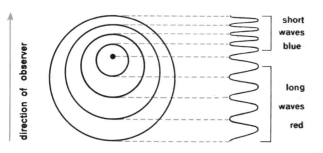

Here a source of light (shown by dot at center of smallest circle) moves toward an observer. As successive crests reach him they are closer together than if the source had been stationary. Light thus appears bluer. To an observer from whom the source is receding, light will appear redder.

We have already remarked on the great strength of the lines produced by calcium atoms in the atmosphere of the Sun. There is a group of stars, the F type stars, in which the hydrogen lines and the calcium lines are roughly comparable in strength. Metal lines, or lines produced by atoms of metals other than calcium, also become noticeable in the F stars, whereas metal lines scarcely show at all in the B and O groups and only occasionally do they show at all strongly in the A group. Next come stars with spectra rather like that of the Sun. Here the calcium lines have become stronger than the hydrogen lines and a tremendous profusion of metal lines, particularly those of iron, begin to show themselves. These are the G type stars.

The next group, the K type stars, also resemble spectra that *can* be observed in the Sun, for the K type stars have spectra similar to those of sunspots. Sunspots do not appear dark because no light at all comes from them; they appear dark only in comparison with the surrounding regions from which considerably more light is received. If we take the precaution to exclude light from the surrounding regions we can obtain the spectrum of a sunspot, and the result differs from the normal solar spectrum in that the hydrogen lines have become greatly weakened. This is the situation in the K type stars.

Finally there are stars in which the lines are produced by molecules as well as by atoms, and where, indeed, the molecular lines become dominant. These are the M stars. Spectroscopists have subdivided these molecular stars into four separate groups, M, N, R and S. It seems likely, however, that these subdivisions arise from chemical differences, whereas the differences we have so far considered arise mainly from the effects of temperature. Since it seems undesirable to mix together the effects of temperature and of chemistry, we shall ignore here the detailed division of the M stars. Hence our groups run as follows: A, B, O, F, G, K, M.

We have already noticed in Chapter 7 that the space between the stars contains fine particles of dust. The size of these particles is in the general range of three thousand angstroms and this fact causes them to absorb and to scatter blue light more readily than red light. Hence the light from a distant star appears to us to be redder than it really is. The observed colors of the stars thereby tend to be falsified, and the farther away a star happens to be, the more its color is falsified in this way. Now stars of the class O are comparatively uncommon, and none of them lies very near to us, so as a group the O type stars are more reddened by the effect of interstellar dust than are the nearer B and A type stars. For this reason it was not immediately clear to the early spectroscopists that the spectral classification outlined above can also give a color classification ranging from blue toward red. To do so, the groups must be rearranged in the following sequence: O, B, A, F, G, K and M. This sequence is easily remembered from the old mnemonic *Oh Be A Fine Girl, Kiss Me.*

Everyday observation tells us that the hotter a fire burns the bluer the light it emits. Hence our sequence of stars from blue to red, or from type O to type M, is a temperature sequence, the O stars being the hottest and the M stars the coolest at their surfaces. It is easy to show that this is true for the G and K sequence. We saw that G corresponds to the normal solar spectrum whereas K corresponds to the sunspot spectrum, and of course the sunspot is dark simply because it is cooler than the solar regions surrounding it.

According to modern work, the temperatures actually involved in the spectral classification scheme are as follows: O type upward of $35,000°$C.; B type from about $11,000°$ to about $35,000°$; A type from $7,500°$ to $11,000°$; F type from $6,000°$ to $7,500°$; G type from $5,100°$ to $6,000°$; K type from $3,600°$ to $5,100°$; M type cooler than $3,600°$. (These are all temperatures at the *surfaces* of the stars; the temperatures in their interiors are enormously higher, as we shall later see.) The temperature range for some groups—the B stars, for example—is very large. To cover the wide range from $11,000°$ to $35,000°$ ten subtypes are introduced. These range from B0 at $35,000°$, through the subtypes B1, B2, B3, etc., up to type B9, corresponding to a temperature of approximately $12,000°$. The other main groups are likewise divided into subclasses, and by studying star spectra the astronomer can classify the stars not only into the main, broad groups but also into the subclasses.

Consider the F stars. At subclass F0, the hydrogen lines are still stronger than the calcium lines, whereas at subclass F8 the reverse is the case. Indeed, the whole sequence of subclasses F0, F1, F2, etc., is based on the relative strength of the hydrogen and the calcium lines. As we pass along the sequence, the hydrogen lines weaken in comparison with the calcium lines. The ability of the astronomer to classify the stars in these subgroups allows his estimates of stellar temperatures to be greatly refined. Among stars of types G and K temperatures can be estimated to within 200°, among stars of type A to within 500°, among type B to within 2,000°, and among type O to within about 5,000°.

Next comes the question of the chemistry of the stars. If our only concern were to recognize which atoms are present in various stars, the problem would be comparatively simple. We should merely have to compare the spectrum lines present in the light of the star with the lines which different types of atom produce in the laboratory. A suitable correspondence in wavelength would then reveal the presence in the star of types of atom already examined in the laboratory. Indeed, it is in just this way that the stars have been shown to contain essentially all the elements that are found here on Earth. But we want to know much more than this. We are not satisfied with a qualitative chemical analysis of the stars; we want to know the concentrations of the various elements, and here difficulties arise.

The first is that we must know the stellar temperature very accurately, and even granted this, there is the further difficulty that different atoms vary enormously in their ability to produce spectrum lines. Whereas helium atoms are very reluctant to produce spectrum lines, even at high temperatures, calcium atoms do so very readily, even at comparatively low temperatures. All these inherent differences between different sorts of atom must be taken into account, and such a feat was far beyond the capacity of early workers in this field.

The first big step was taken about thirty years ago, when the work of Professor Henry Norris Russell of Princeton clearly showed that the compositions of the stars differ in one crucial respect from that of the Earth. The stars contain a vastly higher proportion of hydrogen, helium and other light gases such as oxygen, nitrogen and neon, than the Earth does.

The whole problem of the chemical make-up of stars is still under active investigation, and much remains to be done before the picture is complete. By now, however, we do have a pretty good idea of what the chemical composition of the Sun is like. Hydrogen atoms are about ten times more numerous than helium atoms, while hydrogen and helium atoms together are about a thousand times more numerous than the atoms of all the other elements put together. Of the rest, oxygen and neon are the most abundant elements, followed closely by carbon and nitrogen. After these, and something like ten

times less abundant than oxygen, come magnesium and silicon, then iron, then a whole lot of elements such as aluminum, sulfur, calcium and common metals like nickel and chromium.

The situation, therefore, is that the light group of elements ranging from carbon to neon contribute a little more than one per cent to the mass of the Sun. The elements of which the Earth is mainly constructed, namely magnesium, silicon and the common metals, contribute about a fifth of one per cent. The concentrations of the remaining elements, such as tin, barium, europium, mercury, lead and uranium, are almost negligibly small.

Most of the stars we can see in the sky have compositions very similar to that of the Sun, but we now know that some are markedly different. In particular, there are stars with very low concentrations of the common metals—stars in which the proportion of iron, for example, is only about one hundredth of that in the Sun. At the other extreme

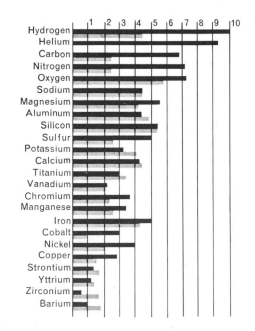

Comparative abundances of atoms of various elements on the Sun (first of each pair of bars) and on the Earth (second of each pair). The horizontal scale is logarithmic, 1 denoting 10^1, 2 denoting 10^2, and so on. Relative abundances are adjusted to agree for the element silicon, which is usually taken as the reference standard in discussions of *relative* abundances.

there are stars with abnormally high concentrations of certain particular elements—of barium, strontium, or zirconium. There are others with high concentrations of the rare earths.

One type of star contains an element which does not exist at all on the Earth. This is the element technetium. Technetium is naturally unstable; that is, it steadily breaks down into other elements. The half-life of its longest-lived isotope is about two hundred thousand years. This means that half of any given quantity of it breaks down into other elements in two hundred thousand years, half of the remainder in the next two hundred thousand years, and so on. At that rate even a very considerable quantity would effectively disappear in, say, twenty million years. None is now found on the Earth for the simple reason that even if there were any to begin with it must all have decayed long ago. Yet technetium is found in certain stars, and the implication is that it has been produced by some form of nuclear transmutation. We shall delve more deeply into this question in the next chapter, and also into the whole problem of why it is that stars differ in their chemical compositions.

Exploring the Surface of the Sun

One of the first triumphs of spectroscopy came in 1868, when with the help of a spectroscope Sir Norman Lockyer detected the presence of a hitherto-unknown element in the Sun. The fact that the Sun has a tenuous outer atmosphere situated above the photosphere had already been verified by direct observation during total eclipses. At such times observers had sometimes seen arched structures in this outer atmosphere, arches with roots descending into the photosphere. These were the prominences. One of Lockyer's outstanding contributions to spectroscopy was to discover that the spectra of prominences could be observed in full sunlight; that is, in the absence of an eclipse. In the course of his observations he came across one spectrum line which did not correspond to any of the characteristic lines that could be produced in the laboratory by any type of atom then known. He suggested that the new line was produced by an entirely "new" element, which he appropriately named helium.

In the last few years of the nineteenth century Sir William Ramsay discovered the presence of helium in certain radioactive materials here on the Earth. Helium is, in fact, constantly being produced by the radioactive materials in the Earth's crust and is constantly leaking away into the terrestrial atmosphere. Incidentally, helium changes from a gaseous to a liquid state at a lower temperature than any other substance. Its boiling-point is $-269°$C, and it was not until 1908 that anyone succeeded in liquefying it. Since then helium in liquid form has given rise to a whole new branch of physics, the branch known as low-temperature physics.

We saw earlier that helium does not readily produce spectrum lines except at high temperatures. How, then, are the spectrum lines of helium produced in the Sun? The answer is that the *outer* atmosphere of the Sun is indeed very hot, for a remarkable situation arises as we go upward from the photosphere. At first the temperature falls. This is

Engraving from Lockyer's *Chemistry of the Sun*, showing apparatus he used in determining coincidences of solar and metallic lines. In the course of his work Lockyer discovered in the solar spectrum lines produced by an element not then known on Earth.

Before the close of the nineteenth century Sir William Ramsay found that this element—helium— does exist on Earth. On the right is a facsimile of some of the notes taken down from Ramsay's dictation on the day the discovery was made.

in the region that produces the dark Fraunhofer lines of the solar spectrum. But then the situation is reversed. Some four or five thousand miles above the photosphere the temperature rises almost discontinuously from about 5,000° to 100,000° and more as we continue upward into the solar corona. (The corona is the great halo that surrounds the Sun and which shows itself so magnificently during a total eclipse of the Sun.) Now why does this hot gas not produce a lot of blue light, like the gas at the surface of a B type star or an O type star? The answer is that here the density of the gas is too low to enable it to emit very much light. But the small amount of light it does emit has the genuine high-temperature property, and this is why the helium spectrum lines are produced.

We can get a clearer notion of one high-temperature property by considering the spectrum lines of the Sun's high corona. For a long time the origin of these lines was fraught with mystery, for in the laboratory scientists could find nothing to match them. Remembering Lockyer's discovery of helium, some thought that these mysterious lines might be produced by other elements not present, or not yet discovered, on the Earth. The problem was finally resolved some thirty years ago by the Swedish physicist B. Edlén. Edlén found in the laboratory that these lines were in fact produced by very well-known elements, such as iron and calcium, but by atoms of those elements from which a considerable number of electrons had been stripped away. For example, one of the brightest lines arises from iron atoms from which 13 electrons have been stripped. The reason

why atoms exist in this state in the solar corona is that, because of the very high temperature there, they are subject to violent collisions. Indeed, the very existence of these lines in the spectrum of the corona is a sure indication that temperatures there *are* extremely high.

We have seen that going upward from the surface of the Sun toward the high corona there is a reversal of temperature. There is a similar reversal as we go upward from the surface of the Earth. The temperature at first decreases, but at a height of some 15 miles it begins to increase again, and at a height of about 35 miles it rises back to normal ground temperatures. Then for a while it drops again, but at about 60 miles above the Earth's surface the rise is resumed, and it continues until temperatures in excess of 1000° are reached in the high atmosphere.

This is the region of the Earth's ionosphere. The ionosphere has two main regions, one called the E region and the other the F region, the latter being subdivided into two parts, F1 and F2. In the E region, which occurs at a height of about 60 miles, X-rays emitted by the corona of the Sun are absorbed by the gases of the atmosphere. The absorption causes electrons to become detached from the atoms; that is to say, the atoms become ionized. The main F region occurs at a height of between 120 and 200 miles. A rather surprising fact, recently established with the aid of rockets, is that ionization in the F region is produced by radiation in the helium lines that occur at a wavelength near 500 angstroms. Thus the main ionosphere of the Earth owes its origins to the radiations emitted by the hot

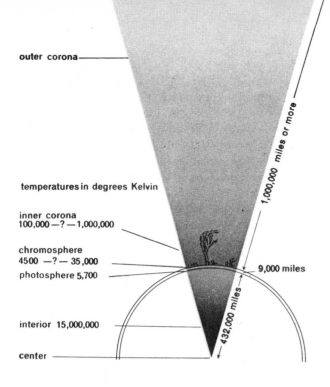

outer corona

temperatures in degrees Kelvin

inner corona
100,000 —?— 1,000,000

chromosphere
4500 —?— 35,000

photosphere 5,700

9,000 miles

1,000,000 miles or more

432,000 miles

interior 15,000,000

center

As we move away from the surface of the Sun the temperature at first falls. Then, as we move farther, toward the solar corona, it rises sharply.

A similar reversal takes place as we move away from the Earth's surface. Temperatures fall up to a height of over ten miles, then begin to increase.

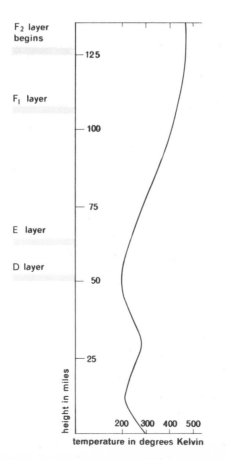

F$_2$ layer begins

125

F$_1$ layer

100

75

E layer

D layer

50

25

height in miles

200 300 400 500

temperature in degrees Kelvin

atmosphere of the Sun. Without these radiations there would be no ionosphere, and long-distance radio transmission, which depends on the reflection of electromagnetic waves from this region, would therefore be impossible.

Some ionization also occurs in our atmosphere at heights well below the E region. This also seems to be caused by X-rays from the Sun, but in this case by X-rays of considerably shorter wavelength than those emitted by the corona. These harder X-rays appear to come from regions down near the photosphere where they are produced by the remarkable phenomenon known as the solar flare. Flares are strongly correlated with sunspots, and at this point it may therefore be as well to examine briefly what astronomers have so far learned about sunspots.

Schwabe, a German apothecary, is usually credited with the discovery that sunspots wax and wane periodically. Schwabe made his announcement in 1843, but toward the end of the eighteenth century Horrebow had already announced that sunspots were probably governed by a law of periodicity; and Sir William Herschel had already boldly speculated that certain events on the Earth, such as the growth of wheat, might be correlated with a periodicity of solar activity. Schwabe's value for the period of sunspot activity was ten years. A few years later, R. Wolf arrived at a value of 11.1 years, remarkably close to the modern estimate.

The frequency of occurrence of sunspots at the maximum phase may be as much as a hundred times greater than at the minimum phase. Almost all the spots lie at latitudes of less than 40°, and they are more or less symmetrically distributed between the two solar hemispheres. At any given moment the spots are usually distributed along two belts, one in the northern hemisphere and the other in the southern. At the beginning of each new cycle, the belts lie at their greatest distance from the equator, at about 40°N and 40°S. As the cycle proceeds these belts gradually drift toward the equator, and by the time of maximum activity their latitudes are usually somewhere between 15° and 20°. By the end of the cycle they have almost reached the equator, but usually they die away at about latitude 5°. The first spots of the next cycle then appear around latitudes 40°N and 40°S.

An individual sunspot starts its life, which may last from a day or two up to several weeks, as a multitude of small dark specks. These specks then coagulate to form a dark spot which may measure

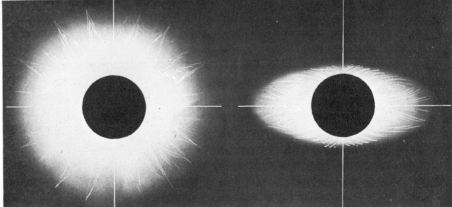

This photograph of the solar corona was taken in the Sudan during the eclipse of February 25th, 1952. The form of the corona is closely related to the phase of the eleven-year sunspot cycle. First diagram shows typical form of corona when spot activity is at maximum, second one shows typical form when spot activity is at minimum.

anything from ten thousand miles to a hundred thousand miles in diameter. Spots usually occur in pairs, one lying almost due west of the other.

We saw in Chapter 5 how Galileo used sunspots to measure the period of rotation of the Sun and arrived at a value of about 27 days. By repeating Galileo's observations more carefully, Carrington and Spörer, in about the year 1860, were able to show that the period of rotation is not exactly the same at different solar latitudes. They found that the Sun rotates most rapidly at its equator, and that at increasing latitudes the period of rotation becomes progressively longer. Indeed, the variation in the time of rotation between equatorial and polar regions of the Sun amounts to three or four days.

A century later this remarkable result is still unexplained. The problem is a famous one, for all the considerations that one might expect to bear on it suggest an exactly contrary situation. All our expectations would be that the Sun should rotate more slowly at its equator.

In the early years of the present century George Ellery Hale made a momentous discovery. Using complex spectrographic methods, he detected the presence of strong magnetic fields inside sunspots. This was the first direct evidence of the existence of magnetic fields in an astronomical problem. Now, in recent times, magnetic fields have come to play a dominant role in almost all our astronomical thinking. Quite apart from the sunspots, photographs of the solar corona taken at total eclipses suggest strongly that a large-scale magnetic field emerges from the solar surface into surrounding space. The movements of prominences and their structure is also strongly suggestive of the presence of magnetic fields emerging at the roots of the prominences from the interior of the Sun.

This brings us back to the question of solar flares, and a terrestrial analogy should help us to understand what these may be. Suppose a high-voltage power line were broken, say in a storm. At first sight one might think that the flow of current in the power line circuit would simply cease. But experience shows this is not so. The current tends to continue, and unless adequate precautions are taken a situation might arise which would cause serious damage to the generators at the power station. It is for this reason that electricity supply companies use elaborate switching arrangements for causing the flow of current to die away whenever a break in the power line occurs. All this can be explained in the following way. Wherever there is a flow of current there is also a magnetic field, and in the case of a large current the magnetic field carries a large amount of energy. This energy does not simply cease to exist as soon as the power line is broken. It must somehow be dissipated, and this is precisely what the electricity supply companies arrange to do with their elaborate switching devices. Violent spark discharges occur at the switches, and it is these discharges that dissipate the energy of the magnetic field.

It seems likely that on the Sun, too, there are situations in which magnetic fields are annihilated. There, just as in the terrestrial case, the energy carried by the fields does not suddenly cease to exist. It is dissipated in the form of huge discharges, and these are the solar flares.

In the course of the discharges electrons and atomic nuclei are accelerated to high speeds. This has two important effects. First these high-speed particles, colliding with each other and also with more or less stationary particles, generate the highly energetic X-rays which produce the lowest ionization zone of the Earth's atmosphere. Second, vast numbers of the high-speed particles themselves are shot out of the Sun in a form somewhat like the beam of a lighthouse. If the Earth happens to lie in the path of the beam, the particles impinge on the Earth's outer magnetic field. This produces the so-called magnetic storms. It also seems likely that in

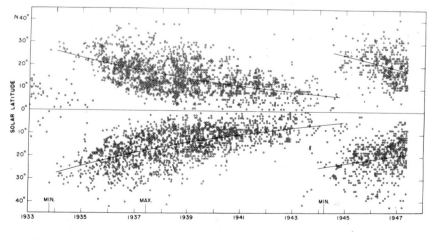

Diagram showing the distribution of sunspots at various solar latitudes (marked on vertical scale) throughout the period 1933-47. Spot distribution moves steadily toward solar equator as activity begins, increases and dies away. First spots of next cycle appear near latitudes 40°N and S.

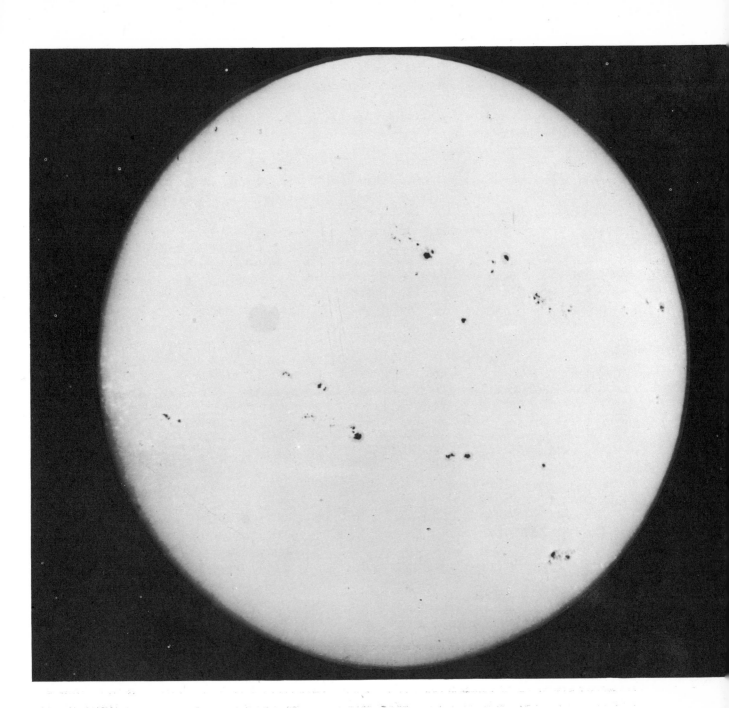

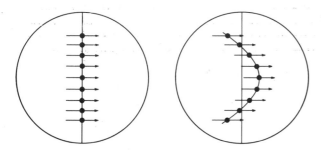

In each pair of spots above, one is almost due west of the other. Specks may later coagulate into big spots. If spots were lined up on a single meridian (first diagram) those near equator would increase their longitude more rapidly than those distant from it (second diagram).

the course of the impinging process high-speed electrons are generated, some of which are captured by the Earth, finding their way into the Earth's magnetic field.

It seems to be in this way that the outer Van Allen radiation belt is formed. The Van Allen radiation belts, recently discovered by the technique of space probes, consist of just such high-speed electrons trapped in the Earth's magnetic field. Rocking backward and forward between the north and south poles of the Earth, taking less than a second for each round trip, these electrons are responsible for the spectacular polar aurorae.

We have already seen that there is convincing evidence that the Sun's outer atmosphere is extremely hot, but we have not yet asked *why* it is. The foregoing discussion about how solar flares are produced should help us to understand the answer most favored by astronomers.

We know that the matter below the photosphere of the Sun is in constant convective motion—the kind of motion water has when being heated in a kettle. This motion must tend to produce magnetic energy at the expense of its own mechanical energy. The magnetic fields so generated then emerge from the photosphere into the solar atmosphere where processes of dissipation can take place. The solar flare is an extreme example of such a process, but for the most part the discharges are far more gentle and less spectacular. Even so, they generate a great deal of heat; not as much as is produced in the flare, where high-speed particles are blasted outward from the Sun into space, but quite enough to heat the Sun's atmosphere to a very high temperature.

In short, most astronomers now think that the Sun's atmosphere derives its energy from the convective motions that take place below the photosphere. The importance of the magnetic field lies in its role of energy-conveyor. It takes up the energy of motion of the material below the photosphere and transports it into the solar atmosphere where, in a process of dissipation, it emerges as heat.

Much of what we know and much of what we believe about the surface and the atmosphere of the Sun depend on our knowledge of magnetic fields. Since magnetic fields first entered into astronomical problems after their detection in sunspots, it is not unreasonable to ask what we have since learned about sunspots. We suspect that magnetic fields play an important part in producing the dark appearance of sunspots because they interfere with the efficiency with which convective motions carry energy from the immediate subphotospheric regions out to the photosphere itself. Beyond that, we have learned surprisingly little. Just why sunspots wax and wane in a time of about 11 years, just why they form belts around the Sun, and just why those belts drift toward the equator as the cycle proceeds, we still do not know. We can only suspect that we are up against extremely subtle and complex processes of which the explanations are far from simple.

The study of activity at the surface of the Sun and of its relation to the Earth has been vigorously pursued for upward of a hundred years, and a truly vast number of observations have been made. What has all this great effort achieved in comparison with achievements in other branches of astronomy? It seems to me that the answer cannot be a particularly

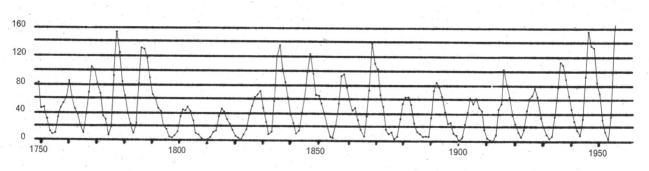

Graph showing sunspot activity from 1750 to 1950. Numbers in the vertical scale are *Wolf numbers*, in which each spot visible through a particular telescope used as a standard reckons as one and each group of spots as ten.

Telescopic photograph of sunspots taken from a balloon over 80,000 feet above the Earth. The spots are cores of relatively cool gases associated with strong magnetic fields. Wisps of hotter gases envelop them.

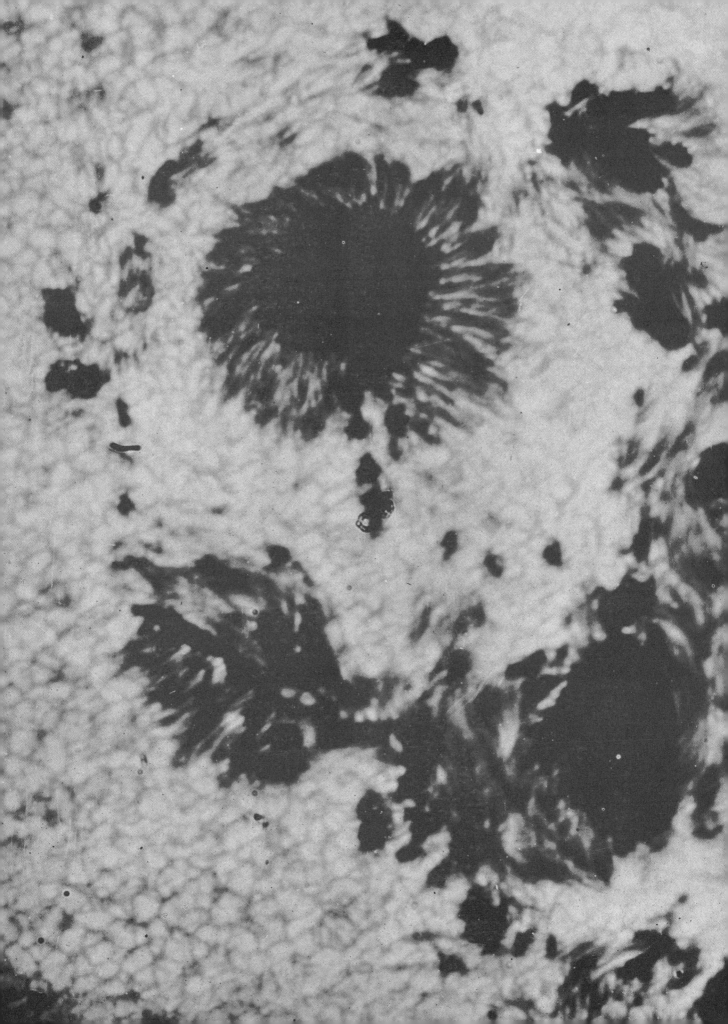

cheerful one. The most interesting and useful developments have emerged only recently, in our increased understanding of the importance of magnetic processes. But progress as a whole has undoubtedly been slight compared with that in the rest of astronomy.

These considerations have a special importance for British astronomy. With the coming of spectroscopy and of interest in the solar cycle, British astronomers lost most of their interest in the larger problems. The lines of research started by such men as Herschel were abandoned, and because large telescopes are not necessary for observing the Sun, no telescope of appreciable aperture has been built in Britain during the past fifty years. As this book goes to press, Britain does not possess a telescope with an aperture equal to that of the largest of Herschel's instruments. This woeful lack can be traced to the over-emphasis that has been placed on solar research. That is not to say that the investigation of the surface activity of the Sun is without importance. What *is* being said is that it is not of such great importance that it should be allowed to override the interests of the rest of astronomy.

All this has an important modern connotation, for space research is in large measure simply a continuation of the investigation of the surface activities of the Sun. And the emphasis now being placed on space research, particularly in the United States and Russia, is similar in many ways to the emphasis that has been placed on solar research in Britain during the last hundred years. Just as a false sense of proportion led British astronomers to forgo the larger problems of astronomy, so overemphasis on space research may again produce a situation in which the main problems are lost sight of.

To give substance to these remarks, we may well quit the surface phenomena of the Sun and consider some of the fascinating problems that arise when we examine its interior. Here we shall encounter phenomena that are of importance for the stars in general and which also have application to the universe in the large.

Inside the Sun

If you throw a ball into the air, it falls back to the ground. It does so because it is pulled downward by the force of gravity. Now gravity does not stop acting when the ball touches the ground, so why doesn't the ball continue to fall until it reaches the center of the Earth? The answer is, of course, that the ground presses upward on the ball with a force equal to that with which gravity pulls it downward. The same is true about all the material in the Earth, and our whole planet is in equilibrium because gravity is everywhere balanced by the pressures that exist throughout the body of the Earth.

This applies equally to the atmospheric gases. These, too, would fall downward under the action of gravity if it were not for the pressure within them. The pressure that supplies the balancing upward force at sea level is the so-called normal atmospheric pressure, about 15 pounds per square inch. The pressure existing at the center of the Earth is some ten million times greater than this.

The same considerations apply to the Sun, but because the Sun is much heavier than the Earth the pressures inside it have to be correspondingly greater. The pressure at the center of the Sun is about a hundred thousand million times greater than the pressure of the terrestrial atmospheric gases at sea level.

How do we know this? In Chapter 6 we saw that the mass of the Sun can be determined from the motions of the planets. We also know the distance of the Sun and hence its true size. Given the mass and size of the Sun, it is a simple matter to work out the pull of gravity at its surface. This turns out to be about thirty times greater than the pull of gravity at the surface of the Earth. At first sight the difference is not very great, but it rapidly becomes more marked as we penetrate inward from the surface of

The top photograph shows giant loop prominences on the edge of the Sun's disk. The movements and structure of prominences strongly suggest the presence of magnetic fields emerging at their roots from the interior of the Sun. In fact, magnetic fields cause the ordinary atomic lines of a spectrum to split into a number of components, and by using complex spectrographic methods it is thus possible to detect them.
The small photograph of the Sun's disk was taken on July 18th, 1953. Beside it is a magnetic map of the Sun for the same date. It shows the location, intensity and polarity of weak magnetic fields in the photosphere, apart from sunspots.

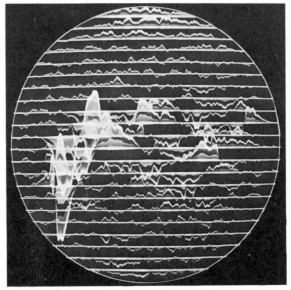

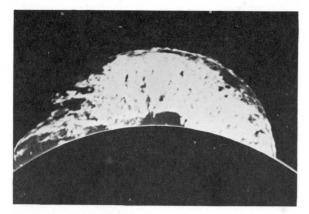

Time: 16h 03m (U.T.)   Time: 16h 36m

Series of photographs of an eruptive
prominence, taken on June 4th, 1946.
Small circle above first picture
shows the Earth to same scale.

the Sun. Because the Sun contains so much more material than the Earth does, the weight of the overlying layers becomes vastly greater as we near its center, and it is to withstand this great weight of the overlying layers that such tremendous pressures are necessary.

The next question is how are the requisite pressures maintained? Nineteenth-century physicists already understood that ordinary solids and liquids cannot withstand more than a certain limited pressure, and that they fall far short of being able either to supply or to withstand pressures of the order that must exist inside the Sun. So the deep interior of the Sun cannot possibly be solid or liquid, as William Herschel imagined it to be. But nineteenth-century discoveries concerning the nature of gases showed that the necessary pressures would be forthcoming from gases if they were sufficiently hot.

The pressure existing in a gas depends on three things: density, temperature, and the nature of the particles that make up the gas. Let us take these in turn. In the seventeenth century Robert Boyle had already established that the pressure of a gas increases with its density, and provided the density is not too great the pressure is directly proportional to it; that is to say, if the density is doubled, the pressure is doubled. This is known as Boyle's Law. In the eighteenth century J. A. Charles showed that there is a similar direct proportionality between temperature and pressure: if the temperature of a gas, as measured from Absolute zero, is doubled then the pressure is also doubled. We can write

these discoveries in the form of a simple equation. If we use P for pressure, T for temperature, and the Greek letter ρ (rho) for density, we can set up the equation: $P = A \times \rho \times T$. In our equation A is a constant that depends on the nature of the particles that make up the gas.

To determine the constant A we need to know two things: first, the chemical composition of the gas—the concentrations of the various types of atoms in it; second, the condition in which those atoms exist. As we have already seen, we now know the chemical composition of the Sun, and of many other stars, but this information was not available to the early investigators. Nevertheless, at least one early investigator, J. Homer Lane, made a surprisingly good guess at the answer to the second part of the problem—concerning the condition in which atoms exist in the Sun's interior—close on a century ago. Lane argued that at the very high temperatures probably existing inside the Sun there would be fierce collisions between atoms which might cause them to be torn asunder. This is just what modern physics teaches us to expect. The atoms are torn asunder in the sense that the electrons which normally surround the heavy central nucleus are largely stripped away. Thus the nuclei of the atoms move around freely by themselves without carrying their normal retinues of surrounding electrons with them, and the stripped electrons themselves move around freely too. So the gas inside the Sun consists of two kinds of particles moving freely and separately: the bare nuclei of atoms and electrons. Knowing this,

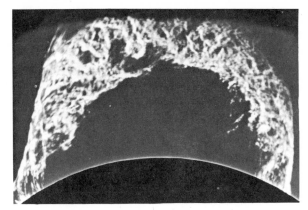

Time: 16h 51m

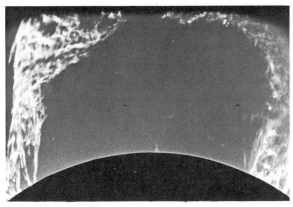

Time: 17h 03m

and knowing the relative proportions of the different types of atom and the degrees to which they are stripped of their electrons, we can determine the quantity A. Provided we also know the density and the temperature of the gas, we can thus use our formula to calculate its pressure; alternatively, if we know the pressure and the density, we can use the same formula to calculate the temperature.

Now we do, in fact, know the general order of the pressures, P, that must exist inside the Sun from our gravity argument. Because we know the mass and the size of the Sun we also know the general order of the density, p. The constant A is determined by the considerations in the last paragraph. Hence we can use our equation to give us a general idea of what the temperature T must be.

A rough calculation of this kind shows immediately that it must be in the region of ten million degrees. The calculation is rough in the sense that it does not determine the precise temperature. It is not rough in the sense that it might permit of an order-of-magnitude change in the result it gives; that is to say, the result cannot be, at most, more than three times too great or three times too small. The temperature could be a little lower or a little higher, so far as our argument is concerned, but it must be *in the region of* ten million degrees. In fact the modern value, given by a far more precise calculation, is close to fifteen million degrees at the extreme center of the Sun.

Since the inside of the Sun is far hotter than the surface regions, there must be a tremendous leakage of heat from the central regions to the photosphere, for heat in matter always flows from a region of higher temperature to a region of lower temperature. This explains why the Sun is a bright luminous object whereas a body like the Moon emits no light of its own, but shines only by reflecting light from the Sun. The basic difference between a planet or a satellite on the one hand and a star on the other is that inside a planet or a satellite the pressures needed to counterbalance the pull of gravity are comparatively small, and can be provided by ordinary solids and liquids. Hence the temperatures inside planets and satellites need not be very high as they must be inside the stars; and just because the temperatures are not very high there is no large-scale leakage of heat from their central regions to their surfaces.

How exactly is energy conveyed from the central regions of the Sun to the photosphere? Heat travels along a metal bar from the hotter end to the cooler end by conduction; that is, the hot particles of metal do not move along the bar but simply pass on some of their heat to neighboring cooler particles. But it is easy to check by calculation that the outflow of heat in the Sun could never be carried by conduction, for it is far too slow a process. The next possibility is that it is carried by convection, that is, by the actual movement of hot particles such as occurs when water in a kettle or air in a room is heated.

The first mathematical investigation of the structure of the Sun, made by J. Homer Lane in 1869, was based on the assumption that the outward

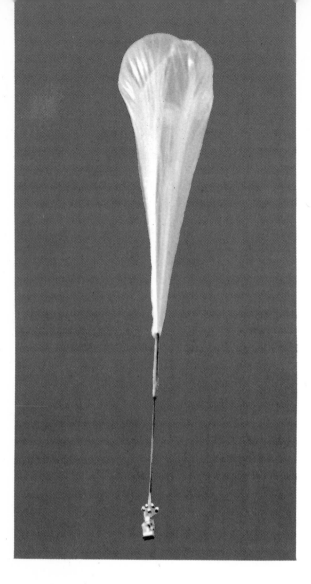

flow of energy from its center is carried in just that way—by convection. If, knowing the chemical composition of the Sun and hence the value of the constant A, one makes this assumption, it is possible with the help of the formula $P = A \times \rho \times T$ to compute the structure of the Sun in precise mathematical terms. The temperature at the center then turns out to be quite close to ten million degrees. The density turns out to be about 50 grams per cubic centimeter, or about fifty times as great as the density of cold distilled water at sea level.

This raises a question that was a serious worry until about forty years ago. Can we rightly regard matter with such high densities as gases, and if we can, is it reasonable to expect them to conform to the simple pressure formula given above? It will be recalled that Boyle's Law, which tells us that the pressure of a gas is directly proportional to its density, is applicable only if the density is not too high. The validity of the law in a terrestrial laboratory certainly ceases at densities as high as 50 grams per cubic centimeter. Why should the law not also cease to be valid at similar densities inside the Sun or inside the stars?

The answer is to be found in the extremely high temperatures that prevail there. By stripping the electrons from the nuclei of atoms these high temperatures enable matter, even at very high densities, to behave just as gases do on Earth. Thus Boyle's

In recent years American astronomers have obtained clearer photographs of the Sun's surface than ever before from unmanned balloons at heights where "bad seeing", produced by the Earth's atmosphere, is eliminated. Photographs show preparations for launching and actual ascent during such a flight made in September, 1957. Diagram shows telescope mounting.

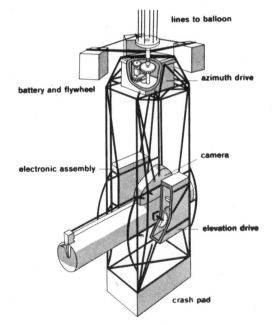

lines to balloon

azimuth drive

battery and flywheel

camera

electronic assembly

elevation drive

crash pad

Law is made applicable at far higher densities than we might at first sight expect. In fact, at very high temperatures, serious discrepencies do not arise until the density climbs to about 1000 grams per cubic centimeter. Hence our simple pressure formula holds good everywhere inside the Sun.

Returning now to the flow of energy from the internal regions of the Sun toward its surface. Nineteenth-century astronomers were aware of the possibility that some or all of this flow might be carried not by convection but by radiation, as energy is carried across space from the Sun to the Earth. The problem was how to calculate the effect of radiation, and the basic plan for doing this was discovered by Karl Schwarzschild only as recently as 1906. Modern work has now demonstrated that the energy flow deep inside the Sun does indeed take place in accordance with the mathematical equations which Schwarzschild worked out. That is to say, the transport of energy there is by radiation and not by convection as earlier workers such as Homer Lane had assumed.

But although this is true in the deep interior, convection does become important nearer the surface layers of the Sun, as the series of photographs shown below would lead us to expect. The situation, therefore, is that in any thoroughgoing discussion of the structure of the Sun, both radiation and convection must be carefully considered.

We need not be satisfied with merely specifying in a qualitative way the mode of transport of energy inside the Sun. It is possible to make a quantitative calculation. The result of such calculation is a prediction of what the brightness of the Sun should be, and this we can check by observation. In modern work the check between observation and theory has become most satisfactory, but before we come to that we must look at the pioneer work which Eddington did in this field.

Let us think now not just of the Sun but of any star. The temperature at its center will not necessarily be the same as in the Sun. It will depend upon the mass of the star and upon its size. These factors are important because they determine the strength of gravity, and hence the pressure required to withstand it. The larger the mass of a star, the greater the gravitational force it exerts. This implies that the temperatures necessary to provide for support against gravity inside stars of large mass will be higher than the temperatures necessary inside stars of smaller mass; and because the internal temperatures are higher, the flow of radiation from the inner regions to the surface will also be greater. Hence we expect stars of large mass to be more luminous than stars of small mass. This is indeed the case, as we shall shortly see.

The effect of the radius of a star on its luminosity can also be considered in a similar way. If two stars

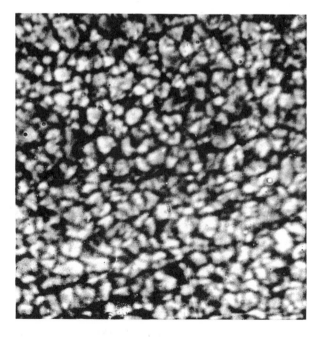
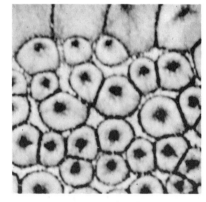
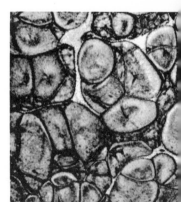

Flying telescope view of Sun's surface (left) shows light spots (columns of hot, rising gas) and darker areas (sinking masses of cooler gas). First small photograph shows convection pattern produced by heating shallow layer of paraffin gently; second one shows convection pattern produced by heating deeper layer more rapidly. Second resembles granulation of Sun.

are of equal mass but of different radii, gravity will be less in the star of larger radius. Hence the internal pressure and the internal temperature will also be less, and for this reason the leakage of energy from the inner regions to the surface will be smaller. In other words the larger star will be less luminous than the smaller one.

These are the ideas that Eddington subjected to calculation. He was able to obtain mathematical formulae from which he could deduce the value of the luminosity from the mass and the radius. By a fortunate circumstance it happens that the radius does not enter the calculations in a sensitive way. Without any substantial loss of accuracy, it is possible to omit a precisely-determined radius and to substitute suitably averaged observed values. For example, if we wish to determine the luminosity of a star of known mass but of unknown radius, we simply insert in our calculation the average radius, determined by actual observation, for stars of that particular mass. In any given instance the actual radius will probably differ from the average value used, but this will not appreciably affect the result. Hence it is possible to calculate a luminosity for each value of mass.

Eddington's results are shown in Figure 8.1, where the solid line gives the outcome of the calculations. The vertical scale on the left represents the luminosity (L), while the horizontal scale at the bottom represents the mass (M). The mass (M) is plotted logarithmically. It is convenient to take the unit of

M as the solar mass, so that mass values in terms of the Sun are easily read off from the figure. But the situation is more complicated for the scale of luminosity. This is a *magnitude* scale, which calls for some explanation.

From a modern point of view the magnitude scale could hardly be more arbitrary or more inconvenient. Yet it is a scale with historical associations going back to Hipparchus and Ptolemy, and for that reason it is not lightly to be abandoned. A difference in luminosity of one magnitude corresponds to a factor of approximately 2.512. That is to say, if two stars differ by one unit of magnitude, one is 2.512 times more luminous than the other; if they differ in magnitude by five units, one is 100 times (or 2.512^5 times) more luminous than the other. Note that the magnitudes go apparently the wrong way, so that the brighter of two stars has the smaller magnitude. Thus if star A is 2.512 times brighter than star B, the magnitude of A is one unit *less* than the magnitude of B.

The magnitude difference between two stars is simply a measure of their difference in luminosity. So provided we take any one star of known luminosity and give it some arbitrarily-fixed magnitude value, we can also give magnitude values to all other stars of known luminosity. But which star shall we use as our yardstick, and what arbitrary magnitude number shall we assign to it? One might have expected that the Sun would be chosen, and assigned a magnitude value of 0 or perhaps 1, but not so. In

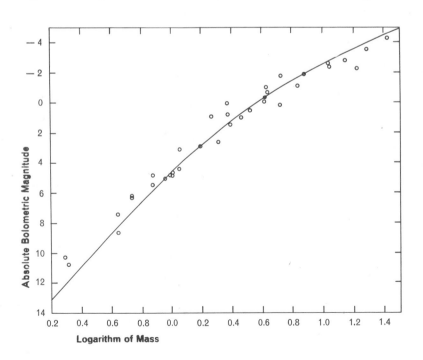

Figure 8.1
The mass-luminosity relation.
If we know the mass of a star, and also the average radius of stars of similar mass, we can calculate its absolute luminosity. Eddington (above) discovered this relationship and in 1924 wrote of it as shown opposite.

fact, for historical reasons which are here irrelevant, the Sun is assigned a magnitude of 4.7; and given this arbitrary choice, all the other magnitudes follow.

There is one other feature of magnitudes that must be mentioned. Magnitudes expressing the *true* luminosities of stars, that is, the amount of radiation they actually emit, are known as *absolute* magnitudes. This is to distinguish them from *apparent* magnitudes, which express the apparent luminosities of stars. The apparent luminosity of a star is its brightness as it appears to us, not its true brightness. Two stars with the same true brightness can have quite different apparent luminosities simply because they are at different distances from us. Thus apparent luminosities and apparent magnitudes differ from absolute luminosities and absolute magnitudes in that they are affected by the different distances of the stars.

The true luminosity of a star includes the whole of the radiation it emits, and the word *bolometric* is sometimes included to emphasize this point. Thus we may talk of bolometric luminosity or bolometric absolute magnitude to indicate that we are referring to the totality of the radiation emitted by a star. This point derives its force from the fact that when we observe a star neither our eyes nor our photographic plates are sensitive to the whole of the light from it. Indeed, not all of it penetrates down to us through the gases of the Earth's atmosphere. Measured luminosities, then, cannot in their nature be bolometric luminosities. Astronomers allow for this

fact by referring to visual luminosities, blue luminosities, or ultra-violet luminosities, each of these being defined as the amount of light that a star emits within a prescribed range of wavelengths. In the case of visual luminosity the prescribed range of wavelengths is approximately that to which the human eye is sensitive; blue luminosity refers to a range of wavelengths that is systematically less than that involved in a visual luminosity measurement; ultraviolet luminosity refers to a range of still shorter wavelengths.

From all this it is clear that bolometric luminosities cannot by their very nature be determined by actual observation. They are determined partly from observation and partly by calculation. The calculation is necessary to allow for the part of the light that fails to get through our atmosphere and to which our detecting instruments are not sensitive.

Now that we understand the meaning of the scales employed, we may profitably look again at Eddington's luminosity diagram (Figure 8.1). The solid line refers to the calculated bolometric luminosity values and the marked points to bolometric luminosities of particular stars. The agreement between theory and observation is remarkable, clearly demonstrating the general accuracy of the physical ideas on which the calculations were based.

Luminosities, Radii and Masses of Stars
How does the astronomer come to grips with the problem of determining the luminosities, radii and

The important result emerges that β depends only on the mass and molecular weight, and is independent of the radius or density of the star. Moreover it is independent of the coefficient of absorption k.

From (20) and (23), we obtain the rate of radiation of energy by the star

$$L = \frac{4\pi c G}{k} M (1-\beta) \tag{29}$$

The density of the star does not appear in this formula; at the most it can only affect the rate of radiation of energy indirectly by its influence on k. If k is the same for all stars, we have the result —

The total radiation of a giant star is a function of its mass only, and remains unaltered as the star changes in density in the process of evolution

If k is not constant, the radiation varies inversely as k

masses of stars? To determine the true luminosity of a star we must know its distance. A method for determining the distances of the nearest stars, the parallax method based on the annual motion of the Earth, was described in Chapter 6. For more distant stars other methods must be used, however, and it will be convenient to defer a discussion of these until a later chapter. For the moment we will suppose that we are equipped with the knowledge of the distance of any particular star we wish to examine. The next step is to determine the apparent luminosity for a particular range of wavelengths, for example, the visual range. This can be done most accurately by the use of photoelectric techniques. Then a simple calculation (based on the fact that the degree of brightness we see varies in inverse proportion to the square of the distance of the source of light) determines the absolute luminosity for the wavelength range in question. The final step is to make a correction to allow for the portion of the star's radiation that was not included in our chosen range of wavelengths. This gives the absolute bolometric luminosity of the star.

Just how accurate is the final result likely to be? When a photoelectric technique is used, the inaccuracy of the actual observation is very slight. Virtually the whole of any error therefore arises from the estimate of distance and from the final correction to allow for radiation not included in the range of wavelengths used in the observation. For stars with

surface temperatures between about 4,000° and 20,000° this correction is expected to be comparatively accurate, so that the error in such cases is likely to be almost wholly due to the distance measurements. But for stars of very high surface temperature and stars of very low surface temperature the correction factors are uncertain. Indeed it is possible that errors of as much as 100 per cent could arise in our estimates of the luminosities of these stars, simply from errors in the correction factor alone. Provided we are not concerned with very distant stars, errors arising from distance measurements will not usually be as large as this. It may, of course, happen that these two kinds of error have a cumulative effect, but it may equally happen that each affects the result in the opposite sense, and so tend to cancel each other out.

Our next problem, determining the radius of a star, is readily solved provided we know its absolute bolometric luminosity and its spectrum type. Luminosity, radius and surface temperature are related by the equation $L = D \times R^2 \times T^4$, in which L stands for luminosity, R for radius, and T for temperature; D is a constant whose precise value we know from physics. Now D is known precisely, and T can be determined from the spectrum type of the star in question, in the manner described earlier in the present chapter. Thus, once the luminosity L has been determined from the considerations of the previous paragraphs, it is an easy matter to calculate the radius, R.

The masses of the stars are more difficult to determine than either their luminosities or their radii. Most of our very limited knowledge in this field is derived from binary systems, that is, from systems containing two stars. We saw in Chapter 6 how Herschel discovered the existence of such systems and how the persistence of such men as Friedrich Wilhelm Struve resulted in determining the orbits in which the two stars move around their common center of gravity in a number of binary systems.

Since the time of Struve the work of observing binaries has been carried on by many enthusiastic observers. Let us examine how such an observer sets to work in an ideal case. He sees the two stars of a double system separated from each other on the sky. The imaginary line joining them turns round as they move about each other, and the time the line takes to move once round in a complete turn determines the period of orbital motion. The period may be one of many years, but with sufficient patience

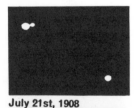

July 21st, 1908

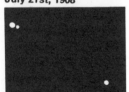

September 2nd, 1915

July 10th, 1920

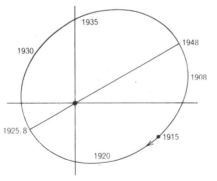

Much of our knowledge of star masses is derived from orbits of binaries. At the left we see the two stars of the binary Kruger 60, together with a neighboring star. Above we see how, from a series of such observations, the apparent orbit of Kruger 60 was eventually determined.

on the part of the original observer—and possibly a long line of successors—it can be successfully determined in this way.

Although both stars of the double system are moving with respect to the pattern of distant stars, there is a point lying somewhere between them that stays almost fixed with respect to the distant background; and it is on this point that the line joining the two stars appears to pivot. This is their so-called common center of gravity. In favorable cases the motion of the center of gravity against the background of distant stars is so slight that for the purposes of our idealized case we can neglect it. At any given moment, then, we have the two stars and their center of gravity lying at a point somewhere on the line joining them. In fact the center of gravity divides the line into two parts and we can very easily determine the ratio of these parts: and from that ratio we can determine the ratio of the masses of the two stars. If, for example, the center of gravity divides the line in the ratio 2:1, then the star nearer the center of gravity has twice the mass of the star farther from it. This, of course, determines only the mass *ratio*. Determining absolute masses involves quite other considerations.

Observations of the positions of the two stars, even extended over a complete orbital period, does not in itself determine the true orbit of the binary system except in the special case where the line of sight to the Earth happens to be perpendicular to the plane of the orbits of the stars around each other. In all other cases what we see is the true orbit projected against the sky; that is to say, projected on a plane perpendicular to the line of sight, as in Figure 8.2. So the next problem is to reconstruct the true orbit. This is a tricky matter, but if the original observations were made accurately enough, it can be done by dint of careful calculation and sheer persistence.

When it *is* done, one thing more remains. In order to fix the true scale of the orbits, we must know the distance of the binary system. There are several ways of doing this, and one—the parallax method—has already been described in Chapter 6. Knowing the shape of the orbits and their true scale, it is then an easy matter to work out the average distance between the two stars over the whole of the orbital period. To determine the absolute masses of the stars we now use Kepler's third law. This tells us that the ratio of the combined masses of the two stars to the mass of the Sun is equal to the ratio of the cube of the average distance between them to the square of the orbital period. Thus if we call the two stars S_1 and S_2 our equation is:

$$\frac{(\text{Mass of } S_1 + \text{Mass of } S_2)}{\text{Mass of Sun}} = \frac{(\text{Average distance between } S_1 \text{ and } S_2)^3}{(\text{Orbital period})^2}$$

In this equation the average distance is measured using the distance of the Earth from the Sun as the unit of measurement; the orbital period is measured in years. Since we already know the mass of the Sun, the average distance between S_1 and S_2, and the orbital period, our equation now gives us the combined masses of S_1 and S_2 in absolute terms. This result, together with our previous determination of the *ratio* of the masses of the two component stars, determines their separate masses in absolute terms.

In some cases the stars of a double system may be so close together that they cannot be separately distinguished even with a large telescope. Yet so long as one star is not enormously brighter than another it is still possible to know that we are dealing with a double system. Both stars produce spectrum lines, and because both are in motion in their orbits around each other, these spectrum lines exhibit the wavelength shift discussed near the beginning of the present chapter. Since the effect of the orbital motion is to cause one star to move toward us while the other moves away from us, as in Figure 8.3, one set of spectrum lines will shift toward blue while the other will shift toward red. Moreover, the effects

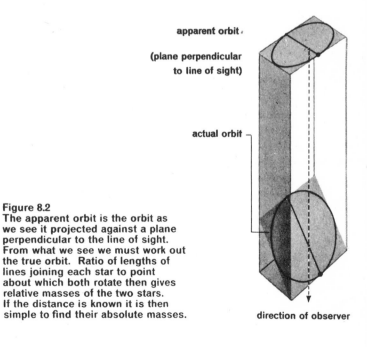

apparent orbit

(plane perpendicular to line of sight)

actual orbit

Figure 8.2
The apparent orbit is the orbit as we see it projected against a plane perpendicular to the line of sight. From what we see we must work out the true orbit. Ratio of lengths of lines joining each star to point about which both rotate then gives relative masses of the two stars. If the distance is known it is then simple to find their absolute masses.

direction of observer

vary as the two stars move around each other, for the one that is moving toward us now will later be moving away from us, and *vice versa*. Hence the shifts of wavelength vary from moment to moment. By detecting this variation, we can infer that we are dealing with a double system.

It is often simpler to determine the relative masses of the components in binary systems where the two stars are comparatively close together than in systems where they are widely separated. For the orbits of close systems, the so-called spectroscopic binaries, are nearly always very close to circles, whereas in cases of wide separation they may be highly elliptical. When the spectrum lines of both star-components can be separately distinguished it is a relatively easy matter to determine the velocities of both stars in their orbits. This immediately gives us the ratio of the masses of the two stars, for the ratio of the velocities is equal to the ratios of the sizes of the two orbits. This must be so since the two stars have exactly the same periods.

We can seldom go beyond this, for in most cases we must perforce remain in ignorance of the angle between the line of sight and the plane of the orbit of the two stars. There is one special case, however, in which this angle can be determined to a good approximation, namely the case where the angle is near zero. In this case the line of sight lies nearly in the plane of the orbit, and at certain moments one star will pass almost directly in front of the other and

eclipse it. This eclipsing effect is made evident by the variation in the light that we receive from the system. We can put the matter the other way round and say that when we observe such an eclipsing effect we can safely assert that the angle between the line of sight and the plane of the orbit must be near zero.

In such a case, a knowledge of the velocities of the two stars in their orbit, together with the orbital period, determines the absolute sizes of the orbits. Then, from Kepler's law, we can deduce the combined absolute masses of the two stars; and by using the ratio of the masses, obtained from the ratio of the velocities, we can estimate their individual masses in absolute terms.

In Figure 8.4 we have a typical case of the light variations that occur in such an eclipsing system. It will be seen that there are two dips in the light, one deeper than the other. The deeper dip obviously occurs when the fainter star passes in front of the brighter one; the shallower dip occurs when the brighter star passes in front of the fainter one.

The Hertzsprung-Russell Diagram

What conclusions can we draw from our knowledge of the luminosities, radii and masses of stars? Before answering this question it is necessary to take stock of just what we do know.

Spectra are available for a great many stars, and for all of these we know the approximate surface temperatures. The number of stars for which we also have reasonably accurate estimates of distance, and for which we therefore know the luminosities and radii as well as the surface temperatures, is considerably more restricted. Far more restricted still is the number for which, in addition to all these other things, we also have an accurate estimate of mass. Indeed, this last group is so small that it cannot provide a sufficient basis for a consideration of the properties of stars as a whole. For this we must rely on the intermediate and reasonably numerous group for which we know spectrum types, luminosities and radii.

A method of representing these stars was invented independently by E. Hertzsprung of Leyden and by Henry Norris Russell. Their representation, now known as the Hertzsprung-Russell diagram, is shown in Figure 8.5. Along the vertical axis we have the absolute visual magnitude. (As we have already seen, absolute visual magnitudes correspond more directly to observation than bolometric magnitudes, but, unlike bolometric magnitudes, they do not represent the total emission of radiation from a star, but only the radiation in a restricted range of wavelengths.) Along the horizontal axis of the diagram we have the spectrum type, starting with types O and B on the left, and ranging through A, F, G and K to type M at the right.

The stars plotted here are a sample of those in the region of the Milky Way lying comparatively close by the Sun. Now it will be recalled that a star's spectrum type is a measure of its surface temperature, and that when both surface temperature and luminosity are known the radius can readily be determined. Hence, when a star's position on the Hertzsprung-Russell diagram is known its radius can be found provided we make an appropriate correction from its visual magnitude to its bolometric magnitude.

A pronounced feature of the star distribution in the diagram is the concentration toward a line stretching from bottom right to top left. This is known as the main sequence. There is also a strong concentration of stars at about spectrum type K and with absolute visual magnitudes around 0.0. These are stars of large radii, known as giants. These are the two main features that stand out of the Hertzsprung-Russell diagram for stars of the solar neighborhood. If stars from more distant parts of the Milky Way are plotted, some of them are found to fall in quite different places. For example, very highly luminous stars with visual magnitudes approaching – 8 and at spectrum types F and G can be found. These are known as supergiants.

What is the reason for the differing positions of the stars on the Hertzsprung-Russell diagram? Before attempting to answer this question in detail it will be best to look at the first of the theories put forward—the giant and dwarf theory proposed by Henry Norris Russell.

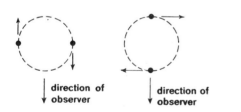

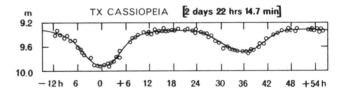

Figure 8.3
When one star of a binary system is moving toward us the other is moving away from us. Spectrum lines of first star are displaced toward blue and spectrum lines of second star are displaced toward red. Thus the lines of the whole system are doubled. Some quarter of a revolution later neither star is moving either toward or away from us. Lines produced by both of them are then superposed. At left are spectra of Mizar, a binary in the constellation Ursa Major.

Figure 8.4
If the line of sight lies nearly in the plane of the orbit of a binary system, then each star will periodically eclipse the other. We can then calculate their relative masses from their velocities and the orbital period. The diagram shows variations in luminosity from an eclipsing binary. Deep dip comes when fainter star eclipses brighter one, shallow dip when brighter eclipses fainter.

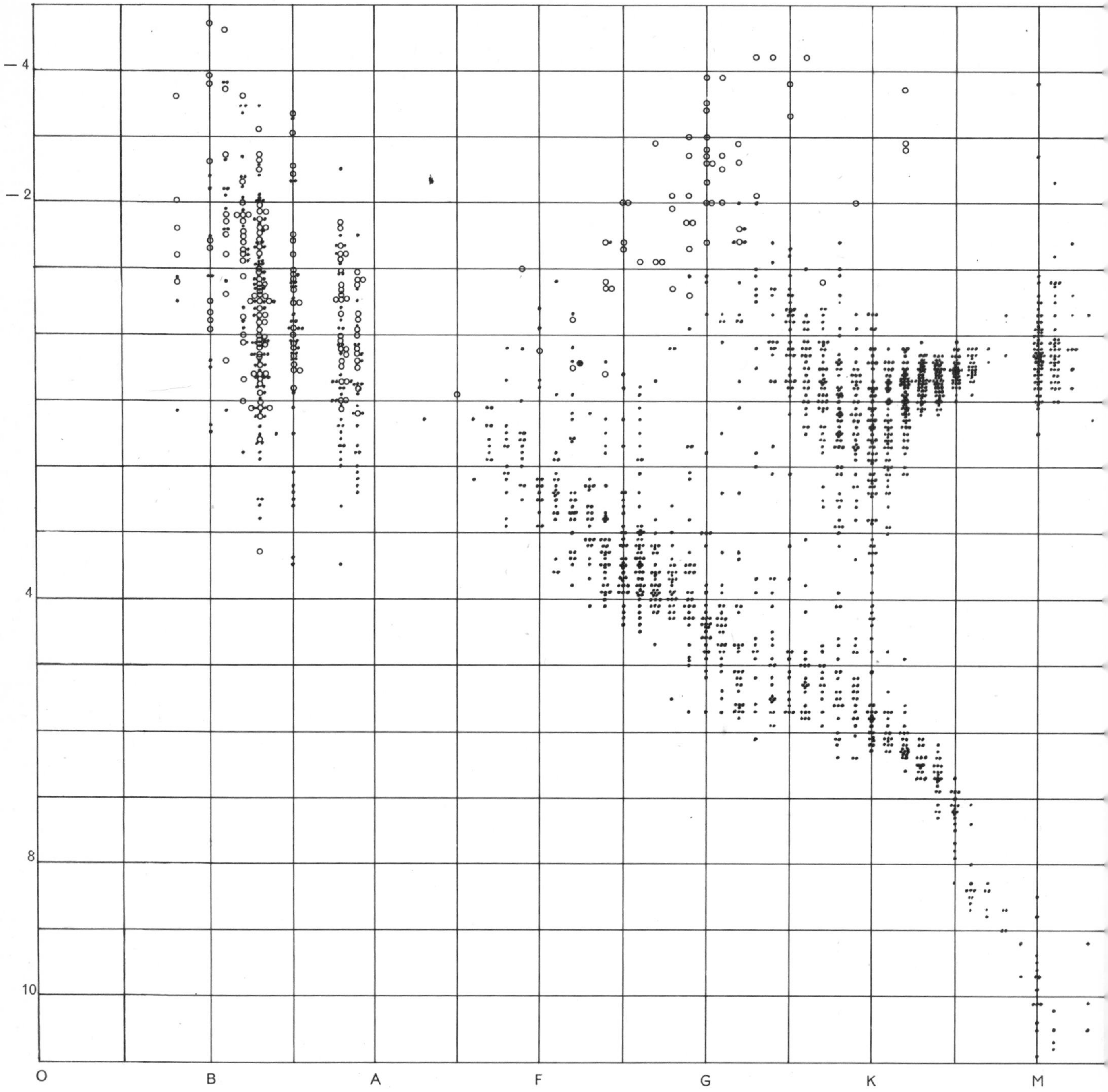

Figure 8.5
The Hertzsprung-Russell diagram, on which absolute visual magnitudes of stars (vertical axis) are plotted against their spectrum types. Stars plotted here are a sample of those in the region of the Milky Way, comparatively close by the Sun.

Since the time of Kant, and possibly even before, most scientists have thought of the stars as originating by a process of condensation from a diffuse gaseous medium in interstellar space. Indeed, we now know that such a gaseous medium does exist and that new stars are continually forming out of it. Russell's idea was that primitive stars, before they had finally condensed, would be large and diffuse and would have low surface temperatures. This would cause them to lie on the right side of the Hertzsprung-Russell diagram. He suggested that perhaps such condensing stars were the giants. Hence, according to Russell's view, these giants, as they continued condensing, should gradually move toward the main sequence which he regarded as the normal condensed position of the stars. If one asked what determined the particular position that a star occupied on the main sequence, Russell answered that it was its mass; the larger the mass the higher the star would lie on the main sequence. And Russell went one step further. He thought that after reaching the main sequence, stars might evolve down it. His idea was that in the first place they would reach the main sequence toward the upper left-hand corner of the diagram, and that they would then move down toward the right-hand bottom corner, implying a steady loss of mass.

Some of these ideas correspond with modern theory. Newly forming stars will certainly appear far away to the right of the diagram, and as they condense they must move toward the left until they reach the main sequence. So far so good, but as we shall see in the following chapter, these newly condensed stars are not the giants. The situation for the giants is precisely the reverse of what Russell suggested.

It turns out that the giants are stars which once lay on the main sequence but which, as a result of nuclear processes that have taken place inside them, have moved away from the main sequence toward the right. That is, the giants are mainly moving toward the right, not toward the left in the diagram. Eventually the rightward motion is halted, however, and stars finally move leftward again. That is to say, after expanding into giants they contract again, their surface temperatures rising as they do so. Such questions are under active investigation by astronomers at the present day. Problems of very great mathematical difficulty arise in their investigation.

Do newly condensed stars, once having reached the main sequence, move down it? Do they, in fact, lose mass? This old proposal of Russell takes us right to the center of a modern controversy. Many Russian astronomers believe that such a loss of mass does in fact take place, but this point of view has not found any general favor outside Russia.

Any examination of this controversy or any further discussion of the Hertzsprung-Russell diagram raises questions relating to nuclear physics. The topics that then arise are of such importance that they must be given a chapter to themselves.

Henry Norris Russell of Princeton, one of the two men who independently invented the important type of diagram shown opposite. In 1929 Russell also made one of the first comprehensive determinations of the comparative abundances of atoms of various elements in the Sun.

Chapter 9   Stars as Thermonuclear Reactors

The very tiny fraction of the Sun's energy that falls on the Earth—estimated at about five parts in a hundred million million—is about 100,000 times greater than all the energy used in the world's industries. The *total* energy the Sun emits in a single second would be sufficient to keep a one-kilowatt electric fire burning for 10,000 million million years. Put in a different way, the energy the Sun emits in one second is greater than the whole amount of energy the human species has consumed throughout its entire history.

We have considered how this vast amount of energy is conveyed within the Sun, but we have not yet asked how it is produced. It is certainly not produced by any ordinary process of combustion. If the Sun were simply a gigantic coal fire it would be reduced entirely to ashes in about a thousand years. Even the most violent forms of chemical combustion, such as that which occurs when hydrogen and oxygen combine to form water, would supply the Sun's energy for only some two thousand years. So the idea that the Sun derives its energy from any process of chemical combustion can be dismissed.

In the nineteenth century the scientists Kelvin and Helmholtz offered an explanation of how the Sun might go on producing its colossal output of energy for a period much greater than a mere two thousand years. Their explanation depended on gravity, and we can best begin to understand it by noting what happens when a stone drops from a high tower. Pulled downward by the Earth's gravity, the stone gains speed and energy during its fall, and when it strikes the ground much of this energy is converted into heat. In a similar way, heat would be released if a stone were to fall into the Sun. Indeed, since the Sun's gravitational field is much stronger than that of the Earth, the stone would attain a much greater speed and would consequently release a much greater quantity of heat on impact. Suppose, now, that instead of one stone falling into the Sun the whole surface of the Sun were subject to a constant rain of falling bodies from outside, for example, a steady rain of meteorites; then energy would be released all over its surface. Could this explain the origin of the energy that the Sun constantly radiates away into space?

The answer must be no, for two reasons. First, if there were any such rain of falling bodies, we ought, with modern instruments, to be able to detect it, but in fact we cannot. Next, as we saw in the previous

This photograph of the Sun, taken in hydrogen light, gives a tremendous impression of power. In fact the Sun emits more energy in one second than the human species has consumed in its entire history. During the nineteenth century scientists asked themselves how this vast output of energy could have been maintained over a period of millions of years.

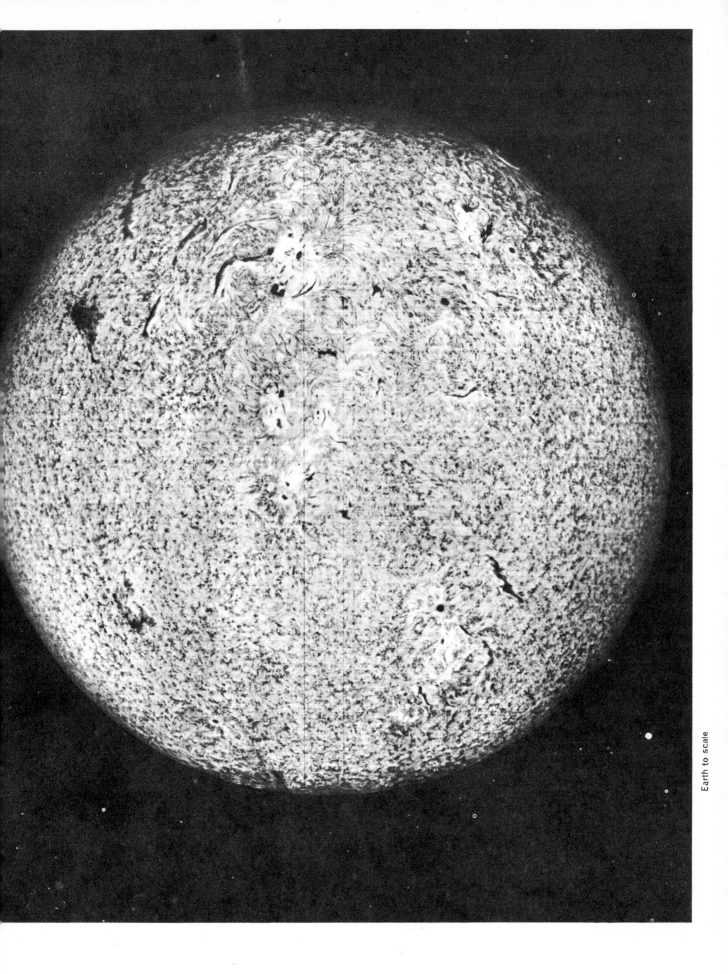

Earth to scale

233

chapter, the Sun's radiation represents the flow of energy outward from its inner regions, so clearly we must seek for a source of energy inside the Sun, not simply at its surface. But the main idea of energy being produced by gravity can be modified to meet both these objections. Instead of assuming a rain of material from outside on to the surface of the Sun, we may suppose that the whole body of the Sun is shrinking very slightly all the time. The Sun would then be falling slightly inward *as a whole*, and energy would be released in the same way as before. It is true that if we assume the rate of infall to be very slow, the energy yield from each ounce of matter involved would be far less than the energy yield from each ounce of matter falling on to the Sun from outside. But the whole of the material in the Sun would now be involved, and because that amount is so huge, the energy obtainable in this way would, indeed, be enormous. In fact it would be about 10,000 times greater than could be provided by even the most powerful chemical reaction.

This, then, was the theory that Helmholtz and Kelvin put forward, and it would certainly suffice to explain how the Sun could go on emitting vast quantities of energy for many thousands of years. Calculation shows that, on this theory, a reduction in the diameter of the Sun of only some fifty yards a year would be sufficient to account for its known output of energy. This would imply a shrinkage of only about fifty miles in the Sun's diameter since the Roman invasion of Britain. Even if the measuring equipment of antiquity had been equal to that

of today it would be quite impossible to detect so small a shrinkage as this.

Nevertheless, if the theory of Helmholtz and Kelvin were correct, the diameter of the Sun would have diminished markedly over periods of several million years. But we know from geological evidence that it has not done so. From fossil evidence it is known that some genera of animals—brachiopods, the tuatara and some lizards, for example—have persisted relatively unchanged for upward of a hundred million years. This is convincing evidence of a constancy of physical environment on the Earth that would be impossible if the Sun had changed its diameter a very great deal during that period. In fact we know from fossil records that the Sun must have been shining pretty much as it is now for at least a thousand million years. Thus the idea that a slow shrinkage of the Sun accounts for the energy it radiates into space is simply not tenable.

In brief, the ideas of Kelvin and Helmholtz could explain a source of energy 10,000 times more potent than any form of chemical combustion; but in view of what the fossil record reveals, we must seek for an explanation that will account for a potency 10,000 times as great again. Such an explanation is indeed available if we think of the Sun as a vast thermo-nuclear reactor; and the transference of the problem from chemistry to nuclear physics may be said to symbolize the entry of astronomy into its most modern phase.

Nuclear processes are about a hundred million times more potent in their energy yield than are

If the Sun's energy were derived from chemical combustion, it could not have been maintained for more than about two thousand years. Kelvin (left) and Helmholtz (adjacent) suggested that the whole body of the Sun might be steadily shrinking. It might be slowly falling inward, releasing energy in the process. This accounted for a vast output of energy over several million years, but it also presupposed that the Sun's diameter must have shrunk markedly over such a period.

chemical processes. For example, the burning of one pound of an ordinary chemical fuel yields only enough energy to keep a one-kilowatt electric heater burning for about an hour, but the consumption of one pound of the most effective nuclear fuel would keep it operating for about ten thousand years. To understand why this great difference arises we must consider something of the physics of nuclear and chemical processes.

Gravitational, Electrical and Nuclear Fields

Let us return for a moment to the falling stone which we thought about in the context of the Kelvin-Helmholtz theory. The stone gains energy as it falls because it is accelerated toward the Earth's center by the attractive force of gravitation. A similar acceleration with a consequent gain of energy can, in fact, be produced by any other attractive force.

The forces that control chemical processes are electrical in nature, and whereas the gravitational force between two bodies is always attractive, the electrical forces between them can be either attractive or repulsive. Whether they are the one or the other depends on just how the bodies are made up from their elementary constituents, electrons and protons, which represent the two stable forms of electric charge. It turns out that for the most part the forces between atoms are attractive, which is why they tend to combine into groups. These groups are called molecules, and they may range in complexity from simple structures, such as the molecule of common salt which contains only one atom of

sodium and one of chlorine, to the complicated molecules encountered in biological structures which may contain something of the order of a million individual atoms.

Now when the electrical force between atoms is attractive, the atoms gain speed as they approach each other. If, after approaching, the atoms were to draw apart again there would, of course, be a compensating loss of energy; that is, the atoms would gain speed, and hence energy, as they approached and would then lose speed and energy as they separated. When chemical combination takes place, however, there is no such compensating loss of energy, for the atoms do not separate; they stay together in the combined molecule. Hence there is a gain of energy, and this energy ultimately appears as heat. This, then, is the source of chemical energy. It arises from attractive electrical forces and is similar in principle to the source of energy of a falling stone. The difference arises from the difference in the nature of the force that promotes the attraction.

And when we come to nuclear energy the situation is still, in principle, the same. Again we have an attraction between particles, but now it is an attraction promoted neither by a gravitational field nor by an electrical field, but by the nuclear field. Two kinds of particles, protons and neutrons, are directly affected by the nuclear field, and we must later look at both of them, but let us first see how nuclear attraction operates.

There is a vital difference between the nuclear force and electrical or gravitational forces. Two

If the Sun's diameter had in fact changed a great deal, it would have been impossible for any form of life to persist relatively unchanged for many millions of years. Yet we know that some have done so. At left is a fossil of the primitive *lingula* of Ordovician times, some 400,000,000 years ago; above is the *lingula* which still lives in the Pacific Ocean. Only if we think of the Sun as a vast thermonuclear reactor can we explain how it has steadily emitted energy over such an immense time.

bodies attract each other gravitationally even when they are a very great distance apart. The Sun, for example, is appreciably attracted by the gravitational field of stars several light-years away. The situation is the same for electric forces. Two electrified particles still continue to attract or repel each other when their distance apart increases. It is true that the effect of the force weakens as the distance between them increases, but it does not cease altogether. It declines as the inverse square of the distance apart of the two particles; that is to say, for each doubling of the distance apart the effectiveness of the force decreases to one quarter of its value.

Electrical forces thus operate over great distances, in precisely the same way as gravitational forces. But their long-range effectiveness tends to be disguised in astronomy for a very simple reason. We have already noted that there are two kinds of electric charge, the negative charge (−) being carried by electrons and the positive charge (+)by protons. The force between one electron and one proton is attractive, but the force between two electrons, or between two protons, is repulsive. Now large bodies such as stars are only weakly electrified because they contain essentially the same number of protons and electrons, and attractive and repulsive effects therefore tend to cancel each other out. With gravitational forces, which are *always* attractive, no such canceling can occur, and it is for this reason only that gravitational fields, rather than electrical fields, dominate large-scale phenomena.

Quite unlike electric forces or gravitational forces, the nuclear force is effective only over very small distances. The nuclear force between two particles, whether two neutrons, two protons, or one neutron and one proton, operates only if the two particles are not more than about one ten-million-millionth part of a centimeter apart. The nuclear force becomes quite negligible if the distance is appreciably greater than this, but it is powerfully attractive at distances of this order. Hence, if protons and neutrons—the particles affected by the nuclear force—approach close enough to each other they will gain speed due to the action of the nuclear force. The situation is now exactly analogous to the case of a chemical reaction. Atoms attracted together by electrical forces, and which combine into molecules, yield chemical energy. Protons and neutrons attracted together by nuclear forces, and which combine into a permanent structure analogous to molecules, yield nuclear energy.

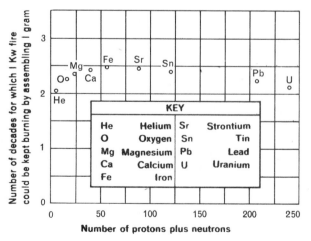

Electron (negative charge) Proton (positive charge) Neutron (no charge)

Hydrogen atom

Oxygen atom

One oxygen and two hydrogen atoms combined as one molecule of water.

Hydrogen Helium Lithium Beryllium

Boron Carbon Nitrogen Oxygen

Nuclei of the commonest isotopes of the eight lightest elements.

Figure 9.1 (Below)
Comparison between gains of energy produced by assembling one gram of nine different chemical elements.

KEY

He	Helium	Sr	Strontium
O	Oxygen	Sn	Tin
Mg	Magnesium	Pb	Lead
Ca	Calcium	U	Uranium
Fe	Iron		

Number of decades for which I Kw fire could be kept burning by assembling I gram

Number of protons plus neutrons

Before we go on to see just what these structures are, let us look at the two kinds of particle involved. Neutrons carry no electric charge, so that *only* the attractive nuclear force operates between them. Protons, on the other hand, all carry a positive electric charge; hence both the attractive nuclear force and a repulsive electric force operate between them. But when we isolate the effect of the nuclear force from that of the electric force, it appears that the nuclear force between two protons is the same as that between two neutrons, or between one neutron and one proton.

What are the combined structures which neutrons and protons yield? They are the nuclei, or heavy cores, of atoms. Stated the other way round, the nuclei of atoms are simply combined structures of protons and neutrons, and every possible stable combination of this sort is represented somewhere or other among the chemical elements. The nuclei of atoms must be very small compared to the size of the whole atoms because of the short range of the nuclear force; for only when the protons and neutrons are very close to each other will the nuclear forces between them operate to hold them together into a coherent structure. The dimensions of the cloud of electrons surrounding the nucleus of an ordinary atom are more than ten thousand times greater than the dimensions of the nucleus.

Why do electrons surround the nuclei of ordinary atoms? Because of electrical forces. The protons present in the nucleus exert an attractive electrical force on the surrounding electrons. Unless the temperature happens to be very high, as it is in the central regions of the stars, the electrical force is adequate to hold the electrons to the nucleus, always provided that there are not more electrons in the surrounding cloud than there are protons in the nucleus. In fact the normal neutral form of an atom has a number of electrons equal to the number of protons in the nucleus.

Nuclear Energy

We have seen that there is a gain of energy when protons and neutrons come together to form the nuclei of atoms. But the amount of the gain varies with the different number of particles that go to make up the nuclei of various elements. How, for example, does the amount of nuclear energy produced in the assembling of one gram of oxygen compare with the amount produced in the assembling of one gram of iron? The answer to this and to other similar questions is contained in Figure 9.1. The vertical axis represents, in units of ten years, the length of time for which the yield of nuclear energy could keep a one-kilowatt electric fire burning. The horizontal axis represents the number of protons plus neutrons which must be assembled to form the nucleus of the element in question.

There is one further point to notice about the number of particles shown for the nucleus of each element in our figure. The chemical properties of an atom are determined by the number of electrons that surround its nucleus, and this, in turn, is determined by the number of protons contained in the nucleus. Hence the chemical properties are ultimately determined solely by the number of protons in the nucleus. This means that two atoms having the same number of protons but a different number of neutrons in their nuclei will still have essentially identical chemical properties. They will be what are called different *isotopes* of the same chemical element. In fact many of the elements do have two or more different isotopes, but the values given in our figure refer in each case to the commonest one, that is, to the one which occurs in the greatest abundance on the Earth.

The figure shows that we obtain most energy by assembling nuclei of iron. The energy yield increases with the number of neutrons and protons contained in the nucleus, until that number reaches sixty or thereabouts. After that the energy yield slowly falls away. Why is there this maximum to the energy yield? Why does it not go on increasing indefinitely as more and more neutrons and protons are added to the nucleus?

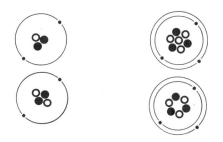

Left: Structures of two different isotopes of helium. Right: Structures of two different isotopes of lithium. Different isotopes of the same element contain the same number of protons and the same number of electrons. They differ only in the number of neutrons contained in their nuclei.

To answer these questions we must bear in mind that electrical forces may be at work as well as nuclear forces. When a neutron is added to a nucleus no electrical force is involved. In order that a neutron can be captured by a nucleus it must clearly be fired very accurately toward its target, for otherwise the short-range nuclear forces will never come into operation at all. If, however, the firing *is* accurate and the neutron *is* captured by the nucleus, energy is yielded. The conditions required for adding a proton to a nucleus are even more rigorous. Not only must it be aimed very accurately, so as to stand a chance of coming within range of the nuclear force; it must also have a very high initial speed in order to overcome the repulsive electrical force existing between it and other protons already in the nucleus. Without that high initial speed it will simply be turned back before it comes within range of the nuclear force. Even if the incident proton should reach the nucleus and be captured by it, the energy made available will be less than in the case of the neutron, simply because the proton has lost speed during the early part of its flight due to the repulsive electrical force. And clearly this repulsive force will become stronger as the nucleus contains more and more protons.

We can now see why Figure 9.1 reveals a maximum beyond which a law of diminishing returns begins to operate. As long as the number of neutrons and protons in the nucleus is small, the effect of the electrical forces on the energy yielded by adding more particles is comparatively unimportant. Eventually, however, the number of protons in the nucleus becomes so large that the electrical force increases, thus reducing the energy yield very appreciably. Indeed, there comes a point where the gain of energy due to the attractive nuclear force is more than offset by the loss of energy due to the repulsive electric force. It is for this reason that the building-up of atoms containing large numbers of protons and neutrons gives a smaller yield of energy than the building-up of iron atoms.

Our figure also enables us to answer other important questions. Suppose we add three helium nuclei together to form carbon; because carbon lies higher in our diagram than helium, energy will be yielded by this fusion process. Similarly, if we add two carbon nuclei together to form magnesium we again obtain energy, since magnesium lies higher in such a diagram than carbon. This situation holds good for all the lighter elements, that is, for

the elements that contain comparatively few neutrons and protons in their nuclei. If we fuse them together we obtain energy. But the situation is reversed for the heaviest nuclei. There we gain energy not by fusion but by the opposite process of fission. If, for example, we break the nucleus of uranium into two comparable pieces, then energy will be released. This follows because the two pieces lie higher in the diagram than the original uranium does.

Nuclear Processes in Main Sequence Stars
We have seen that in order to build up a light nucleus into a heavier one by the addition of protons, the protons must have a high initial speed; otherwise they would be unable to reach the nucleus because of the repulsive electrical force acting on them during their journey. Where does this high initial speed come from? In the stars it comes from the high temperature existing deep in their interiors. Indeed, it is because high temperatures are necessary to promote the building process that the word *thermonuclear* is used to describe it.

Since the repulsive electrical forces become larger as nuclei of greater and greater atomic number are involved, it is obvious that higher initial speeds, and therefore higher temperatures, will be needed to build heavy nuclei than to build light ones. To build the simplest light nucleus, namely the helium nucleus which contains two protons and two neutrons, temperatures of about ten million degrees are needed. The building of the other common light nuclei, such as carbon, oxygen and neon, needs temperatures of about one hundred million degrees. To build magnesium, silicon, sulfur, or calcium demands temperatures in the region of a thousand million degrees, and to build iron the temperature must be around three thousand million degrees.

How does all this help us to answer the questions about the Hertzsprung-Russell diagram which were left unanswered at the end of the previous chapter?

Carbon Oxygen Neon	Magnesium Silicon Sulfur Calcium		Iron
0	1000	2000	3000

temperature in millions of degrees.

The building-up of heavy nuclei demands higher temperatures than the building-up of light ones. Here we see the temperature-range at which nuclei of various elements form.

With reference to Russell's giant and dwarf theory, it will be recalled that newly forming stars appear toward the right of the diagram; that as they condense they move toward the left until they reach the main sequence; and that during the process of shrinkage their internal temperature rises. This part of Russell's theory clearly corresponds closely to the idea of Kelvin and Helmholtz. During its formation and condensation a star does indeed derive energy through its gravitational field. Part of this energy is radiated away into space and part is taken up in producing the steadily rising temperature of the interior. Evidently the first nuclear reactions to take place will be those that require the lowest temperature, and these, as we have just seen, are the reactions in which helium is formed. Hence our expectation is that the first nuclear reactions to occur inside a newly-condensed star will be those in which helium nuclei are assembled from their constituent particles.

Why do stars stop moving toward the left in the Hertzsprung-Russell diagram once they reach the main sequence? The answer is that the main sequence marks the stars in which the production of helium has begun. In other words, it marks the position of stars that have begun to behave as thermonuclear reactors.

We saw in the previous chapter that overwhelmingly the most abundant atoms inside the Sun are those of hydrogen, and this is true of all stars at the time of their formation. Now a normal neutral hydrogen atom has a nucleus consisting of only one proton, and an outer "shell" consisting of only one electron; but inside the stars hydrogen atoms do not exist in their neutral form. Because of the high temperature, the electrons are separated from the protons, forming a gas in which electrons and protons move freely and independently of each other. And the protons form the raw material out of which the helium nuclei are built. Yet since a helium nucleus contains two protons and two neutrons one may well ask where do the neutrons come from? In fact a free neutron changes spontaneously into a proton and other particles; and for similar but rather more complex reasons it is possible for a proton to change into a neutron.

Let us take the simpler case first. There is a general rule in physics that provided the necessary processes are available, matter will always tend to reach its lowest possible energy state. (In fact, as can be inferred from our discussion of Figure 9.1, the lowest form of energy arises when iron is formed. The reason why all the matter in the universe does not assemble itself into nuclei of iron atoms is that no relevant physical processes are available except inside certain stars where temperatures are in the region of three thousand million degrees; at temperatures lower than this the incident protons cannot reach the iron nucleus because of the strongly repulsive electric forces operating.) Now when a free neutron changes spontaneously into a proton, an electron and a third particle known as an anti-neutrino, it *does* attain a lower energy state. The proton and the electron together have a slightly smaller mass than the original neutron, and this implies that they also have a slightly smaller energy. (The anti-neutrino has an almost negligible interaction with matter and plays no part in the production of energy inside a star, so we shall here make no further mention of it.)

Yet although a proton by itself has less mass (and hence less energy) than a neutron, a nucleus composed entirely of a given number of protons would not have less energy than a nucleus composed of a suitable mixture of protons and neutrons. One reason for this lies in the repulsive electric forces involved; another depends on the way the particles pack themselves together, the details of which need not concern us. The main point of present importance is that if we attempt to build a nucleus containing too many protons it will actually have a *higher* energy state than if it were composed of mixed protons and neutrons. In accordance with the general rule of physics we have already noticed, one or more of the protons will then change into a neutron. The nucleus thereby attains a lower energy state than it had before.

The very fact that protons can change into neutrons is sufficient to explain how, starting with protons only, it is possible to build up nuclei containing both protons and neutrons; but we may pause here to see just *how* the change comes about. We have seen that a neutron changes into a proton by emitting an electron and an anti-neutrino. Similarly, when a proton changes into a neutron two other particles are involved, a positron and a neutrino. The neutrino, like the anti-neutrino, has only an extremely feeble interaction with matter and need not further concern us. The positron which the proton emits on changing into a neutron can best be described as an electron carrying a positive instead of a negative charge.

Protons already begin changing into neutrons if we try to build a nucleus consisting of only two protons. One of the two then becomes a neutron, thus forming a nucleus in which one proton and one neutron are bound together. This is called a deuteron, and it is the nucleus of heavy hydrogen, a constituent of heavy water. Deuterons produced in this way can then pick up a further proton so that a nucleus containing two protons and one neutron is formed. This is the nucleus of an isotope of helium. Although it contains only one neutron, it also contains two protons; atoms with such nuclei would therefore have just the same chemical properties as ordinary helium atoms, whose nuclei contain two neutrons and two protons.

But how is ordinary helium formed in the thermonuclear reactor of a star? The answer is somewhat complicated, since the conversion can be brought about in a variety of ways. Inside the Sun the main process is one in which two nuclei of this light form of helium come into collision. Since each of them contains two protons and one neutron, if they were to fuse the resulting new nucleus would have four protons and two neutrons. This would be a light-weight form of the element beryllium; but this form is not stable and it can reach stability in either of two ways. One of the four protons could change into a neutron, yielding a nucleus with three protons and three neutrons. This would be the nucleus of an isotope of lithium which forms a vital component of the hydrogen bomb. The other possibility is that the light-weight beryllium nucleus might eject two protons, leaving a nucleus consisting of two protons and two neutrons. This would be the nucleus of our ordinary form of helium, and the overwhelming probability is that this second process is what actually occurs inside the Sun.

We have thus traced a continuous line of reactions starting from protons only and ending with ordinary helium nuclei; and energy is generated at several stages along the line. The two protons ejected at the last stage move at high speeds. Inside the Sun most of their motion is quickly lost by collisions with other particles, and their energy of motion appears in a general increase of motion of *all* the particles, that is to say in the form of heat. Energy is also emitted to a lesser extent in the other reactions. In the first stage, when two protons collide and one of them changes into a neutron, a positron is emitted. This positron quickly combines with one of the electrons that it encounters in its motion. The elec-

tron and the positron then mutually annihilate each other, yielding a quantum of radiation. The third source of energy comes from the addition of a proton to the deuteron. A quantum of radiation is also emitted in this process. In total, therefore, energy is made available partly in the form of radiation and partly in the form of heat. This is the resolution of the age-old question of where the Sun's energy comes from.

The temperature inside the Sun is not high enough to allow more complicated nuclear processes to take place with appreciable frequency. As an example of a more complicated process we might consider the collision of a proton with a nucleus of carbon. Provided the proton has a sufficiently high initial speed to overcome the repulsive electrical force between itself and the carbon nucleus, a reaction can occur in which the proton is added to the carbon nucleus, thus producing the nucleus of a light isotope of nitrogen. Energy, in the form of radiation, is also produced by this process.

Such processes do not have any great importance inside the Sun simply because the temperature there is too low to give the protons the necessary initial speed. We, however, in the previous chapter that the temperatures inside stars of the main sequence increase as we move up the sequence from the position of the Sun to the top left-hand corner of the Hertzsprung-Russell diagram. In other words, the internal temperature is higher inside main sequence stars with masses greater than that of the Sun, which is precisely why such stars are more

The first nuclear reactions to occur inside a newly-condensed star are those in which helium nuclei are assembled. Our diagram shows the main process by which helium nuclei are built up inside the Sun.

Two protons collide, one becomes a neutron, and they combine to form a deuteron (heavy hydrogen nucleus).

Deuteron gains a proton, forming nucleus of light isotope of helium.

Two such nuclei collide and eject two protons, leaving nucleus of the common form of helium (see page 236).

luminous than the Sun. At these higher temperatures nuclear reactions of the kind just described take place on an important scale.

In fact it turns out that there is a sequence of processes which begins with the formation of nitrogen from carbon and ultimately results in the production of helium nuclei. The light-weight isotope of nitrogen (seven protons and six neutrons) produced from carbon changes into a heavy isotope of carbon (six protons and seven neutrons). The latter nucleus then acquires a further proton to give the common form of nitrogen (seven protons and seven neutrons). This common form of nitrogen then acquires still another proton; but one proton of the resulting nucleus very quickly changes into a neutron. The result, a structure consisting now of seven protons and eight neutrons, is the nucleus of a heavy isotope of nitrogen, an isotope that is indeed present in the gases of the Earth's atmosphere but only in a very low concentration. This structure next picks up yet another proton, thereby forming a nucleus with eight protons and eight neutrons. This is just the common form of oxygen. But the oxygen nucleus so formed is initially in a state of violent agitation; that is, the eight protons and eight neutrons are moving violently around inside the nucleus, far more violently than they do inside the nucleus of an ordinary oxygen atom.

Two possibilities now arise. The agitated nucleus could get rid of the motion of its particles by emitting radiation, in which case an ordinary stable oxygen nucleus would be formed. The alternative is for it to eject a helium nucleus (two protons and two neutrons). This second possibility is far the more probable, so that in the great majority of cases a nucleus of oxygen is not permanently formed. Indeed, after ejecting the helium nucleus the structure that remains is a nucleus containing six protons and six neutrons; *and this is just the common form of carbon from which the whole process began.* We may express this by saying that the carbon acts as a catalyst. It serves to generate a series of reactions as a result of which it is itself reproduced in the overwhelming proportion of cases.

Hence there is a second way of producing helium, and this second way is far more important in stars of large mass than it is inside the Sun, simply because the temperatures in more massive stars are appreciably higher than in the Sun. Indeed, this carbon-nitrogen cycle, as it is called, provides the main process for the production of helium in stars

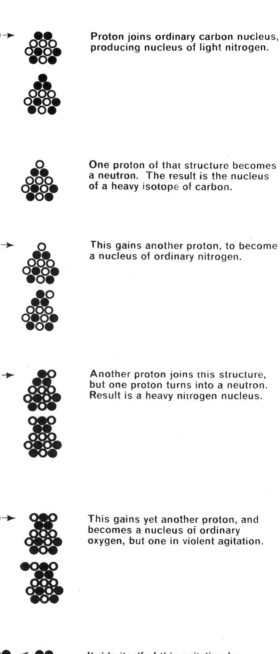

In main sequence stars with masses greater than that of the Sun, internal temperatures are higher. Our diagram shows one of the nuclear processes which then takes place

Proton joins ordinary carbon nucleus, producing nucleus of light nitrogen.

One proton of that structure becomes a neutron. The result is the nucleus of a heavy isotope of carbon.

This gains another proton, to become a nucleus of ordinary nitrogen.

Another proton joins this structure, but one proton turns into a neutron. Result is a heavy nitrogen nucleus.

This gains yet another proton, and becomes a nucleus of ordinary oxygen, but one in violent agitation.

It rids itself of this agitation by ejecting two protons and two neutrons (together a helium nucleus). There remains a nucleus of ordinary carbon.

with masses more than about twice that of the Sun. All stars lying on the upper part of the main sequence generate an overwhelming proportion of their energy through the operation of the carbon-nitrogen cycle rather than through the simpler processes that take place inside the Sun.

The different modes of energy-generation inside massive stars (carbon-nitrogen cycle) and inside stars of small mass, which we may describe as solar-type stars, lead to an interesting difference in their internal structures. This is illustrated in Figure 9.2. In the shaded parts of each star energy is transported mainly by convection, while in the unshaded parts transport of energy is entirely by radiation, except for a negligible contribution from conduction. The two cases are thus completely opposite in character. In massive stars we have convection near the center and radiation outside, whereas in solar-type stars we have radiation carrying the energy throughout the inner portions and convection on the outside. It is transport of energy by convection in the outer regions of the Sun that probably accounts for much of the highly complicated behavior of the gases of the solar atmosphere, discussed in the previous chapter.

Evolution Away from the Main Sequence
In the convective region of a star, any helium produced by nuclear reactions will be mixed more or less uniformly. Thus in the massive star shown in Figure 9.2 the helium produced in the hot central regions is thoroughly mixed throughout the inner part of the convective core. But in the solar-type star (at left of Figure 9.2) there is no mixing except in the outer parts, where the production of helium is negligible because temperatures are not high enough to promote nuclear reactions. In the solar-type star, therefore, the helium stays put where it is produced, and the helium concentration accordingly rises higher in the central regions than anywhere else. As more and more hydrogen is converted into helium the chemical composition of the star thus becomes more markedly nonuniform.

This has, indeed, already happened in the case of the Sun. In the outer parts the composition is still much the same as it was when the Sun first formed from its parent cloud of gas: the hydrogen concentration is about 70 per cent by mass. But now, after some 5,000 million years, the hydrogen concentration at the center of the Sun has fallen to about 30 per cent.

The effect of this steadily growing nonuniformity of chemical composition is to cause a star to move toward the right of the Hertzsprung-Russell diagram. The general features of this motion are shown in Figure 9.3. Stars high on the main sequence—that is, stars lying toward the upper left-hand side of the Hertzsprung-Russell diagram—move more or less directly to the right. They enter the region of the diagram which marks the so-called super-

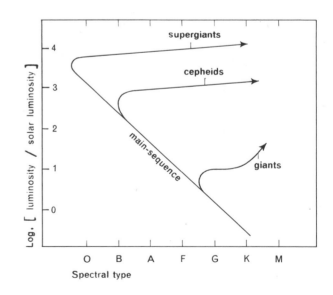

Figure 9.2 (Above)
Left: Star with mass similar to that of Sun. Right: More massive star, on upper part of main sequence. In each case shading denotes region where energy is transported mainly by convection. In unshaded region transport is by radiation.

giants. Such stars are rare, partly because not many of them are born, and partly because they are short-lived. None is found close to the Sun, and this explains why none appears in the diagram given in the previous chapter.

Stars that begin to move to the right from points somewhat lower down the main sequence pass through a region marked as the Cepheid variables. These are stars that pulsate in quite regular periods, their radii alternately expanding and contracting. During the expansion phase the radius increases by something like 10 per cent of its mean value. The period of oscillation of a Cepheid variable is directly related to its absolute luminosity, in the manner shown in Figure 9.4. This means that such stars can be used as indicators of distance. The relation between period and luminosity in Cepheid variables was discovered in 1913 by Miss Leavitt, of Harvard College Observatory, in her now-classic observations of the Magellanic Clouds; and it was the American astronomer, Harlow Shapley, who first used the discovery for determining distances.

The method is not difficult to understand. Suppose there is a Cepheid whose distance we wish to determine. Because the distance is so far unknown, we can measure only its apparent brightness, not its absolute brightness. But we can also measure the period of its oscillation, simply because its luminosity varies during the oscillation. Hence from our curve shown on Figure 9.4 we can simply read off the absolute luminosity. Then, knowing both the absolute luminosity and the apparent luminosity, we can very easily calculate the distance of the star.

Although the Cepheid variables have played an important part in astronomy over the last fifty years, and although much theoretical work has been done on their structure, no one has yet been able to offer an entirely satisfactory explanation of the cause of their oscillations. These stars occur only in one part of the Hertzsprung-Russell diagram, and they seem to undergo their oscillations as they pass through this region along tracks which start on the main sequence and ultimately move far toward the right.

When we consider stars that start lower and lower down the main sequence we find evolutionary tracks which not only move toward the right, but which also ascend in the diagram. Thus all the tracks from the lower half of the main sequence tend to converge and concentrate in one particular region, namely that occupied by the giants, the stars of large radius discussed at the end of the previous chapter. These stars are far more numerous than either the supergiants or the Cepheids, partly because the number of stars populating the lower half of the main sequence is much greater than the number on the upper half, and partly because the time required for evolution is much greater for the fainter stars. In fact the stars of the solar neighborhood include quite a number that fall in the giant region. This explains the distribution of the stars in the

Figure 9.3 (Left)
Only in the convective region of a star is the helium produced by nuclear reactions uniformly mixed. Hence in solar-type stars helium stays put where it is produced. The chemical composition of such stars thus becomes increasingly non-uniform. This causes them to move rightward in the Hertzsprung-Russell diagram, as shown.

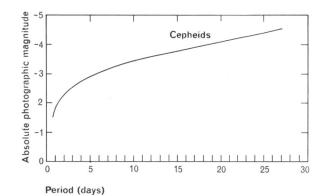

Figure 9.4 (Above)
Cepheid variables pulsate in regular periods, their radii alternately expanding and contracting. The period of oscillation is directly related to the star's absolute luminosity in the manner here shown. This fact enables astronomers to use Cepheid variables as indicators of distance.

Hertzsprung-Russell diagram as given in the previous chapter, where comparatively nearby stars tend to concentrate on or near the main sequence or else in the giant region. It was stated in the previous chapter that the giants are not newly forming stars moving toward the left, as Russell originally thought, but that they are stars moving from the main sequence toward the right. Now we have justified this statement. The stars are moving toward the right because of the increasing concentration of helium in their central regions.

Calculation shows that no significant motion to the right takes place until the concentration of hydrogen in the extreme central regions has fallen to zero. In fact, it is the exhaustion of hydrogen in the central regions, causing a cessation of energy production there, that produces the evolution into the giant region. The situation is depicted in Figure 9.5. The star has an inner core consisting mainly of helium, throughout which the hydrogen has been exhausted by nuclear reactions. But outside the core hydrogen is still present, and it is in the hydrogen immediately surrounding the core that the main energy-production of the star now takes place. This causes more and more helium to be added to the surface of the core, which therefore grows steadily in mass. By the time the star enters the giant phase of its evolution, the growing core of helium accounts for some 30 per cent of its total mass.

In Figures 9.6 and 9.7 we see the stars of two well-known clusters plotted in the Hertzsprung-Russell diagram. The positioning of the stars indicates their evolutionary paths. Figure 9.6 shows the stars of the Hyades cluster, while Figure 9.7 shows those of the cluster Messier 67. Here, then, we have direct observational evidence for the forms of evolution shown in Figure 9.3.

We saw in the previous chapter that a knowledge of the spectral type of a star implies a knowledge of its surface temperature. Hence when we know the

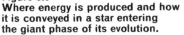

Figure 9.5
Where energy is produced and how it is conveyed in a star entering the giant phase of its evolution.

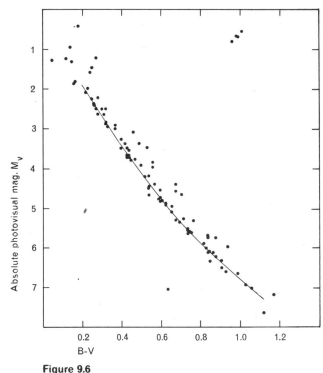
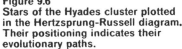

Figure 9.6
Stars of the Hyades cluster plotted in the Hertzsprung-Russell diagram. Their positioning indicates their evolutionary paths.

Left: Part of outer region of the Great Spiral in Andromeda, M 31. The marked star near the center is a Cepheid variable with a period of approximately 18¼ days. Here it is at its maximum luminosity.

Figure 9.7 (Right)
H-R representation of the stars of the cluster Messier 67.

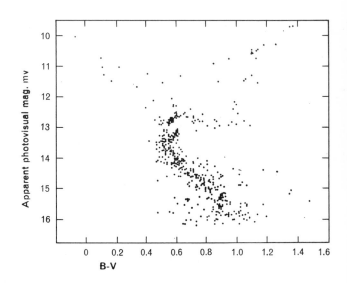

position of a star in the Hertzsprung-Russell diagram, we know both its absolute luminosity and its surface temperature. From these the radius of the star can readily be computed with the help of the equation $L = D \times R^2 \times T^4$ mentioned in Chapter 8. (It will be recalled that in this equation L stands for luminosity, D for a constant, R for radius, and T for surface temperature.) Accordingly, when we know the position of a star in the Hertzsprung-Russell diagram we also know its radius.

Figure 9.8 shows three lines superimposed on the Hertzsprung-Russell diagram. One joins points where the radius of each star is equal to that of the Sun; the second joins points where the radius is ten times that of the Sun; and the third joins points where the radius is one hundred times that of the Sun. It will be seen that the line drawn for a radius of one hundred Suns passes through the giant region of the diagram. Hence we see that the giants are indeed stars with very large radii. The radius of the Earth's orbit is a little more than 200 times the radius of the Sun. If the Sun were a giant—and indeed it will become one at some time in the future—the Earth would lie comparatively close to its surface. In fact, the Earth might even lie inside the Sun.

Because a giant has such a huge radius, gravity at its surface is very much weaker than it is at the surface of the Sun—anything between 10,000 and 100,000 times weaker. For this reason disturbances taking place at the surfaces of such stars, disturbances similar to those that take place at present on the Sun, must cause material to be thrown outward to vastly greater distances than in the case of solar surges. In fact, disturbances comparable with those that normally occur on the Sun would result in material being thrown so far outward into space that it would escape entirely from the gravitational field of a giant star. Observational evidence has, indeed, come to hand to show that giant stars, and supergiants too, are steadily showering off material from their surfaces. The outer layers of such stars are hence peeled steadily away. Granted that enough of the outer layers are thus peeled off, the inner regions, where nuclear processes have been taking place, will gradually be revealed. It is thus possible for the products of nuclear reactions that once took place in the deep interior to appear at the surface of a star. And once this happens those products are subject to observation by means of the spectroscopic techniques which were discussed in the previous chapter.

Let us look at some of the evidence of the products of nuclear processes and see what it implies. It will be recalled that stars of spectral type M have surface temperatures lower than about 3,600°. The dominant contribution to the spectra of such stars normally comes from molecules of zirconium oxide, but in the giant class there are some stars whose spectra are dominated by lines produced by carbon molecules. These stars, then, evidently have a high concentration of carbon at their surfaces. How does this come about?

We have seen that as a star moves rightward toward the giant region of the Hertzsprung-Russell diagram it develops an inner core composed very largely of helium and containing no hydrogen. As the star evolves and continues to move rightward the temperature inside this core rises steadily. Calculation shows that it reaches about 100 million degrees as the giant region is reached, and at such temperatures interesting new nuclear reactions begin to operate. The first is one in which three helium nuclei (each with two protons and two neutrons) fuse together to form a nucleus of carbon (six protons and six neutrons). The subsequent addition of further helium nuclei produces first oxygen and then neon. Here we have an example of what was emphasized above, that the higher the temperature inside a star the more complex the nuclear reactions that can take place. The situation, then, is that at temperatures of the order of 100 million degrees occurring inside giant stars, the helium that was

Figure 9.8
Curves showing positions on the Hertzsprung-Russell diagram of stars with radii equal to that of Sun (1), ten times that of Sun (10), and one hundred times that of Sun (100).

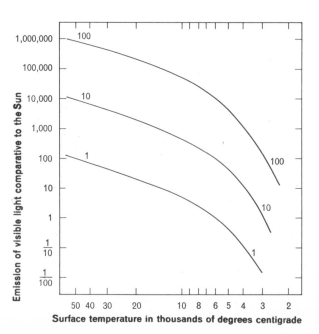

first produced from hydrogen can itself fuse to produce important new elements, namely, carbon, oxygen and neon. And the production of carbon explains how it comes about that we can observe certain stars with quite exceptional concentrations of carbon at their surfaces. These are stars from which the outer layers have been removed by the shedding process already described.

As a by-product of the helium fusion which produces carbon, oxygen and neon, a reaction occurs in which neutrons are set free. At the temperatures in question these neutrons are not absorbed to any appreciable extent by carbon, oxygen or neon, nor are they absorbed by the helium; and since the initial hydrogen was long ago exhausted, they cannot be absorbed by hydrogen either. It turns out that they are added to the much heavier nuclei present only in low concentrations at the time when the star was formed. Iron is an example of such a nucleus. We saw in the previous chapter that the initial concentration of all the nuclei as heavy as iron is a small fraction of one per cent. This is so low that the absorbing nuclei tend to be overwhelmed by neutrons. In other words they do not pick up merely one neutron, but a whole sequence of neutrons. In this way, atoms of iron are gradually built into atoms of heavier and heavier elements: first cobalt, then nickel, copper, zinc and so on to strontium, zirconium, etc. In some cases, elements as heavy as tin, barium, the rare earths and even lead are formed.

There is striking observational confirmation of these results. In the giant region of the Hertzsprung-Russell diagram we can observe stars in which strontium, zirconium, barium and the rare earths are particularly abundant. Most remarkable of all, some contain the element technetium. Technetium is not found on the Earth, for the reason that it is so unstable. In a time scale of the order of a hundred thousand years it changes, due to the decay of a proton into a neutron, into molybdenum. But technetium *is* observed in certain stars—those called the S stars, and which also contain abnormal abundances of strontium, zirconium, etc. The clear implication is that the technetium has there been produced very recently—that is within the last hundred thousand years or so—by nuclear reactions.

Does a star undergo any further evolution after it has reached the giant region of the Hertzsprung-Russell diagram? Figure 9.9 shows an example of a cluster of stars in which such a further evolution almost certainly takes place. The final phase of the evolutionary track shown in this figure turns sharply to the left, and the stars in this final phase are said to belong to the "horizontal branch." So far no reliable calculations are available for such stars, but there is reason to believe that this swing-back to the left, during which stars reach a higher level of luminosity than at the beginning of their evolution, is caused by a lack of hydrogen, not only in the innermost regions but throughout the whole body of the stars in question. Such a lack of hydrogen can arise

Sizes of orbits of the first four planets compared with sizes of two giant stars, Mira and Orionis.

Figure 9.9
Stars of the globular cluster M 3 plotted in the Hertzsprung-Russell diagram. Stars of horizontal branch have evolved beyond the giant stage. Characteristic of them is a lack of hydrogen and increased luminosity.

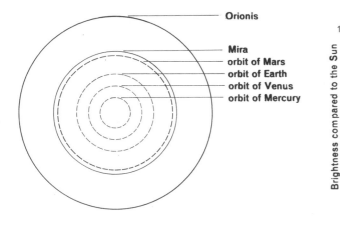

Orionis

Mira
orbit of Mars
orbit of Earth
orbit of Venus
orbit of Mercury

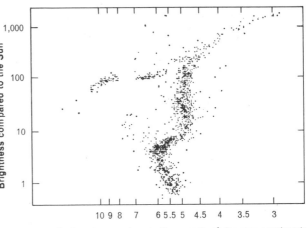

Brightness compared to the Sun

1,000

100

10

1

10 9 8   7   6 5.5 5   4.5   4   3.5   3

Surface temperature in thousands of degrees centigrade

either as a result of nuclear reactions or by the shedding off of surface material into space during the giant stage.

These considerations, again, are confirmed by observation. Astronomers have found one star, lying far to the left of the Hertzsprung-Russell diagram, whose atmosphere contains no detectable trace of hydrogen whatever.

If we ask what happens when a star reaches the end of the track shown in Figure 9.9, we must seek the answer by looking at a class of stars very different from any so far mentioned—the white dwarfs. A white dwarf is characterized by a very small luminosity and a very small radius; the radius, in fact, is comparable with that of one of the larger planets, such as Saturn. And because of this very small radius the density with which material is packed inside a white dwarf is extremely high, so high that nothing at all comparable is known on Earth. One well-known white dwarf is the Pup, companion of the Dog-Star, Sirius. So densely packed is the material at its center that a single matchboxful would weigh several tons. Clearly the white dwarfs are stars that have reached the end of their evolution, stars in which nuclear processes have ceased. The thermonuclear reactor is dead and the ashes are now cooling off. The white dwarf state is the graveyard that all stars will ultimately reach.

But what are the evolutionary changes through which a star passes between the time when it begins its swing-back to the left and the time when it reaches the white dwarf state? The honest answer is that we do not yet know, either from theory or from observation. And the difficulty that stands in our way is this. Stars that lie far to the left in the Hertzsprung-Russell diagram have very high surface temperatures—temperatures probably exceeding 100,000 degrees. Now the light emitted at such temperatures lies mainly in the far ultraviolet, and therefore fails to penetrate through the gases of the Earth's atmosphere; indeed, much of it is probably absorbed by the gases that lie between the stars, and thus never reaches the Solar System at all. So our telescopes can reveal little about what is happening in stars of very high surface temperature.

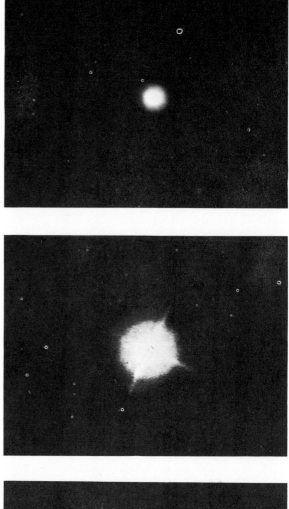

Nova Aquilae increased enormously in brightness during 1918. These photographs, taken at Mount Wilson in 1922, 1926 and 1931 show the expansion of the gaseous shell surrounding the nova.

Gases expelled from Nova Persei
in 1901 have formed the nebulosity
shown above. The photograph was
made with the 200-inch Hale telescope.

But we do have some interesting fragmentary evidence. It seems almost certain that a spectacular class of stars actually observed by astronomers does lie far to the left in the Hertzsprung-Russell diagram. This is the class of exploding stars, of which the supernova provides the most violent example. A supernova is a stellar explosion in which vast quantities of material are thrown violently outward at speeds of the order of a thousand miles a second. The famous Crab Nebula, shown below, is composed of material flung out by a supernova which Chinese astronomers saw blazing out in A.D. 1054. During the last nine centuries the material has continued to move outward at enormous speed until it now forms a nebula measuring some 40 million million miles across.

Furthermore, there are theoretical reasons for believing that the temperature *inside* stars continues to rise as they move toward the left in the Hertzsprung-Russell diagram. We have already noticed that temperatures of the order of a hundred million degrees are attained in the giant phase; during the swing to the left internal temperatures may well soar above 1,000 million degrees. At this stage new nuclear reactions begin. At about 1,000 million degrees the carbon and oxygen, produced during the giant phase, themselves begin to fuse, producing such elements as magnesium, silicon, argon and calcium. But still there is no production of iron. For this, temperatures in excess of 3,000 million degrees are

needed. Only when such temperatures build up does matter plunge into its lowest energy state, which, as we have seen, is reached with the production of iron, together with a few neighboring elements such as titanium, vanadium, chromium, manganese, nickel, cobalt and copper.

We have already traced how, beginning with hydrogen, the simplest of all the elements, the thermonuclear reactors of the stars build up various light elements: first helium, then the carbon and nitrogen which largely make up our own bodies, then the oxygen that we breathe. In later stages, these materials are used in the building-up of heavier elements: the magnesium and silicon that form so large a part of the Earth's crust, and the common metals such as iron and copper, of which we make such widespread daily use.

How is it that such elements, produced only at fantastically high temperatures inside stars, form our Earth? This is a subject we must postpone to the next chapter, where we shall consider the structure and origin of the Milky Way, with particular emphasis on the origin of the Solar System.

There is yet another question implicit in this chapter which has not been answered. We have seen how it is possible to trace the origin of all the elements, beginning only with hydrogen. Does it mean anything to go further and ask about the origin of hydrogen itself? This is a far deeper question, and must be reserved until the final chapter.

Eastern astronomers saw a supernova blaze out in A.D. 1054. Material flung from it moved outward at enormous speed to form the famous Crab Nebula (left), now 400 million million miles across. The still-expanding Veil Nebula in Cygnus, shown opposite, may owe its origin to some similar but unrecorded happening.

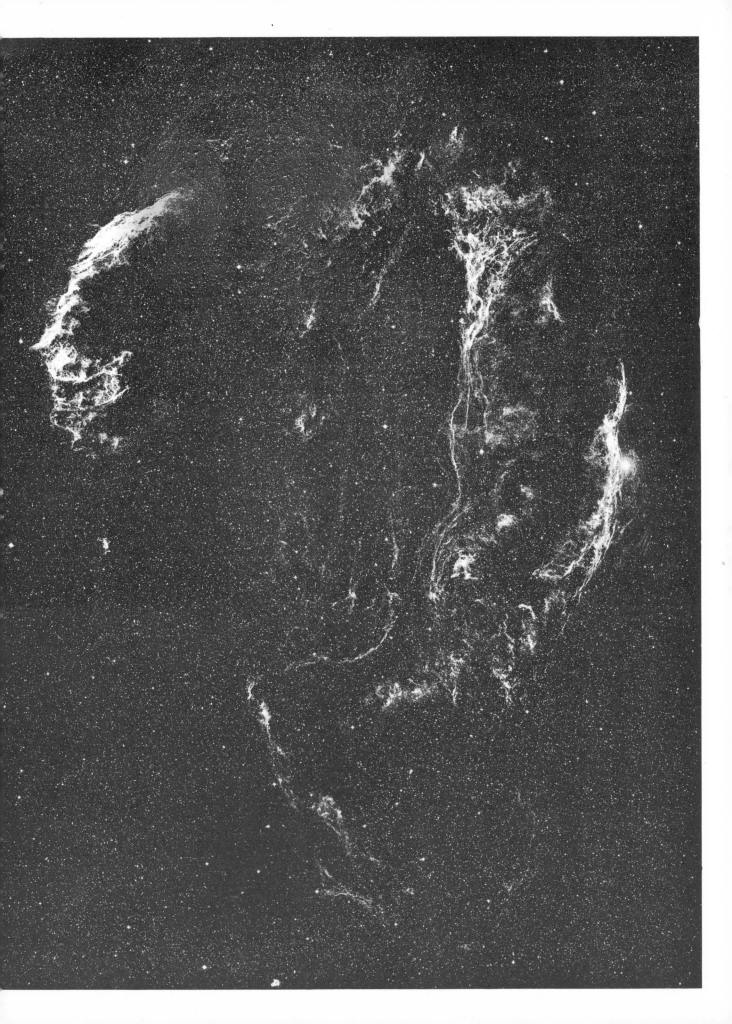

Chapter 10   The Structure of Our Galaxy

Perhaps we can best approach the problem of planet formation by first seeing what is known of the structure and content of our galaxy as a whole. And we may well start by asking how astronomers have set to work to measure the dimensions and to assess the motions within the Milky Way, a galaxy comprising some 100,000 million stars. The task has been and is a colossal one. The motions involved include not only line-of-sight motions, directly toward or directly away from the terrestrial observer; they also include transverse motions—motions across the observer's line of sight. Most distances involved are so great that they cannot be measured by trigonometrical methods. How, then, do we begin?

We saw in Chapter 8 that astronomers do possess a powerful and accurate method for determining the speed of motion of any object directly toward or away from the Earth. Such a motion produces a shift in the spectrum lines. If the motion is away from us the lines are shifted toward the red end of the spectrum; if it is toward us, they are shifted toward the blue end of the spectrum.

Unfortunately there is no such powerful method of determining motions across the line of sight. Figure 10.1 shows a star whose motion is made up of two components, one along the line of sight from the Earth, and the other across it. The motion along the line of sight can readily be determined from the shift of the star's spectrum lines, but the transverse motion is much more difficult to measure, since it produces no detectable effect on the spectrum lines. Indeed, the transverse motion shows itself only in a slowly-changing direction of the star. This can be seen from Figure 10.2. Assuming for simplicity that the Earth is fixed, the star lies at one moment at the point S_1 and at a later moment at the point S_2. Hence the line joining the Earth to the star has changed its direction. If we can measure this change, we can arrive at an estimate of the star's transverse motion, since in practice it is always possible to make allowance for the Earth's motion around the Sun.

However, such a procedure is difficult and awkward. It is difficult because very small changes of angle are involved; and it is awkward because the two moments of time must be as widely spaced as possible, since the longer the time interval the greater will be the change of angle and the easier it will be to measure that change. In practice, the desirable interval is at least fifty years.

Top: A multitude of stars in part of the Milky Way, photographed with the 48-inch Schmidt telescope. The task of measuring dimensions and motions within a galaxy made up of some 100,000 million stars has been and still is a colossal one.

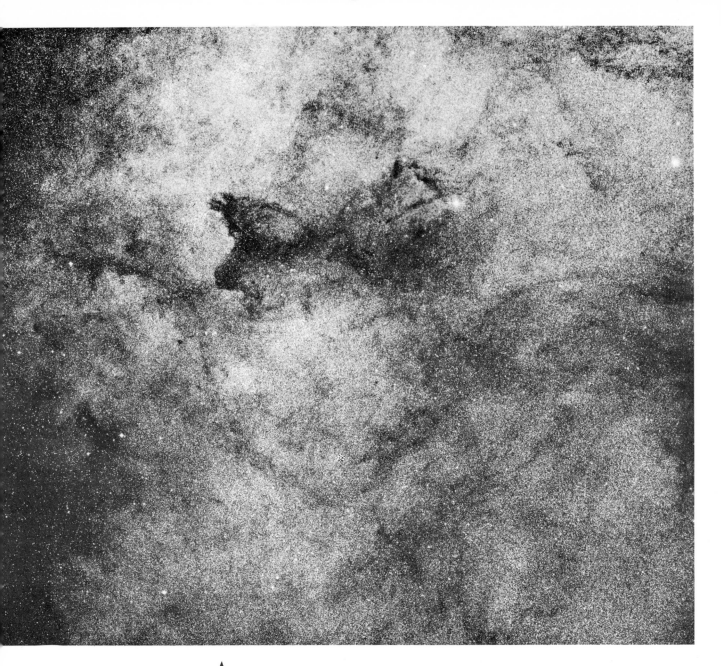

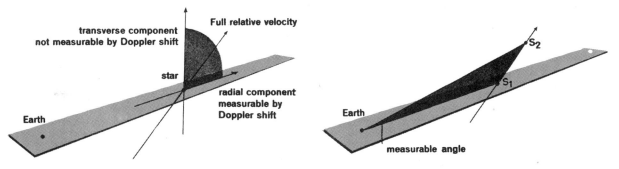

Figure 10.1
Only the radial component of a star's
motion can be measured by the shift
of its spectrum lines.

Figure 10.2
Transverse motion shows itself only
in the slowly-changing direction of
the line from the Earth to the star.

This raises practical problems. Telescopes are not completely rigid structures; they bend very slightly. Can we be sure that the degree of bending is the same today as it was fifty years ago? If we use the same telescope we *can* be reasonably sure of this. But it is not always possible, for practical reasons, to use the same telescope, and indeed if we attempted to do so we should prevent any improvements in telescopic technique from ever being employed in the measurements. We should perforce be obliged to work with instruments that were fifty years out of date. For these reasons, the available estimates of the motions of stars across the line of sight are of comparatively poor quality, and in any case they are available only for comparatively nearby stars. For the most part, then, astronomers are compelled to make do with a knowledge of motions along the line of sight.

With modern techniques it might be possible greatly to extend the measurement of transverse motions. But anyone who embarks on such a program must necessarily start from scratch; that is, he will have to wait about fifty years before the results become available. Such a program demands a degree of patience and resignation that not many scientists possess. Yet any young astronomer prepared to devote his efforts to such a task would be sure to earn the gratitude of a future generation. Transverse motions can sometimes be inferred from theoretical calculations but mostly they remain unknown.

In order to determine the structure of our galaxy we must have methods for determining the distances of the stars as well as their motions. We saw in Chapter 6 that we can measure the distances of the nearest stars by the parallax method—a direct trigonometrical method depending on the motion of the Earth around the Sun. This motion causes a slight annual oscillation in the direction of every star. If this tiny effect can be measured then the distance of the star in question can easily be determined. But in practice this can be done with a reasonable measure of accuracy for only about 10,000 stars, these being the 10,000 that happen to lie closest to us, all within a distance of less than 100 light-years, or about 600 million million miles.

Although this is only a small sample compared with the 100,000 million stars of the whole Milky Way, it is sufficient to allow astronomers to calibrate a more powerful method for measuring much greater distances. When we *do* know the distance of a star,

we can easily convert its measured apparent magnitude into its absolute magnitude, and, of course, we can always determine its spectrum type. Hence each of the stars for which a good trigonometrical distance *is* available can be plotted on the Hertzsprung-Russell diagram. Our sample of 10,000 stars of measured distance is then sufficient to determine the lower part of the main sequence with considerable accuracy, although there are not sufficient measurements for stars high on the main sequence to enable us to delineate that part of the sequence with adequate accuracy.

Shown opposite are the Large and Small Magellanic Clouds. By observing Cepheid variables in the Small Cloud, whose stars can all be regarded as lying at virtually the same distance from the Earth, Miss Leavitt was able to show that the relation between period and apparent magnitude is the same as that between period and absolute magnitude. Thus once we can measure the distance of one Cepheid we can fix the distances of others by direct observation of their periods and apparent magnitudes. By means of the main sequence method of measurement (which is calibrated from the trigonometrical parallax method) astronomers *have* determined the distances of several Cepheids. Thus other Cepheids, which are bright stars observable from great distances, can now be used to measure the vast dimensions of our galaxy. The bottom picture opposite, showing the Small Magellanic Cloud, is from Miss Leavitt's negative.

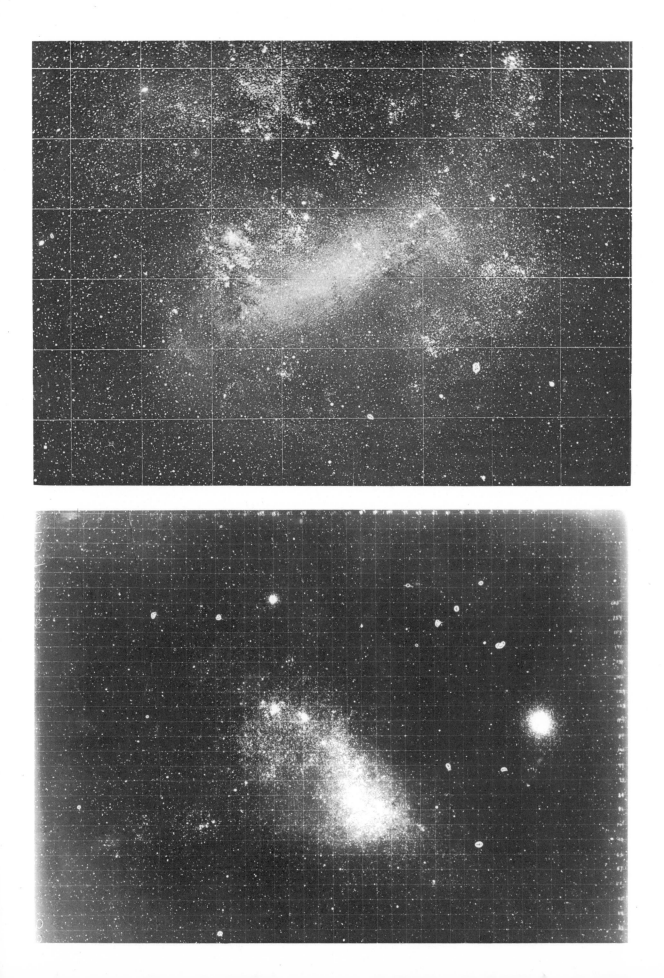

Knowing, then, the lower part of the main sequence, we can use it to determine the distances of a much larger sample of stars. Consider a star that is too far away for its distance to be measured accurately by the trigonometrical method, but which is nevertheless close enough to allow us to determine its spectrum type. Suppose its spectrum type is similar to that of the Sun. This implies that the star lies on or very close to the main sequence, and hence that its absolute luminosity is also similar to that of the Sun. Knowing the absolute magnitude of the star, we can compare this with its measured apparent magnitude and so infer its distance. The distance of *any* star that falls on the lower part of the main sequence can be determined in this way once its spectrum type is accurately known.

Although this method is a great gain on the trigonometrical method, it does not enable us to extend distance measurements enormously far out into space, since unfortunately it works only for comparatively faint stars—those that lie on the lower part of the main sequence. To obtain a still more powerful system of measurement we must turn again to the Cepheid variables, briefly mentioned in the preceding chapter. We there saw that the use of the Cepheid variables as distance indicators depends on the remarkable relation between their absolute magnitudes and their periods of oscillation. This relation was plotted in Figure 9.4, and we may here ask how this figure was obtained.

The original observations of Miss Leavitt were made on the Cepheid variables in the Magellanic Clouds. Both Clouds, the large one and the small one, contain many such variables, the periods of oscillation differing from one star to another. The small one contains far less obscuring dust than does the large one and therefore gives the observer a better opportunity of determining the apparent magnitudes of the Cepheids with accuracy. What Miss Leavitt did was to compare the measured apparent magnitudes of the Cepheids with their periods. Then by plotting apparent magnitudes on one axis of a graph and periods on the other, she obtained a line like that of Figure 9.4. We must now bear in mind that the Magellanic Clouds are very small compared to their distance from the Earth. We can therefore regard all the Cepheids in either the Small Cloud or the Large Cloud (but not in both together) as lying at essentially the same distance away from us. Thus the relation between apparent magnitude and absolute magnitude is the same for all of them. It is thus clear that there is a similar relation between apparent magnitude and period as there is between absolute magnitude and period.

Now if we are to use Cepheids for the purpose of distance determination, we must know the relation between absolute magnitude and period, and this is not given by observation of the Magellanic Clouds, for the simple reason that we have no *initial* knowledge of the distances of the clouds. All we know to begin with is that they are very far away from us. (It eventually turns out that their distances exceed 100,000 light-years.) To convert the relation between apparent magnitude and period into a relation between absolute magnitude and period, we must determine the distance of at least one Cepheid, for only then shall we know the relation between apparent and absolute magnitude for that Cepheid. Then, since for all Cepheids there must be the relation between apparent magnitude and period that was shown in Figure 9.4, the absolute magnitude scale in this figure will become fixed.

But how can we determine the distance of at least one Cepheid, remembering that none is close enough for the trigonometrical method to be employed accurately? By good fortune a number of cases have recently been discovered of Cepheids present in a comparatively compact cluster of stars. The stars of a cluster all lie at essentially the same distance away from us, and in the cases in question the distance is not very great. So if we can determine the distance of *any* star in the cluster, we have also determined the distance of the Cepheid member of the cluster. And luckily this has been done in several cases, using the main sequence method of measurement described above. Hence we now know the distances of a small handful of Cepheids and this information enables us to calibrate the curve of Figure 9.4. This curve can then be used for distance measurement in the manner described in Chapter 9.

The importance of the method lies in this. The Cepheids are bright stars, and can therefore be observed at great distances. Moreover, the oscillation of their light is a readily distinguishable feature. Hence they can be used for measuring distances far greater than those for which the main sequence method can be employed.

We can now see that there is a whole chain of methods of measuring distance. So far we have noted four links. The first is the measurement of distances inside the Solar System, especially the distance of the Earth from the Sun. This is the fundamental measurement, since the size of the Earth's orbit forms an essential datum in the trigonometrical method of measuring distances of nearer stars.

This trigonometrical method—the parallax method—is the second link in the chain. The main sequence method, calibrated from the trigonometrical method, is the third link. And now we have the fourth link—the Cepheids method—which in turn is calibrated from the main sequence method. Each successive link allows distance measurements to be carried to greater and greater depths into space, and each link depends for its calibration on the preceding link. In the last chapter we shall add two further links beyond the Cepheids. These further links are necessary only when we come to look beyond our galaxy and consider distances outside the Milky Way. For the present the four links of our chain will be sufficient.

Shape, Size, Motion and Make-up

Almost two hundred years ago it was already clear to Thomas Wright, a Durham sailor, and to William Herschel that the Milky Way is a flat plate-like structure, and that the Sun and Solar System are immersed inside the plate. But without the means of measurement that modern astronomers command, the early investigators were quite unable to determine the size of the whole structure, the precise position of the Sun within it, and the general nature of the motions of the stars. All these things were still matters for speculation, but some of the guesses were surprisingly near the mark. As long as two hundred years ago J. H. Lambert conjectured that all the stars of the galaxy might be moving around a common center, much as the

planets all move around a common center in the Solar System. This idea has proved to be correct. The stars do indeed move around a common center, namely the central bulge of our galaxy.

The general features of the modern picture of our galaxy are shown schematically in Figures 10.3 and 10.4. The first gives an edge-on view and the second a face-on view. From Figure 10.3 we see that the Sun lies well out toward the edge of the galaxy, its distance from the center being about 25,000 light-years. In the central regions of the galaxy, the plate-like structure tends to disappear. It is replaced by a distinct bulge, the thickness of the bulge being, perhaps, about 10,000 light-years. The region of the bulge is known as the nucleus of the galaxy, and an important characteristic of this nucleus is that the density of stars within it is higher than the density in the outer plate-like region. In particular, it is probable that the star density becomes very high near the extreme center of the galaxy.

The Sun moves in an almost circular orbit around the center of the galaxy, the speed of the motion being about 150 miles per second. This motion is not apparent to us here on the Earth simply because the Sun and planets all have it in common. For the most part, other stars also move around the center in almost circular orbits. The relation between the speed in these orbits and the distance from the center is shown in Figure 10.5. It will be seen that the speed rises to a maximum at a distance of about 15,000 light-years from the center. Thereafter it declines slowly. The Sun lies on this declining part of the curve.

Figure 10.5 gives no indication of speeds for the stars of the nucleus, that is for stars lying at distances of less than about 5,000 light-years from the center. The reason for this is that the motions of the

Figure 10.3
Schematic edge-on view of galaxy.

Sun

Figure 10.4
Schematic face-on view. The spiral structure represents the positions of highly luminous stars recently formed from the interstellar gas.

stars inside the nucleus are probably not simple. Such stars probably do not move around the center in circular orbits. Indeed, some stars just as distant from the center as the Sun is do not move in orbits that are even approximately circular. These stars are known as high-velocity stars, a name derived from the fact that those close by the Sun are moving at high speeds with respect to the Sun. This property arises simply because of the differences between the orbit of the Sun and the orbits of the stars in question. It is not an indication that those stars have particularly high speeds in their orbits; it is just that their orbits have a different shape from that of the Sun's orbit. The kind of difference is shown in Figure 10.6, below.

So far, we have dealt only with the *stars* of the galaxy, but as we noted in earlier chapters, gas occupies the spaces between the stars and this is also an important component of the galaxy. Contained within the gas are fine particles of dust—the dust that produces the troublesome obscuration mentioned in Chapter 6. We have little or no certain knowledge of the chemical composition of this dust, but many astronomers believe it to consist largely of ice particles. It was only after astronomers had discovered the presence of interstellar dust and had learned to allow for its effects that they were able to measure the dimensions of our galaxy with any show of accuracy.

Although the dust makes its presence only too readily felt, the gas is peculiarly difficult to detect.

Nevertheless this gas causes spectrum lines to appear in the light of distant stars. These lines are dark like the Fraunhofer lines of the Sun's spectrum (see page 199) and they are produced in an essentially similar way. It will be recalled that the Fraunhofer lines are produced because light with a continuous range of color, emitted from the photosphere, passes through cooler gas lying above the photosphere; the atoms within this cool gas then absorb the light at their own characteristic wavelengths, so that these particular wavelengths tend to be missing when the light reaches the Earth. A similar situation arises as the light from a distant star passes through the interstellar gas. Atoms within the gas absorb light at their own characteristic wavelengths.

The effect is particularly marked for atoms of sodium and calcium and it would not therefore be very noticeable in the case of a star whose spectrum already contained dark lines produced by sodium and calcium atoms in its own atmosphere. We have already seen, however, that the spectra of stars of high surface temperature, the B and O type stars, contain essentially only the lines of hydrogen and helium. The reason why no lines of sodium and calcium appear in the spectra of such stars is that at their high surface temperature the sodium and calcium atoms have so many electrons stripped away that their absorptive powers cease to be important. Consequently it was suspicious when dark lines of sodium and calcium were found in the light of distant stars with high surface temperatures. The

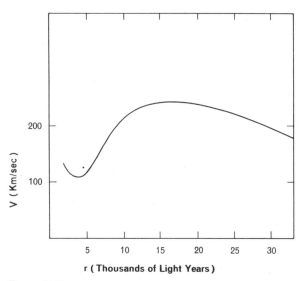

Figure 10.5
Relation between distance of stars from center of galaxy and speed in their orbits around that center.

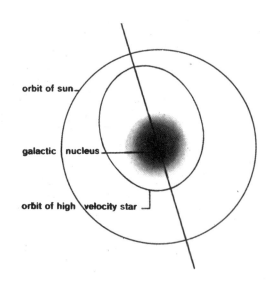

Figure 10.6
Orbits of Sun and high-velocity star.

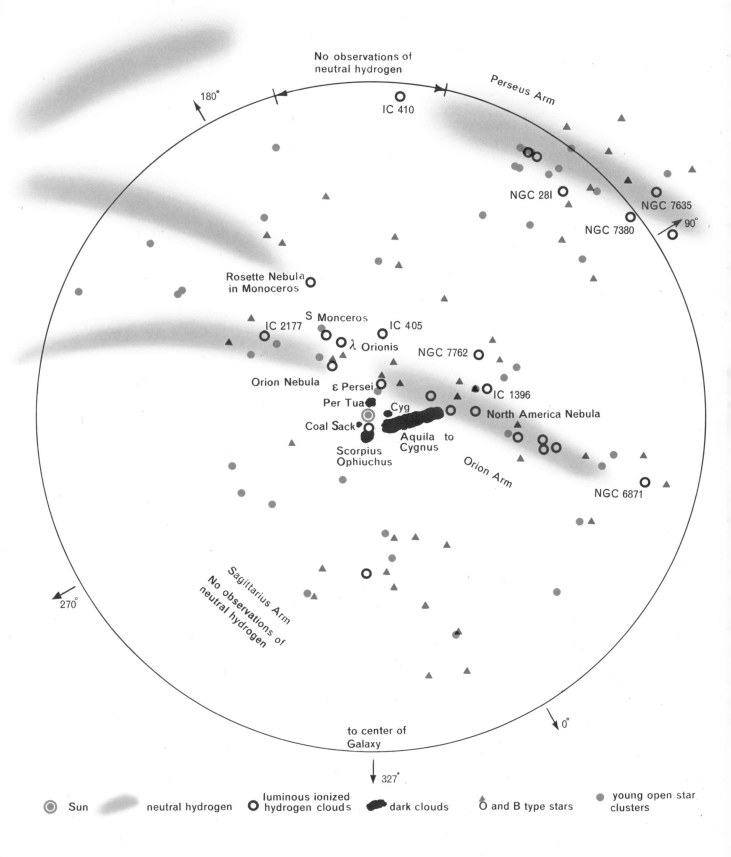

No observations of
neutral hydrogen

180°

IC 410

Perseus Arm

NGC 7635

NGC 281

NGC 7380

90°

Rosette Nebula
in Monoceros

S Monceros

IC 2177

IC 405

λ Orionis

NGC 7762

Orion Nebula

ε Persei

IC 1396

Per Tua

Cyg

North America Nebula

Coal Sack

Scorpius
Ophiuchus

Aquila   to
Cygnus

Orion Arm

NGC 6871

270°

Sagittarius Arm
No observations of
neutral hydrogen

0°

to center of
Galaxy

327°

| Sun | neutral hydrogen | luminous ionized hydrogen clouds | dark clouds | O and B type stars | young open star clusters |

Some features of the region of our
galaxy in the vicinity of the Sun,
as revealed by modern observation.
Names refer to dark and bright
hydrogen clouds. The arrows with
figures in degrees show galactic
longitudes. The circle, drawn with
the Sun as its center, has a radius
of about 10,000 light-years.

correct interpretation of their presence was given by Sir Arthur Eddington, namely that they are produced by sodium and calcium atoms lying in the interstellar gas.

Although sodium and calcium lines were thus important in revealing the presence of the interstellar gas, they do not reveal the most common constituents of it, which are atoms of hydrogen and helium. It was first realized that hydrogen must be a very much more common constituent of the interstellar gas than either sodium or calcium when faint radiations from the hydrogen were detected some twenty-five years ago. The observations of T. Dunham at the Mount Wilson Observatory then revealed the presence of hot patches of hydrogen with temperatures of the order of 10,000°. The concentration of hydrogen atoms in these patches was about a million times greater than the concentrations of sodium and calcium atoms. At first it was thought that the whole interstellar gas was as hot as this, but we now know that such hot patches of hydrogen are comparatively rare. Indeed, most of the interstellar gas is very cool, with temperatures around 100° on the Absolute scale (i.e., the scale on which the melting point of ice is 273°).

Now cool hydrogen gas cannot be detected by direct optical means. Provided the atoms exist by themselves—that is, provided they are not combined together into molecules—the hydrogen *does* emit a spectrum line, but the characteristic wavelength of the line is close to 21 centimeters, so that it falls into the radio wave band and can therefore be detected only by radio techniques. Thus although optical astronomy fails to detect the presence of neutral hydrogen atoms in the interstellar gas, radio-astronomy is able to supply this missing information.

Figure 10.7 shows a map of the distribution of hydrogen as determined by the radio method. It was produced by Dutch and Australian radio astronomers working in collaboration, measurements in the northern sky being made by the Dutch and those in the southern sky by the Australians.

The radio method has the disadvantage that it cannot detect molecules of hydrogen, but only neutral atoms by themselves. Hence our map is necessarily incomplete in that it does not include the contribution of molecular hydrogen. How important this may be is uncertain. Astronomers differ widely in their views on this question, some believing that molecules are probably the main constituent of the gas, others believing that they are quite unimportant. If the molecules are indeed unimportant, then the total mass of the interstellar gas amounts to only two or three per cent of the total mass of the stars. If, on the other hand, they prove to be important, then the total mass of the gas will be correspondingly higher.

Magnetic Fields and Cosmic Rays

It is strongly suspected that a magnetic field pervades our galaxy. Although its exact structure is not yet determined there are some things that can be said about it. A magnetic field is most easily thought of in terms of magnetic lines of force. When iron filings are placed near an ordinary bar magnet they arrange themselves in a pattern that readily shows up the lines of force, as shown in Figure 10.8. The direction of a line of force at any point is simply the direction of the magnetic field. It will be recalled from Chapter 7 that the presence of a magnetic field is shown by the effect it exerts on a moving charged body.

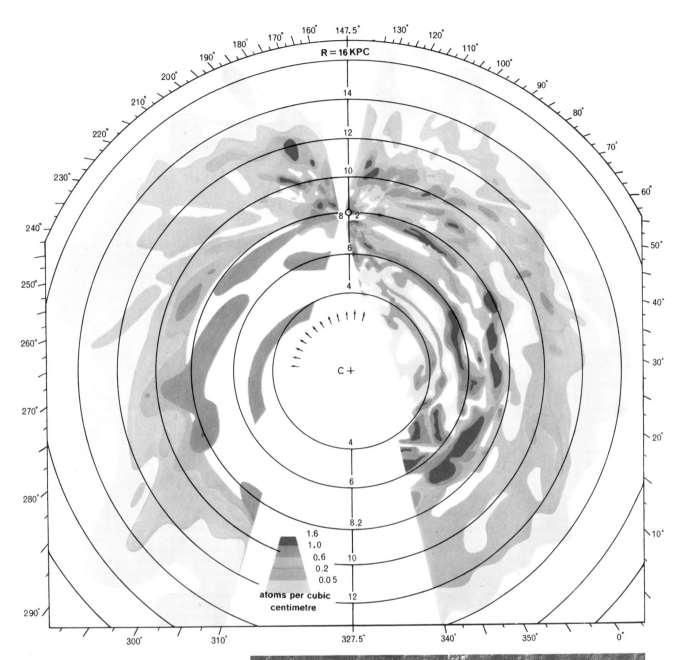

R = 16 KPC

1.6
1.0
0.6
0.2
0.05

atoms per cubic
centimetre

C +

Figure 10.7
Map showing distribution and density
of neutral hydrogen in the galaxy.
Measurements in the northern sky
were made by Dutch astronomers,
measurements in the southern sky
by Australian astronomers.
On this page is a Dutch radio
telescope at Dwingeloo and on the
opposite page is the Mills Cross
telescope near Sydney, Australia.

The lines of force within the interstellar gas seem to be aligned mainly parallel to the plane of the galaxy, but this may not be the whole story. Lines of force probably emerge from the nucleus of the galaxy into a huge halo that entirely surrounds the distribution of stars, as shown schematically in Figure 10.9. Thus the whole galaxy is probably contained within a huge magnetic bubble; and this magnetic bubble serves to contain the cosmic rays.

These are particles—mainly protons—with tremendously high energies. Indeed, some of them have even higher energies than it has been found possible to impart to protons in the laboratory, even with such huge machines as are now available, for example, at the CERN laboratory at Geneva. There is as yet no entirely satisfactory theory of the origin of cosmic rays. Such rays, of comparatively low energy, are certainly produced by the Sun, probably during solar flares. But stars like the Sun cannot be the principal source of production. Many astronomers and physicists believe that the main production occurs in the explosion of supernovae. Their view is that cosmic rays are constantly produced by exploding stars, and that instead of traveling freely away in space outward from the galaxy, they remain trapped inside the great magnetic bubble. There is some suspicion, however, that the origin of cosmic rays may be a still larger-scale phenomenon. A decision between these points of view remains for the future.

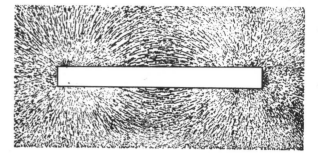

Figure 10.8
Iron filings reveal lines of force in magnetic field of a bar magnet.

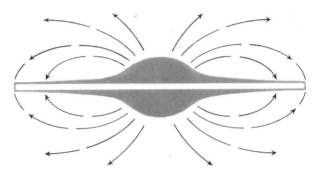

Figure 10.9
Schematic representation of magnetic field of galaxy. Lines of force seem to be aligned mainly parallel to galactic plane. Others probably emerge from nucleus to form a halo surrounding the entire distribution of stars. This magnetic bubble serves to contain the cosmic rays.

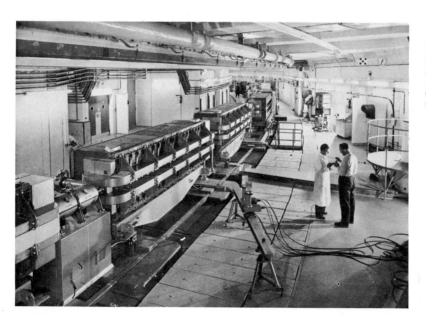

Interior view of the ring building of CERN's 28,000 million electron-volt alternating gradient proton synchrotron. Here protons have been accelerated up to 99.9 per cent of the speed of light. Cosmic rays consist of particles—mainly protons—some with even higher energies.

It seems unlikely that the whole of the interstellar gas is confined to the disk of the galaxy, as in Figure 10.7. Rather does it seem that it must occupy the whole of the bubble shown in Figure 10.9. There is this difference, however. The gas of Figure 10.7 is comparatively dense and its temperature is low, whereas the gas within the bubble, or halo, must have a high temperature—probably in excess of a million degrees—and its density must be comparatively low. But though the density of the halo gas must certainly be very much lower than that of the disk gas, this does not necessarily imply that the total mass of halo gas is smaller than the total mass of the disk gas, for the volume of the halo is vastly greater than the volume of the disk. There is no general agreement among astronomers about the mass of the halo gas. Some believe it is more or less comparable with that of the disk gas; others suspect it may be very much greater, simply because of its huge volume.

High-energy cosmic rays, moving at speeds close to the speed of light, occasionally collide with the halo gas and in such collisions electrons and positrons of high energy are produced. Being particles with electric charges, these electrons and positrons are deflected by the magnetic field: they are made to turn corners, as it were. The protons of the cosmic rays are also electric particles and they, too, are made to turn corners by the magnetic field. But since the protons have a far greater mass than the

electrons, their deflections are much weaker—the corners they turn are less steep. Now whenever an electric particle is made to turn a corner it radiates energy, and the steeper the turn the more powerful the radiation. So the magnetic field causes both the protons and the far lighter electrons and positrons to radiate, but the electrons and positrons are much more effective because they are made to travel in tighter curves.

This radiation occurs at wavelengths which do not produce spectrum lines; in fact the whole range of wavelengths concerned falls in the radio wave band. Hence the radiation emitted by electrons in the halo of the galaxy must necessarily be detected by the radio astronomer rather than by the optical astronomer.

Thus our galaxy is not only an emitter of light, it is also an emitter of radio waves. An overwhelming proportion of the light comes from the stars, and is derived from the energy produced by nuclear processes inside them. The radio waves come from high-speed positrons and electrons moving for the most part in the magnetic bubble surrounding the galaxy. (There are also electrons moving in the interstellar gas in the disk of the galaxy, but the radio emission from this component is appreciably less than that contributed by the halo.) The emitting electrons are probably derived from the cosmic rays, which in turn may be derived from the stars, by means of the explosion of supernovae, for example. In total,

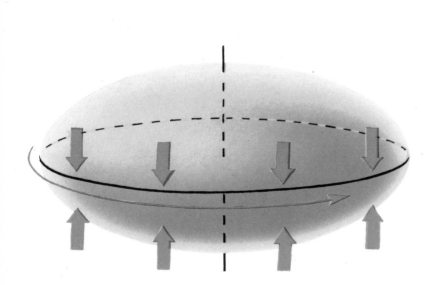

Figure 10.10
Most astronomers believe that the galaxy formed from a vast, slowly-rotating cloud of gas. As this gas condensed, the speed of rotation increased to such an extent that further contraction could no longer take place toward the axis of rotation, but only parallel to the *direction* of rotation. This would explain the shape of Figure 10.3.

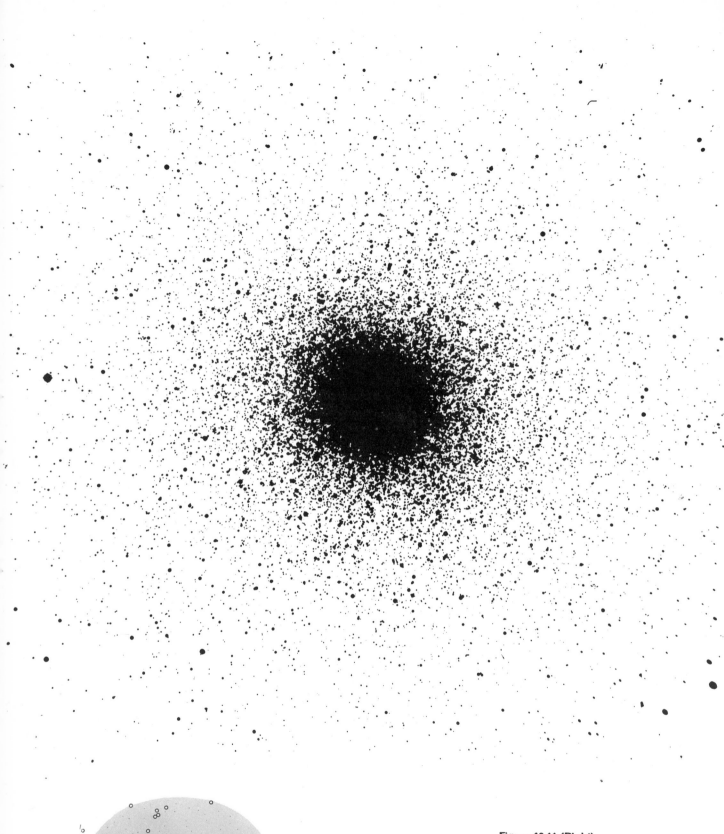

Above: The globular cluster M 13 in
Hercules. Such clusters occur mainly
in the halo of the galaxy and consist
of stars formed at an early stage
in the galactic condensation process.
The total mass of stars in the halo
is only 10 per cent of that of the disk
stars. Diagram at left shows general
distribution of globular clusters
in relation to galactic plane.

Figure 10.11 (Right)
Positions in the Hertzsprung-Russell
diagram of the cluster NGC 188, a
photograph of which is also shown.
Figure 9.3 (page 242) shows the kind of
evolutionary tracks which stars
follow on the diagram, and the time
taken to move along a given track
can be calculated. Such a calculation
for this track shows that NGC 188
is about 15,000 million years old.

the radio emission of the galaxy is weaker than the optical emission by a factor of something like a hundred thousand.

The Formation of the Galaxy

The great majority of astronomers believe that the galaxy was formed from a cloud of gas of very large dimensions, certainly with a diameter of many hundreds of thousands of light-years. To begin with the cloud was rotating very slowly, but as it condensed the rotation gradually speeded up, causing the cloud to become more and more flattened. Eventually the rotation became so rapid that any further contraction toward the axis of rotation was prevented. Only contraction parallel to the direction of rotation could then take place, as shown in Figure 10.10. The ultimate result was a condensation to the disk-like structure we saw in Figure 10.3.

During this period of condensation, only a sprinkling of stars was formed, and this sprinkling now surrounds the main structure of the galaxy. These are the stars found in the halo of the galaxy, and their total mass is about ten per cent of that of the disk stars. Sometimes the halo stars are found in clusters. These are the globular clusters, of which an example is shown in the photograph opposite.

But the great bulk of the gas reached the disk-like shape of Figure 10.3 before it condensed into stars. Once this stage was reached, star formation may have taken place with great rapidity, the bulk of the gas soon disappearing. A little remained uncondensed into stars, however, and it is this small fraction that constitutes the interstellar gas of the disk. Similarly, another small fraction remained behind in the halo, and this is the gas that we believe to be present in the halo today.

This picture of the formation of the galaxy is very qualitative, and there is no certainty that it is correct. It does, however, stand up to one explicit test.

We saw in Chapter 9 that all the elements other than hydrogen are produced only by thermonuclear reactions which take place inside the stars. Thus the iron and calcium which show so strongly in the spectra of many stars must themselves have been produced by such reactions. If our picture of the formation of the galaxy is reliable, we should expect the initial cloud of gas to contain scarcely any heavy nuclei, since such nuclei are produced only inside stars; we should therefore expect that the spectra of the earliest stars to be formed would reveal only traces of iron and calcium. At a later stage, when many stars were already formed and had had time to produce such elements, we might expect the still-condensing cloud of gas to contain more heavy nuclei. This, in turn, would lead us to expect that the spectra of stars formed at a later stage in the condensation process would reveal a higher concentration of iron and calcium. On this basis the stars of the halo should contain lower concentrations of such elements than do the stars of the disk.

This expectation is confirmed by observation. The concentrations measured in certain halo stars are as low as 1 per cent of the concentrations found in the Sun. Besides supporting the above general picture of the formation of the galaxy, this observation also gives strong support to what was said in the previous chapter, that hydrogen is the basic building block from which all the other elements are made.

It must be added, however, that although this observation agrees with what we should expect on the basis of our picture of the formation of the galaxy, it does not prove that this picture is correct. For there are other ways in which the low concentrations of iron and calcium in the halo stars might be explained. Beyond this cautionary mention we shall not here consider such possibilities, for they would lead us on to extremely speculative ground.

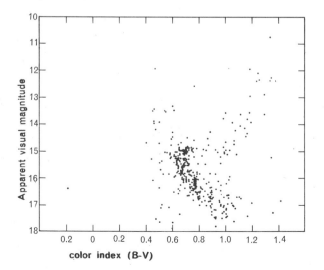

This photograph of the Orion Nebula
shows huge dark areas consisting of
dense clouds of gas and dust. There
the formation of stars in our galaxy,
which began 15,000 million years
ago, almost certainly still goes on.

© California Institute of Technology.

Returning to our general picture, we may well ask how long ago did all this happen—how old is our galaxy? The techniques of observation and calculation described in the previous chapter allow us to get to grips with this question. Look again, for a moment, at Figures 9.3, 9.6 and 9.7. We saw that the exhaustion of hydrogen in the central regions of a star causes it to move away from the main sequence toward the right-hand side of the Hertzsprung-Russell diagram, and a number of evolutionary tracks are shown in Figure 9.3. It can be shown by calculation that the stars move along tracks of this kind, and calculations can also determine how long the evolution takes. For stars high on the main sequence the time is much shorter than for stars lower down the main sequence. The evolution times are longest for stars comparatively low down on the main sequence that follow tracks which not only move simply to the right but also steeply upward in the Hertzsprung-Russell diagram.

In Figures 9.6 and 9.7 we saw examples of actual clusters of stars. If we carry out calculations of an evolutionary track that matches the distribution shown in Figure 9.7 the length of time calculated for the evolution will represent the age of the Messier 67 Cluster. A similar procedure for Figure 9.6 will determine the age of the Hyades group of stars. The results of the two calculations will not necessarily agree, and in fact they do not do so. The reason is, of course, that the two clusters were formed at different epochs. The Messier 67 Cluster is older than the Hyades group. The situation, therefore, is that if we take a whole series of clusters we shall obtain a corresponding series of age determinations; and the age of the whole galaxy must be at least as great as the age of the oldest of our clusters. If we have been lucky enough to include a cluster that was formed during the earliest phases of the history of the galaxy, then we shall have a close estimate of the age of the galaxy itself.

In Figure 10.11 we have the positions in the Hertzsprung-Russell diagram of the cluster NGC 188, believed to be one of the oldest clusters in the galaxy. Calculation shows its age to be about 15,000 million years. This, then, is the answer to our question, for that figure must be close to the age of the galaxy.

The Sun and the Solar System are much younger. Evidence from the rocks of the Earth's crust and from the meteorites suggest that the age of the Solar System is about 5,000 million years, or only about

NGC 6611. Here a vast cloud of gas is expanding, probably as a result of radiation from newly-formed stars. Only when the cloud has become even more diffuse will it be possible to see into it and observe whether or not it contains newly-formed stars.

a third as old as the galaxy itself. Our Sun was not among the first stars to form by a very considerable margin. In fact it is a comparatively young star.

The Formation of Stars

Because gas is still present in the disk of the galaxy, it is still possible for new stars to form; and a very simple argument shows it is extremely probable that stars *are* still forming.

In the previous chapter, our discussion of Figure 9.3 made it clear that stars high on the main sequence go through their evolution in a comparatively short time. Indeed, the most luminous known stars take only about a million years to complete their evolution. Since we can actually observe such stars—not any great number of them, it is true—it must follow that they were formed within the last million years. It would obviously be unrealistic to suppose that star formation, which began 15,000 million years ago and which quite clearly went on until at least a million years ago, suddenly ceased, say, a hundred thousand years ago. Hence, although we do not actually *see* new stars being formed at the present moment, it is nevertheless quite clear that such a process of formation is almost certainly still going on.

The reason why we do not literally see new stars being formed is easy to understand. New stars are born in dense clouds of gas and dust, such as the Orion Nebula shown on page 266. Because of the large amount of dust, we cannot see into the interior of these clouds to the places where the actual star formation takes place. We must wait until after the stars have actually formed. Once a very bright star begins to radiate, it quickly heats up the surrounding cloud of gas, and this causes the cloud to expand. As the cloud thus becomes more diffuse, it eventually becomes possible to see into it, and at this stage we do indeed observe recently-born stars. This is so in the case of the Orion Nebula.

It appears to be a necessary condition for star formation that there should be dense clouds of gas and dust, so we are naturally led to consider the location and origin of such clouds. Now the gas in the halo of the galaxy is too diffuse and too hot to

The Lagoon Nebula in Sagittarius, photographed with the 200-inch Hale telescope. This is an emission nebula. In such nebulae the density of hydrogen is many times greater than the average in interstellar gas.

permit the formation of clouds like the Orion Nebula. Hence there seems to be little or no new star formation taking place in the halo. Nor is there much star formation in the nucleus of the galaxy, the reason being that the nucleus seems to be largely devoid of gas. The densest gas occurs in the outer parts of the disk of the galaxy—in other words, in the sort of region where the Sun lies.

The clouds are probably formed by a cooling process. If there were no cooling the presence of existing stars would soon lift the gas to a temperature of about 10,000°. That is why astronomers used to believe that the interstellar gas had such a temperature. They had overlooked one thing: the cooling power of dust and molecules in the gas. The dust particles in interstellar space probably play an important part in causing atoms to combine into molecules. What happens is that individual atoms strike and stick to the surfaces of dust particles. This brings them into contact with each other, enabling them to combine into molecules. The molecules then evaporate away from the surfaces of the dust particles.

This dust, which probably plays such a vital part in the formation of molecules, and in the cooling of the gas, and so in the origin of stars, is not uniformly distributed in the interstellar gas. Almost any photograph of the Milky Way shows apparently dark regions. These are not places where stars are absent; they are simply places where patches of dust intervene between the Earth and the stars that lie beyond. The fact that such regions are irregularly scattered about the galaxy shows quite plainly that the dust is not uniformly distributed. And because of this the cooling effect of the dust is not uniform. Some local regions must cool far more effectively than others.

Where the dust is most dense the cooling of the gas is most rapid. Pressure within the cooled region declines, and becomes less than the pressure in surrounding regions. The surrounding regions press the gas of the cooled regions inward, thereby producing a localized dense cloud. Here we have a possible mode of formation of localized regions of higher density within which stars can begin to form.

We would expect stars to derive two important characteristic properties from their parent clouds of gas: a magnetic field and a rapid speed of rotation. Consider the magnetic field first. We have seen that a magnetic field exists within the interstellar gas. If the gas increases its density, the lines of force of this field become compressed together; and since the rise of density is enormous when a star is formed, the rise of the magnetic intensity is expected to be correspondingly great. Thus even if the magnetic field in the interstellar gas is initially rather weak, the field produced inside a star can still be very strong. It is believed that the stars do, in fact, derive their magnetic fields in this way. They are simply fields that have been produced by the compression of the initial lines of force pervading the interstellar gas from which the stars were formed. Very probably the magnetic field of the Sun was derived in this way. We saw earlier that the Sun's magnetic field plays a crucial role in many of the phenomena we observe at its surface. These, then, may owe their origin to the conditions within the original gas cloud from which the Sun condensed.

Let us turn now to the second hereditary characteristic we should expect the stars to possess, namely rapid rotation. The interstellar clouds that we observe all have some degree of random swirling motion, and this means that any portion of such a cloud which condenses into a star will also have a rotation. At the beginning of the condensation process the rate of rotation is small and comparatively unimportant, but as condensation proceeds the speed of rotation increases, and calculation shows that speeds of many hundreds of miles a second must finally be reached by the time a star is formed.

Two questions now arise. Do all stars possess magnetic fields and do they all have rapid speeds of rotation? The answer to the first question is that many stars have, indeed, been shown to have strong magnetic fields. This work, carried out by Babcock at the Mount Wilson and Palomar Observatories, could not be expected to reveal the presence of a magnetic field except under special circumstances. For example, if we were to observe the Sun from a great distance, using Babcock's method, we should not be able to detect the magnetic fields that do in fact exist. Hence we can answer our first question in two parts: on the positive side we can say that many stars quite certainly do have strong magnetic fields; on the negative side, we can say that there is no evidence to suggest that some stars lack a magnetic field.

Measuring the rotation of a star is considerably easier than measuring the strength of its magnetic field. If a star is rotating, some parts of its surface will be moving toward us and other parts away from us. These motions produce slight displacements of the spectrum lines coming from different parts of the star's surface. The wavelengths of the lines from those parts that are moving away from us are slightly increased, while the wavelengths of the lines from those parts that are moving toward us are slightly decreased. This causes the spectrum lines to be broadened. Unfortunately, there are other causes which may also produce a broadening of spectrum lines, but provided these other causes can be correctly allowed for it is possible to estimate the degree of rotation of a star.

It turns out that stars lying high on the main sequence do, indeed, rotate rapidly, in accordance with our expectation; but stars low on the main sequence rotate only very slowly, as the Sun does. Here we have a very definite departure from what we would at first sight expect. How do we explain this apparent contradiction? The answer leads us directly to a consideration of the whole problem of planet formation.

The Origin of the Planets

The surprising thing is that if all the planets were scooped up and placed inside the Sun, then in spite of the insignificance of their total mass compared with that of the Sun, the solar speed of rotation would be greatly increased. In fact, it would be increased almost a hundredfold. This arises because of the great distances of the planets from the Sun.

Further consideration suggests that if all the original planetary material were placed inside the Sun, its speed of rotation would be increased still further. We can best understand this point by taking a brief look at the chemical make-up of the planets. The large outer planets, Uranus and Neptune, contain very little hydrogen and helium, in contrast with the large inner planets, Jupiter and Saturn, both of

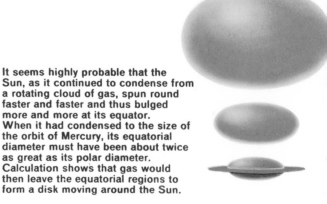

It seems highly probable that the Sun, as it continued to condense from a rotating cloud of gas, spun round faster and faster and thus bulged more and more at its equator. When it had condensed to the size of the orbit of Mercury, its equatorial diameter must have been about twice as great as its polar diameter. Calculation shows that gas would then leave the equatorial regions to form a disk moving around the Sun.

which have high concentrations of hydrogen and helium. Indeed, the compositions of Jupiter and Saturn are so nearly the same as that of the Sun as to suggest that the original planetary material had exactly the same chemical composition as the Sun itself. In this case hydrogen and helium must at some stage have escaped from the periphery of the Solar System, otherwise their absence from Uranus and Neptune could not be explained.

It is easy to see how such an escape might have come about. Hydrogen and helium are the lightest gases, and at the outskirts of the Solar System the restraining influence of the Sun's gravitational field on them was weak. Hence these gases simply evaporated away into space. If the mass of these "lost" gases, together with the mass of the planets, could be placed inside the Sun, its speed of rotation would be increased almost a thousandfold. And this is just what our calculations on star formation would lead us to expect.

It seems highly probable, therefore, that our expectation with regard to the rotations of the stars is in principle correct, but that somehow the rotation of the Sun, and of other stars low on the main sequence, became transferred to an outlying system of planets.

So let us follow our ideas on star formation a little further. As the still-forming Sun continued its condensation, it must have spun round faster and faster, and this caused it to bulge more and more at the equator. By about the time it had shrunk to the diameter of the orbit of the planet Mercury, the innermost planet of the Solar System, its equatorial diameter must have become about twice as great as its polar diameter. Somewhat complicated calculations show that at this stage gas would leave

the rapidly-swirling equatorial regions and form a disk moving around the Sun and lying outside it. And the soundness of these calculations appears to be borne out by actual observation. Certain stars lying high on the main sequence, which are indeed in rapid rotation, do seem to possess just such a disk of gas lying outside the main body of the star and moving around it in a circular path. One example is Pleione, an important member of the Pleiades.

More than a hundred years ago Laplace put forward a theory of planet formation that had similarities with all these considerations. He held that a nascent star could develop a surrounding disk of gas in just this way, and that planets could then form out of the material of the disk. But his theory did not secure universal acceptance among astronomers, particularly in the early part of the present century, for one important reason. Merely saying that a star may throw off a disk of gas does not begin to explain why this should slow down its rotation. Indeed, Pleione has a very rapid rotation, so the mere growing of a disk is certainly not the whole story.

In order to account for the slowing down of rotation we must be able to show that there is some coupling between the star and the disk—a coupling that conveys the torque of the star to the disk. This would not only explain the slowing down; it would also explain how the disk itself is pushed farther and farther outward, and hence how planets formed from it can lie at such great distances away from the parent star. The stumbling block to acceptance of Laplace's theory, then, was that until comparatively recently astronomers could not show the nature of any such torque coupling. How, for instance, could the Sun ever have been connected with an outlying disk of gas? What influence could possibly

Figure 10.12
The mere throwing-off of a disk of gas would not explain why the Sun rotates more slowly than the theory of its formation leads us to expect. But this *is* explained if lines of magnetic force, behaving like elastic strings, provided a torque coupling between Sun and disk (later between Sun and planets formed from disk).

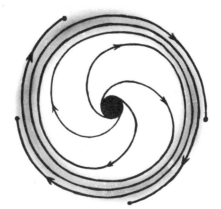

have crossed the wide space between the Sun and the disk, a space that must have increased as the disk of gas was pushed outward?

For the answer we must come back to the strong magnetic field which we have seen was present in solar condensation. When the disk of gas became separated from the Sun it is probable that magnetic lines of force continued to connect the material of the disk with the material of the Sun, in spite of the growing distance between them. Now it has been known since the time of Faraday that magnetic lines of force behave in many ways like stretched elastic strings. Such strings connecting the Sun with an outer disk could indeed play the role of a torque conveyor. The situation is shown in plan in Figure 10.12. Lines of magnetic force emerge from the solar equator, cross the space between the Sun and the disk, and then enter the material of the disk. So long as the Sun rotates faster than the disk, the lines of force become twisted, as shown in the figure. Remembering that they behave like stretched elastic strings, it is easy to see that they not only tend to slow down the rotation of the Sun but also to force outward the material of the disk.

So far we have an explanation of how the Sun could develop an outer disk of gas, and of how that disk could slow down the Sun's rotation; but we have not yet examined how planets could form from the material of the disk. What was the first step? Almost certainly it was not a simple aggregation of gaseous material, for the strong gravitational effect of the Sun itself would prevent any such process of aggregation from taking place within the disk. But what the gravitational field of the Sun *cannot* prevent is the formation of small solid, and perhaps liquid, particles within the gas. We saw in Chapter 8 that the Sun contains not only atoms of hydrogen and helium, but also—though in very much smaller proportions—atoms of oxygen, neon, carbon, nitrogen, magnesium, silicon and the common metals as well as very small quantities of tin, barium, mercury, lead and uranium. So from the disk of solar material, particles of these elements, or of combinations of these elements, can form. Such particles form rather like the raindrops in the clouds of the Earth's atmosphere. Yet although the Sun's gravitational influence does not prevent this type of condensation, its radiation does have an important effect. For example, neither water drops nor drops of ammonia will form if the gas is too hot; hence, only as the gas in the disk moves steadily farther away from the Sun and cools more and more will a stage be reached where water and ammonia begin to condense. It turns out that the distance in question, at any rate for ammonia, though perhaps not for water, is comparable with the radii of the orbits of the planets Jupiter and Saturn. Thus the planetary gases had to move outward until they reached the neighborhood of these orbits before ammonia was able to condense out of the gas.

But particles of rock and metal would readily condense at higher temperatures, and hence closer to the Sun. In fact, they could condense already at the distances of the inner planets from the Sun—the distances of Mercury, Venus, the Earth and Mars. At one stroke this explains three outstanding characteristics of the inner planets: first, their unusual composition—the fact that they contain very high concentrations of such elements as magnesium, silicon and iron, elements that must have been comparatively rare in the original planetary material, amounting in mass to no more than about one-tenth of one per cent, exactly as we find in the Sun today; second, their small masses; and third, the fact that they lie comparatively close to the Sun. We now see that all these three characteristics are closely interlinked. The first two are directly complementary to each other: the inner planets are of small mass simply because they are composed of elements that were present only in low concentrations in the original planetary material. These elements had the property that their solid forms were able to condense as particles from the gas at comparatively high temperatures; and this explains why the rock and iron planets lie comparatively close to the Sun.

We can now readily visualize the sequence of events. As the torque coupling operated to slow down the Sun's rotation, the planetary gases moved rapidly outward. As they moved through the regions now occupied by the inner planets, small particles of rock and metal condensed out of the gas and were left behind while the main bulk of the gas continued to be pushed farther and farther outward. Gradually the particles of rock and metal that were left behind began to aggregate. Eventually, quite a number of bodies of a considerable size—say comparable with the size of the Moon—were formed. In the final phase these bodies became fused together into the small handful of inner planets that we now find. At the outskirts of the region of rock and metal condensation—that is beyond the orbit of

Mars—there were insufficient particles to form a planet of tolerable size, however, and this is just why we still find there a situation of partial condensation. This is the region still populated by a host of small bodies, namely the asteroids, or minor planets.

By the time the inner planets had aggregated into bodies with appreciable gravitational fields, the main bulk of the planetary gases had swept out to the regions of the great planets, Jupiter and Saturn. The gravitational fields of the inner planets were thus unable to gather up very much gas because only a little was then available. The small amount that was still available we now find, for example, in the nitrogen of the terrestrial atmosphere, in the water of the oceans and in carbon dioxide.

Let us turn now to the great planets. We have already seen that ammonia condensed in the region of the present orbits of Jupiter and Saturn. Once solid particles of ammonia became aggregated into bodies with appreciable gravitational fields, these primitive bodies were able to pull in large quantities of gas, for here the situation was very different from the case of the inner planets. The gas of the disk had not effectively been all pushed beyond the orbits of Jupiter and Saturn, so much of it remained to be picked up through the gravitational influence of the aggregating primitive planets. And it is because of the addition of large quantities of gas, particularly of hydrogen and helium, that the masses of Jupiter and Saturn are so large in comparison with those of the inner planets.

The formation of Uranus and Neptune differed from that of Jupiter and Saturn in one crucial respect. By the time the first primitive condensations grew large enough for their gravitational fields to be capable of pulling in gas, the bulk of the gas had disappeared; for when the disk gases had moved outward that far, the hydrogen and helium had evaporated away entirely from the Sun's gravitational influence. Thus only gases such as methane and carbon monoxide remained behind in the region of Uranus and Neptune. These gases were, indeed, picked up by the primitive condensations. Their abundances were high enough to give Uranus and Neptune much larger masses than those of the inner planets, but not masses comparable with those of Jupiter and Saturn.

There is just one further point to note. Yet another planet, Pluto, lies beyond the orbit of Neptune. It has only a small mass and is in no sense similar to Uranus and Neptune. But as Lyttleton has point-

ed out, Pluto may well be an escaped satellite of Neptune, in which case it cannot properly be considered as a planet at all. We shall consider the class of satellites in a moment, but it will be as well first to say something of the physical characteristics of each of the planets, beginning with the innermost one, Mercury.

Mercury

Because Mercury's orbit lies inside that of the Earth and because Mercury shines by reflected sunlight, the part of its illuminated hemisphere that we see undergoes phases similar to those of the Moon. Mercury lies almost in the plane of the ecliptic, so that it appears either to follow or to precede the Sun, according to the position of the planet in its orbit. Indeed, owing to its motion in its orbit, Mercury appears to oscillate backward and forward, lying first behind the Sun, then in front of it, then behind it again, and so forth. When Mercury lies behind the Sun we see it near the western horizon in the evening sky; when it precedes the Sun we see it in the eastern sky near dawn. In antiquity it was not realized that these different observations were in fact observations of one and the same planet. The ancients gave the name Hermes, or Mercury, to the evening aspect and the name Apollo to the morning aspect.

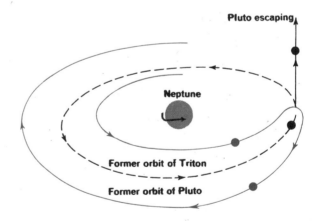

Pluto may well be regarded not as a planet but as an escaped satellite of Neptune. The diagram shows how the present satellite, Triton, may at some stage have overtaken Pluto in its orbit around Neptune. Such an encounter would have speeded up Pluto enough to enable it to escape. It would also have reversed the direction of Triton's motion.

Under the most favorable circumstances, Mercury is an easily visible object, with a brightness comparable to that of the star Sirius. When such favorable occasions arise they must be seized, for Mercury changes its position very quickly. Viewed from the Earth, it executes one complete oscillation —from behind the Sun to in front, to behind again —in only 116 days. Its actual period of motion around the Sun is 88 days, and, if we exclude Pluto, its orbit is more highly elliptical than that of any other planet.

Its diameter is roughly 3,000 miles, or 40 per cent greater than that of the Moon, and its mass is some four or five times greater than the mass of the Moon. Incidentally, the internal density of Mercury seems to be higher than the densities of the other three inner planets. This high density would appear to imply that Mercury contains a higher proportion of metals than does Venus, the Earth or Mars. Venus and the Earth seem to contain about the same proportion of rock to metal; Mercury contains more metal and less rock, while Mars contains more rock and less metal.

Since Mercury has little in the way of atmospheric gases we can see through to its surface, which seems to be very similar to the surface of the Moon; and because we can see its surface, we can readily determine its rate of rotation. During last century Schiaparelli showed that Mercury's period of rotation is the same as the period of its motion around the Sun, namely 88 days. This means that Mercury always keeps the same face directed toward the Sun, so that one half of the planet is in perpetual sunshine and the other in perpetual darkness. Hence

Mercury has the distinction of possessing not only the hottest place but also the coldest place in the whole planetary system.

Venus

Venus also lies nearer to the Sun than the Earth does, and like Mercury it also shows phases similar to those of the Moon. Because it lies nearly in the ecliptic, and because of its motion around the Sun, it appears sometimes behind the Sun and sometimes in front of it. This means that we see it sometimes in the evening sky after sunset and sometimes in the morning sky before dawn. The Greeks had two names for it—Hesperus when it appeared in the evening sky and Phosphorus when it appeared in the dawn sky.

Venus is almost a twin of the Earth. It is only slightly smaller in mass and diameter, has almost the same internal density, and probably much the same composition. This has raised the question of whether its surface features are also similar to those of the Earth. Unfortunately this question cannot be settled by direct observation, since Venus is perpetually shrouded in a mantle of white cloud. And this cloud not only obscures our view; it also obscures the problem of assessing the probability of whether the surface of Venus is partly covered with oceans.

The atmosphere of Venus is known to contain a huge quantity of carbon dioxide, and very recently, as a result of observations made from balloon flights over the United States, a minute quantity of water has also been detected in it. Now this new discovery can be interpreted in two different ways, depending upon what temperature we assign to the

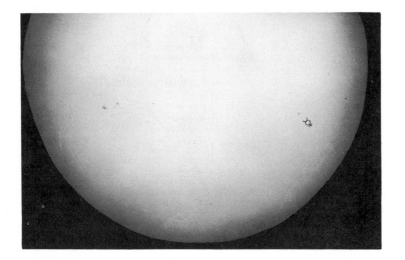

Mercury, the innermost and smallest of the planets, seen against the disk of the Sun. The photograph explains how easy it was for early observers to mistake sunspots for the passage of Mercury across the Sun's disk.

This reproduction of one of the best recent drawings of Mars, made by Dr. de Vaucouleurs of Harvard College Observatory, shows the visible markings of the planet and what seems to be a yellow dust storm sweeping across its surface.

Venus—almost a twin of the Earth in mass, diameter and composition—seen at crescent phase. Since it is perpetually shrouded in a mantle of cloud, astronomers cannot yet tell whether its surface features are also like those of the Earth.

clouds of Venus. If their temperature is fairly high, then the fact that only a small quantity of water has been detected forces us to the conclusion that there can be very little water indeed on the surface of Venus. If, however, the clouds are very cold we should not expect to find more than a very small quantity of water lying above them, however much might lie beneath. (Obviously we can only observe the content of the atmosphere that lies above the clouds, and not that which lies below them; and if the clouds and the regions above them are very cold, then almost all the water will be frozen out.)

This second interpretation has to face up to a serious difficulty. Unless the temperature is as low as −75 C. more water vapor would exist than is actually found. How can the clouds maintain a temperature as low as this when they are constantly subjected to intense heat from the Sun? In fact they could do so only if they possess the remarkable property of being able to reflect and transmit sunlight without absorbing it. In such a case, part of the incident sunlight would be reflected back into space and the rest of it would penetrate through the clouds to the regions below; virtually none of it would be absorbed in heating the clouds. If this is what actually happens, the problem of the nature of the clouds can be solved very simply. They could be no more than a haze produced by fine particles of solid carbon dioxide, and ordinary clouds of water vapor might well lie far below them. Hence it would be possible for Venus to have oceans of water like those of our own Earth. A decision between these two points of view will probably be made within the near future.

The Earth

Only recently have photographs of the Earth been taken from rockets and artificial satellites. One of them is shown on page 11. They give the best impression yet available of the Earth as a planet.

Mars

Mars, since its orbit lies outside that of the Earth, never exhibits crescent phases as do Mercury and Venus. When nearest to us it lies in the opposite direction to that of the Sun, in distinction to Venus which, at its nearest, lies in approximately the same direction as the Sun. Thus Mars lies in the night sky when it is closest to us. This is a highly favorable circumstance for the astronomer, and the situation is made still better by the fact that Mars has only a tenuous cloud cover. Even so, it must be remembered that a view of Mars through the best telescope under the most favorable circumstances is still inferior to a view of the Moon with the naked eye.

Observation of distinct surface markings shows that Mars makes one complete rotation on its axis in 24 hours 37 minutes 23 seconds. Thus, while Mars takes almost two terrestrial years to move once round its orbit, the Martian day is of almost the same length as the terrestrial day. Moreover, the Martian axis of rotation is inclined at almost exactly the same angle to the ecliptic as is the Earth's axis. These similarities have prompted the question as to whether there could be life on Mars. What we know of the chemistry of the Martian atmosphere does not rule out such a possibility. The atmosphere of Mars probably contains small quantities of water and carbon dioxide, and perhaps a somewhat greater quantity of nitrogen. Nor can we say that Martian temperatures preclude the possibility of life. White pole caps develop during winter in each hemisphere, but these melt so readily when summer comes that they cannot be deep. Probably they are simply thin caps of hoar frost.

It is possible, then, that life exists on Mars, but if so, it is likely to be confined to low forms of plant life. In general, temperatures are too low and the whole physical and chemical environment too sparse and primitive for any luxuriant flora or fauna to be reasonably expected. In this connection, Sindon, working at the Lowell Observatory at Flagstaff, Arizona, has found the spectrum of Mars to show features that correspond closely to those found in the light reflected by certain terrestrial flora.

Percival Lowell's "map" of Mars, made in 1901. Lowell held that Mars was criss-crossed by canals made by intelligent beings. (On the original map many of these "canals", drawn as perfectly geometrical lines, were given names.) Few people then and still fewer now would draw such a conclusion from the scant visual evidence available.

Many astronomers interpret this observation as clear evidence of the existence of plant life on Mars. One must note as a matter of caution, however, that this evidence cannot be regarded as conclusive unless it can be shown that no inorganic material could have caused the spectrum effects in question. This negative demonstration is, of course, hard to make, and in fact it has not yet been made. Strictly speaking, therefore, the proof is incomplete.

Some fifty years ago there was a heated controversy about whether or not any higher forms of life exist on Mars. Percival Lowell, on the one hand, maintained that the surface of Mars was criss-crossed by a network of lines, or canals, and that the geometrical regularity of the network, together with its variations through the Martian year, indicated it to be an artefact constructed by intelligent beings. At the other extreme were the views of E. E. Barnard, views with which the great majority of astronomers now agree. Barnard said Mars gave him the impression of "a globe whose entire surface had been tinted with a slight pink color on which the dark details had been painted with a greyish colored paint supplied with a very poor brush, producing a shredded or streaky and wispy effect in the darker regions." Suggesting, perhaps, that it was unwise to draw over-firm conclusions from such scant visual evidence, he added that "no one could accurately delineate the remarkable complexity of detail of the features which were visible in moments of the greatest steadiness."

What Barnard meant by this last remark is that the shimmering effect of our own atmosphere prevents us from viewing the fine detail of the Martian surface with any great accuracy. This defect may well be remedied by the program now being carried out by Martin Schwarzschild in the United States. During the next year or two Schwarzschild intends to carry a telescope of considerable aperture on a balloon at such a great height that the disturbing effects of the Earth's atmosphere will be largely eliminated.

Jupiter

When seen in even a small telescope Jupiter is a remarkable-looking body. Its surface shows a great variety of detail and it is very rich in color, with dominant reds and browns and occasional greenish tints. The details change continuously as the planet rotates on its axis. The markings are arranged mainly in belts more or less parallel with the equator. The belts themselves change slowly over the years, varying in their widths and in their numbers; usually there are about four such belts.

Besides these ever-changing features, Jupiter also has markings which appear to preserve their identity over long periods of time. The best known one is the famous red spot. Such markings are probably connected with the internal structure of the planet itself—perhaps with the configuration of a magnetic field, for it seems likely that Jupiter has a strong magnetic field. Certainly powerful electrical disturbances occur within its atmosphere, and intense bursts of radio waves emitted from these disturbances seem to be associated with particular points on the surface.

The main constituents of the atmosphere of Jupiter seem to be hydrogen and helium, methane and

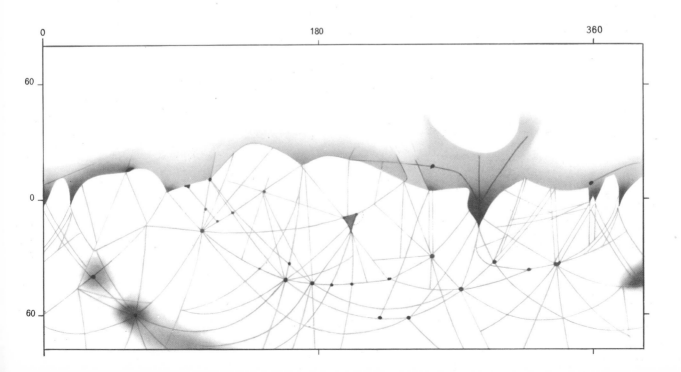

ammonia. Calculation suggests that this atmosphere, surprisingly enough, is rather shallow. A penetration into Jupiter would soon encounter solid or liquid material. Certainly much of the interior must be solid or liquid hydrogen, and the remarkable feature of this hydrogen is that it exists in a metallic form. In the extreme central regions there may well be a denser core representing the primitive condensation around which the hydrogen and helium have collected.

Nothing is known about the temperature inside Jupiter. Possibly it is quite high.

It is attractive to suppose that some form of energy-source exists inside this massive planet—perhaps a concentration of radioactive materials, such as uranium. Such an energy-source could serve to produce convective motions in liquid metallic hydrogen, leading to marked and powerful electrical effects. Indeed, the interior of Jupiter could behave as a vast dynamo, generating a great and powerful magnetic field. Such a possibility would account for the disturbances we observe at the surface of the planet, particularly the electrical storms that seem to occur there.

Left: This painting of about 1700 by Donato Creti shows astronomers observing Jupiter, depicted as their telescopes would then have revealed it, with red spot and satellites clearly visible. Below is a modern color drawing of Jupiter, the most massive planet of the Solar System.

Saturn

The main body of Saturn is probably similar in all essential features to that of Jupiter, but the belts observed at the surface of Saturn are less marked and less variable than those of Jupiter. There is also much less in the way of red and brown colors; rather do the equatorial regions of Saturn appear yellow, and the polar regions green. Probably the colors in both planets arise from the condensation of small liquid particles, the conditions being different in the two cases because the atmosphere of Saturn is colder than that of Jupiter.

To the eye the most striking feature of Saturn is its magnificent system of rings—three flat concentric rings lying in the plane of the planet's equator. Galileo glimpsed the rings indistinctly in the year 1610, and the main division between the two outer rings was first observed by Cassini toward the end of the seventeenth century. It was not until the middle of the nineteenth century that Bond first observed the faint innermost ring.

Although so striking visually, these rings are quite insubstantial. They consist of a swarm of tiny particles, probably crystals of ice.

This drawing of Saturn shows the magnificent system of rings which are its most striking visual feature. Though impressive, they are quite insubstantial. If all the particles of which they are made could be swept into one body, it would be only a tiny satellite of Saturn.

Uranus and Neptune

Uranus and Neptune probably consist mainly of water, ammonia, methane and perhaps carbon monoxide. They lack the great masses of hydrogen and helium which characterize Jupiter and Saturn, for the reasons already seen. In fact these two outer planets are probably similar to the cores of Jupiter and Saturn. Not much can be said about their appearances, for they are undistinguished objects even when seen with the aid of a large telescope. They present small greenish disks, their color resembling that of Saturn rather than that of Jupiter.

The Satellites of the Planets

A full discussion of all the details of the Solar System would occupy many volumes. Here we shall consider only one, the origin of the satellites of the planets.

Two distinct processes can be distinguished. One is a simple process of capture—the process by which the gravitational pull of a comparatively massive planet causes a less massive body that comes near it to keep orbiting around it. The small satellites of the great planets Jupiter, Saturn, Uranus and Neptune seem to have been acquired in this way. Possibly, too, the Earth acquired the Moon by a process of capture. It is clear, however, that the *main* satellites of the great planets, such as the four Galilean satellites of Jupiter, cannot be accounted for in this way. It is far more likely that they were formed from their parent planets in much the same way as the planets themselves were formed from the Sun.

The great planets, as they were formed, rotated very rapidly. This caused them to shed a disk of gas in essentially the same way as the Sun had done. The gravitational fields of the planets, however, were not as strong as that of the Sun. Hence the lightest gases—the abundant hydrogen and helium—evaporated away from the disks, leaving behind solid and liquid particles, notably water, and perhaps some particles of rock and metal. These particles aggregated to form the larger class of satellite belonging to the great planets.

It seems likely that magnetic fields did not play the same part in the formation of satellites as they did in the formation of the planets. This would explain in a very satisfactory way the notable difference between the system of planets and the systems of satellites. The formation of the planets slowed down the Sun's rotation because a strong magnetic field supplied a torque coupling between the Sun and the disk of gas that it shed; but there was no magnetic torque coupling to connect the planets with their surrounding disks of gas, and hence the planets were not slowed down. If this theory is correct, the disks of gas would not have been pushed very far away from their parent planets, and we

Almost all the thousands of millions of stars of small mass in the Milky Way have a slow rotation. This is an indication that almost all have formed their own planetary systems. Since the conditions which make life possible on Earth are not so special as was once believed, it seems highly probable that life itself is not the monopoly of our own small planet.

would therefore expect the satellites to lie comparatively close in to their parent planets. And indeed this is actually the case.

Here, then, we have striking confirmation of the importance of a torque coupling in slowing down the speed of rotation of a heavenly body which sheds a disk of gas.

The Abundance of Planetary Systems

The key point in the theory of the origin of the planets outlined above is, of course, the slow rotation speed of the Sun. We have seen that this slow speed of rotation is explained by the origin and existence of the planets. If we wish to know how many stars other than the Sun also possess planetary systems, it is therefore natural to consider how many stars rotate slowly, as the Sun does. It turns out that effectively *all* stars of small mass do so. In accordance with our argument, we should thus expect all such stars to have planetary systems. Their number in the Milky Way is known to be about 100,000 million. Hence our argument indicates that there are probably about 100,000 million planetary systems within our galaxy.

We can follow up this somewhat startling conclusion by an equally startling question. Were the conditions that promoted life here on the Earth in any way special to the Solar System, or can they be regarded as quite typical, in the sense that they might well have occurred in a considerable proportion of the 100,000 million other cases? At first sight there seem to be many very special requirements for the existence of life, but this consideration tends to recede as we look more closely at the problem. It seems, rather, that only our ignorance has made them look special.

Take, for instance, the distance of the Earth from the Sun. At first sight this looks to be very specially adjusted to give the correct temperature for biological phenomena here on the Earth. What chance is there that a planet will lie at just the right distance from its parent star? In fact the chance is quite high, simply because the central star does not have a constant luminosity. We have seen that stars become brighter as they age, so that provided a planet is initially somewhat too far away from the central star to enable it to have a high enough temperature to support life, the increase of luminosity will sooner or later produce a situation in which the temperature is exactly right. This, indeed, is just what has happened on the Earth. Originally the Sun was

significantly fainter than it is today. Over the history of the Earth the luminosity of the Sun has increased by some fifty per cent over its initial value. Originally the Earth was probably *not* too cold to have precluded the possibility of life, but its temperature must certainly have been well below an optimum value.

Further, the situation concerning the chemistry of the planets is now seen to be no accident. Small rock and iron planets like the Earth and Venus will always lie on the inside of every planetary system, and for the same reason. Carbon, nitrogen and oxygen will always be present among the original planetary gases, because these are elements found in every star. Nitrogen probably condensed into the material from which the Earth was formed as ammonium chloride; oxygen was contained in water; carbon probably derived from carbon monoxide.

Perhaps the most critical feature of conditions here on the Earth is the amount of water in the oceans. This is only a small fraction of the total mass of the Earth, and if the fraction were just a little larger the whole surface of the Earth would be inundated. Yet this, presumably, would not have stopped the emergence of life; it would merely have stopped the migration of life from the oceans on to the land. How far the amount of water on the surface of the Earth is due to chance we do not know. The intricate details of the condensation of the planets is still too imperfectly understood. Moreover, for all we as yet know to the contrary, it could be that a great deal of water still exists inside the Earth—that the amount we find on the surface is simply the amount exuded from the interior, along with the rocks of the continents. If this is so, if there is a rough proportionality between the amount of water and the amount of continental rock, then it may well be no accident that a proportion of the rock is lifted above the level of the water. It could be a *necessity* for there to be both oceans and land. In that case almost the last of the apparent coincidences necessary for the development of life here on the Earth would disappear.

We have already seen that astronomers are now actively investigating the problem of whether or not Venus, so similar to the Earth in mass, size, and chemistry, possesses oceans. If the answer should prove to be yes, then almost the last barrier will be removed to our acceptance of the strong probability that a vast number of planets within our galaxy are just as capable of supporting life as is our Earth.

Chapter 11   Galaxies and the Expanding Universe

We have seen that the Sun is but one member of a vast aggregation of stars, the aggregation that we call the galaxy. Other aggregations, other galaxies, exist within the universe. Of those that are comparable to our own in size and in mass, the nearest is shown in the accompanying picture. (A few comparatively minor aggregations actually lie closer to us.) This is the famous galaxy in the constellation of Andromeda. Its position is shown on map 8, page 28 (M 31). With this map as a guide it is easy to pick up the Andromeda Nebula, as a faint blur of light, with the naked eye. The blur appears yellowish in color because what you see is only the bright central part of the galaxy, the part that appears yellow in the picture.

The Andromeda Nebula has a special interest in that it is very closely similar to our own galaxy. Its general shape is that of a flat circular plate with a central bulge. The reason why we do not see it as circular is that we are looking at the plate from an oblique direction.

Most of the gas and dust in our own galaxy, and also in the Andromeda Nebula, lies well out from the central regions. This means that new stars do not form with any appreciable frequency in those regions. The central regions therefore consist almost wholly of old stars, stars of comparatively small mass lying low down on the main sequence, like the Sun, or stars that have evolved away from the main sequence in the Hertzsprung-Russell diagram toward the region of the giants. In fact, most of the light that comes from the central bulge is emitted by giant stars, and it is just because such stars are big and have low surface temperatures that the light from the central bulge has the yellowish color we have already remarked on. Well out from the central bulge, or nucleus, as astronomers call it, some of the newly-formed stars are much more massive than the Sun. They lie high on the main sequence and are blue in color, which is why the outer parts of the Andromeda Nebula present a bluish aspect in the picture. Thus the coloring of the Andromeda Nebula (and of our own galaxy, if we could see it from a distance) arises basically from the presence of gas and dust in the outer parts, and from their absence in the inner parts.

What an ordinary optical picture of the Andromeda Nebula does *not* prepare us for, is the discovery of recent years that that nebula, our own galaxy, and very likely most other large galaxies,

The Andromeda Nebula—the nearest aggregation of stars comparable in size and mass with our own galaxy. The yellowish light of the central part comes from old stars with low surface temperatures. The blue of the outer regions comes from hot stars newly formed from gas and dust.

are surrounded by halos of very hot gas. These halos emit X-rays rather than ordinary light, and hence we do not see them with our telescopes; for quite apart from the fact that the emission is rather feeble, the X-rays fail to penetrate the Earth's atmosphere, and so do not reach the telescope at all. But the halos also contain extremely energetic electrons, electrons moving with speeds close to that of light. These electrons are deflected in their motion by the magnetic fields that pervade the halos, and this deflection causes them to emit radio waves. These waves do penetrate our terrestrial atmosphere and can therefore be detected by the radio astronomer. Indeed, it is because of the findings of the radio astronomers that we know about the halos, these bubbles of hot gas that surround the galaxies. Although, judged by terrestrial standards, the emission of radio waves from the Andromeda Nebula is enormous, it is feeble compared with other cases that we shall have occasion to notice later.

The accompanying pictures show a number of galaxies with different structural forms. The classical method of classifying galaxies is due to the American astronomer, Edwin Hubble (1889-1953). Hubble's classification, based on whether or not a galaxy possesses spiral structure, consists of three sequences. First we have a sequence without spiral structure, the elliptical galaxies. At one end of the

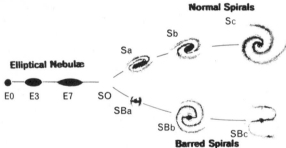

Normal Spirals

Sc

Sb

Sa

Elliptical Nebulæ

E0   E3   E7   S0

SBa

SBb   SBc

Barred Spirals

The classical method of classifying galaxies is due to the American astronomer, Edwin Hubble. Below his photograph the essentials of the system are shown diagrammatically. E denotes ellipticals, S spirals, and SB barred spirals. Figures after E and small letters after S or SB indicate various sub-groups.

Here and on the opposite page are photographs of nine galaxies, taken with the 60-inch reflector at Mount Wilson. Each is labelled according to Hubble's system of classification. Ellipticals, in increasing numerical order, become increasingly flattened. In both spirals and barred spirals the spiral structure is more highly marked when the nucleus is small than when it is large. It is believed that in barred spirals rotary and magnetic forces are comparable while in spirals rotary forces dominate.

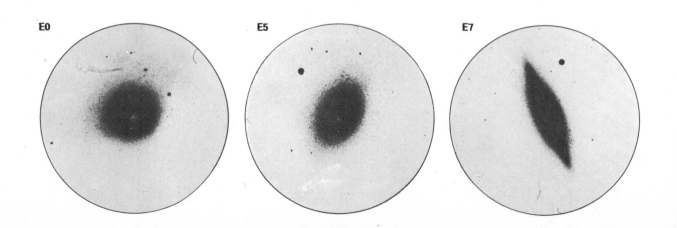

E0

E5

E7

elliptical sequence we have almost spherical forms —galaxies that seem to consist of huge balls of stars; at the other end are galaxies flattened into plate-like structures, but possessing central nuclear bulges. The galaxies at this end of the elliptical sequence are somewhat similar in general shape to our own galaxy, although our galaxy is known to belong to the spiral class and not to the ellipticals. Indeed the whole of the spiral class is similar to the extreme form of flattened elliptical galaxy so far as general overall shape is concerned, but the spirals differ from the ellipticals in that they contain appreciable quantities of gas and dust.

The spirals form two sequences, based on whether or not their structure possesses a central straight bar. The reason why some galaxies possess such a bar and others do not is imperfectly understood, but it is believed to be connected with an interplay between the effects of rotation and the effects of a magnetic field. In spirals with a straight bar, the magnetic and the rotary forces are thought to be comparable with each other, whereas in spirals without a bar the rotary forces are thought to be dominant.

In Hubble's system of classification all spiral galaxies without a bar were denoted by S, and all barred spirals by SB. The contraction S or SB was followed by either a, b, or c, the purpose of these letters being to indicate the relative importance of the central nucleus. It was found that galaxies with large nuclei tended to have a rather weak spiral structure, whereas galaxies with small central nuclei tended to have a highly marked spiral structure, as appears in the photographs shown below. Hubble denoted the elliptical galaxies by the letter E, followed by a number ranging from o for those of almost spherical form up to 7 for the most flattened elliptical galaxies.

There was some uncertainty as to whether the three sequences of galaxies, S, SB and E, should be connected together. Hubble himself appears to have favored such a connection, at a galactic type which he referred to as So. This connecting type So was similar to the elliptical galaxies in that it had no discernible spiral structure; but it was also similar to the spirals in that it was more flattened than any of the ellipticals—more flattened than even type E7. Indeed, an So galaxy was like an Sa galaxy from which the weak spiral structure had been removed.

The remarkable thing about Hubble's classification was that something like 97 per cent of all the large galaxies that he observed could be fitted into it. Among the exceptions were a few ellipticals which appeared to possess gas and dust, and certain galaxies which showed no clear-cut structure at all. The latter Hubble termed the irregulars, and he regarded them as being of very uncommon

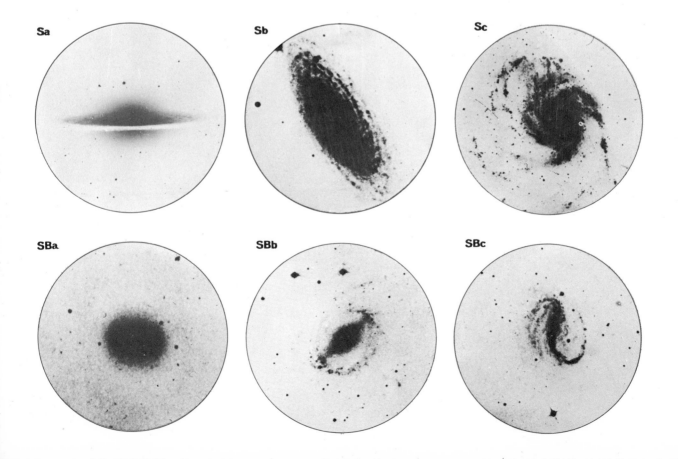

Sa   Sb   Sc

SBa   SBb   SBc

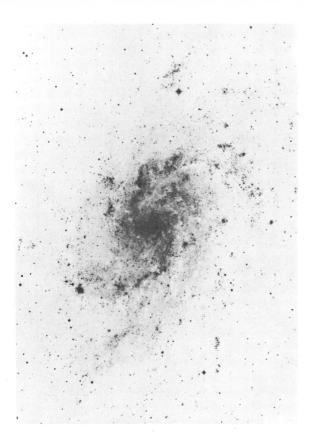

The photograph at the left, taken
with the 48-inch Schmidt telescope,
shows an Sc galaxy in Triangulum.
A negative of the same galaxy, above,
emphasizes the characteristically
well-marked spiral arms.

This galaxy in Sculptor, NGC 253,
represents a special sub-group of
Sc galaxies. In this case the arms
are defined as much by dust clouds
as by light from stars.

occurrence. But if we take into account the vast
number of minor galaxies that are known to exist,
then the proportion of irregulars is much higher.
Indeed, the irregulars then probably outnumber
the massive galaxies with regularly defined structures by a considerable margin.

Nevertheless, Hubble's system of classification
makes it very clear that the larger galaxies, at any
rate, fit into a smooth range of types. Although in
recent years some astronomers have preferred a
different system of classification, it is also a feature
of the newer systems that they present a continuous
gradation of types rather than a set of discrete
examples. The interesting implication is that the
structure of a galaxy does not arise from random
effects, but rather from smoothly-varying physical
factors. One example of a smoothly varying
physical factor is the degree of rotation that
galaxies possess. It is very clear that the sequence of
elliptical galaxies from E_0 to E_7 is a sequence
characterized by increasing rotation. More or less
spherical galaxies at E_0 can have little rotation,
whereas galaxies at E_7 are highly flattened by a
marked degree of rotation. The latter situation also
arises in all spiral galaxies.

Now the degree of rotation of a galaxy is a factor
that could be present at the time when the galaxy
was formed. If *all* the relevant physical factors
were present at the birth of the galaxies, then the
sequence of structural forms would simply reflect
the differing conditions of origin. One galaxy
would be an elliptical and another a spiral simply
because the initial conditions were different in the
two cases. On this basis there would be no reason to
believe that a galaxy changes its structural form
with time. It is, however, possible to take an opposite point of view. One can argue that the present
observed properties of any given galaxy were only
partially determined by initial conditions; that
during its lifetime a galaxy changes from one type
to another; that there is a continuous evolution
among the galaxies.

In fact, when we examine the available evidence
the presence of some degree of evolution can hardly
be doubted. Let us look first at the spirals. Spiral
structure in galaxies is known to be closely associated with the presence of gas and dust. Because
the outer parts of a galaxy rotate more slowly than
the inner parts, there is a constant tendency for
distributions of bright new stars formed within
the gas to be drawn out into spiral structures.

287

Although this is certainly not the whole story of how spiral forms originate, it is undoubtedly an important component of the story. Now the amount of gas and dust within a galaxy must change with time. This change must be reflected in the rate at which new stars are formed, and in the degree of prominence of the resulting spiral structures. At the present time gas and dust are thought to comprise some five per cent of the total mass of our own galaxy, and about the same proportion of the total mass of the Andromeda Nebula. Possibly this estimate may be too low, the true amount being nearer 10 per cent.

An interesting way in which one structural type of galaxy could change into another was pointed out some years ago by Lyman Spitzer of Princeton University and the late Walter Baade. From time to time galaxies must collide with each other. So far as their widely-spaced stars are concerned, the two galaxies involved in such a collision could pass smoothly through each other. But the situation would be very different for their gaseous components. The gas in one galaxy would collide with that in the other, and at the expected speed of collision it would become so hot that it would simply evaporate away into space, leaving its parent galaxies altogether. In this way it would be possible for two spiral galaxies to collide and to lose their gaseous components in the process. No further new star formation could then take place in either of them, so that their spiral structure would tend gradually to disappear.

They would then be very much like galaxies of type So, and Baade and Spitzer suggested that So galaxies might indeed originate in just this way. It was also pointed out that once no new bright stars were formed in the outer parts of such a galaxy, those outer parts would become much fainter than before. This would mean that when viewed from a distance the outer parts would be difficult to observe, and could be missed altogether for galaxies at very great distances. For these, the observer would see only the much brighter inner parts, which would appear to him to possess just the characteristics of an elliptical galaxy. Hence after a collision between distant spiral galaxies the observer might well judge those galaxies to be of elliptical type. In this way a change of type, as judged by the terrestrial observer, could arise from the passage of time.

Probably this idea does correctly explain the origin of galaxies of type So, but the work of the last few years has shown clearly that it does not explain the most notable examples of galaxies of the elliptical type, for it would imply that the elliptical galaxies are necessarily fainter and less massive than the colliding spirals. In fact the reverse situation holds for the outstanding giant elliptical galaxies. These are from about two to five times more luminous than the brightest spiral galaxies, and they have masses as much as ten times greater. This allows us to say one of two things. Either there are no major switches of type with the passage of time, or else the changes are more drastic than the kind envisaged by Baade and Spitzer. Indeed, for spiral galaxies to change into giant elliptical galaxies it is necessary for a large increase of mass to take place, perhaps at the expense of a universal gaseous medium filling the space between the galaxies.

While there is as yet no certainty as to which of these very different points of view is correct, radio astronomy has shown that the massive elliptical galaxies are certainly not dead structures. The

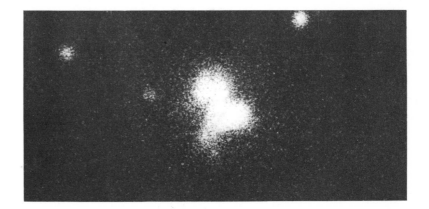

Left: NGC 5128, a strong emitter of radio waves. The picture may represent a collision between two galaxies, one globular and the other spiral. In such a collision both galaxies may lose their gaseous components so that no further star formation can take place. In the photograph on the right the fuzzy object near the center depicts the colliding galaxies—both probably large spirals—in Cygnus. This is among the most powerful of all known sources of radio waves.

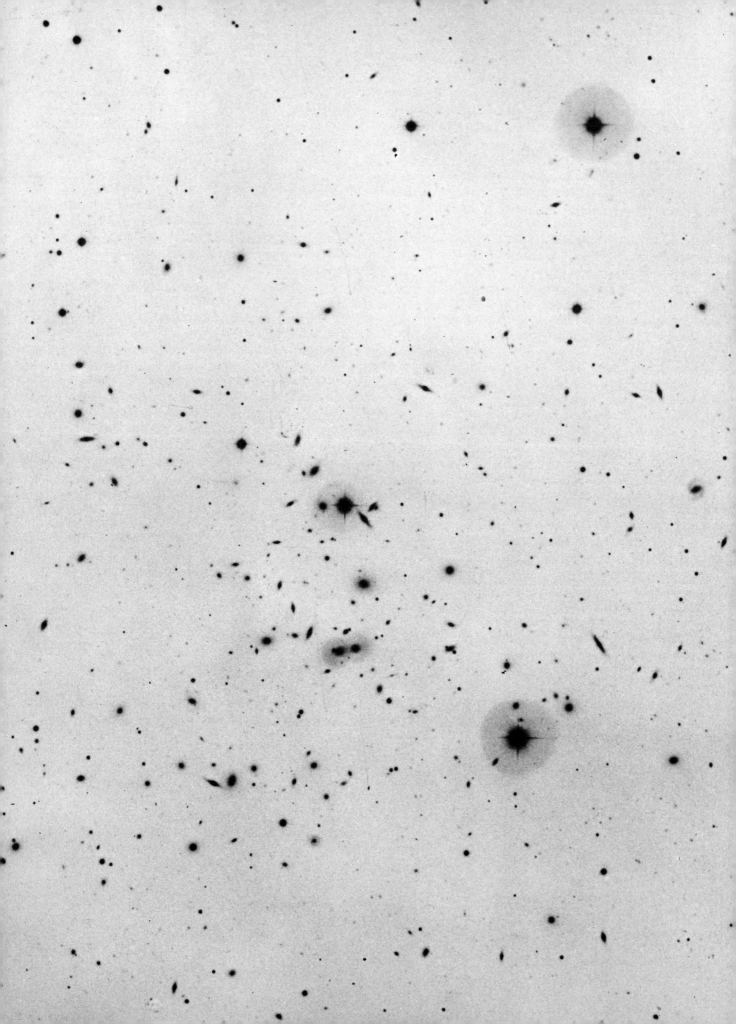

accumulated evidence of the last few years shows that the strongest radio sources are just these elliptical galaxies of great mass. This is not to say that *all* such galaxies are strong radio sources; what is being said is that the strongest sources are mainly to be found among the class of massive elliptical galaxies. From such sources the emissions of radio waves are of the order of a million times more intense than from our own galaxy or the Andromeda Nebula. This is a certain indication of the presence of intensely active physical processes in the E type galaxies.

A very different observation shows that the giant ellipticals also play a dominant role among other galaxies. So far nothing has been said about the distribution of galaxies in space. Space is strewn with them. The distances between neighboring galaxies is, on the average, only about a hundred times greater than the dimensions of an individual galaxy. Thus if we think of a galaxy as being about a yard in diameter we can think of the average distance between neighboring ones as about a hundred yards. This situation is very different from that of the spacing of individual stars within a galaxy, for if we think of a star as being a yard in diameter, then the comparable

distance between neighboring stars would be about 10,000 miles. So in relation to their individual sizes, the stars are very widely spaced, whereas the galaxies are comparatively close together. And there is a circumstance that makes the galaxies seem still closer, for they tend to occur in groups. So while their average distances apart are as we have already seen, the distances within a particular group can be considerably less. Indeed, in the centers of certain rich groups the galaxies seem to be almost touching each other. Small groups contain about ten members, whereas large ones may contain several thousand. The small groups are very much more common than the large ones.

Now it is very typical for a small group of galaxies to be dominated by a giant elliptical. Most members of such a group are commonly spirals, some three or four times fainter than the dominating elliptical. This makes it clear that the massive elliptical galaxies play a role outside themselves, as it were. They appear to control the situation within their particular group. This is another fragment of evidence indicating that the large elliptical galaxies are active structures.

Here it may be useful to summarize the main points so far made. On the basis of their visible

Left: Individual stars of a galaxy are very widely spaced, but galaxies themselves, in relation to their size, are comparatively close together. They also tend to occur in clusters. The photograph shows the cluster in Corona Borealis. The small round spots and objects with "spikes" are stars. Other structures are galaxies.

Below, projected on the plane of the Milky Way, we first see our local group of galaxies and comparable objects. Next, shown on a far smaller scale, our entire local group is reduced to a small dot at the center of the diagram. Like the other small dots it represents a cluster of fewer than fifty galaxies. Large dots indicate clusters of more than fifty galaxies.

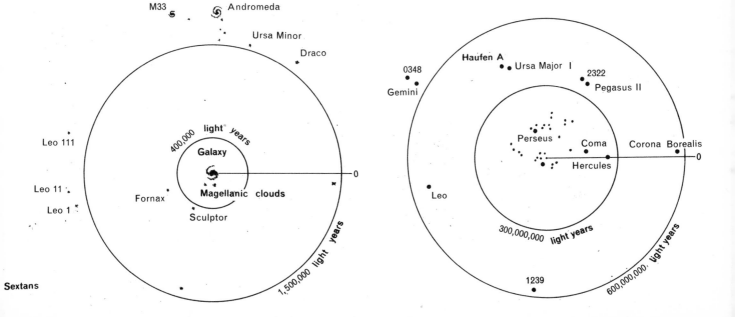

structural forms, the galaxies can be fitted into a simple empirical scheme of classification in which one type changes smoothly into another. This indicates that the structural features of a galaxy are controlled by clear-cut physical factors such as the degree of rotation, rather than by mere random chance. The major issue of whether all the main physical factors were decided at the time of origin of a galaxy, or whether the galaxies are in fact in the process of constant change with time, is still undecided.

The Expansion of the Universe

The galaxies apparently stretch away into space without end. Within the range of the largest telescopes there are about a thousand million of them. Yet although local irregularities certainly exist in their distribution—irregularities of local clusters for example—on a large scale there seems to be no important difference between one part of space and another. In other words, the general distribution of galaxies seems to have large-scale homogeneity. Moreover, there seems to be no difference between the observations we make in one direction and the

observations we make in another. Space is isotropic —that is, it manifests the same physical properties in all directions.

All this can readily be summed up in everyday terms. Suppose you are an observer placed at random in space, then by observing the large-scale distribution of galaxies you cannot find out where you are. And if you are in motion with respect to the system of galaxies, then it doesn't matter where you are going: a journey in one direction will show you the same things as would a journey in any other direction.

Do the galaxies themselves possess any motion? The answer is that they do, and that this motion constitutes the expansion of the universe.

We saw in Chapter 8 that the spectrum lines emitted by the atoms in a distant object are shifted in their wavelengths if a relative motion exists between ourselves and the distant object. If there is a motion away from us the wavelengths are increased and the lines are shifted toward the red end of the spectrum. If there is a motion toward us the wavelengths are decreased and the lines are shifted toward the blue end of the spectrum. We also saw

In this photograph, the clear round dots are stars in our own galaxy. The cluster of faint hazy spots near the center are the remotest galaxies whose distances had been determined by June, 1960 (3c-295 in Boötes). They are receding from us at a rate of about 70,000 miles per second.

In each of the oblongs at the right the fixed pattern shows positions of H and K spectrum lines produced in a terrestrial laboratory. The central band shows positions of corresponding lines emitted from the galaxy concerned. In each case the lines of the band are shifted to the right—toward the red end of the spectrum—indicating that the galaxy is moving away from us. The more distant the galaxy, the greater the red shift, and the greater the speed at which it is receding.

that the rate at which the distances are increasing or decreasing can be inferred from the measured amount of the displacement of the spectrum lines relative to the same lines emitted by similar atoms in the terrestrial laboratory. The fractional change of wavelength, $\Delta\lambda \div \lambda$, is equal to $V \div c$, where V represents the velocity between source and observer and c the velocity of light.

Here two provisos must be mentioned. First, the velocity between source and observer is measured as positive when the distance is increasing and as negative when it is decreasing. Second, the simple formula given above is applicable only when the velocity V is small compared to the velocity of light. The corresponding formula when V becomes comparable to the speed of light is:

$$1 + \frac{\Delta\lambda}{\lambda} = \sqrt{\frac{1 + V/c}{1 - V/c}}.$$

When the velocity is small compared to the velocity of light, the square root in this equation takes a value close to $1 + V/c$, so that the equation then becomes exactly the one we had before. But when the velocity V is comparable with c the correct form with the square root must be used.

Now let us consider the observed situation concerning spectrum lines emitted by the stars in distant galaxies, particularly the so-called H and K lines of calcium atoms. The results obtained for a number of galaxies are shown in the accompanying picture. First it should be noted that the galaxies become fainter and fainter as we pass from the top to the bottom of the picture, implying that we are dealing with galaxies at increasingly great distances away from us. Next, the farther the H and K lines are displaced toward the right in relation to the fixed pattern above and below the central band, the larger is the value of $\Delta\lambda$. (It should be noted that the fixed pattern above and below the central band in each case simply represents the positions of the corresponding lines as given by atoms in the terrestrial laboratory.)

Now there are two clear implications to be drawn from the picture. First, the lines are displaced in such a direction as to indicate that the galaxies are all moving away from us, not toward us. In other words $\Delta\lambda$ is always a positive quantity. Second, as the distances of the galaxies increase, the velocity V also increases. In Figure 11.1 explicit

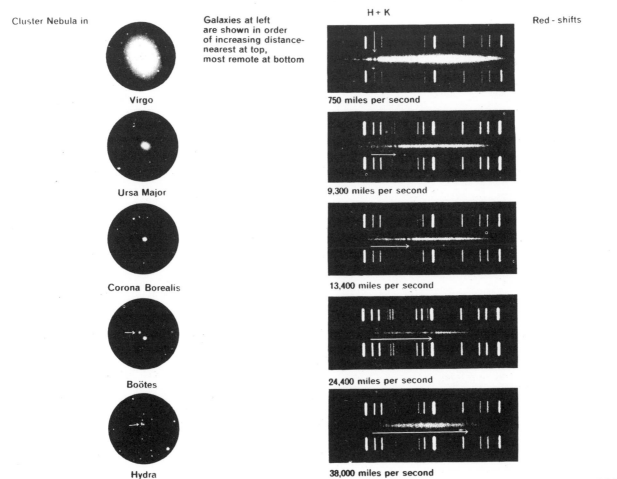

Cluster Nebula in

Galaxies at left are shown in order of increasing distance- nearest at top, most remote at bottom

H + K

Red - shifts

Virgo

750 miles per second

Ursa Major

9,300 miles per second

Corona Borealis

13,400 miles per second

Boötes

24,400 miles per second

Hydra

38,000 miles per second

293

values of V for a number of galaxies are plotted against their apparent magnitudes.

If we now make two suppositions, Figure 11.1 can be shown to have a simpler intuitive meaning. Our first supposition is that all the galaxies in question have the same intrinsic brightness, the same absolute luminosity. This will certainly not be *exactly* the case, but if our galaxies have been chosen suitably, then our assumption of equal luminosities should at least be approximately correct. Our second supposition is that space has the geometry of Euclid (and here we come to the issues of geometry raised in the first chapter). If this is so, then it is possible to express the scale of apparent magnitudes in Figure 11.1 as a distance scale, the unit of distance depending on what intrinsic luminosity we take the galaxies to possess.

Figure 11.2 is drawn on the basis that we are dealing with galaxies having an intrinsic brightness

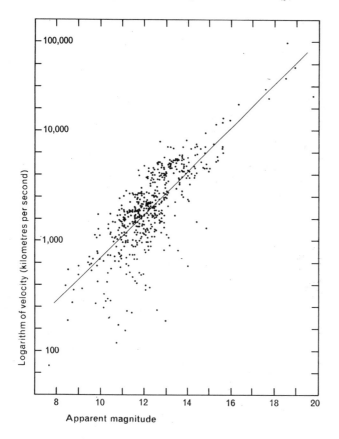

Figure 11.1
The relation between the apparent magnitudes of a number of galaxies (horizontal scale) and the velocities at which they are moving away from us (vertical scale).

about the same as that of our own galaxy. We now see that Figure 11.2 reveals an important relation between the distance of a galaxy and its velocity. The velocity V is closely proportional to the distance. Double the distance and the velocity doubles. We can express this by writing $V = H \times R$, where R is the distance, and H is a constant known as the Hubble constant, named after Hubble in memory of his discovery of this remarkable relation.

Before we go on to examine the implications of this velocity-distance relation, we may well ask whether the observations really mean what we suppose them to mean. Do the measured values of Δz really imply that the galaxies are receding from us, or could there just possibly be some alternative explanation? Apart from one or two exceptions, astronomers and physicists are unwilling to believe in the possibility of an alternative interpretation, for a reason that can readily be understood.

We noted above that the distribution of galaxies possesses large-scale homogeneity and isotropy. That is, an observer at an arbitrary point of space is unable to discover any special feature either about his position or about the different directions in space. Now this statement referred to a particular moment of time. If we allow that the galaxies may move, changing their positions with time, but also assume that such motions must not destroy spatial homogeneity and isotropy, what motions of the galaxies can possibly take place? The answer can be worked out mathematically, and it turns out that the only permitted motion is precisely the motion of expansion envisaged above. This correspondence between the observations and the mathematical demands of homogeneity and isotropy is so striking that almost all scientists feel that the observations really do mean exactly what ordinary physics tells us they mean: that the distances between the galaxies are steadily increasing. The notion sometimes put forward in popular commentaries, that there might be some mysterious process at present unknown to science that would also produce the observed results, seems quite improbable.

This is a suitable moment, before returning to our main topic, to consider the question of distance measurement in a little more detail. It was said above that the distance scale of Figure 11.2 has been determined on the assumption that we are dealing with galaxies having an intrinsic brightness about the same as that of our own galaxy.

What grounds do we have for believing that this is true? Indeed, how does the astronomer go about the problem of determining the intrinsic brightness of the galaxies? The answer is by an extension of the system of distance measurement described in the early part of Chapter 10.

The starting point of distance measurements is the trigonometrical method, using the motion of the Earth around the Sun. This method enables the distances of about ten thousand nearby stars to be determined with great accuracy. Although the distances measured in this first step are small, even compared to the size of our own galaxy, an accurate determination of the faint end of the main sequence can be made from this sample.

Then a more distant cluster of stars is considered, but not so distant that its fainter stars cannot be distinguished. A fit of the faint end of the main sequence of the cluster to that of the local stars is

then made. This determines both the distance of the cluster and the form of the main sequence for the brighter stars of the cluster. Indeed, if the cluster has been suitably chosen, we now have the form of the main sequence extending upward to quite bright stars. In this way the full form of the main sequence can be found, together with the distances of many clusters. In certain of the clusters special types of star can sometimes be found, for example the Cepheid variables, discussed in Chapters 9 and 10.

With the distances of a few Cepheid variables determined from the star clusters, the whole group of Cepheid variables becomes calibrated in the manner described in Chapter 10. The Cepheids are intrinsically bright stars, and therefore they can serve as distance indicators over a very much greater volume of space than the small region we started from in the trigonometrical method. In fact, the Cepheids serve to determine distances throughout our own galaxy, and can even be used to determine the distances of a small handful of nearby galaxies, those of the local group. The latter determination then leads to the final steps in the process of distance measurement.

We now treat each nearby galaxy as a single huge collection of stars. With the distance known, from the Cepheids, we know the distance of every individual star that can separately be distinguished in the galaxy, since we can consider all the stars of the galaxy to be at essentially the same distance away from us.

The curious point now emerges that the most luminous stars seem to have just about the same intrinsic brightness in all these very nearby galaxies. We now make the assumption that the same is true for all other galaxies of similar type—that their very brightest stars all have the same intrinsic luminosities. This plausible hypothesis allows the range of distance measurement to be extended farther than is possible by means of the Cepheids, since, although as stars go the Cepheids are undoubtedly very bright specimens, they are certainly not the brightest of all stars. The Cepheids can be used to a distance of perhaps 5 million light-years, whereas the very brightest stars can be used to a distance of about 25 million light-years. The last important point now emerges. Fortunately, the distance of 25 million light-years is sufficiently great to include a reasonable sample of galaxies—a thousand or more of them. With their distances

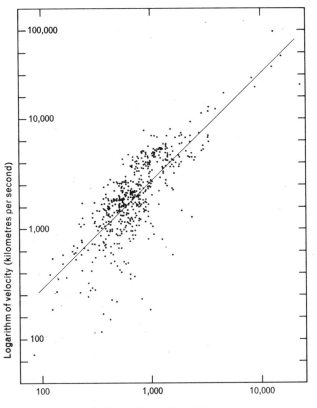

Figure 11.2
Assuming absolute magnitudes to be the same, and assuming space to have the geometry of Euclid, Figure 11.1 can be re-drawn to reveal a relation between distance and velocity.

known, we now have information not merely about individual stars, but about the total intrinsic brightnesses of whole galaxies. This leads us back to the question asked above: how do we know the intrinsic brightnesses of the galaxies? From those we measure in our sample, the sample lying within a range of about 25 million light-years. Finally, given the intrinsic brightnesses of whole galaxies, the vast distances of Figure 11.2 are determined in the manner already discussed.

The remarkable feature to notice in this train of argument is how the very greatest distances of thousands of millions of light-years are determined by a method that proceeds step by step from the elementary trigonometrical system based on the motion of the Earth.

If, now, we refer back to our equation $V = H \times R$, it is clear that if R is sufficiently large, the velocity V will rise to the velocity of light. This forces us either to deny that the equation will continue to hold good as R increases and assert that the velocity will not rise to the velocity of light, or else to dispense with our supposition that the geometry of Euclid continues to hold good when R becomes sufficiently large. The reason why we are forced into one of these alternatives is that we know from the physics of Einstein's special theory of relativity that *under the conditions of Euclidean geometry* no material body *can* move at a velocity relative to ourselves greater than the velocity of light.

Thus the point about Euclidean geometry is crucial. Many non-physicists and non-mathematicians fail to notice this requirement about the nature of the geometry to be used. The point is of great importance because most astronomers believe that the resolution of the issue lies in the second alternative. That is, they believe that at sufficiently large distances Euclidean geometry ceases to hold good, for in view of the facts, it would be a bold man who would say today that the velocities of galaxies cannot rise to the velocity of light. The latest observations by Rudolf Minkowski for the galaxy shown in the photograph on page 292 give a value of V equal to over a third of the velocity of light, and this is about twice as great as the velocities that were measured before the year 1960. Steadily over the last forty years the measured velocities have increased from about one per cent of the speed of light to nearly forty per cent, and it is a safe prediction that they will continue to increase in the future as observational techniques continue to improve.

Besides, the physics of Einstein's general theory of relativity (not his special theory) shows that in any case we must abandon Euclidean geometry when very large distances come under our review.

Let us return now to the phenomenon of expansion. If at a particular moment of time we choose an arbitrary finite number of galaxies, spaced at considerable distances apart, we can regard the galaxies so chosen as forming a lattice of points. At a later moment of time we can again choose the same galaxies and they will again form a lattice of points. What expansion in accordance with Hubble's law implies is that the second lattice will have exactly the same form as the first one; only its scale will have changed. For example, if we choose three galaxies to form the three points of a triangle, the triangle will have the same shape at a later moment as it did at an earlier moment. The only change will be that the lengths of all three sides of the triangle will have increased.

One other point must be mentioned. The homogeneity and isotropy of space imply that there can be no center of expansion, otherwise an observer at the center would be able to judge that he *was* at the center, and would hence be able to distinguish his particular position in space. How, then, is it possible for all the galaxies to be moving away from us without our being at the center of the universe? A very simple experiment provides the answer. Mark a number of dots at random on the surface of a balloon, then blow it up a little. The distance between *every* pair of dots will increase, in analogy to the situation for the galaxies; but obviously there is no central dot in this case. Whichever dot you choose, all the others move away from it.

In measuring the distance of a galaxy we use the same unit as that used in measuring distances within a galaxy. For example, we could decide to use the distance from the Earth to the Sun as our unit, or we could decide to use a mile as the unit, or indeed we could use any standard yardstick. When we say that the distance between us and a galaxy is increasing, we mean that as time passes the number of units of distance that separate us from that galaxy is increasing. Hence we are really saying that distances outside our galaxy are increasing in relation to distances within the galaxy—in relation to the distance from the Earth to the Sun, or from the Sun to the center of our galaxy, or in relation to the size of the Earth itself. This means that *within* a galaxy there is no participation in the general expansion. In other words it is the ratio between distances external to the galaxies and distances internal to the galaxies that changes with time. Hence when we speak of the expanding universe, all we can properly assert is a change in this ratio. Indeed, it would be possible to maintain that the external distances remain fixed but that the individual galaxies and everything inside them, including ourselves, are shrinking with time. But this point of view seems somehow deflating to our own ego, so that we find it more pleasant to think of ourselves as remaining a fixed size; and when we do this we must take the distances between the galaxies to be steadily increasing with time. It is this increase that constitutes the expansion of the universe, the increase in the scale of our lattice described above.

Before we go on to consider the implications of this expansion, there is one last point of detail that is worth mentioning. We have already noted that galaxies tend to occur in groups, the common groups having about ten members, and the large, much less common, groups several thousand members. What of the clusters, do they also expand? Certainly the distances between different clusters increase, but the situation within many of the clusters is similar to that within individual galaxies. The distances within many clusters do not increase with time; the clusters stay together without expansion. It must be mentioned, however, that some recent observations have suggested that there may be clusters that *are* in a state of expansion, although probably the general rate of expansion for the whole universe is more rapid than it is within these special clusters.

Cosmological Theories

Observation suffers from the inherent handicap that it can never tell us unequivocally how things change with time, for over the period of a human life, or even over the whole time scale of human history, few astronomical objects change in any detectable way. (There are exceptions—in the Crab Nebula, for instance—but these need not detain us.) The best that observation can do is to present us with a continuous range of cases, such as a range of stars at different stages of evolution. By seeing the different examples at different stages, it may then be possible to infer how one particular example changes with time, and this, indeed, can be done for stars. But this is only because we possess a reliable physical theory of the structure and evolution of stars. Where such a theory is not available, as in the case of the gradation of structural forms of galaxies, observation cannot present us with an unambiguous situation. The straightforward observation of the sequence of structural types cannot of itself tell us whether the galaxies were born in the sequence in question, or whether it is the case that individual galaxies evolve along that sequence during their lifetimes.

The expansion of the universe in accordance with Hubble's law implies that if, at a given moment, we regard a number of galaxies as forming a lattice of points, then at some later moment the same galaxies will form a second lattice which differs from the first only in scale and not in shape. Here only the *scale* of the triangle ABC changes with expansion.

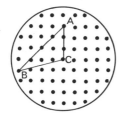

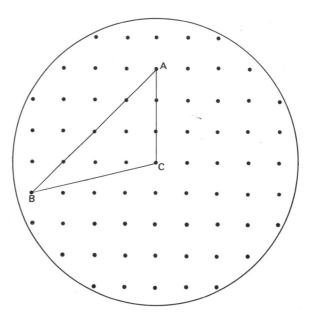

This weakness of the observational method shows itself most acutely when we come to consider the past or the future of the universe as a whole. Observation, of itself, simply cannot tell us what an observer living five thousand million years ago would have seen, nor can it tell us what an observer living five thousand million years hence might see. To answer such questions a cosmological theory must be added to the observations. In this respect the situation is no different from what it is in the case of the evolution of stars; but a big practical difference arises from the fact that no present-day cosmological theory possesses anything like the same degree of validity and precision as do our theories of the physics of stars. Of necessity, any statements that we make about the past history or the future of the whole universe lies at the very frontiers of our knowledge, and must today be considered uncertain and tentative.

With these reservations in mind, the moving apart of the galaxies can be followed out in its theoretical implications. Just as we expect the galaxies to be farther apart in the future than they are now, so we expect that they were closer together in the past. But how close together? Consider this question first on the basis that the galaxies have always been moving apart at their present rates. Then with those rates measured from observation we arrive at the conclusion that the galaxies were all pressed tightly together some ten to twelve thousand million years ago. This length of time is quite close to the age of our own galaxy that we

discussed in the previous chapter, namely about fifteen thousand million years. While it is obviously true that our galaxy cannot be older than the universe, a discrepancy between an age of fifteen thousand million years for our galaxy and twelve thousand million years for the whole universe is one that might well lie within the errors of measurement.

The discrepancy becomes worse, however, if we allow for variations in the rates of expansion. The expansion itself is regarded as coming from an initial state of explosion of the whole universe. Gravitation, as it is ordinarily understood in physics, supplies an attractive force that tends to reduce the speed of the explosion, that is, to reduce the speed of separation of the galaxies, and we might therefore expect that they were moving apart at a greater velocity in the past than they are now. When this effect is allowed for, the estimated age of the universe is cut by some 30 to 40 per cent, that is, to between seven and eight thousand million years, which is only about half the age of our galaxy. The discrepancy is now too large to be explained away except on the basis that a mistake has been made somewhere—either in the estimation of the age of our own galaxy or in the rate of expansion of the universe. That such a mistake has been made is by no means impossible. The discrepancy may be genuine, however, and the balance of evidence is perhaps in favor of the view that it *is* genuine. If so, we are forced into a situation where the most straightforward consideration of the expansion of the universe—in terms of ordinary physics—is

Given that all clusters of galaxies are expanding apart, one can reason that they must once have been packed tightly together. Given that the pace of expansion is constant (or slowing down at a calculable rate) one can estimate how long it is since that tightly-packed matter started to spread out. These considerations give rise to cosmological theories in which the universe had a finite and ''explosive'' origin. In most theories the estimated age of the universe then turns out as less than that of our own galaxy. In Lemaître's finite-origin theory, here summarized in diagrams, the discrepancy is avoided. (1) Shows the primeval galactic atom just after its explosion. Very soon afterwards (2) its temperature has fallen from several billion to 1000 million degrees, and particles are combining to form nuclei of atoms. In 30 million years (3) temperatures are down to a much lower level; gas and dust accumulations from which galaxies will form are already present. (4) Shows today's universe, 20,000 million years after explosion. Arrows indicate rates of expansion.

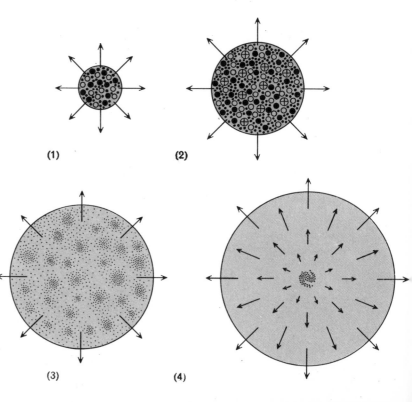

(1)   (2)

(3)   (4)

rendered untenable. In other words we are faced with a situation that demands a change in our present physics.

Some cosmologists, notably the Abbé Lemaître, have found a theoretical method of avoiding the discrepancy we have noted. In their cosmology the behavior of gravity differs from that of ordinary experience. According to this theory, once the galaxies have become sufficiently separated, gravitation tends to speed up their expansion apart rather than to retard it. Hence in Lemaître's cosmology we cannot argue that the rates of separation were always greater in the past than they are at present. During a certain period in the past, the rates of expansion could have been substantially less than they are now. Our initial calculation of twelve thousand million years for the total time of expansion is then too low, not too high. Hence in this cosmology there is no conflict between the age of the universe, as deduced from the rates of expansion, and the age of our own galaxy.

Although it modifies the law of gravitation, Lemaître's cosmology does not differ from the straightforward cosmology, considered first above, in one crucial respect: it still demands a definite origin for the whole universe. This origin is conceived of as an infinitely dense state of matter at an infinitely high temperature. A difference arises, however, as to the amount of matter involved. In some theories the amount is infinite and in others it is finite. Particularly in Lemaître's cosmology, the amount is finite. Since the density of matter is initially infinite in all the theories concerned, the total amount of matter cannot be finite unless space begins with a zero volume. In such a case we can think of the universe as having a point origin.

In all the theories so far considered, as time proceeds the density of matter falls rapidly. In cosmologies such as Lemaître's, as the density of matter falls space increases from a point to a finite volume, a volume that grows rapidly in order to maintain the constant finite amount of matter. With the further passage of time, the density of matter falls lower and lower, and the volume of space becomes larger and larger. We can ask at what stage, within the framework of these cosmologies, did the galaxies form? The answer is at a stage where the density had fallen to a very low value, not a great deal more than its present-day value. This leads to the further question of why the galaxies should have formed at this particular

stage and not before. No really convincing answer to this latter question has yet been offered. The beginnings of an answer can be given in Lemaître's cosmology, but not, I suspect, in the other cases.

It is the duty of scientists to cover all possible forms of theory. Then observation is used to decide which of the possibilities put forward by the theoretician are to be allowed to survive and which must be rejected. It is therefore important to ask whether a theory can be built up to explain the observed expansion apart of the galaxies without requiring the universe to have had a definite origin. One such theory proposes that the universe has an infinite past and an infinite future, passing through an infinity of cycles of expansion and contraction.

A serious difficulty in this theory lies in the reversal of the contracting phases. One can understand how an expanding phase can be replaced by a contracting phase, but no convincing explanation has yet been found for how a contracting phase can be replaced by an expanding phase. It seems as if contraction must proceed until space shrinks to a point, until the density of matter becomes infinite, and indeed until the universe ceases to exist. The difficulty lies in explaining how expansion begins from this state.

The theory of an oscillating universe raises an interesting point. It is necessary that there be no net change of chemistry from one cycle to the next. Now with hydrogen being systematically converted into helium within the stars during every cycle, it is clear that if there were no reconversion of helium

The Abbé Lemaître. His theory makes the age of the universe greater than that of our galaxy, as logic demands, by assuming that the rate at which the galaxies move apart, so far from decreasing, has actually increased. This modifies the law of gravitation as it applies to ordinary experience.

back to hydrogen, then by now, after an infinity of cycles, there could be no hydrogen left in the universe. And this, of course, contradicts observation. To provide for a reconversion of helium back to hydrogen it would be necessary that the universe should contract sufficiently for the density of matter to become very high, of the order of the densities found in the nuclei of atoms. This means that all galaxies and all stars would have to be destroyed during the contracting phase.

We see, therefore, that the oscillating theory does not avoid the requirement that the matter of the universe shall have been through a phase of very high density and very high temperature. On the contrary, it requires that matter shall have been through such a phase an infinite number of times. Indeed, all the theories so far considered postulate a stage of high density and high temperature, and this raises a very important issue. Can we find any direct observational evidence to show that matter has ever actually been in this state of extremely high density? The answer seems to be that we cannot. It is just possible that some of the helium that we observe in the stars of our own galaxy, and in neighboring galaxies, might have been produced during a very high density phase, but it does not seem that any of the other elements were produced on a literally universal scale. Rather have they originated inside individual stars, in the manner described in Chapter 9.

The absence of any clear-cut evidence in favor of a high-density-high-temperature phase in the history of the universe is a suspicious circumstance, at the very least. In order to preserve any of the theories so far mentioned we are compelled to say that although all the matter of the universe has passed at least once through a most remarkable high-density condition, during which a profusion of nuclear reactions must have taken place, nothing of its effects survives except, possibly, in the case of helium; in other respects, while the world around us bears ample evidence of being processed inside stars, it bears no significant evidence of ever having been processed in a high-density-high-temperature phase of the universe.

In view of all this, it seems justifiable to ask whether any theory can be found that does not require the matter of the universe to have passed through a high-density-high-temperature phase. Investigation shows that if we restrict ourselves to normal physical ideas we cannot find any such theory. But are we bound to restrict ourselves to normal physical ideas? Let us approach the answer this way. Many different types of field are known to the physicist: the gravitational field, producing the phenomenon of gravitation; the electromagnetic field, producing the phenomena of electricity and magnetism; the nuclear field, holding together the particles of the atomic nuclei. And from time to time new fields are discovered by experiments in the laboratory—for instance, the meson fields of modern physics, discovered during the last twenty years. Hence it is by no means certain that the physicist yet possesses a complete inventory of all possible fields. The possibility therefore arises that some new field, not at present known from terrestrial experiment, might be important on the cosmological scale. If one makes this hypothesis, then a new type of theory avoiding the requirement of a high-density-high-temperature phase for all matter can indeed be found. Postulating what is almost the simplest type of new field, one arrives mathematically at what has become known as the steady state universe.

The theory of the steady state universe is based on a physical field that causes new matter to originate. There is nothing particularly revolutionary in this idea, for the fields already known to physics can cause matter to originate. (Ordinary gamma-rays, for example, can produce pairs of electrons.) The problem differs in detail but not in principle from the situation already known to exist. What is new in detail is that a coupling can be found between the expansion of the universe and the rate of creation of matter. This coupling is of such a nature that if one knows the rate of creation of matter then one can deduce from the theory the rate of expansion of the universe. Conversely, if one knows the rate of expansion of the universe, as indeed we do from observation, then the rate of creation of matter is specified by the theory. It turns out that the required rate is very slow, amounting to about one atom per century for each unit of volume corresponding to that of the largest man-made building. So it is not at all difficult to understand why the process, if it really occurs, has not been detected in the terrestrial laboratory.

In spite of this very slow rate, the effect of such creation of matter on a large scale would be enormous. The coupling between the expansion of the universe and the creation of matter operates in such a way that the average density of matter in space remains constant. Although expansion tends to reduce the density, this tendency is precisely compensated by the creation of new material. We therefore expect that a diffuse gas will exist throughout space, and that new galaxies may form continuously out of it. Thus although expansion carries already-existing galaxies apart from each other, the average density of galaxies in space can remain constant because of the formation of new ones. This is quite a different picture of the way the universe behaves with time than that given by the other theories. In the other theories, the galaxies move apart from each other, so that an observer in the future would find space to be more sparsely populated with galaxies than it is now. In the steady state theory, on the other hand, the situation remains constant. At every epoch an observer would see exactly the same large-scale picture. Individual galaxies change with time, or can change with time, just as individual humans change with time; and just as the young replace the old in the human species, so newly-formed galaxies take the place of older galaxies as the latter move farther apart.

This represents an important change in outlook on space-time symmetry. It was pointed out above that an observer cannot discover anything special about his position in space. We are now adding the further vital point that he cannot distinguish anything special about his particular epoch. The

universe in the large looks the same from all points of both space and time. And, of course, because things look the same at all times, there is no beginning to the universe, and there will be no end.

How do we go about deciding between these different theories? By taking the different predictions they make and checking up on those predictions by observation. Here we may take a brief look at how things stand at the present moment.

We have already seen that some systems of cosmology encounter the considerable difficulty of arriving at an estimate of the age of the universe that is less than the estimated age of our own galaxy. We saw, too, that the age criterion favors Lemaître's cosmology. It also favors steady state cosmology, for in the latter the universe possesses an infinite age, and there can therefore be no question of our own galaxy being older than the universe. On the other hand, a recent observation goes against both Lemaître's cosmology and against steady state cosmology, so that at the present time the situation would appear to be rather evenly balanced.

Suppose we consider all galaxies to have exactly the same intrinsic brightness. We can then work out purely from theory how we would expect the speeds of recession of the different galaxies' to vary with their distances or, more usefully, with their apparent magnitudes. For galaxies that are not too far away from us the results are the same for all the

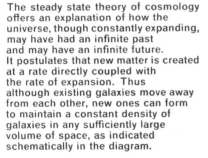

The steady state theory of cosmology offers an explanation of how the universe, though constantly expanding, may have had an infinite past and may have an infinite future. It postulates that new matter is created at a rate directly coupled with the rate of expansion. Thus although existing galaxies move away from each other, new ones can form to maintain a constant density of galaxies in any sufficiently large volume of space, as indicated schematically in the diagram.

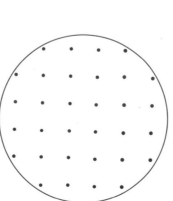

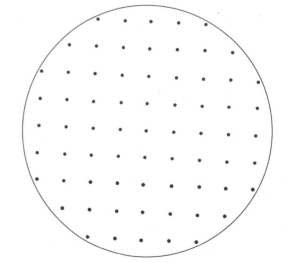

theories. Indeed, they are just the results already given in Figure 11.2. But for galaxies sufficiently far off, the departures from Euclidean geometry must be considered, and these departures are different for the different theories, as can be seen in Figure 11.3. In this figure the case of steady state cosmology is given together with that of the simple, straightforward cosmology considered at the outset, in which the universe originated a finite time ago.

Here observation seems to favor the cosmology considered at the outset. In particular, a recent similar observation by W. Baum of a very distant galaxy is thought by some astronomers to be in serious discrepancy with the prediction of steady state cosmology, and also with Lemaître's cosmology. But of course the assumption that all galaxies have the same intrinsic brightness is certainly not correct in itself. Galaxies vary from one to another by at least a hundred per cent in their intrinsic

Figure 11.3
Assuming all clusters of galaxies to have the same absolute brightness we can work out from theory how we would expect speeds of recession of different clusters to vary with their apparent magnitudes. For the remote clusters different theories, assuming varying departures from Euclidean geometry, lead to different expectations. Here observed results for eighteen very distant clusters are compared with the expectations of simple "exploding" cosmologies and of the steady state theory.

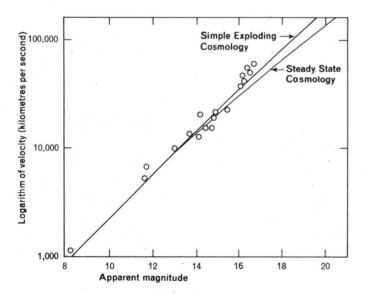

luminosities, and this is the order of the discrepancy involved. So it could be that Baum has simply observed a particularly bright galaxy. It is too early to anticipate the outcome of this argument.

One of the features of the steady state theory is that galaxies must form all the time. The theory requires that they form initially as quite insignificant objects which continue to grow with time, so that the largest galaxies are the oldest ones. On this basis the giant elliptical galaxies considered at the beginning of the present chapter should be the oldest of all. Evidence has indeed begun to accumulate to show that new galaxies do form, hence providing some measure of support for the steady state theory. But whether galaxies grow steadily in size and in mass is still unknown. One group of astronomers believes that galaxies are in a state of continuous evolution, as the steady state theory requires; others believe that once a galaxy is formed it stays nearly constant throughout its entire life.

The last of the observational tests of steady state cosmology that must be mentioned here is that devised by Martin Ryle and his colleagues at Cambridge, who have made extensive counts of the number of radio sources that they can detect in the sky. Some of these sources have a high intensity and others are much weaker. What Ryle does is to count the numbers in different intensity ranges—the number of strong sources, the number of slightly weaker sources, the number of still weaker ones, and so on—defining the various categories, of course, by experimental measurements. More precisely, a level of apparent brightness is specified, and the number of sources brighter than the specified level is counted. This is done for a set of values of the specified level. The results are shown diagrammatically in Figure 11.4 (right). One curve on this figure (dotted line) represents the expected number of sources, calculated on the basis that their frequency in space is uniform and that the geometry of space is that of Euclid. Now the vital point of interest is that the second curve (solid line), which closely coincides with the results of observation, rises more steeply than the first one.

At first sight one might interpret the fact that the experimental curve rises more steeply than the expected curve as a further demonstration that the geometry of space is not that of Euclid, for quite certainly a change of geometry changes the expected curve. But unfortunately things go the wrong way. A change from the geometry of Euclid to that of Einstein turns out to *decrease* the slope of the expected curve, thereby increasing the discrepancy.

The sense of the discrepancy, as our figure shows, is that there are too many faint sources in comparison with the number of intense sources. Ryle has interpreted this in the following way. Radio waves travel at the same speed as light, and just as light takes time to reach us from a distant source, so do radio waves. The time required for radiation to reach us from a star within our own galaxy may be measured in years, in centuries, or in thousands of years; but the time required for light or radio waves to reach us from a galaxy must be measured in millions, in hundreds of millions, or even in thousands of millions of years. Indeed, the radio waves from some of the most intense of the sources under consideration took more than 500 million years to reach us. In other words they were actually emitted from their source at a time when the first primitive

forms of life had only recently appeared in the oceans of our Earth. And the radio waves from the faintest of Ryle's sources may have taken some two, three, or four thousand million years to reach us. They may have started on their journey across space at about the time that our planetary system was first formed.

The second of the two points on which Ryle's explanation of his results is based depends on the fact that the chance of a particular galaxy being a strong radio source—that is, of its being strong enough to be included in Ryle's survey—is very small. Only about one galaxy in a million is thought to be of the type that is under consideration, a proportion that we may here call p. Now our observations of very distant galaxies tell us not about their situation today but about their situation many hundreds of millions of years ago. Thus Ryle argues that the fact that p is higher than expected for very distant galaxies indicates that the quantity p was significantly larger in the past than it is today, that there were then more sources of radio waves.

If this argument is correct, it disposes of the steady state cosmology, for according to the steady state theory things must be essentially the same at one moment of time as at another, so that the quantity p could not be greater in the past than it is now. According to the steady state theory, if the quantity p is measured as an average for a sufficiently large volume, then the resulting quantity will be the same at all places and at all times. So it follows that if the observations have been correctly made the theory is forced into the supposition that the quantity p has not been measured for a sufficiently large volume.

At first sight this would seem an unlikely form of defense, for certainly Ryle's observations extend over a huge volume of space, a volume even larger than that which is surveyed by the largest optical telescopes. There is, however, just one possible loophole. If any property, such as that of being a radio source, increases in probability with sufficient rapidity as a galaxy ages, it cannot be defined by comparatively small volumes. Indeed, if a property increases in probability more rapidly than does the weakening effect of the expansion of the universe, a curious situation arises in which it is not possible to define the average property of a small region of space. In such a case, the chances of finding a galaxy with the required property increase with the age of the galaxy in such a way that most of our

Figure 11.4
Here observed numbers of radio sources above a specified apparent brightness (horizontal scale) are compared with what we should expect if their frequency in space is uniform and also if space has the geometry of Euclid. The difference between expectation and observation actually increases if we change to the geometry of Einstein.

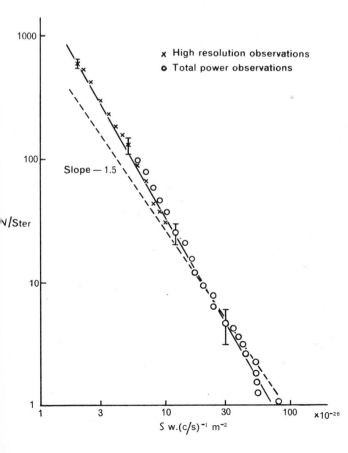

observations will be concerned with galaxies at very great distances. In mathematical terms, there is a tendency toward divergence of the property for galaxies at increasing distances, a divergence that is only prevented by the non-Euclidean character of the geometry.

The upshot is therefore as follows. According to Ryle's point of view it was more probable for a galaxy to be a strong radio source in the past than it is now; in other words, a galaxy is more likely to be a strong radio source during the early part of its life history than it is later on. If this point of view is correct, then steady state cosmology would seem to be wrong, for steady state cosmology requires either that the observations are wrong or else that a galaxy is more likely to become a strong radio source as it grows older.

The question therefore arises as to which way round things really are, but it is a question to which no definite answer can be given. We have already seen that a large proportion of the strong radio galaxies are giant elliptical systems, systems that we believe to contain old stars and very little gas and dust. The presence of the old stars would seem to support the steady state point of view, that these galaxies are indeed very old systems. At all events, the steady state cosmology is consistent in that it places the galaxies in an age sequence in which the elliptical galaxies are the oldest, and this placing agrees with the quite independent requirement that we have just considered for the radio sources.

When we know *why* a galaxy is a strong radio source, it will undoubtedly be much easier to arrive at a definite answer to our question. At one time it was thought that strong radio sources arise from collisions between galaxies. If this were so, then Ryle's argument must be judged better than the steady state argument; for in all cosmologies other than the steady state cosmology, the density of galaxies was higher in the past than it is now, and collisions could therefore be expected to occur more frequently then than now. Thus all cosmologies other than the steady state cosmology would be consistent with Ryle's observations. But the tendency among radio astronomers in recent years has been away from the idea that strong radio sources arise from the collisions of galaxies, for on such a basis it is difficult to understand the predominance of giant elliptical galaxies among the strong radio sources. And here, at this very uncertain point, the question must be left.

Essential Differences Between Cosmologies

The various cosmologies can be divided into two kinds: those that require the universe to have had a very definite origin and those in which the universe had no origin at all. In cosmologies of the first kind, the present-day situation is not only a consequence of the laws of physics but also of the particular way in which the universe started off. In cosmologies of the second kind, the present-day situation is a consequence purely of the laws of physics. In the terminology of the physicist, we may say that in the former case the present-day properties of the universe depend both on the laws of physics and on initial boundary conditions; in the latter case there are no initial boundary conditions.

In so far as one can assert any general principles by which to judge where the balance of probability lies between the two classes of cosmology, one might begin by saying that nature commonly appears to avoid starting with a complex situation. Complex situations arise out of the operation of physical laws. For example, complex atomic nuclei are built from the simplest element, hydrogen, by processes which take place within the stars; there was no *starting* with the complex nuclei. Exactly the same situation applies in chemistry. Beginning with single atoms, molecules were formed—at first relatively simple molecules, but then more and more complex ones until the vastly intricate processes of life were reached. Things did not *start* with life already existing.

If one accepts this idea of evolution from simple forms to much more complex forms, then cosmological theories of the first kind, those that require the universe to have had a definite origin, must surely be excluded; for such cosmologies require the main properties of the universe as we observe it today to have been already built into the starting conditions. An example is the formation of galaxies. According to cosmologies of the first kind, the galaxies formed because things were started in a very particular way. In cosmologies of the second kind, in particular in the steady state cosmology, there is no possibility of appealing to special conditions. Everything, including the formation of galaxies, must follow from the physical laws.

Some preliminary work has been done on this in steady state cosmology, on the basis that the general gas in space is very hot, as indeed it must be if newly-created matter is in the form of neutrons. The neutrons decay spontaneously into hydrogen atoms, and energy released in the decay heats the hydrogen to very high temperatures. Cooling within the hot gas then leads to a situation in which galaxies, and indeed clusters of galaxies, can be formed. Earlier in this chapter it was mentioned that our own galaxy and the Andromeda Nebula possess halos of very hot gas. These halos would represent regions of transition between the much cooler, denser gas lying within the flat plate-like structure of those galaxies and the entirely external world of high-temperature gas. The effects of cooling within the hot gas can produce speeds of motion of the order of two thousand miles per second. This is so large as to suggest that powerful electromagnetic effects should occur in intergalactic space. There should be processes of particle acceleration, perhaps leading to the production of cosmic rays. High-speed electrons among the cosmic rays should then lead to the emission of radio waves. Indeed, the whole subject of extragalactic radio astronomy becomes intimately connected with this external high-energy world.

So the steady state theory presents us with a remarkable view of the conditions that may exist in intergalactic space. According to this theory, intergalactic space is a place of great activity. It is a place in which galaxies are constantly being formed, and in which already-existing galaxies are steadily changing with time. In other words, already-existing galaxies are in interaction with the medium that surrounds them. This picture is entirely different from that presented by the other cosmologies, in which intergalactic space is a dead region in which little or nothing is supposed to take place.

Probably it will be upon this difference that the theories will finally be judged as more and more evidence is gathered. Sooner or later it must be possible to decide by observational techniques whether or not a high-energy world really does exist outside the galaxies. Perhaps one might say that in the phenomena of cosmic rays and cosmic magnetic fields, and through extragalactic radio astronomy, we already do possess at least some evidence to favor the existence of such a world.

Milton Humason who, together with Hubble, established the relation between distance and velocity of recession of galaxies. The spectra shown earlier (on page 293) were obtained by Dr. Humason.

Appendix on the Epicyclic Constructions of Hipparchus and Ptolemy

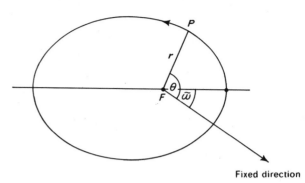

Fixed direction

Figure A.1

In Figure A.1 we have a body P moving around an ellipse of eccentricity e and semi-major axis a. The angle of the radius vector from a fixed direction through the focus F is θ and the line of apses makes angle $\tilde{\omega}$ with this fixed direction.

The equation of the ellipse requires

$$r = \frac{a\,(1 - e^2)}{1 + e\,\cos\,(\theta - \tilde{\omega})} \qquad (1)$$

The conservation of angular momentum requires

$r^2 \dot{\theta} = \text{constant} = h$ say,

so that

$$\dot{\theta} = \frac{h}{a^2\,(1 - e^2)^2}\,[1 + e\,\cos\,(\theta - \tilde{\omega})]^2. \qquad (2)$$

Since the epicyclic constructions of Hipparchus and Ptolemy only represented the elliptic motion at best to terms of the first order in e, the above formulae will be approximated by neglecting terms containing the square and higher powers of e, viz.,

$$r = a\,[1 - e\,\cos\,(\theta - \tilde{\omega})], \qquad (3)$$

$$\dot{\theta} = n\,[1 + 2e\,\cos\,(\theta - \tilde{\omega})], \qquad (4)$$

where $n = h/a^2$. (N.B. When the square of e is not neglected, n is usually defined as $h/(a^2\,(1 - e^2)^{\frac{1}{2}})$.) Equation (4) can be integrated by successive approximations

$$\theta = nt + \tilde{\omega} \qquad (5)$$

in first approximation, provided $t = 0$ is chosen as a moment when the body is nearest to the focus. Substituting into the cosine term of (4) gives

$$\dot{\theta} = n\,[1 + 2e\,\cos\,nt]$$

so that in second approximation

$$\theta = nt + 2e\,\sin\,nt + \tilde{\omega}. \qquad (6)$$

Substituting in (3) gives

$$r = a\,[1 - e\,\cos\,(nt + 2e\,\sin\,nt)] = a\,(1 - e\,\cos\,nt), \quad (7)$$

neglecting a term involving e^2.

For the purpose of comparing the elliptic motion with constructions composed from circles, it is convenient to express the position of P as a complex number $r\,\exp\,(i\theta)$. Thus

$$r\,exp\,(i\theta) = a\,(1 - e\,\cos\,nt)\,\exp\,i\,(nt + 2e\,\sin\,nt + \tilde{\omega}). \qquad (8)$$

By expanding $exp\,(2ie\,\sin\,nt)$ as $1 + 2ie\,\sin\,nt$ and by neglecting the term in e^2 arising from the multiplication with $(1 - e\,\cos\,nt)$ we obtain

$$r\,exp\,(i\theta) = a\,(1 - e\,\cos\,nt + 2ie\,\sin\,nt)\,\exp\,i\,(nt + \tilde{\omega}).$$

The next step is to express $\cos\,nt$ and $\sin\,nt$ as exponentials,

$$cos\,nt = \frac{1}{2}\,[exp\,(int) + exp\,(-int)],$$

$$sin\,nt = \frac{1}{2i}\,[exp\,(int) - exp\,(-int)],$$

giving

$$r\,exp\,i\theta = a\,exp\,(i\tilde{\omega})\,[exp\,(int) - e +$$
$$\frac{e}{2}\,(exp\,2int - 1)]. \qquad (9)$$

We now compare this result, correct to order e for elliptic motion, with an assumed motion in an epicycle, as shown in Figure A.2, where a is the radius of the main circle, hereafter called the *deferent*, and ae is the radius of the epicycle. Take ω_d as the angular velocity of the center of the epicycle about the center of the deferent, and ω_e as the angular velocity in the epicycle, both reckoned in an anti-clockwise sense, from the same fixed direction. At $t = 0$ the center of the epicycle is taken as having argument $\tilde{\omega}_d$, and the argument of P' is taken relative to C as $\tilde{\omega}_e$. Then the position of P' is given by

$$a\,exp\,i\,(\omega_d t + \tilde{\omega}_d) + ae\,exp\,i\,(\omega_e t + \tilde{\omega}_e). \qquad (10)$$

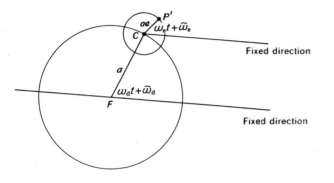

Figure A.2

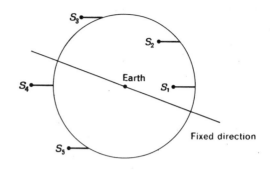

Figure A.3

Evidently (9) and (10) represent the same position at $t = 0$ if $\tilde{\omega}_d = \tilde{\omega}$ and $\tilde{\omega}_e = \tilde{\omega} + \pi$. Moreover if $\omega_d = n$, $\omega_e = 0$, (9) and (10) are always the same apart from the extra factor $exp\,(2int) - 1$ appearing in (9). This extra factor vanishes when the body is at either of its apses. With these choices for ω_d, ω_e, $\tilde{\omega}_d$, $\tilde{\omega}_e$, (10) is in fact just

$$a\,exp\,(i\tilde{\omega})\,[exp\,(int) - e].$$

This gives Hipparchus's theory of the Sun and of the unequal seasons. In Figures A.1 and A.2, F is the Earth. P is the Sun in Figure A.1, and in Figure A.2, P' is Hipparchus's position for the Sun. The two differ only by

$$\frac{ae}{2}\,exp\,(i\tilde{\omega})\,[exp\,(2int) - 1].$$

Hipparchus's picture of the solar motion is illustrated in Figure A.3. S_1, S_2, S_3, S_4, S_5 are positions at various points of the orbit, S_1 being perihelion and S_4 aphelion. The Sun is held, as it were, in a constant direction on the end of a stick of length ae*.

The position becomes more interesting when we turn to the case of the Moon. We have seen that in our third phase of sophistication the major axis of the Moon's orbit must be considered as slowly turning in its own plane. This we can represent in terms of the elliptic motion by writing

$$\tilde{\omega} = \omega t + \tilde{\omega}_0$$

where ω, $\tilde{\omega}_0$ are constants. The magnitude of ω

* Dreyer, in his authoritative *History of the Planetary Systems from Thales to Kepler*, remarks that Hipparchus determined a value $e = 0.04166$ from comparison with the observed lengths of the seasons. He adds that this was "fairly correct". This appears to be an oversight, since the true value of e is 0.0167. Hipparchus could not possibly have made so large an error.

is small compared with n, so that the line of apses hardly changes from one revolution of the Moon to the next. (The period $2\pi/\omega$ is about 9 years, as compared with 27 days for $2\pi/n$.) Substituting in (9), the elliptic representation gives

$$re^{i\theta} = a\,exp\,i\tilde{\omega}_0\,[exp\,i\,(n+\omega)\,t - e\,exp\,(i\omega t) +$$
$$\frac{e}{2}\,exp\,(i\omega t)\,(exp\,2int - 1)]. \qquad (11)$$

If again in the epicycle picture we do not seek to represent the term in $exp\,2int - 1$, which still vanishes at the apses, the remaining terms are given by putting $\omega_d = n + \omega$, $\omega_e = \omega$, $\tilde{\omega}_d = \tilde{\omega}_0$, $\tilde{\omega}_e = \tilde{\omega}_0 + \pi$, in (10). Thus the Moon is not attached to a stick that maintains a constant direction, but to one that turns, relative to a fixed direction, with angular velocity ω, this being just the angular velocity of the apse line.

This was Hipparchus's theory of the Moon. It brings out the advantage of an epicyclic theory (when only circular motions are allowed) and well illustrates the dilemma of Aristarchus.

In fact the Moon's motion is, of course, far more complex than this. The Sun causes the Moon to speed up in some parts of its orbit and to slow down in others (the so-called *evection*). This Ptolemy was able to represent by an extension of Hipparchus's theory, an extension in which the center of the deferent circle ceased to fall exactly at the Earth, and in which ω_d was no longer a uniform angular motion. But rather than pursue Ptolemy's theory of the Moon, it will be more instructive to consider similar ideas applied to the planetary motions.

In Figure A.1 let F represent the Sun, and let P represent any planet. Give all quantities a subscript P. Thus the position of P is given by (9) but with the subscript P added, viz.,

$$r_P \exp i\theta_P = a_P \exp(i\tilde{\omega}_P) [\exp(in_P t) - e_P +$$
$$\frac{e_P}{2}(\exp 2in_P t - 1)]. \tag{12}$$

The position of the Earth is given by writing an exactly similar equation but with subscript E. *Provided we assume the planes of the orbits to be the same*, the position of the planet as seen from the Earth is therefore

$$a_P \exp(i\tilde{\omega}_P) [\exp(in_P t) - \frac{3}{2}e_P + \frac{e_P}{2}\exp(2in_P t)] -$$
$$a_E \exp(i\tilde{\omega}_E) [\exp(in_E t) - \frac{3}{2}e_E + \frac{e_E}{2}\exp(2in_E t)]. \tag{13}$$

Next we consider Ptolemy's famous construction, shown in Figure A.4. Here the center of the deferent circle is at O, not at the Earth E. Moreover, the center C of the epicycle does not move with uniform angular velocity about O, but about a point Q on the line EO. (Q is the so-called *punctum aequans*.) Provided the distance OQ is small compared with OC, then OQ^2 may be neglected in

$$OC^2 = OQ^2 + QC^2 + 2OQ \cdot QC \cos(\omega_d t + \tilde{\omega}_d)$$

when we work only to first order. Hence

$$QC = OC - OQ \cos(\omega_d t + \tilde{\omega}_d)$$

in first order. The position of P' is thus

$$EQ + [OC - OQ \cos(\omega_d t + \tilde{\omega}_d)] \exp i(\omega_d t + \tilde{\omega}_d) +$$
$$CP' \exp i(\omega_e t + \tilde{\omega}_e).$$

Expanding the cosine in exponentials we obtain

$$EQ - \frac{1}{2}OQ + OC \exp i(\omega_d t + \tilde{\omega}_d) -$$
$$\frac{1}{2}OQ \exp 2i(\omega_d t + \tilde{\omega}_d) + CP' \exp i(\omega_e t + \tilde{\omega}_e). \tag{14}$$

The question now arises as to how far the direction and relative distance of P', as given by (14), can be made to agree with the direction and distance of P. In the first place no complete equivalence is possible, but a partial agreement can be achieved, especially if either $a_P e_P$ is large compared with $a_E e_E$ or if $a_P e_P$ is small compared with $a_E e_E$. The worst case is where these quantities are comparable with each other. Fortunately this is not the situation for any planet. Indeed $a_P e_P$ is large compared with $a_E e_E$ for all planets except Venus, where the opposite is the case (as can be seen from Tables 1 and 2, given at the beginning of Chapter 3).

Consider the case where $a_P e_P$ is large compared with $a_E e_E$. First we note that the complex number (14) is taken with the line EQ as real axis. We can, however, choose a real axis through E such that the argument of EQ is $\tilde{\omega}_0$, say. Then in place of (14) the position of P' is

$$\exp(i\tilde{\omega}_0) [EQ - \frac{1}{2}OQ + OC \exp i(\omega_d t + \tilde{\omega}_d) -$$
$$\frac{1}{2}OQ \exp 2i(\omega_d t + \tilde{\omega}_d) +$$
$$CP' \exp i(\omega_e t + \tilde{\omega}_e)]. \tag{15}$$

We make no attempt to represent the terms involving e_E in (13), but the term $-a_E \exp(i\tilde{\omega}_E) \exp(in_E t)$ must, of course, be represented. This requires $\omega_e = n_E$, $\tilde{\omega}_0 + \tilde{\omega}_e = \pi + \tilde{\omega}_E$, and $CP' = a_E$. The π appears because of the minus sign. The other main term in (13), viz. $a_P \exp(i\tilde{\omega}_P) \exp(in_P t)$ appears in (15) when we put $OC = a_P$, $\omega_d = n_P$, $\tilde{\omega}_0 + \tilde{\omega}_d = \tilde{\omega}_P$. The term $-\frac{3}{2}a_P e_P \exp(i\tilde{\omega}_P)$ appears if $\tilde{\omega}_0 = \pi + \tilde{\omega}_P$, $EQ - \frac{1}{2}OQ = \frac{3}{2}a_P e_P$. Finally, the term $\frac{1}{2}a_P e_P \exp(2in_P t + \tilde{\omega}_P)$ appears if $OQ = a_P e_P$, $\tilde{\omega}_0 + 2\tilde{\omega}_d = -\pi + \tilde{\omega}_P$. Collecting all these requirements

$$CP' = a_E, \quad OC = a_P, \quad EO = OQ = a_P e_P.$$
$$\omega_e = n_E, \quad \omega_d = n_P.$$
$$\tilde{\omega}_0 = \pi + \tilde{\omega}_P, \quad \tilde{\omega}_e = \tilde{\omega}_E - \tilde{\omega}_P, \quad \tilde{\omega}_d = -\pi. \tag{16}$$

With these choices the position of P' in the epicyclic picture is

$$\exp(i\tilde{\omega}_P) \left[-\frac{3}{2}a_P e_P + a_P \exp(in_P t) + \right.$$
$$\left. \frac{1}{2}a_P e_P \exp(2in_P t) \right] - a_E \exp i(\omega_e t + \tilde{\omega}_E). \tag{17}$$

Only terms in $a_E e_E$ appear in (13) but not in (17). Ptolemy's construction therefore represented the elliptic motion, to first order in the eccentricity, except for these small omitted terms.

Several further points must be noticed. In the first line of (16) the distances could be written

$$CP' = ka_E, \quad OC = ka_P, \quad EO = OQ = ka_P e_P \tag{18}$$

where k is any constant, without the direction of P' being changed, and without *relative* distances being falsified in any way. Since absolute distances were not known to Ptolemy, (18) should really replace the first line of (16).

Ptolemy's choices for the distances EO, OQ were made empirically, so as to get the best fit to the observations. It is of great interest that his actual choices did give EO substantially equal to OQ. Moreover his values for EO were close to $a_P e_P$ in the cases of Mars, Jupiter, Saturn. The cases of Venus and Mercury require separate comment. Let us take Mercury first since, like the outer planets, $a_P e_P$ is substantially larger than $a_E e_E$, because of the very large eccentricity of the orbit of Mercury (0·2056, as compared with 0·0167 for e_E).

The situation emerges that because a_P is smaller than a_E for Mercury, OC must be smaller than CP'. Hence our discussion really requires the use of the eccentric circle picture rather than the epicycle picture. In point of fact, Ptolemy preferred to work with the epicycle picture. This naturally forced him to modify his geometrical construction. He need not have done so if he had wished to use the eccentric circle picture. (Dreyer remarks that the construction used for the outer planets "failed" in the case of Mercury. It did not really fail. It was replaced by an equivalent construction.)

Turning last to the case of Venus, $a_E e_E$ is in this one case appreciably larger than $a_P e_P$. We change the construction simply by interchanging the subscripts P and E in (16) (or in (18) if we wish to be strict, instead of the first line of (16)). Thus

$$CP' = ka_P, \quad OC = ka_E, \quad EO = OQ = ka_E e_E$$
$$\omega_e = n_P, \quad \omega_d = n_E$$
$$\tilde{\omega}_0 = \pi + \tilde{\omega}_E, \quad \tilde{\omega}_e = \tilde{\omega}_P - \tilde{\omega}_E, \quad \tilde{\omega}_d = -\pi. \qquad (19)$$

Because of the interchange of subscripts, OC is again larger than CP', as it is for the outer planets. The picture is therefore the epicyclic one, and not the eccentric circle one. Thus Ptolemy did not need to modify his construction for Venus. But EO must now be chosen as $a_E e_E$, not as $a_P e_P$. Ptolemy's empirical choices for EO and OQ were again substantially equal, and EO was roughly equal, but not exactly equal, to $a_E e_E$. (Once again, Dreyer's comment on this point appears to arise from an oversight. He notes that EO is no longer close to $a_P e_P$, but fails to notice the reason. In a footnote he implies that the change was a weakness in Ptolemy's construction. This was obviously not so.)

The above analysis is based on the planes of the orbits of the planets and of the Earth being coincident. To take some account of the effect of the inclinations of the planetary orbits, Ptolemy introduced the additional complication of requiring the plane of the epicycle to be not quite the same as that of the deferent. Although it is not profitable to include a detailed discussion of this feature (no new matters of principle being involved), it is worth noticing as a further indication of the subtlety of Ptolemy.

Figure A.4

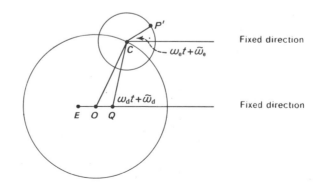

Acknowledgments

Key: (T) ... top   (M) ... middle   (B) ... bottom
(L) ... left   (R) ... right

Brit. Mus. ... Courtesy of the Trustees of the British Museum

Mt. W. & P. Obs. ... Courtesy of Mount Wilson and Palomar Observatories, California, USA

Frontispiece: Veil Nebula in Cygnus, part of NGC 6992 photographed in color with the 48-inch telescope. Photo: Mt. W. & P. Obs.

11 (T) Clouds over southern Greece.
Photo: Swissair.
(B) Mexico from High Altitude Rocket.
Official U.S. Navy Photograph.

12 Arabic edition of Euclid translated by Ishâq ibn Honeim, MS c. 1350.
From *The World of Mathematics* Vol. I. by D. E. Smith, 1900 (Ginn & Co., New York).

16 Star Trails, 1½ hr. exposure.
Photo: Observatoire de Haute Provence du Centre National de la Récherche Scientifique.

18 (T) Chart of Atlantic by W. J. Blaeu c. 1630.
Courtesy: Trustees of the National Maritime Museum, Greenwich.
(B) Prime Meridian at Greenwich Observatory.
Photo: Gerald Howson.

19 *24 New and Accurate Maps of . . . France*
by Herman Moll, 1708.
Brit. Mus. (BM–MAPS 18.a.23)

24-5 *Harmonia Macrocosmica*, Andreas Cellerius 1660. Brit. Mus. (MAPS C.6.c.2)

26-8 Star Maps from *Astronomy*, John C. Duncan 1955. (Harper & Bros., New York.)

29 From Persian MS *Sũr Al-Kawãkab* of 17th century.
Courtesy: Victoria & Albert Museum.

31 (T) 200-inch Hale telescope.
Mt. W. & P. Obs.

31 (B) From *The Pagan Tribes of Borneo*, Hose and McDougall, 1912. (Macmillan & Co. Ltd.)

34 (T) Nuremburg clock. Repro–Gebühr enthalten.
Belegexemplar Erbeten.

35 Equatorial Sundial, woodcut of about 1550.
Courtesy: Bibliothèque Nationale, Paris.

36 (T) Replica of Merkhet of 6th century B.C. in Berlin.
Courtesy: Science Museum, London.
Photo: David Swann.

37 (R) Triquetrum. From *Astronomiae Instauratae Mechanica*, Tycho Brahe 1602. Radio Times Hulton Picture Library.

40 (TL) Tycho Brahe's Azimuth quadrant from *Astronomiae Instauratae Mechanica*, Tycho Brahe 1602.
Photo: Science Museum, London.
(BL) From *Antarctica*, Emil Schulthess 1961.
Photo: Schulthess/Black Star, London.
(BR) Sculpture in Florence said to be of Ptolemy.
Mansell Collection. Photo: Alinari.

41 (T) Great Equatorial Armillary from *Astronomiae Instauratae Mechanica*, Tycho Brahe 1602.
Photo: Science Museum, London.
(B) Diagrams from an article by John Christianson in the February 1961 issue of *Scientific American*.

42 *Treatise on the Astrolabe*, Geoffrey Chaucer (MS.–Dd. 3.53) Courtesy: Cambridge University Library.

43 14th-century Astrolabe, probably French.
Courtesy: Museum of the History of Science, Oxford. Photo: David Swann.

45 (L) Apian's Torquetum of c. 1530. From *Astronomicum Caesareum*, Petrus Apianus 1540.
Photo: Science Museum, London.
(R) Torquetum of Nicholas of Cusa. Rheinisches Landesmuseum, Trier, Germany.

50 (T) Mare Imbrium. Mt. W. & P. Obs.
(B) Drawing of Moon by Galileo. Courtesy: Biblioteca Nazionale Centrale, Florence, Italy.

52 (L) Transit Circle of 1806. Courtesy: Science Museum, London. Photo: David Swann.
(R) From *Cycle of Celestial Objects*, Vice-Admiral W. H. Smyth 1860. Courtesy: London Library.

54   200-inch Hale telescope, Mt. Palomar.
Mt. W. & P. Obs.
45-inch Cassegrain telescope, Melbourne, Australia in 1860. Mansell Collection.

56   (T) Replica of Newton's telescope of 1668. Courtesy: Science Museum, London. Photo: David Swann.
(B) Lassell's 48-inch Newtonian telescope. From R.A.S. *Memoirs* Vol. 36, 1866. By permission of the Royal Astronomical Society, London.

57   (T) Nasmyth's 20-inch telescope. Courtesy: Science Museum, London. Photo: David Swann.
(B) Nasmyth at his telescope. From *History of the Telescope*, H. C. King 1955. (Charles Griffin & Co. Ltd., London.)

59   (T) Model of equatorial Coudé telescope. Courtesy: Science Museum, London. Photo: David Swann.
(B) Engraving of equatorial Coudé at Paris Observatory. Courtesy: Musée des Arts Decoratifs, Palais du Louvre, Paris.

63   (T) Rosse 6-ft. reflector in 1840s. Crown Copyright, Science Museum, London.
(B) From *Practical Astronomy*, W. Pearson 1824. Brit. Mus. (BM–533.i.11).

64   (T) 40-inch telescope, Yerkes Observatory.
Photo: Yerkes Observatory (No. BI 53)
(M) 40-inch lens of Yerkes refractor.
Photo: Yerkes Observatory. (No. B, 197)
(B) 200-inch mirror of Hale reflector, Mount Palomar. Mt. W. & P. Obs.

65   Schmidt 48-inch telescope, Mt. Palomar.
Mt. W. & P. Obs.

67   (T) *Harmonia Macrocosmica*, Andreas Cellerius 1660. Brit. Mus. (MAPS C.6.c.3).
(B) Babylonian Tablet, observations of Jupiter from B.C. 131/0 to 59/8. Brit. Mus. (BM–34,750 rev.)

71   Greek Bell-Krater Vase (E 502) showing Omphalos. Brit. Mus.

75   Munich Planetarium. Photo: Erich Lessing-Magnum.

76   Cast of Sarcophagus cover of Prophet Mut. Photo: Metropolitan Museum of Art, New York.

78   Photographed in mid-air over Canary Islands, 2nd October, 1959. Photo: Courtesy McDonnell Aircraft Corporation, USA.

79   From a miniature by Tolomeo (Marc. Gr. z. 388). Courtesy: Biblioteca Nazionale di S. Marco, Venice, Italy.

80   (T) Babylonian Tablet. Lunar observations from B.C. 174/3 to 151/0. Brit. Mus. (BM–45,688 obv.).
(B) Boundary stone of Gula-Eresh. Brit. Mus. (BM–102,485).

82   (T) "The Commission for the Reformation of the Calendar." Courtesy: Archivio di Stato di Siena.
(B) *An Election Entertainment*, from "The Election" Series by Hogarth c. 1754. Courtesy: The Trustees of Sir John Soane's Museum, London.

86   Greek conception of the spherical cosmos altered from *Und es ward Licht* by Rudolf Thiel, 1956. (Rowohlt Verlag GmbH, Germany). English edition *And There Was Light*, 1958. (André Deutsch Ltd., London.)

88-9   *L'Art d' Eudoxe* (N 2325). Courtesy: Dept. Egyptian Antiquities, Musée du Louvre. Photo: Les Services Photographique des Musées Nationaux.

93   *L'Universo*, a fresco by Piero di Puccio. Courtesy: Campo Santo, Pisa. Photo: Nardi, Pisa.

95   (TL) Ulagh Beg MS *Silsilanana* (8457. p. 96). Courtesy: Ethnographical Museum, Ankara.

95   (TR) *Shahinshshanana* (MS–F 1404. p. 57a)· Courtesy: Istanbul University Library, Turkey.
(B) Based on diagrams in a work on Ulagh Beg, 1950, by Karui-Niyazov.

96   From *Nicholaus Coppernicus*, Leopold Prowe 1883/4. Courtesy: London Library.

97   (L) Portrait of Nicholas Copernicus c. 1600. Courtesy: Cracow University. Photo: Erich Lessing-Magnum.
(R) From the portrait in the possession of the Seminary of Braunsberg, Poland, prior to 1939.

99   (T) The Geometry Room at Cracow University. Photo: Erich Lessing-Magnum.
(B) Lesson in Dissection from *Fascicolo di Medicina*, Johannes de Ketham 1493. Brit. Mus. (BM–IB.21041).

101   (T) Copernicus' Room at Frauenberg. Photo: Erich Lessing-Magnum.
(B) Frauenberg. From *Nicholaus Coppernicus*, Leopold Prowe 1883/4. Courtesy: London Library.

103   (L) *De Libris Revolutionum . . . . Narratio Prima*, Joachim Rheticus 1541. Brit. Mus. (BM–531.c.3(1)).
(R) *De Revolutionibus . . .*, Nicholas Copernicus 1543. Courtesy: London Library.

104   (L) From *Nikolaus Kopernikus Gesamtausgabe* Vol. 1, a facsimile of original MS of *De Revolutionibus* edited by Fritz Kubach, 1944. (R. Oldenbourg Verlag, Munich.)
(R) From the portrait in the possession of the Copernicus Grammar School, Torun, Poland, prior to 1939.

105   From *De Revolutionibus . . .*, Nicholas Copernicus 1543. Courtesy: London Library.

106   (L) Tycho Brahe painted about 1597. Royal Observatory, Edinburgh. Courtesy: The Astronomer Royal for Scotland. Photo: J. B. Watson Ltd., Edinburgh.
(R) From *Astronomiae Instauratae . . .*, Tycho Brahe 1648. Courtesy: London Library.

107   Tycho Brahe's Mural Quadrant. From *Atlas Major . . .* Vol. 1. Jan Blaeu 1663. Brit. Mus. (BM–MAPS C.5.b.1).

108   (T) Uraniborg Observatory from *Atlas Major . . .* Vol. 1. Jan Blaeu 1664. (BM–MAPS C.4.d.1).
(B) Stjerneborg Observatory from *Atlas Major . . .* Vol. 1. Jan Blaeu by Courtesy of the Science Museum, London. Photo: David Swann.

109   (T) Adapted from *Tycho Brahe's Uraniborg and Stjerneborg on the Island of Hveen*, F. Beckett, 1921. By permission of Selskabet til Udgivelse af Skrifter om danske Mindesmaerker.
(B) Map of Hveen from *Atlas Major . . .* Vol. 1, Jan Blaeu 1664. Brit. Mus. (BM–MAPS C.4.d.1).

110   (T) Kepler, painted in oils c. 1620. By courtesy of Foundation Saint-Thomas, Strasbourg.
(B) From *Mysterium Cosmographicum . . .*, Johannes Kepler 1596. Brit. Mus. (BM–C.54.bb.34).

111   (B) . . . *Mysterium Cosmographicum*, Johannes Kepler 1621. Brit. Mus. (BM–532.K.11(1-3)).

112   *Tabuli Rudolphinae*, Johannes Kepler 1627. Brit. Mus. (BM–48.f.7).

113   Tomb of Tycho Brahe in the Týn Church, Prague. Photo reproduced by Courtesy of the State Institute for the Care of Historical Monuments, Prague.

114   From the Kepler MSS on the calculations for the orbit of Mars. Preserved in the Archives of the Academy of Sciences, Leningrad. Photo: Courtesy of the Director of the Pulkovo Observatory.

116 (R) Observatory at Prague. Photo: Erich Lessing-Magnum.

117 (L) From *Astronomia Nova* . . . , Johannes Kepler 1609.

118 *Somnium* . . . . Johannes Kepler 1634. Brit. Mus. (BM–531.K.13(9)).

119 (L) From *A History of Astronomy from Thales to Kepler*, J. L. E. Dreyer (Cambridge University Press).
(R) Horoscope by Kepler from *And There was Light*, Rudolf Thiel 1958 (André Deutsch).

121 (T) One of a series of astronomical paintings by Donato Creti *c.* 1700. Courtesy Director General, Monumenti, Musei e Gallerie Pontificie. Photo: Photographic Archives of the Vatican Museums & Galleries. (See also p. 278.)
(BL) Portrait of Galileo Galilei by Attavio Leoni (*c.* 1578-1630). Courtesy: Biblioteca Marucelliana, Florence, Italy. Photo: Dr. G. B. Pineider, Florence.
(BR) Reconstruction from Galileo's drawing, by courtesy of the Directors of the Science Museum, London. Photo: David Swann.

122 (BL) *Istoria e dimostrazione intorno alie Macchie Solari* . . . , Galileo Galilei 1613. Brit. Mus. (BM–60.c.19).
(BR) Day-by-day record of sunspot group of March-April 1947. Photo: Mt. W. & P. Obs.

123 *Rosa Ursina* . . . , Christophoro Scheiner 1626-30, Frontispiece to Book III. Photo: Science Museum, London.

124 (L) *Sidereus Nuncius* . . . , Galileo Galilei 1610. Brit. Mus. (BM–C.112.c.3).

124 (R) From *Discoveries and Opinions of Galileo*, translated by Stillman Drake. Copyright 1957 by Stillman Drake. Reprinted by permission of Doubleday & Co., Inc., New York.

125 (L) Replica of telescope made by Galileo in 1610. Courtesy of the Director of the Science Museum, London. Photo: David Swann.
(R) *Sidereus Nuncius* . . . , Galileo 1610. Brit. Mus. (BM–C.112.c.3).

127 Opening page of Galileo's notes on Jupiter's satellites. Courtesy: Biblioteca Nazionale Centrale, Florence.

128 (T) *Dialogo di Galileo Galilei* . . . . 1632. Brit. Mus. (BM–C.28.i.4).
(B) Frontispiece from *Opere di Giordano Bruno* . . . Vol.I. Adolfo Wagner 1830. Brit. Mus. (BM–1113.i.7)

129 (L) Translation of Galileo's Abjuration from *The Sleepwalkers*, A. Koestler 1961.
(R) Contemporary copy of Galileo's Abjuration. Courtesy: Archivio di Stato, Moderna.

132 Portrait of Huygens by Netscher. Collection Municipal Museum, The Hague, Holland.

134 Paris Observatory. Radio Times Hulton Picture Library.

135 Frontispiece from *Recueil de plusieurs traitez de Mathématique de l'Academie Royale des Sciences*, 1676. Brit. Mus. (BM–789.1.41).

136-7 (T) From *Cantabrigia Illustrata*, David Loggan 1690. Brit. Mus. (BM–129.h.3).
(BL) Redrawn from *The Mathematical Principles of Natural Philosophy*, the English translation of Newton's *Principia*, by Andrew Motte 1729. Brit. Mus. (BM–233.f.22).
(BM) Sir Isaac Newton, painted by Sir Godfrey Kneller in 1702. Photo: Courtesy: National Portrait Gallery, London.
(BR) Woolsthorpe Manor. Courtesy: National Trust. Photo: David Swann.

139 (T) Halley's Comet painted by Samuel Scott (*c.* 1702-1772). Formerly in possession of Messrs. M. Bernard, London.
(B) From the Bayeux Tapestry in Bayeux Cathedral.

140 Original minutes of the Royal Society for 28 April 1686. Courtesy the Royal Society. Photo: David Swann.

141 *Principia Mathematica*, Newton 1687. Brit. Mus. (BM–C.58.h.4).

143 (T) John Harrison's No. 1 Timekeeper 1735. Courtesy: Trustees National Maritime Museum, Greenwich. Photo: David Swann.
(BL) Kendal's copy of John Harrison's No. 4 Timekeeper 1770. Courtesy: Trustees National Maritime Museum, Greenwich. Photo: David Swann.
(BR) Capt. James Cook's Journal, *A Voyage Towards the South Pole*, 1772-75, showing last page, July 1775. Courtesy: Trustees National Maritime Museum, Greenwich.

144 (T) Satellites of Jupiter on 27-8 April 1945. Photo: Griffith Observatory, California, USA.
(B) *Nautical Almanac & Astronomical Ephemeris for 1767*, by Commissioners of Longitude, 1766. Brit. Mus. (BM–PP.2373.m).

144-5 *English Ships in a Strong Breeze* painted by C. Bouwmeester. Courtesy: Trustees National Maritime Museum, Greenwich. Photo: David Swann.

147 (T) Octagon Room, Greenwich Observatory, showing Maskelyne's Observing Suit. Courtesy: N. M. Arnold-Foster and Trustees National Maritime Museum, Greenwich. Photo: David Swann.
(BL) *Atlas Coelestis*, John Flamsteed 1729. Brit. Mus. (BM–48.i.17).
(BR) The Octagon Room, from an old print. Photo: Science Museum, London.

148 (BR) From *Astronomy*, John C. Duncan (Harper & Bros., New York).

150 Grahame's Zenith Sector made for Bradley, from *Miscellaneous Works and Correspondence of James Bradley*, 1832. Brit. Mus. (BM–532.i.24).

151 (T) Grahame's Zenith Sector. Courtesy: Trustees National Maritime Museum, Greenwich. Photo: David Swann.
(B) Bradley's MS note of observation of Gamma Draconis, 21 December 1725, from *Miscellaneous Works and Correspondence of James Bradley*, 1832. Brit. Mus. (BM–532.i.24).

153 Römer at his transit instrument of 1684, from *Basis Astronomiae* . . . , Petro Horrebow 1735. Brit. Mus. (BM–531.h.17).

154 (L) Portrait of Edmund Halley by Thomas Murray. Courtesy: Curators of the Bodleian Library, Oxford.

154-5 *Men of Science*, in the Library of the Royal Institute of Great Britain in 1807-08, engraved by Walker & Zobel. Courtesy: National Portrait Gallery, London.

156 (T) The *Resolution* and *Adventure* at Tahiti, 1772-75. Painted by William Hodges. Lent by the Admiralty to the National Maritime Museum, Greenwich. Photo: Film Strip Distributors.
(B) Chart of Matavie Bay. Brit. Mus. (BM–Add.MS. 7085.8).

157 (T) Mappemonde of Transit of Venus of 1769. Courtesy: Observatoire de Paris.
(BL) "Mr. Banks shows the Indians the Planet Venus on the Sun" from *Voyage to the Southern Hemisphere or Nature Explored*, London *c.* 1775. By permission of Sir Maurice Holmes.

157 (BR) Cape Venus, Tahiti; detail from map of Matavie Bay. Brit. Mus. (BM—Add.MS. 7085.8).

158 Trails of Asteroids. Photo: Landessternwarte Heidelberg-Königstuhl.

159 (BL) Apparatus used by Cavendish, from *Philosophical Transactions of the Royal Society*, Vol. 88, 1798. Brit. Mus. (BM—L.R.292).

159 (BR) Pencil and wash portrait of Cavendish by William Alexander. Brit. Mus. (BM print P.4.I.8-137)

160 Portrait of William Herschel by J. Russel. Courtesy: Trustees National Maritime Museum, Greenwich. Photo: David Swann.
     (R) Extract from Herschel's journal, reproduced from *Sir William Herschel's Collected Scientific Works*, Vol. I, pl.I. Courtesy of the Royal Astronomical Society. Photo: Gerald Howson.

162 (T) Illustration of 20-ft. reflector of Herschel. Photo: Palais de la Découverte, Paris.

162-3 (B) Extract from the journal of Caroline Herschel. Courtesy: Humanities Research Center, University of Texas.

164 From *John Couch Adams and the Discovery of Neptune*, Sir Harold Spencer Jones. By permission of the Cambridge University Press.

166 From the *Scientific Papers of Sir William Herschel*, 1917. Courtesy: The Royal Astronomical Society. Photo: Gerald Howson.

167 North America Nebula photographed in color with the 48-inch Schmidt telescope. Photo: Mt.W.&P.Obs.

168 (BL) Based on Fig. 8 in *From the Aratus Globe to the Zeiss Planetarium*, Dr. H. Werner.
     (BR) From *The Scientific Papers of Sir William Herschel*, 1917. Courtesy: The Royal Astronomical Society. Photo: Gerald Howson.

170-1 Map of Milky Way. Lund Observatory, Sweden.

172 Portrait of Friedrich Wilhelm Bessel (1784-1846). Radio Times Hulton Picture Library.

174 Oxford Heliometer, made by A. & G. Repsold of Hamburg, 1848. On loan from the Trustees of the Radcliffe Observatory, Oxford. By courtesy of the Director of the Science Museum, London. Photo: David Swann.

175 Details of the Oxford Heliometer. By courtesy of the Directors of the Science Museum, London. Photo: David Swann.

177 *Opticks*, Isaac Newton 1704. Brit. Mus. (BM—59.g.18).

179 Ripple Tank photographs by K. A. Rose, Lecturer in Acoustics, Nottingham.

180 (BL) By permission from *Fundamentals of Optics*, 3rd edn. by F. A. Jenkins and H. E. White. Copyright 1957 (McGraw-Hill Book Company Inc.).

181 (BR) As above.

183 (T) Blythswood Ruling Engine, built on Rowland's system by Otto Hilger. By Courtesy of the Science Museum, London. Photo: David Swann.
     (M) From a paper by R. G. N. Hall and L. A. Sayce in the *Proceedings of the Royal Society*, A, Vol. 215, 1952. Courtesy of the Royal Society.
     (B) Unblazed diffraction grating made at The National Physical Laboratories, Teddington, Middlesex. By Courtesy of the Science Museum, London. Photo: David Swann.

186 By permission from *Fundamentals of Optics*, 3rd edn., by F. A. Jenkins and H. E. White. Copyright 1957 (McGraw-Hill Book Company Inc.).

189 (T) *A Treatise on Electricity and Magnetism*, James Clerk Maxwell 1892.

189 (B) James Clerk Maxwell. Photo: Radio Times Hulton Picture Library.

190 (T) *Novi Prefectus in Historia Electricitatis . . .*, C. A. Hausen 1743. Brit. Mus. (BM—538.l.5(2)).
     (B) A Coulomb torsion balance. Courtesy: Science Museum, London. Photo: David Swann.

191 Lightning photographed over Moscow. Reproduced from *Soviet Union* published in Moscow.

192 Replica of apparatus used by Hans C. Oersted in 1820. By courtesy of the Directors of the Science Museum, London. Photo: David Swann.

193 Faraday's Laboratory in the Royal Institution, painted by his niece. Reproduced by permission of the Royal Institution of Great Britain.

194 (L) Heinrich Hertz, from *Signalling Across Space without Wires*, Oliver J. Lodge 1898. Courtesy: London Library.

195 Early Marconi wireless in a lightship at the turn of the century.

196 (T) X-ray photograph of 1897. Photo: Gernsheim Collection, London.

198 (M) Spectrum lines of strontium chloride and of sodium vapor. Both from *Chemistry of the Sun* by Sir Joseph Norman Lockyer 1887. Courtesy: London Library.

199 Part of spectrum of sunlight. From *Chemistry of the Sun* by Sir Joseph Norman Lockyer 1887. Courtesy: London Library.

200 Bowl of Jodrell Bank Radio Telescope under construction. Photo: Park Pictures (Manchester) Ltd.

201 Control Room at Jodrell Bank. Photo: Park Pictures (Manchester) Ltd.

202 (L) Mobile aerial at the Mullard Radio Astronomy Observatory, Cambridge. Photo: Courtesy: Mullard Ltd.
     (R) Fixed aerial at the Mullard Radio Astronomy Observatory, Cambridge. Photo: Courtesy: Mullard Radio Astronomy Observatory, Cambridge.

203 Contours of radio brightness at 160 Mcs from *Galactic Background Survey and the Galactic Halo*, 1958, a paper in the Paris Symposium on Radio Astronomy 1958. Courtesy: Prof. J. E. Baldwin, Cambridge.

205 From *Publications of Sir William Huggins's Observatory*, 1899. Brit. Mus. (BM—8752.1).

206 Sequence of stellar spectra. Courtesy of Curtiss and Rufus, University of Michigan Observatory.

209 Based on Fig. 61 in *Our Sun* by Donald H. Menzel, revised edn. 1959. Courtesy: Harvard University Press.

210 (L) From *The Chemistry of the Sun* by Sir Joseph Norman Lockyer, 1887. Courtesy: London Library.
     (R) Sir William Ramsay. Courtesy: The Librarian, University College, London.

211 Note on Ramsay's discovery of helium. Courtesy: The Librarian, University College, London.

212 (T) Diagram reprinted with permission from *Astronomy* by Theodore G. Mehlin, 1959 (John Wiley & Sons Inc.).
     (B) Based on Fig. 5 in *Atlas of the Universe*, Br. Ernst and Tj. E. de Vries, edited by H. E. Butler 1961. (Thomas Nelson & Sons Ltd., Edinburgh.)

213 (T) Solar corona photographed in Sudan on 25 February 1952. Photo: Yerkes Observatory.
     (B) Based on diagrams from *The Sun*, Giorgio Abetti 1957. (Faber & Faber Ltd., London.)

214 Sunspots recorded according to Spörer's system

15 Reprinted from *Du*, August 1952. Photo: Eidge-nössische Sternwarte, Zurich.

16 Based on Fig. 68 in *Our Sun*, Donald H. Menzel, revised edn. 1959. Courtesy: Harvard University Press.

17 Sunspots. Photo: Perkin-Elmer Corp., USA.

19 (T) Loop prominence of 4 June 1946. Photo: High Altitude Observatory of the University of Colorado, USA.
(BL) Sun photographed in white light.
(BR) Magnetogram of Sun, July 1953.
Both photos: Mt. W. & P. Obs.

20-1 Loop prominence on Sun. Photo: Sacramento Peak Observatory, USAF, Sunspot, New Mexico, USA.

22 (T) Balloon in ascent.
(BL) Telescope and camera.
Official US Navy photographs.
(BR) Diagram of camera and telescope mounting. Courtesy: *Scientific American*.

23 (L) Surface of Sun photographed with the balloon telescope.
(M & R) Two experiments with paraffin wax by Dr. Martin Schwarzschild. Project Stratoscope of Princeton University, sponsored by the US Office of Naval Research, the National Science Foundation and the National Aeronautics and Space Administration of the USA.

24 (L) Mass-luminosity diagram from *Internal Constitution of the Stars*, A. S. Eddington 1926. (Cambridge University Press.)
(R) Prof. Arthur Stanley Eddington in 1931 at Cambridge. Photo: Ramsay & Muspratt Ltd., Cambridge.

25 Eddington's MS from *Sir Arthur Stanley Eddington*, A. Vibert Douglas 1956. (Thomas Nelson & Sons Ltd.).

26 (L) Krüger 60 photographed in 1908, 1915 & 1920. Photo: Yerkes Observatory.
(R) Diagram of orbit of Krüger 60 from *Astronomy*, R. H. Baker 7th edn. Copyright 1959. (D. Van Nostrand Company Inc., Princeton, New Jersey, USA.)

28 Mizar (Zeta Ursae Majoris). Ap. period 20.5 days. Photo: Yerkes Observatory. (SS191)

29 Light curves of TX Cassiopeia, from *Astronomy* Vol. II, by Russell, Dugan and Stewart 1955. (Ginn & Company, Boston, Mass., USA.)

30 Hertzsprung-Russell diagram from *Stellar Evolution*, Otto Struve 1950 (Princeton University Press, Princeton, New Jersey, USA).

31 Henry Norris Russell, from *Biographical Memoirs of the Royal Society*, Vol.III, page 173. With permission of The Royal Society.

33 Sun photographed in hydrogen (Hα) light, 12 August 1917. Photo: Mt. W. & P. Obs. (Neg. 225)

34 (L) William Thomson, 1st Baron Kelvin of Largs.
(R) Hermann L. von Helmholtz. Both photos: Radio Times Hulton Picture Library.

35 *Lingula* murphiana King, from Australian waters and *Lingula* sp. of Ordovician times. Courtesy: The Trustees of The British Museum (Natural History).

43 Diagram reprinted with permission from *Astronomy*, Theodore G. Mehlin 1959. (John Wiley & Sons Inc.)

44 Southern portion of Andromeda Nebula, M 31 (NGC 224), photographed with the 100-inch Hooker telescope on 24 August 1925. Photo: Mt. W. & P. Obs. (No. 101).

245 (T) From *Frontiers of Astronomy*, Fred Hoyle 1959 (Heinemann Educational Books Ltd., London)
(M) Diagram based on Fig. 1 in an article by H. L. Johnson and A. R. Sandage in *Astrophysical Journal*, Vol. 124, page 478. Published by the University of Chicago Press. Copyright 1956 by the University of Chicago.
(B) Diagram based on Fig. 3 in an article by O. Heckmann and H. L. Johnson in *Astrophysical Journal*, Vol. 121, page 619. Published by the University of Chicago Press. Copyright 1955 by the University of Chicago.

246 From *Frontiers of Astronomy*, Fred Hoyle 1959. (Heinemann Educational Books, Ltd., London)

247 (L) Diagram from *Astronomy*, John C. Duncan 1955. (Harper & Bros., New York)
(R) From *Frontiers of Astronomy*, Fred Hoyle 1959. (Heinemann Educational Books Ltd., London)

248 Nova Aquilae (1918)
(T) 20 July 1922.
(M) 3 September 1926.
(B) 14 August 1931.
Photo: Mt. W. & P. Obs. (Neg. G-136).

249 Expanding nebulosity around Nova Persei (1901). Photograph taken with the 200-inch Hale telescope. Photo: Mt. W. & P. Obs. (Neg. 6)

250 Crab Nebula photographed in red light. Photo: Mt. W. & P. Obs. (Neg. 7)

251 Veil Nebula in Cygnus photographed in red light with the 48-inch Schmidt telescope. Photo: Mt. W. & P. Obs. (Neg. 159)

253 Photographed in red light in region of Sagittarius with the 48-inch Schmidt telescope. Photo: Mt. W. & P. Obs.

254 Miss H. S. Leavitt. Photo: Harvard College Observatory.

255 (T) Large Magellanic Cloud photographed at the Cape of Good Hope on 15 November 1903. Courtesy: Royal Astronomical Society.
(B) Small Magellanic Cloud. Photo: Harvard College Observatory.

259 Diagram based on Plate 61 in *Atlas of the Universe*, Br. Ernst & Tj. E. de Vries, edited by H. E. Butler 1961. (Thomas Nelson & Sons Ltd., Edinburgh)

260 Radio telescope of the Radiophysics Laboratory of the Radio Astronomy Observatory near Sydney, Australia.

261 (T) Distribution of neutral hydrogen in the galactic system from *Paris Symposium on Radio Astronomy*, July-August 1958, edited by Ronald N. Bracewell. Courtesy: Stanford University Press, USA.
(B) The radio telescope at Dwingeloo, Holland. Photo: Courtesy Royal Netherlands Embassy, London.

262 (T) Reproduced from *Magnets*, Professor Francis Bitter 1959. Courtesy: Doubleday & Co., Inc., New York.
(B) Proton synchrotron of the laboratories of the European Organization for Nuclear Research, Geneva. Photo: CERN.

264 (T) Globular cluster in Hercules (M13) photographed by J. S. Plaskett at the Dominion Astrophysical Observatory, Victoria, B.C. (Neg. k288). Courtesy: Royal Astronomical Society.
(B) Diagram showing distribution of globular clusters in relation to the plane of the galaxy. Librarie Larousse, Paris.

265 (L) Diagram by A. R. Sandage. Mt. W. & P. Obs.
(R) NGC 188.
Photo: Harvard College Observatory.

266 Great Nebula in Orion, photographed in color with
the 200-inch Hale telescope, Mt. Palomar. Photo:
Mt. W. & P. Obs. (s-23)

267 Nebula in Scutum Sobieski M 16 (NGC 6611) in red
light. Photo: Mt. W. & P. Obs.

268 Lagoon Nebula in Sagittarius (M 8), photographed
in color with the 200-inch Hale telescope at Mt.
Palomar. Photo: Mt. W. & P. Obs. (s-25)

271 Based on diagram from *Quarterly Journal of the Royal
Astronomical Society*, Fig. 2, p. 39, Vol. 1, No. 1,
September 1960. Courtesy: Royal Astronomical
Society.

273 From *Man's View of the Universe*, R. A. Lyttleton
1961. (Michael Joseph, London.)

274 Mercury in transit, photographed at Greenwich on
7 November 1914, (E448). Reproduced by permission of the Royal Greenwich Observatory.

275 (T) Drawing of Mars by Dr. de Vaucouleurs of
Harvard College Observatory. Prepared for McDon-
nell Aircraft, St. Louis, Missouri, by John Patrick
Starrs Advertising Agency, New York, USA.
(B) Venus in blue light, 200-inch Hale telescope.
Photo: Mt. W. & P. Obs.

277 Map of Mars based on Percival Lowell's map of 1901.

278 One of a series of paintings by Donato Creti *c.*1700.
Courtesy Director General, Monumenti, Musei e
Gallerie Pontificie. Photographic Archives of the
Vatican Museums & Galleries. (See also p. 121.)

279 Drawings of Jupiter and Saturn by Terence Maloney.

280 Milky Way in Cygnus, photographed with the Lick
6-inch telescope on 20 October 1892. Photo: Lick
Observatory.

283 Great Andromeda Nebula, M 31 (NGC 224),
photographed in color with the 48-inch Schmidt
telescope. Photo: Mt. W. & P. Obs. (s-24)

284 (T) Edwin Powell Hubble at the 48-inch Schmidt
telescope at Mt. Palomar. Photo: Planet News.
(M) Based on diagram in *The Realm of the Nebulae*,
E. P. Hubble 1936. Yale University Press, copy-
right 1958. (Dover Publications Inc., and Constable
& Co. Ltd.)

284-5 Nebulae from *The Realm of the Nebulae*, E. P. Hubble
1936. Photographed at Mt. Wilson Observatory.
Photo: Yerkes Observatory.

286 Galaxy in Triangulum, M 33 (NGC 598), photographed in color with the 48-inch Schmidt telescope.
Photo: Mt. W. & P. Obs. (s-28)

287 (T) Galaxy in Triangulum, M 33 (NGC 598),
photographed in red light with the 48-inch Schmidt
telescope. Photo: Mt. W. & P. Obs. (No. 158).
(B) Galaxy in Sculptor (NGC 253), photographed
in color with the 48-inch Schmidt telescope. Photo:
Mt. W. & P. Obs. (s-27)

288 Probable collision of a globular and spiral galaxy
(NGC 5128). Photo: Mt. W. & P. Obs.

289 Radio Source in Cygnus "A", photographed with
the 200-inch Hale telescope. Photo: Mt. W. & P.
Obs. (No. 53)

290 Cluster in Corona Borealis. Photo: Mt. W. & P. Obs.

291 Diagrams from p 94 5, *Man's View of the Universe*,
R. A. Lyttleton 1961. (Michael Joseph Ltd., London)

292 Boötes showing farthest galaxies yet photographed
(1961). Photo: Mt. W. & P. Obs.

293 Relation between red shift (velocity) and distance.
Photo: Mt. W. & P. Obs. (No. 313)

294-5 Two diagrams based on Fig. 10 in a paper by M.
L. Humason, N. V. Mayall and A. R. Sandage in
the *Astronomical Journal*, Vol. 61, No. 1237, 1956.

298 Cosmology of Canon Georges Lemaître from *Atlas
of the Universe*, Br. Ernst and Tj. E. de Vries, edited
by H. E. Butler 1961. (Thomas Nelson & Sons, Ltd.,
Edinburgh)

299 Canon Georges Lemaître, reproduced from *Stellar
Populations*, symposium at the Vatican, May 1957,
edited by D. J. K. O'Connell, S. J. (North Holland
Publishing Co., Amsterdam; and Interscience Pub-
lishers, Inc. New York)

302 (L) Diagram based on a figure appearing in
Scientific American, September 1956.

303 Diagram from Monthly Notices of The Royal
Astronomical Society, Vol. 122, No. 5. Courtesy:
Professor M. Ryle, F.R.S.

305 Photograph of Dr. Milton M. Humason. Photo:
Mt. W. & P. Obs.

Artists: A. Ball, K. Bendall, G. Cramp, J. Early, N. Jones,
A. T. Lockwood, J. Messenger, S. A. Parfitt, P. Sullivan.
Photographers: K. Dustan, J. R. Freeman, G. Howson,
Studio 51, D. Swann.